Kant

Kant

Alexandre Kojève

Translated by Hager Weslati

VERSO
London • New York

This work was published with the help of the French
Ministry of Culture – Centre national du livre
Ouvrage publié avec le concours du Ministère français
chargé de la culture – Centre national du livre

This English-language edition first published by Verso 2025
Translation © Hager Weslati 2025
First published as *Kant*
© Éditions Gallimard 1973

The manufacturer's authorized representative in the EU for product safety (GPSR) is LOGOS EUROPE, 9 rue Nicolas Poussin, 17000, La Rochelle, France contact@logoseurope.eu

All rights reserved

The moral rights of the author and translator have been asserted

1 3 5 7 9 10 8 6 4 2

Verso
UK: 6 Meard Street, London W1F 0EG
US: 207 East 32nd Street, New York, NY 10016
versobooks.com

Verso is the imprint of New Left Books

ISBN-13: 978-1-80429-065-1
ISBN-13: 978-1-80429-066-8 (UK EBK)
ISBN-13: 978-1-80429-067-5 (US EBK)

British Library Cataloguing in Publication Data
A catalogue record for this book is available from the British Library

Library of Congress Cataloging-in-Publication Data

Names: Kojève, Alexandre, 1902-1968, author. | Weslati, Hager, translator.

Title: Kant / Alexandre Kojève ; translated by Hager Weslati.
Description: London ; New York : Verso, 2025. | "First published as Kant © Éditions Gallimard 1973"—Title page verso. | Includes bibliographical references and index.
Identifiers: LCCN 2025001856 (print) | LCCN 2025001857 (ebook) | ISBN 9781804290651 (trade paperback) | ISBN 9781804290675 (ebook)
Subjects: LCSH: Kant, Immanuel, 1724-1804.
Classification: LCC B2798 .K6313 2025 (print) | LCC B2798 (ebook) | DDC 193—dc23/eng/20250201
LC record available at https://lccn.loc.gov/2025001856
LC ebook record available at https://lccn.loc.gov/2025001857

Typeset in Minion by Hewer Text UK Ltd, Edinburgh
Printed and bound by CPI Group (UK) Ltd, Croydon CR0 4YY

Contents

Translator's Introduction	vii
A Note on the Translation	xix
Kojève's Cited References	xxv
French Editor's Note	xxvii
On Kant (1952–3)	1
Hegel's Energo-logy	231
Index	233

Translator's Introduction

When Alexandre Koyré took up several visiting professorships at the University of Cairo, between 1933 and 1941, he tasked his mentees and assistants Maurice de Gandillac and Alexandre Kojève with covering his teaching at the École des hautes études in Paris. The latter delivered a six-year lecture course on the religious philosophy of Hegel and another semester course on Pierre Bayle, while working as part-time librarian and contributing occasional review essays to research journals such as *Revue Philosophique de la France et de l'Etranger*, *Recherches Philosophiques*, and the early issues of *Zeitschrift fur Sozialforschung* of the Frankfurt School. Kojève never expounded his philosophy in monographs that were published in his lifetime. Convinced that he had nothing more to say at the end of his brief career in teaching on the margins of academic philosophy, he transitioned to civil service and spent a major part of his working life travelling the world on diplomatic trade missions in the company of high-ranking French government officials. At his sudden death in the summer of 1968 in Brussels, he was in the middle of a meeting with fellow members of supra-national Committee 113 of the European Common Market.

Scholarship on Kojève has grown exponentially in recent years. Although curiosity about his personal life, and the considerable interest generated by his famous lectures on Hegel, have continued unabated, there has been a flourishing of secondary literature concerned with his works of the 'early' and 'middle' periods.[1] Conversely, his post-war philosophical writings, spanning from the early 1950s to the first half of the 1960s, are still largely neglected and hardly ever read. *Kant* belongs to this uncharted area of Kojève's self-described posthumous oeuvre.[2] Written over roughly two months, and not originally conceived as a self-contained monograph, this lengthy text fragment was lifted from a larger corpus of manuscripts, which have been archived in fourteen boxes at the National Library of France, under the generic label *Système du Savoir* (SdS). The present translation is based on Gallimard's 1973 print edition of the text, which corresponds, in manuscript form, to folios 369 to 482, and 483 to 571, respectively dated 24 December 1952 to 10 January 1953 and 18 January to 17 February 1953.[3]

Plucked out of context and published in its raw unedited manuscript form, *Kant* is a challenging read, not only owing to its subject matter but also to its abrupt opening and closing lines and its lack of chapter divisions or subject headings. In addition to its unusual form and method of presentation, the text is strewn with lengthy footnotes addressed at unnamed philosophical interlocutors who were familiar with the author's unorthodox reading of Kant. This introduction will neither put forth a closed interpretation of the text nor attempt a summary of its main articulations. It is, however, essential to provide some background to the book to highlight its pivotal position both in the source manuscript and in the broader systematic context of its author's philosophical project.

---

[1] Some strands in contemporary legal philosophy, and recent works dedicated to the history and theory of the political economy of European integration, were quick to recognise the importance and relevance of Kojève's 1940s political writings. Similarly, his 'early' studies on Buddhism, Soloviev, the philosophy of religion, modern physics, and Kandinsky's art theory are also beginning to attract critical attention.

[2] In a letter addressed to Strauss, dated 6 April 1961, Kojève writes: 'I have completed my Ancient Philosophy. Over 1,000 pages. Taubes has had them photocopied. In my view it is by no means "ready for publication". But if Queneau insists, I will not refuse. (To refuse would, in this case, also amount to taking oneself seriously!).' 'The Kojève–Strauss Correspondence', in Leo Strauss, *On Tyranny*, ed. Michael Roth and Victor Gourevitch (University of Chicago Press, 2013), p. 305.

[3] The Kant manuscript has recently been relocated to Box 17, sub-folders II-1 to II-3.

The location of *Kant* in its source manuscript

Several clues, phrased as directly addressing the reader, are indicative of the author's indecision as to whether his draft study on Kant should take the form of a single work or be broken down into smaller fragments to be elaborated upon in separate monographs. When Kojève drafted the initial outline of his three-plane system of knowledge, he did not set out to write a book on Kant. The latter was meant to be a key reference in the exposition of the intermediary systematic plane dealing with objective-reality. Conceived as the metaphysical plane of the system, 'objective-reality' is interposed between the ontology of 'discursive being' and the phenomenology of 'empirical-existence'. *Kant* is thus located in the first working draft of 'Part I, Section II, of the Exposition of the SdS' (in folios numbered 191 to 503). This part of the source manuscript begins with a lengthy discussion on 'the objective-reality of space-time' (started on 12 October 1952) and proceeds to an elaborate narrative on the philosophical discovery of objective-reality, starting with Parmenides and Thales.

Kant is introduced on folio 221, in reference to the 'feeling of ill and well-being' as the basic sense-datum via which objective reality reveals itself, in contradistinction to the idea of 'anguish' in the ontological discourse.[4] The historical elucidation of objective-reality is resumed from Parmenides to Democritus, and then in reverse order, from Plato (folio 274) to Aristotle (folio 313) before it abruptly jumps to Descartes (starting on folio 327). This entire section, which precedes the one starting on folio 369 and coinciding with the opening paragraphs of the print version of *Kant*, places the Kantian system in direct conversation with the Cartesian notion of extension in relation to thought. This is the missing part which may help the reader make sense of the disorienting opening paragraphs of the book.[5]

---

4 Readers familiar with the French edition of *The Introduction to the Reading of Hegel* may note that the very same argument is expounded in Kojève's lecture course of the academic year 1933–4, which was edited out of Bloom's abridged English version of the text.

5 The reader will find in the text itself a summary of the Descartes–Kant fragment on pages 66–9 (of the French edition). These may be read first before moving to the opening line (page 1).

The source manuscript is continued on folios 572 to 602, which sheds light on the intriguing and seemingly out of place concluding sub-headed paragraph in *Kant*. In manuscript context, the paragraph in question, titled, 'Hegel's Energology', refers to the discussion started on folio 572 with the following statement:

> I have collected under the title Energology all the component parts pertaining to Objective-Reality qua constituent element of the system of knowledge . . . Hegel on the other hand, who was pursuing a systematic goal, undertakes in the *Science of Logic* a discursive development, which is continued uninterrupted from the primordial notion of Given-Being to the absolute-Idea. (NAF 28320, Box 17, Folder II)

In the rest of the manuscript, Kojève engages in a lengthy discussion on the concept of energology from the standpoint of classical and modern physics. He notably agrees with Kant's strict observation of the principles of Newtonian physics while he derides the wrong turn taken by Hegel via what he describes as the 'absurd' speculative physics of Schelling. In his view, every philosopher should reflect awareness and understanding of the findings of physics in their time.

In the process of writing the first drafts of *Kant*, Kojève sharpened the conceptual terminology of his metaphysics. In the main subheadings used in the source manuscript, as in the sub-folders which contain the fragment on Kant, the word 'Energo-logy' is added in red ink above the crossed-out word 'Cosmo-logy'. These insertions were probably made after the completion of the first draft of *Kant*. The source manuscript suggests that the book is a fragment from a lengthier study on the systematic function and content of 'objective-reality'. It therefore constitutes a thematic continuity between Kojève's early and later work insofar as it continues and expands upon the argument put forth in *Zum Problem einer diskreten Welt* (1929) and *L'idée du déterminisme* (1932).[6] In these early works, Kojève laid down the fundamental principles of the

---

6 Alexandre Kojève, *Zum Problem einer diskreten Welt* (Verlag, 2023), and *The Idea of Determinism*, trans. Robert B. Williamson (St. Augustine Press, 2023). See also Kojève's review essay 'Compte rendu des Archives d'histoire de sciences et des techniques de Leningrad [Archiv istorii nauki I techniki]', *Thalès* 2 (1953), pp. 237–53.

metaphysical part of his system in conversation with the crisis of modern physics and its consequences for contemporary philosophy.[7]

Kant in the context of Kojève's 'later' works

The subsequent form that the source manuscript took in a posthumously published series of volumes cast the fragment on Kant into a decontextualised single work, thus obscuring its position and function in Kojève's 'system of knowledge'. In place of their original title, these works were presented to readers and came to be known as historical studies on 'pagan philosophy' terminating in the 'Christian transition' to the Kantian system of critical philosophy. Published as a single work, *Kant* thus became another fragment in the vexing puzzle of the Kojèvean philosophical corpus, far removed from its role and function in the source manuscript described above.

It is often believed that Kojève may have gradually lost control over his unfinished 'magnum opus' as he strayed further into pagan philosophy. Both his biographers and commentators concur in this criticism. But Kojève was not wavering between different possible ways to articulate his system.[8] There is, however, a more plausible explanation for the apparent inconsistencies in the confusing SdS manuscripts. It may well be the case that Kojève revised his plans for his post-war philosophical writings at the behest of his publisher.[9] He trusted

---

[7] Contrary to the opinion held by biographers and commentators of Kojève, his early studies on and later developments of the concept of 'objective-reality' in the context of the 'crisis of physics' do not simply paraphrase Alexandre Koyré's epistemology; rather, they resonate his familiarity with and endorsement of Lenin's *Materialism and Empirio-criticism* (1909). When Kojève shared early drafts of his work on the question of causality and legality after modern physics with Kandinsky, the latter picked up on his nephew's enthusiasm about the '*Kausalgesetz*', so dear both to the 'masters of the Kremlin' and the agitators in the local Nazi government of Dessau who campaigned for the forced closure of the Bauhaus. (Kandinsky's letter to Kojève, dated 6 October 1932, Fonds Kojève, Box 22-1, sub-folder 9, NAF28320, *BNF*).

[8] Contrary to what is commonly believed, the structure, content, and precise terminology of the Kojèvean system was finalised at least two years before the lectures on Hegel.

[9] 'Kant's Energo-logy', qua the second part of a tryptic on metaphysics, was left unedited. Several annotations and marginal notes (Box 17, sub-folder II-2) describe different options as to how it may be split up into fragments, which were meant to be

Queneau's editorial judgement and often acted accordingly. After all, it was thanks to this self-described '*voyou désoeuvré*' and exceptional storyteller that his *Lectures on Hegel* became a 'literary success'. By the mid-1950s, Kojève may have followed his editor's advice when he began to reframe his three-plane system as a series of self-contained works on the history of Western philosophy. The outlines of this project are presented in Kojève's 1955 short article 'The Concept and Time' for a special issue on Hegelianism in Jean Wahl's journal *Deucalian*. This article contains a succinct introduction to the principal arguments put forth in *Kant*.

A posthumously published draft preface for the Gallimard volumes, dated 23 August 1956, was used by Bernard Hesbois to introduce the 1990 edition of *The Concept, Time, and Discourse* as if it was a print-ready book.[10] Although the *Concept* is another fragment taken from the same source material as *Kant*, it nevertheless announces, in numerous cross-references, the theme of the 'Third Introduction to the SdS' with the descriptive title: '*determination of the position and of the role of Kant in the history of philosophy*'.

The French editor's anecdotal claim, probably penned by Queneau himself, that the author misplaced the lengthy section on Kant as he was preparing his *Essay in a Reasoned History of Pagan Philosophy* for publication, validates Gallimard's designation of the book as the fifth volume in a series of works on the history of Western philosophy, starting with the second edition of the *Lectures* in 1962, and followed by the trilogy on pagan philosophy, posthumously published as *The Pre-Socratics* (1968), *Plato-Aristotle* (1972), and *The Neo-Platonists* (1973).

Describing Kant as 'the big star of the third introduction' to his system of knowledge, Kojève claims that: 'if Hegelianism is nothing else than the Kantian "System" transformed into System of Knowledge, all Philosophy that culminates in the latter appears as a Kantian Philosophy, where the reflection that precedes Kant only prepares for the reflection of Kant himself'.[11] This statement captures the ubiquity of Kant in the

---

added to 'Section B of the Third Introduction to the SdS' on the pivotal position of Kant in the history of philosophy. Sub-folder II-3 contains typed fragments of the text, annotated by Kojève's posthumous editors around 1972–3.

10 Recently translated as *The Concept, Time, and Discourse* by Robert B. Williamson (St Augustine's Press, 2019), pp. 1–7.
11 Kojève, *The Concept, Time, and Discourse*, p. 49.

SdS. Notably, the few commentators who skirted the edges of this forbidden area of Kojève's work would have noticed that, confusingly enough, Hegel is hardly ever mentioned in what is claimed to be an 'updating of Hegel's system of knowledge'. Kant is, indeed, a central figure in the voluminous studies on 'Pagan Philosophy', to such an extent that one wonders whether the Kojèvean system is conceived within the horizon of a post-Kantian world rather than a reflection on a post-Hegelian existence after the infamous 'end of history'.

Although presented as the last volume in the chrono-logical evolution of Western philosophy, the sequence Hegel–Plato–Aristotle–Kant is meant to be read in line with the circular structure of the system of knowledge. *Kant* is, therefore, intended to coincide with the *Introduction to the Reading of Hegel*. According to this circular design, *Kant* is 'automatically' transformed into the lectures on Hegel, while the latter anticipate *Kant*, first, via the 'authentic' philosophies of Plato and Aristotle, and then via the Aristotelianism of the Stoics and the eclecticism of the Neo-Platonists. Confusing as it sounds, this configuration of the history of Western philosophy ties up Kojève's entire oeuvre into a subversive political programme. Although it may, at first, appear as though Kojève was attempting to Hegelianise Kant, such an interpretation will only account for one side of the circle. For, when moving towards Hegel from the standpoint of Kant, it may be said that Kojève became Hegelian thanks to Kant rather than turned to Kant after Hegel. It is, therefore, essential to read Kantian critical philosophy, on the one hand, in the context of Kojève's Hegelianism, and, on the other hand, with reference to his interpretation of the sequences Plato–Aristotle and Stoic Aristotelianism–Eclectic Neeoplatonism in the second and third volumes of *Reasoned History* as two irreducibly antithetical positions for or against Marx.

Kant between Platonism and Aristotelianism

In *History and Class Consciousness* (1923), Georg Lukács argued that the notion of reification in modern bourgeois societies is foreign to 'the problems and solutions of the philosophy of the Ancients'. For that reason, he deemed 'as idle to imagine that we can find in Plato a precursor of Kant (as does Natorp), as it is to undertake the task of erecting a philosophy on Aristotle (as does Thomas Aquinas)'.[12] The reader will find, in Kojève's *Kant*, an intriguing, not to say an outright provocative argument on the continuity of the philosophical tradition otherwise derided by Lukács. In addition to framing the Kantian 'philosophical attitude' with numerous references to Buddhism, which is a prominent theme in Kojève's philosophical education and 'early' writings, the book sets the stage for the three volumes on 'Pagan Philosophy'.

From the outset, *Kant* frames the system of critical philosophy in terms of an internal conflict, within reason itself, between action and discourse. In the gradual unfolding of this internal conflict, we begin to see not one, but two Kants: one drawn closer to Plato and another pulled in the direction of Aristotle. Kojève is thus providing two readings or two genealogies of Kantianism. After the completion of the first draft version of the text, Kojève started to design, for his split Kant, different possible trajectories, in various outlines and lengthy working notes. As 'Part I, Section II of the Exposition of the SdS', *Kant* would be the second volume in a triptych on metaphysics, preceded by 'Plato's Energology' and followed by 'Hegel's Energology'. In the alternative scenario, *Kant* would become the 'Third Introduction to the SdS', preceded by the first introduction via Aristotle, and the second via Plato–Hegel. As a philosophical fragment, *Kant*, therefore, announces the two other Kants which will become central to Kojève's substantial and complex studies on the philosophical systems of Plato, Aristotle, the Stoics, and the Neo-Platonists. The reader unfamiliar with these highly dense works may find in the 1938–9 lectures on 'Eternity, Time and the Concept' the foregrounding premises of Kojève's interpretation of the Kantian philosophical system in relation to Plato–Aristotle. All this is integral to his philosophy of time and the concept. The politics of positioning Kant between Aristotelianism and Platonism is, however, fully disclosed in the opening chapter to volume 1 of the *Essay in a Reasoned History of Pagan Philosophy* (1968).

Insofar as every modern philosopher is Kantian, whether they know it or not, one cannot turn away from Kant without ceasing to be a philosopher. Unless one chooses the Kojèvean path of 'wisdom', the only option left is the one proclaimed in the neo-Kantian slogan 'Zurück zu

---

12 Georg Lukács, *History and Class Consciousness: Studies in Marxist Dialectics*, trans. Rodney Livingstone (MIT, 1972), p. 111.

Kant'.[13] Now, as far as any modern philosopher is concerned, the question is to know whether the 're-turn to Kant' will lead down the path of Aristotle or Plato, Proclus or Plotinus, stoicism or eclecticism. Each path, according to Kojève, will, sooner or later, encounter the looming shadow of Hegelianism. Faced with that prospect, many neo-Kantians 'moved *en masse* towards a more remote philosophical past', and, each time, they find either Aristotle or Plato again, and then Kant, and, once again, Hegel.[14] In his criticism of 'the bad turn' taken by some of his contemporaries, aimed directly at Heidegger and Eric Weil, Kojève evokes the danger entailed in straying further away from the orbit of Plato–Aristotle in relation to Kant–Hegel. In the remotest frontiers of the Ancient philosophical tradition, one is inevitably drawing closer to Parmenides and Heraclitus, that is, to absolute silence and infinite chatter, where 'the bottomless abyss of the Logos' lies hidden. To Kojève's mind, the unresolved question of the Kantian wager and the ubiquity of the spectre of Hegelianism signposts two major tendencies in contemporary philosophical thought. The first is 'sooner or later' driven 'towards Christian theology (through Kant, via Plato)', while the second 'would inevitably be tempted to progress . . . (through Kant, via Aristotle) to Hegel and, therefore, *horribile dictu*: Marx'.[15]

Kant between left and right Hegelianism

Kojève took up the study of academic philosophy between Heidelberg and Berlin in the first half of the 1920s. Back then, the Weimar intellectual scene was torn between two competing camps of neo-Kantians: those who promulgated an epistemological interpretation of Kant, and those calling for a return to or a revival of anthropological philosophy, legal psychologism, life philosophy, and existential theology. Kojève

---

13 The distinction between the post-historical Hegelian 'wise man' and the servile bourgeois philosopher was developed in the last two years of Kojève's lectures on Hegel and subsequently popularised in the 'Strauss–Kojève debate' on tyranny and wisdom. Notably, the first draft on Kant was written when Kojève made a swift exit from this debate, and a month before Stalin's death.

14 Alexandre Kojève, *Histoire Raisonnée de la philosophie païenne*, vol. 1, *Les présocratiques* (Gallimard, 1968), pp. 160–1.

15 Ibid., pp. 165–6.

studied with both camps and took substantial notes on the lecture courses given by Rickert, Maier, and Jaspers.[16] When he settled in Paris in the late 1920s, French academic philosophy was dominated by the 'Platonic and anti-Aristotelian' neo-Kantianism of Brunschvicg.[17] Resonances of all these currents are omnipresent across Kojève's work before, throughout, and long after his lecture course on Hegel.

In the opening section of the first volume of *Reasoned History*, Kant is described as the unassuming hero of 'the universal and homogeneous empire of philosophy'. Since its Eleatic beginning, and throughout its historical evolution, Western philosophy engaged in a losing battle against science and theology. As it kept ceding its territories, philosophy was faced with the mortal danger of being reduced to silence, in the sense that it would be left with nothing to talk about. According to Kojève, when Kant acted with 'the courage of despair' and changed the course of modern philosophy from the territorial struggle over what subjects it can reconquer to the preoccupation with the manner or method of speaking about anything, he saved modern philosophy from a certain death. Likened, in a tongue-in-cheek analogy, to the 'miracle of the Marne', the Kantian 'revolutionary's' albeit risk-free achievement consists in the definition of philosophy as a coherent discourse that can speak of everything and anything while speaking of itself speaking of itself, thus giving an account not only of what it talks about, but also of the fact that the 'truths' it utters are arranged in a meaningful discourse, spoken by a human subject living in the world.[18] Kojève attributed a great deal of significance to a pronouncedly Kantian philosophy of discourse in his 'System of Knowledge'. His 'later' work misled his

---

16 Kojève's notes from Jaspers and Maier's 1921 lecture course on Kant (NAF28320, Box I, sub-folder 1 & 2), notes dated 1922 to 1924 based on Rickert's interpretation of Kant's 'Weltanschauungslehre' [comprehensive doctrine of worldview], notes from Heinrich Maier's 1924 lecture course on Kant's epistemology (NAF28320, Box I, sub-folder 2), and six notebooks containing reading notes on Kant dated 1923 (NAF28320, Box II, sub-folder 5).

17 In his *Memoirs: Fifty Years of Political Reflection*, Raymond Aron evokes the teaching of Léon Brunschvicg, namely his reduction of philosophy to a theory of knowledge, which 'does not preserve the table of categories from Kant's Critique, nor does it accept the solution of the Third Antinomy (immanent determinism, transcendental freedom). Platonic and anti-Aristotelian, [Brunschvicg's brand of neo-Kantianism] aims towards the suppression of all obstacles to the progress of science' (Holmes & Meier, 1990), pp. 29–30.

18 Kojève, *Histoire raisonnée de la philosophie païenne*, vol. 1, pp. 27–8.

biographers and commentators into believing that the radical shift from a philosophy of action, grounded in the dialectic of struggle and work, to discourse is indicative of the failure and unviability of his philosophical project. The earlier 'work of propaganda' on behalf of Hegelianism and revolutionary action is said to have lapsed into post-historical irony and language games. Such claims, relevant as they might be, betray a lack of understanding of Kojève's critique of and continued conversation with the politics of neo-Kantianism in its 'universal and homogeneous empire of philosophy'.

In his famous lectures, Kojève claimed that the culmination of the dialectical movement in the dualism of (Napoleonic) political tyranny and (Hegelian) absolute science had achieved the ends of history. He made a lasting impression on the minds of his contemporaries when he situated the genealogy of all future philosophy in the irreducible opposition of left and right Hegelianism and in its concrete manifestations in economic and political struggles.[19] Kojève's argument that Kant's philosophical system 'Hegelianises' itself by itself into an atheistic, circular, and uni-total system of knowledge goes against the grain of many seminal works on the reception and interpretation of Kant in Marxist scholarship.[20] Lucien Goldmann's study on Kant in the mid-1940s marked a significant departure from the negative theses put forth by Lukács and Marcuse on the incommensurability of Kantianism and left-Hegelianism. His claim that 'Kant was the first modern philosopher to recognize anew the importance of the totality as a fundamental category of existence' is indicative of many other intersections between his and Kojève's *Kant*.[21] Both the former and the latter are at the antipode of Jaspers's rejection of closed totality.[22]

---

19 Alexandre Kojève, 'Hegel, Marx, and Christianity', trans. H. Gildin, *Interpretation* 1, no. 1 (1970), pp. 21–42.

20 Lukács, *History and Class Consciousness*; Herbert Marcuse, *Reason and Revolution: Hegel and the Rise of Social Theory* (Routledge, 2000). Kojève would, however, agree with both Lukács and Marcuse that Kantian philosophy is the expression of bourgeois consciousness. The reader will encounter this argument on 'bourgeois hypocrisy' in numerous lengthy footnotes in *Kant*. Similarly, Marcuse's interpretation of Kantian philosophy in his *Study on Authority* (Verso, 2008) as a 'rationalisation' of bourgeois social authority echoes a similar argument in Kojève's *Notion of Authority* (Verso, 2014) and in his *Outline of a Phenomenology of Right* (Rowman & Littlefield, 2007).

21 Lucien Goldmann, *Immanuel Kant*, trans. Robert Black (Verso, 2011), p. 36.

22 Karl Jaspers, *Kant, From the Great Philosophers*, vol. 1, ed. Hannah Arendt, trans. Ralph Manheim (Harcourt Brace, 1962).

Kojève's *Kant* is a continuation of, rather than a break with, his left Hegelianism. An attentive reader of the *Introduction* would notice the omnipresence of Kant from start to finish. The first three sets of lectures of 1933 to 1936, focused on the Hegelian transitions between sensibility, understanding, and reason, are prominently framed within neo-Kantian theories of value and cognition and a 'dualist ontology' whose origins are explicitly attributed to Kant. The 1938–9 lectures on 'Eternity, Time and the Concept' are picked up almost verbatim in the opening lines of *Kant*. The lectures delivered between 1936 and 1937 foreground the references to 'bourgeois hypocrisy' and the openly Hegelian–Marxist arguments put forth in *Kant*. Those lectures mark the transition from the dialectic of struggle and work to the controversial dyad tyranny-wisdom or Napoleon–Hegel. After a brief and furtive reference to the philosopher of self-consciousness and absolute knowledge who completes history by revealing the tyrant, or the 'man of action' who is fully satisfied with the success of his universally recognised achievement, a more substantial and lengthier analysis is dedicated to the study of the 'Kantian man' and his reaction, in thoughts and feelings, to the Napoleonic universal state. The inherent inconsistencies of Kantian philosophy are thus deliberately put to the test in the context of tyranny. However, on account of its conception of freedom and its limited understanding of objective-reality within the horizon of Newtonian physics, the Kantian philosophy is unable to account for struggle and work, and therefore lacks a clear understanding of history and historical existence. As the prototype of the bourgeois intellectual, the Kantian philosopher does not participate in history and remains indifferent to the state. Paradoxically, and although devoid of any content and not commanding anything, Kantian morality, Kojève notes, is developed within the Napoleonic state. These arguments on the politics of the Kantian philosophical system warrant a different reading, not only of the lectures on Hegel, but also of Kojève's so-called 'political writings' on the notions of right and authority. As such, *Kant* holds a pivotal position in Kojève's oeuvre, and attests to the systematic consistency and coherence of his works.

A Note on the Translation

The source text of the present translation is Gallimard's 1973 print edition of *Kant*, which reproduced the paragraphing, punctuation, hand-drawn diagrams, and even the typos of the original manuscript. The latter has recently been relocated from Box 14 to 17 and now contains, in addition to the typescript prepared for the French edition, additional sub-folders which have only recently been made available for researchers. This new material shows that Kojève revisited the 1952–3 draft version of his study on Kant over more than a decade in the process of developing his multi-volume 'System of Knowledge'.

I adhered as closely as possible, a few typos notwithstanding, to the French edition. The only modification I introduced concerns the use of the word 'Man' in the sense of the human person in general, which I rendered with the gender-inclusive 'human being' and the third person plural 'they'. A few instances of syntactic ambiguity are placed between curly brackets, which I also use to signpost a group of French words with different lexical nuances. In his direct translations from Kant, Kojève provides German words, sometimes italicised and sometimes not, between parentheses. These words have been carried over into the translation as they appear in the original text. I deleted the abbreviation 'ibid' which appears inconsistently with and without italics and capitals. Kojève's sources from the *Akademie* edition of Kant's texts are listed in the Cited References section below.

Written in lengthy notes and, at least initially, intended to be heard rather than read, the 1952–3 draft study on Kant is not print-ready. Any tempering with its authentic stylistic idiosyncrasies would have resulted in the loss of important aspects of its acoustic effects. Paragraph-long sentences interrupted with several parenthetical comments, appositions, and bracketed dependent clauses are used in profusion throughout the text. Rendering *Kant* in English-friendly prose through a transparent translation, or resorting to lexical repetitions to break unwieldy sentences into shorter units, would have doubled the original text in volume, while introducing significant changes in the sequencing of Kojève's 'discursive developments' – to use his own turn of phrase.

The source text presents novel challenges for which there are no precedents in English translations of Kojève. However, my decision on the appropriate word choice, as far as a specific set of conceptual terminology is concerned, had to be made in awareness of precedents set by translations of Kant. For that reason, readers familiar with Kojève will note minor terminological deviations from existing English translations of his work.

The hyphenation used by Kojève to create compound words is familiar to readers of his work and recognised as being central to his conceptual terminology. The hyphens he uses to break words up, as in 'contra-diction', 'de-monstrate' or 'arte-fact', have been retained without the need to find alternative words to convey their intended etymological pun. In other cases, however, hyphenation is used to coin a portmanteau term and not merely as a play on words, as in the prominent case of the *vrai-semblant*, in the Greek sense of *Eikos* or verisimilitude, which I chose to render as 'true-semblant' rather than in more common English terms such as likely, plausible, or true-seeming. The Kojèvean *true-semblant* underpins and informs a broader theme that runs through much of *Kant*, namely the unstable unity of the (discursive) development of philosophy in the 'mode of truth' and the 'mode of as if'. In that context, I rendered the phrase *dire vrai*, in the Nietzschean sense of 'mode of veridiction' (*Wahrsagen*), as 'tell true' rather than 'truth-telling'.

I adhered to the established translation of Kojève's conceptual terminology, except in the case of *objet-chosiste*, which has so far been rendered as 'thingish object'. To avoid the (Marxist) resonance of reification in the *chosisme* of the *nouveau roman*, or closer to us, in the 'thingish horizons' of the new materialists and object-oriented ontologists, I chose the more clinical, unhyphenated term *thinglike*. It is worth noting that *objet-chosiste* is Kojève's own word choice to render the German *Gegenstand* in the (Heideggerian) sense of the *positing of a thing as an object*, but also in the neo-Kantian sense of the autonomous subject of cognition in opposition to the conceived object. I do, however, acknowledge that *Gegenstand* remains a problem-word in translations of Kant, and that it is equally contentious in translations of other philosophical works, from Hegel to Heidegger and beyond.

I translated Kojève's direct translation of lengthy passages from the *Akademie* edition and then checked them against the more recent *Cambridge Edition* of Kant's major works. In terms of its quality, Kojève's translation is very rigorous and well ahead of its time insofar as it comes very close to the more recent English and French retranslations of Kant. In some cases, his word choice appears to be even more accurate than the one used in standard English translations, as in his rendition of the German *Art* as 'mode', rather than 'way' or 'kind'. However, in other instances, Kant's translators and scholars seem to have agreed on a more precise terminology, as in the rendition of *das Beharrliche* as 'permanence' rather than 'persistence', even though the latter is closer to the usage of this word in the context of Kojève's reading of Kant after modern physics. Similarly, he would use 'Inter-action' instead of 'reciprocity', and the rather unusual 'active-conflict' instead of the more commonly used 'opposition'.

There are other instances where Kojève deliberately brings what he calls a 'terminological innovation' to the translation of specific Kantian words. For instance, he translates *Demütigung* as 'humiliation' rather than 'humility', *Achtung* as 'esteem' rather than 'respect' or 'reverence', and *zufrieden* and *Selbst-zufriedenheit* as 'contented' and 'self-contentment' in contradistinction with the idea of 'satisfaction' in *befriedigt*. He renders *Zufälligkeit* sometimes as 'chance' and sometimes with the more common term 'contingency'. Notably, Kojève coins his own conceptual terminology in his direct translation of Kant when he signposts the distinction between the three planes of his own philosophical system. He thus translates *Dasein* as 'empirical-existence', *Wirklichkeit* as 'objective-reality', and *Sein* as 'given-being'.

The distinction between *connaissance* and *savoir* has always been difficult to render in English. In his translation of *Concept, Time, and*

Discourse, Williamson rendered '*connaissance*' and '*connaître*' with a 'c' superscript attached to 'know' and its derivatives. In *Kant* this is not at all necessary insofar as *connaissance* and *savoir* denote the distinction between cognition and knowledge. While this word choice is accepted by readers familiar with Kantian philosophy, it may seem out of place for those who know Kojève through other works in English translation.

The resonance of the Kantian *Sinn* and *Sinnlichkeit* in the French lexicon of *sens, sensibilité, sensualité,* and *sensation* required additional attention to avoid as far as possible the uniform rendition of the French *sens* as 'meaning', even though this is Kojève's intended idea of the 'logos' as discursive essence 'incarnated' in an arbitrary 'morpheme', or, to speak a more common language, the distinction between the signifier and the signified. When it is exclusively a question of (linguistic) meaning, Kojève, in anticipation of a similar choice of word in Derrida, for example, uses the French equivalent for 'signify' or 'signification' to render the German *Bedeutung*.

There is no word in French to convey the English and German distinction between 'multiplicity' (*Vielheit*) and the 'manifold' (*Mannigfaltigheit*). However, Kojève seems to use *multiplicité* or *multiple* in lower case to indicate the former, and the same term in upper case to indicate the latter.[1]

The most challenging cluster of words is the one expressing the idea of 'relation' in the non-categorial sense of the term. Words such as *rapport*, in the sense of *Verhältnis* and sometimes *beziehen*, or *par rapport*, in the sense of *in Anehung*, have been interpreted in line with the idea of 'reference' and 'referring'. The French *liaison, lien, raccorder,* and sometimes *connexion* in the sense of *angeschlossen*, are also used to convey the idea of 'coupling' in *Verknüpfung*, and 'composition', 'nexus', or 'combination' as in *Verbindung* and *verbunden*, or 'binding' as in *zusammenhängt*. Kojève's deployment of this rich lexicon of relation and connection could not be rendered uniformly with the same word. I wanted to restrict the term 'relation' to contexts pertaining to its categorial usage.

---

1   To the extent that capitalisation signposts Kojève's conceptual terminology, it has traditionally been retained in English translations of his work. I chose to follow this tradition while correcting instances of inconsistent use. That said, I do not think that excessive use of capitalisation is at all necessary; its removal would eventually make Kojève in English translation more accessible to a contemporary readership.

A Note on the Translation

The last example of word choice worth mentioning is *Primat*, which is the same in German and French. One of the provenances of Kojève's *théorie des primats* can be traced to Koyré's work. The notion of *Primat* is also known to students of Kant in reference to the 'primacy' of practical over theoretical reason. Although the rendition of *Primat* as 'primacy' is not satisfactory, I chose not to opt for an alternative word evocative of other philosophical projects, such as Heidegger's threefold ecstatic character of time. It is worth noting that Kojève uses *future* in the context of Kant's 'future world', and *avenir* when referring to his own philosophical idea of the primacy of the 'project'. Since there is no English equivalent to render the nuance between *future* and *avenir* (to come), I have inserted the French word between curly brackets whenever it occurs in the text.

Acknowledgement of thanks are due to Bryan-Paul Frost for thoroughly editing the entire manuscript, and to Hugh Gillis, Scott Wilson, Kyle Moore, Evgeni Pavlov, and Howard Caygill, who commented on parts of the translation, in early drafts or in revised versions. A very special thank-you goes out to Zobia Syeda for her generous assistance in helping to reproduce Kojève's hand-drawn diagrams. I am especially grateful to Nina Kousnetzoff for granting me permission to translate this text, and to Jocelyn Monchamp for facilitating access to its manuscript versions. This work is dedicated to the memory of my friend Hassine Ben Azouna.

Kojève's Cited References

These works are listed in Kojève's personal library, now housed at the National Library of France. Each copy is heavily annotated, with reading dates in brackets, at times, spanning the early 1920s, '40s, and '50s.

Emmanuel Kant, *Gesammelte Schriften*. Preußischen Akademie der Wissenschaften, Berlin: Druck und Verlag von Georg Reimer.

Band II (1912) Kant's Werke. Vorkritische Schriften. II. 1757–1777 [III.41]
Band III (1911) Kant's Werke. Kritik der reinen Vernunft: zweite Auflage 1787 [21.IX.21, 3.III.23, 30.III.23, 6.VIII.25, 20.VII.41]
Band IV (1911) Kant's Werke. Kritik der reinen Vernunft (1. Aufl.); Prolegomena [25.IX.21, 8.III.23, 8.VIII.25, 24.VII.41]; Grundlegung zur Metaphysik der Sitten [27.IX.21, 5.III.23, 30.VII.41]; Metaphysische Anfangsgründe der Naturwissenschaft [28.IX.21, 10.III.23, 25.VII.41, 10.XII.52]
Band V (1913) Kant's Werke. Kritik der praktischen Vernunft [30.IX.21, 8.III.23, 11.VIII.25, 15.VIII.41]; Kritik der Urtheilskraft [11.X.21, 7.V.22, 15.III.23, 15.VIII.25, 28.VIII.41]
Band VII (1917) Kant's Werke. Der Streit der Fakultäten [16.I.23, 3.I.42]; Anthropologie in pragmatischer Ainsicht [18.I.23, 20.II.42]

French Editor's Note

In his Introduction to *An Essay in a Reasoned History of Pagan Philosophy*, Alexandre Kojève had amply developed his 'thesis' that Kant is the only great philosopher between Plato–Aristotle and Hegel. But when he wanted to publish his book, he misplaced this portion of the work and had it replaced with a few lines of text. Subsequently found among his papers after his sudden death (in 1968), the section on Kant turned out to be the subject of an entire book, which we present to the reader today, giving them the opportunity to discover a 'Kojèvean' Kant. Having set the conditions for the possibility of every philosophical discourse, Kant is said to be the philosopher who brought philosophy to an end while opening a path to the discursive Wisdom, which is the Hegelian system of Knowledge. Thus, the present work *Kant*, together with the *Essay in a Reasoned History of Pagan Philosophy* and the *Introduction to the Reading of Hegel*, constitute the comprehensive history of Western philosophy such as envisioned by Alexandre Kojève.

On Kant (1952–3)

Having shown his place in the schematic overview of the general history of Western Philosophy, let us now specify the historical position of Kant.

As was said above, the break between the 'ancient' or 'classical', or even the 'naturalistic' or 'theistic' period, including the subterranean pre-atheistic current, and the 'Judeo-Christian' or modern, or even the 'anthropological' and properly atheistic period, somehow finds its way into the Kantian System itself.

On the one hand, Kantian 'empiricism', which is both an integral renewal of anti-Platonic Aristotelianism and a prefiguration of authentic Hegelianism, in fact determines the radically *atheistic* character of Kant's System. Similarly, its identification of what is specifically human with 'pure Volition', that is, with creative Freedom, or, to speak a Hegelian language, with negating Action (acting Negativity), turns the Kantian System into an authentic philosophical expression of the *Judeo-Christian* anthropology which reaches its culmination in Hegel.

But, on the other hand, Kant's upholding of the notion of the Thing-in-itself ranks his System with its classical 'rationalist' counterparts, which (even in Aristotle) are in the final analysis *theistic*ally informed Systems. Similarly, the irreducible dualism of Volition and Reason (*Vernunft*), or Understanding (*Verstand*) to be more exact, that is, of Action and Discourse, turns the Kantian System into a *pagan* or an ancient philosophical System; one in which human 'nature' or 'essence', being always and everywhere identical to itself, is given as a function of the immutable place occupied by the Human being within the Cosmos or the 'natural' World.

Regarding Kant's (Aristotelian) 'empiricism' or 'sensualism', as summarised by him in the relevant passage from the *Prolegomena*, it is easy to see how it amounts to affirming that the sum total of Discourse derives its meaning {*sens*} from the whole fact of Perception (which consists of a variable 'Tonus' and sometimes implies the feeling of Well- or Ill-being).[1] However, not only does such an affirmation deny the possibility to *speak* of the Transcendent, that is, of the non-spatio-temporal whatever it may be, but it also parts ways with the 'rationalist' faith in the existence, for the Human being, of truths *anterior* to human Discourse and accessible in isolation through a direct contact called Proof, which Aristotle (C. /. E) would have not shied from admitting. In other words, the *radical* 'empiricism' of Kant (for whom C. /. T) compels him, in fact, to define the (one and unique) Truth in terms of the coherence of one and the same human Discourse, which integrates all that can be said using sense-endowed words, to the extent that the sense in question is ultimately derived from the detachment from its *hic et nunc* of the content of Perception, which is given in the extended-duration of empirical existence.

In other respects (and contrary to Aristotle), to perceive the Human being in terms of *free* Will in the strong sense of the word, that is, in terms of the creative Action that exists and manifests itself only as the *negation* of the given *whatever it may be*, to the extent that the given in question could be the Human being per se, is to render the latter autonomous vis-à-vis the natural World (the Cosmos), also in the sense that human Discourse can be (become) *true* even if it is (at a given moment) dissonant with the given World to which it refers. This therefore amounts to admitting that the (discursive) Truth (that is, the uni-total Discourse) is *made* {*se* fait} over a time span transformed into History through human Struggles and negating or creative Works, and that it is attained {*faite*} or accomplished, that is, truly or necessarily true or true everywhere and always (at a given moment) only at the end of History, when

---

1 Therefore: the (eternal) C is . /. E *in* T, and not *outside* T. This can already be found in Aristotle. But Kant goes further because for him the (eternal) C is . /. Time (but not = T as in Hegel). [Tr. for a detailed presentation of these 'formulae', see Kojève's 'A Note on Eternity, Time, and the Concept' in *Introduction to the Reading of Hegel*, pp. 101–2].

all human 'Projects', all the 'possibilities' of Struggle and (creative) Work have been exhausted, at least virtually. In other words, this is what the equation of C to T amounts to.

Interpreted in this manner, the Kantian System becomes strictly identical with Hegel's *System of Knowledge*. Although this is how Hegel *interpreted* Kant, he was fully aware that his 'violent interpretation' would do violence to Kant's thought taken in its historical context, because Kant *relates* {*rapporte*} C to T without *identifying* them with one another.

Indeed, if the notion of the thing-in-itself (*Eternity*), which renders the Hegelian interpretation untenable, is 'easily' removable from the Kantian System, thus enabling it to somehow Hegelianise itself by itself, Kant, who witnessed its removal (by Reinhold) during his lifetime, officially took issue with it.

The question concerning the Thing-in-itself (which provides the ultimate basis for every theistic Philosophy [or C. /. E])[2] and its role in the Kantian System is so complex and equally important that it is worth dwelling upon at length.

The following passage, translated from the first edition of the *Critique of Pure Reason*, shows to what extent the notion of the Thing-in-itself played a fundamental role in Kant's thought.

Sensation (*Sinnlichkeit*) [which determines the *spatio-temporal* character of human Intuition (*Anschauung*), the latter limiting to space-time the domain of Discourse and discursive Truth] and its field, namely that of Phenomena, are themselves *limited* by the Understanding, in that Sensation does not pertain to Things (as they are) in themselves, but only to the way in which, on account of *our subjective* constitution, Things appear to *us*. This was the result of the entire Transcendental Aesthetic, and it follows naturally from the notion of a Phenomenon in general (überhaupt) that something

---

2 [Tr. While atheistic systems are defined as the determination of the uni-totality or equation of concept to time (C = T), in their theistic counterparts, the concept 'is a reference [rapport] . . . to something else' or to something other than itself. The differential relation (. /.) introduces internal division in 'the Universe of Ideas-Concepts' in ancient theistic systems (after Plato–Aristotle), and in the 'schematised Concepts-categories' or the 'World of space-time' in modern theistic systems (after Kant). See *Introduction to the Reading of Hegel*, pp. 125–6.]

> (*Etwas*) must *correspond* to it which is not *in itself* Phenomenon, for a Phenomenon can be nothing *for itself* and outside of *our* kind of representation (*Verstellungsart*); thus, if there is not to appear (*Herauskommen*) a constant (*vicious*) circle, the word Phenomenon already indicates a *relation* to something the *immediate* representation of which is, to be sure, sensible (*Sinnlich*), but which *in itself*, even without this constitution of *our* sensation (on which the form of our Intuition is grounded), must be something, that is, an object *independent* of Sensation. (*Akademieausgabe*, IV, 164, 15–27)

To be sure, this slightly bald statement was not retained in the second edition of the *Critique*. However, other passages in the second edition articulate the same idea. Consider, for instance, the following one:

> The notion of a Noumenon, taken merely problematically, remains not only admissible but even, as a notion setting limits to Sensation, *unavoidable*. But in that case, it is not a special intelligible object for *our* Understanding; rather an Understanding to which the Noumenon would belong (*Gehörte*) is itself a problem, namely, [that] of cognising its object not *discursively*, through *Categories*, but *intuitively*, in a *non-sensible* Intuition, [it is the problem of the Understanding] the possibility of which *we* cannot in the least represent (*Vorstellung*). Now in this way *our* Understanding receives a negative extension, that is, it is not limited by Sensation, but on the contrary, it *limits* Sensation by *calling/naming* (*nennt*) Noumena Things [taken] in themselves ([that is,] not considered as Phenomena). But our understanding itself also immediately sets limits for itself, [which consist in the obligation of] not *cognising* these Noumena through any Categories, [and] hence, merely *thinking* them under the *name* of an *unknown* Something. (III, 212, 13–27)

Elsewhere, Kant says [wrongly, as we will see later on] that it is not *impossible* [= contra-dictory] for an Intuition to be *sensible* while being *other* than our *human* sort, the latter being characterised by its spatio-temporal 'form' (which is therefore, for Kant, an irreducible given, to the extent that it does not admit a 'transcendental deduction', neither from the fact of Discourse nor from the Postulate of Truth). Be that as it may, Kant says repeatedly to his heart's content that *non-sensible* Intuition is necessarily *non-spatio-temporal*. Now, it is the Intuition (whatever it may be) that 'gives' the Object to the Understanding, thus rendering it accessible to the 'Cognition' (prone to being *true*). *Sensible* Intuition, 'accidentally' spatio-temporal, 'gives' to the *human* Understanding the Object that Kant calls 'Phenomenon' in such a way that the 'Cognition' of *that* Understanding is by definition necessarily limited to *spatio-temporal* Phenomena. Therefore: C. /. T and not = T. It is *that* Cognition alone that Kant calls *discursive*. Accordingly, Discourse is, for him, a specifically *human* phenomenon, which exists in regard to Human beings (and for their Discourse, that is, for themselves) only qua *spatio-temporal* Phenomenon; it consists in the (coherent) [spatio-temporal] 'discursive' development of the Categories within the frame of the spatio-temporal Intuition which 'gives' to the Human being the Phenomena whence human Discourse derives all its sense. As for *non-sensible* Intuition, it 'gives' to a *non-human* Understanding the Object which Kant calls 'Noumenon', in such a way that the 'Cognition' of *that* Understanding is *limited* to the *transcendent* Noumenon in reference to any Spatio-temporality (that is, in reference to Eternity) (to the extent that the essentially *spatio-temporal* Phenomenon is, by definition, inaccessible to it). *That* Understanding is not *discursive* in this sense that it does not have any 'Categories' prone to being 'developed' (spatio-temporally) within a *spatio-temporal* frame. Thus *its* Truth is not *Discourse* in the sense of *Phenomenon* with an *extended duration*. Consequently, the meaning {*sens*} of *human* Discourse is not a Truth for *that* 'intuitive' (= non-discursive) Understanding, and what is Truth for the latter makes no Sense for the speaking-Human-being for whom 'Noumena do not have any positive *significance* (*Bedeutung*) that can be indicated [verbally]' (III, 230, 19). In other words, from a human standpoint, the Noumenon is essentially *ineffable* and the 'intuitive' Understanding that 'cognises' this Noumenon is radically *mute* for and with reference to the Human being (therefore: no 'Revelation').

There is, certainly, no contradiction in the fact that Kant *speaks* of Silence and *says* that there is the Ineffable, since the possibility to speak of that which does not speak is one of the main implications of the Axiom of Error [presupposed by the Postulate of Truth, itself inexpressible without the preliminary attainment of an awareness of the (raw) Fact of Discourse (that this Postulate, together with its presupposed Axiom, both *define*)]. What he *says* might simply mean that the uni-total Discourse, which integrates all that one may say without contra-dicting oneself (including what is said to express Recognition or to promote an Accomplishment {*Réussite*}), does not only exclude the mass of contra-dictory Utterances {*Paroles*} (which 'develop' notions of the kind 'square circle'), but also Silence strictly so called, such as musical or pictorial Silence. Thereupon, the (one and unique) Truth might be identified with the uni-total Discourse itself, to the extent that all Errors implied therein as statements {*énoncés*} must necessarily (= everywhere and always) be denied so that the whole, which is, by definition, true, can be coherent, that is, precisely non-contra-dictory.

When Kant's (cited) utterances are interpreted in this manner [which is in no way impossible per se], his System would be transformed into a Hegelian System of Knowledge, which achieves and perfects the System of the anti-Platonic Aristotle through its becoming fully aware of the latter. The result would then be a strictly *atheistic* Kantian System, since it would exclude from the discourse in which it is set forth any element of Transcendence whatever, that is, any discursive statement whose Sense refers to what is deemed to be transcendent in reference to Spatio-temporality. It would not be possible to *speak* of a non-temporal and non-spatial 'God' *inside* this System, because according to this, by definition, non-contradictory System, it is possible to *speak* of that 'God' only in the mode of Contradiction, to the extent that the notion 'God' or '*eternal*-Being'/'Eternity-that-is' (in the sense of non-temporal or non-spatio-temporal) is of the type 'square Circle'. As for Silence, all that can be *said* thereof, without self-contradiction, is that it 'refers' to nothing (of which one can speak without self-contradiction) other than itself. Consequently, it must be strictly and absolutely *silent*, if it does not want, by becoming *discursive*, to be *contra-dictory*. More specifically, one cannot *say* without *contra-dicting* oneself that Silence 'pertains' *to* God (= Eternity-that-is) or that there is a silent 'Revelation' *of* '*God*' (in the double sense of the word 'of'), since 'God' is a *Notion* of a *contra-dictory* kind, which qua *Notion* or Sense-endowed word is part of the ensemble of Utterances pronounced and pronounceable by the Human being, but qua *contra-dictory* Notion, it is not part of the uni-total, that is, *coherent* Discourse which implies *all* that one may say without contra-dicting oneself.

However, a similar interpretation of the Kantian System would be 'violent' in the sense that, {even though} possible *in itself* and *for us*, it would be rejected by Kant himself. For in the cited passage, Kant goes, consciously and deliberately, much further than the above interpretation might have wanted to go. In fact, he says in those passages that *discursive*, that is, human, Understanding *limits* 'Sensation' insofar as it *names* (*nennt*) Things-in-themselves 'Noumena' [and could, consequently, name them 'God']. In other words, Kant claims that the 'Noumenon' (= Eternity) is a *Notion* in the proper sense of the term, that is, a *sense*-endowed *word* which is not contradictory in-itself, and that it must accordingly be an integral part of the uni-total Discourse, that is, of the System of Knowledge wherein it is, so he says, 'unavoidable' (*Unvermeidlich*; cf. III, 212, 16).

We thus see that, for Kant, his System is not Hegelian, that is, a radically and consciously atheistic 'Aristotelian' System (C = T), but rather a Platonic System (C. /. E ♂ T) which is, in the final analysis, and often unconsciously, always theistic. Indeed, the Kantian claim that the Noumenon is ineffable would not bother Plato at all, since by the latter's own admission, at least towards the end of his life (in Letter VII), the Agathon-Theos is accessible as such to the human being only in and through 'ecstatic' or 'mystical' *Silence*. Many theologians, be they 'Platonic', Christian, or otherwise, would not see anything disconcerting in this either.

However, one must refrain from identifying Kant's System with Plato's (where C. /. E ♂ T), because, even as a 'violent interpretation', such an identification is *intrinsically* untenable. Indeed, in the cited context, Kant deliberately refrains from *naming* 'God'. When he *names* the Thing-in-itself 'Noumenon', he hastens to add that the latter is an '*unknown* Something' (that is, C. /. E *in* T). Elsewhere, he calls the Thing-in-itself 'Some-thing in general (überhaupt)', 'Object as such', 'Some-thing = X'. And if the notion 'God' intervenes in the 'transcendental Dialectic', it shows up (externally) only to be revealed as discursively 'undevelopable' without contra-diction, that is, as 'inextensible' inside the System. Thus, in contrast with Plato's, Kant's System is (at least in principle) *intrinsically* non-contradictory.

In and for Plato, the One-Agathon-Theos is, to be sure, ineffable *as such*. But, in and for the same Plato, the transcendent One *determines* the Two of Being, in this sense that Being itself is transcendent in reference to the spatio-temporal world and to Spatio-temporality itself: the

Platonic Being is thus Idea-Essence [-Number?] accessible to Discourse (and providing a basis for Discourse by guaranteeing its truth) *independently* of spatio-temporal Perception. The 'notion' of the ineffable One (contra-dictory in itself) is therefore an *integral* part of any (non-Aristotelian) Platonic System, in this sense that it is *discursively developable* (albeit, over the course of human life, only in *connection* {*liaison*} with the Discourse which refers to Perception). Plato himself thought that this discursive development might be non-contra-dictory. However, in fact and for us, this cannot be the case (because if, without contra-dicting oneself, one can *say* that there is the Ineffable, one cannot *say what* it is, that is, *discursively develop* this *ineffable* or this *discursively undevelopable* Notion without contra-dicting oneself). The supposedly *ineffable* notion of the One thus worms its way into the System or the uni-total *Discourse* and distorts it from within to such an extent that it renders it contra-dictory in itself. Conversely, in and for Kant, the uni-total Discourse or the (discursive) System of Knowledge is *intrinsically* non-contra-dictory, because it *excludes* any discursive development of that which is, by definition, for Kant as for Plato, undevelopable in a discursive way.

However, for Kant as for Plato, the 'Thing-in-itself' or, if one prefers the Platonic designation (to the extent that its 'proper name' is, moreover, irrelevant for that non-magical thought which no longer accepts some indissoluble bond between Phoneme and Sense [which Poetry retains, without seeking to gain any 'material' Achievements from it]), the One-Agathon-Theos, is a Notion in the proper sense of the term, with an intrinsically non-contra-dictory meaning.[3] This is otherwise [the] one [and only] 'inconsequence' of Kant (which he inherited from the Platonic tradition) because he never managed to explain why a notion he [wrongly] claims to be non-contra-dictory cannot be

---

3 On the face of it, it might be objected that the Thing-in-itself cannot be called the One because Kant often speaks thereof *in the plural*. But this is most obviously nothing other than 'a manner of speaking' (barely less satisfactory than speaking thereof *in the singular* as Kant does when he says *Etwas überhaupt* or *Etwas* = X). In Kant, Unity and Plurality are, in fact, Categories. However, according to Kant, no Category can be applied to the Thing-in-itself. In fact, the latter is accordingly neither *one* nor *multiple*. But if we *speak* of it (albeit to only *say* that it is ineffable), we are indeed obliged to say (simultaneously or successively, or even interchangeably) that it is one *and* multiple. Additionally, in Plato, the One comes before the Number, even when it is a numbering number, and must not, therefore, be confused with the Unity of numbered Numbers.

developed into discourse without contra-diction, to then be *inserted*, qua constituent-element, in the uni-total Discourse or the System of Knowledge. In any event, qua (discursively undevelopable) 'notion', the Thing-in-itself is an integral element in the System, not to say in Discourse strictly so called. It appears in the System as a 'singular point' so to speak, and although it does not have a proper discursive *extension*, it cannot be eliminated, while it thus *interrupts* the otherwise continuous discursive development in the System of Knowledge. This discursive development can be carried out 'AS IF' the 'singular point' of the Thing-in-itself was some 'ordinary' constituent element in Discourse or in the System. Thus, Discourse becomes *total*, in the sense that (in principle) it implies *all* that can be said (without contradicting itself). But it is not truly *homogeneous*, that is, *one* in itself, owing to the mode of 'as-if' affecting one of its constituent elements. If this 'as-if' is overcome, that is, if the 'singular' character of the 'point' of the Thing-in-itself is ignored and treated as a truly 'ordinary' element, the Kantian System will be transformed into a Platonic (theistic) System. But, in that case, it becomes intrinsically contra-dictory, thus ceasing to be *one* or *uni*-total. To tell the truth, it ceases to be even *total*, because if it makes any sense to say that a/the (non-contra-dictory) Discourse implies/encompasses (at least potentially, virtually, or implicitly) *all* that can be said without *contra-dicting itself*, that notion of *totality* loses all its meaning as soon as contra-diction is allowed in Discourse. This is because contradiction is, by definition, indefinable in a *uni*vocal, and therefore, *indefinite* manner: one is *never* able to say (at any moment) *all* that *can* be said (at any given moment) *while contra-dicting oneself*, since nothing can prevent *all* that has been said (before) from being contra-dicted (at any given moment) nor prevent this contra-diction from being included in a (contra-dictory) discourse, which will encompass *all* that has been said before, including what has just been said in order to contra-dict it.

Kant himself avoids the pitfall of the (explicit or implicit) contra-diction proper to all variants of Platonism or Theism by expressly maintaining the mode of 'as-if' when he *speaks* of the trans-spatio-temporal Thing-in-itself. His System can, therefore, be and remain *total* qua Discourse. But, once again, it ceases for the same reason to be truly *one* or *homogeneous* (or even 'coherent' in the strongest sense of this term). In Kant, Discourse properly so called cannot, in fact and for us, if not for Kant himself, 'justify' or 'deduce' the presence of the 'As-if', neither qua discourse (because were it able to do so, it would have included this As-if within itself, thereby overcoming it qua 'As-if'), nor as Silence (because not speaking of anything at all, Silence cannot *speak* in the mode of 'As-if'). Consequently, when Kant claims that the notion of the Thing-in-itself and the discursive 'As-if' to which it 'refers' are 'unavoidable' (*unvermeidlich*) inside his System, he is not, strictly speaking, contradicting himself, but he is, nonetheless, claiming something which is strictly in-de-monstrable within that same System; in other words, he is claiming this something as an 'article of faith' (= Platonic 'Proof' = theological 'Revelation' or 'revealed Dogma').

If we do not take Kant at his word and note instead, without 'prejudice', as Hegel did, following Reinhold-Fichte-Schelling, that the Kantian trans-spatio-temporal notion of the Thing-in-itself is less 'unavoidable' than it is 'in-de-monstrable' (besides being contradictory as soon as it is discursively *developed* otherwise than in the mode of As-if, which in any case cannot be 'justified' discursively within the System), and overcome this notion accordingly, Kant's System will be automatically transformed into the System of Hegel. This is because the 'As-if' mode, which was introduced by Kant in Philosophy (even though it was [unconsciously?] initiated by the Platonic 'Myth'), allowed him to develop the properly discursive part of his System 'as if' the discourse in the 'As-if' mode were not there. Therefore, all we need to do is to take this other Kantian 'as if' seriously (which is, in any case, within anyone's grasp), that is, eliminate from the Kantian System all that pertains, in any shape or form, to the trans-spatio-temporal (or even 'divine') Thing-in-itself, while leaving virtually *intact* the properly discursive part of this System or the part which does not refer (directly or indirectly) to the notion of the Thing-in-itself (developed discursively in the mode of 'As if'), to 'automatically' obtain the authentically, even radically and consciously, atheistic Hegelian System of Knowledge. And it is that 'automatic' transformation of (Platonising) Kantianism into (Aristotlising) Hegelianism which manifested itself in the history of (Western) Philosophy in the form of an avalanche of Systems, which were successively elaborated, after Reinhold, by Fichte and Schelling.

In summary, the notion of the 'Thing-in-itself' is the 'singular point' that prevents Kant's total System from being truly one in its own self, that is, 'circular' in the Hegelian sense of the word. Kant's System closes in upon itself only on condition that its discourse passes through a segment of the circle indicated by the dotted line, or when developed discursively in the mode of As-if. When this segment is overcome, leaving everything else genuinely intact, that is, when thought freezes that segment and prevents it from moving dialectically by itself in such a way that the gap thus opened is 'overcome' (with a view to safeguarding the idea of the Truth identified with the *totality* of [the coherent] Discourse), we end up with an '*open*' or '*sceptical*' Discourse unworthy of the name System, and, if it remains true to form, it would lay no claim to being called one. Rather, it is a Discourse that develops indefinitely without ever completing itself by coming back to its starting point, and would not, therefore, be identified with the Truth, which is, by definition, everywhere and *always* identical to itself. That Discourse might validate itself merely qua permanent *Discussion*, of which one should not even say that it is discussing the *True*-semblant since, by definition, it excludes the transposition of the so-called true-semblant into Truth. And that is how, in the history of Western Philosophy, (Platonising) Kantianism, disencumbered of the notion of the Thing-in-itself, but otherwise frozen in the very same form it took before the said elimination, appeared in the guise of the Neo-scepticism inaugurated by *Aenesidimus-Schulze* and subsequently put forth under different names, including Positivism (in the same way Plato's System, disencumbered of the ineffable One, but otherwise left intact, gave rise to Academic Scepticism).

But if, after overcoming the notion of the Thing-in-itself, the residual Kantian System, that is, its properly discursive part, is allowed to develop within an immanent dialectical movement, it ultimately closes in upon itself (via Reinhold–Fichte–Schelling and lesser known others) while remaining a Discourse properly so called. And this Kantian Discourse without a 'singular point', that is, closed in upon itself or 'circular', is nothing else but the truly uni-total Discourse, since it is one in its own self (coherent in the strong sense of the word) while encompassing *all* that can be said without contradicting itself, which is the discourse of the *Hegelian System of Knowledge*, the one which can accomplish the feat of being *atheistic* without being 'sceptical'.

This situation can be illustrated with the following graph.[4]

---

4   In Hegel, the 'double Point' is the counterpart of the 'irreducible gap' of 'Kantian' Scepticism and of Kant's own 'As-if'. This 'Point' is 'double' in the sense that it is both the 'starting' and 'endpoint' of the circular uni-total Discourse ('Beginning' = 'Result'), but without causing any 'interruption' {*solution de continuité*} and can be arbitrarily placed

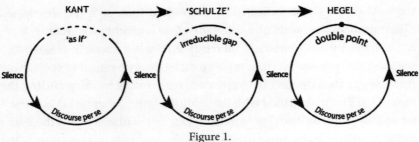

Figure 1.

Furthermore, Kant himself became perfectly aware of that situation, as evidenced by numerous passages from his writings, and particularly this one (which I have picked at random) from the *Critique of Pure Reason*, and which can be translated as follows:

> The notion (*Begriff*) of the Noumenon(*a*) is therefore not the notion of an Object (*Objekt*) [in the common sense of the word, that is, in the sense of an 'object of *discourse*', or even of 'Experience' or Perception; because the Noumenon will be defined a little further on as '*transcendental* Object'], but rather a problem (*Aufgabe*) unavoidably (*unvermeidlich*) bound with the *limitation* of *our* Sensation and [which comes down to the question of knowing] whether there may not be thinglike-objects (*Gegenstände*) entirely exempt from the aforementioned Intuition (that is, *sensible*, or even spatio-temporal); a question

anywhere on the circle. Similarly, the Platonic or theistic System also consists of a 'double Point', but that 'Point' is 'singular' in the sense that when discourse passes through it, it can be developed in two opposite 'directions' {*sens*}, making it thereby contra-dictory. We can, therefore, say that the Point in question *imposes* an escape into Silence (when it is truly 'singular', that is, if it engages Discourse on a path which has already been travelled 'in the opposite direction' {*sens*}, which would therefore be an 'impassable' one), as does the Sceptical 'gap'. This can be illustrated with the following graph:

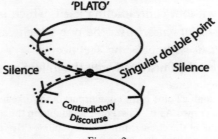

Figure 2.

that can only be given the indeterminate (*unbestimmt*) answer, namely [by saying] that, since *sensible* Intuition does not pertain to *all* things without distinction, *room remains* for *more* and *other* thinglike-objects [than the objects of sensible experience, which alone are available to Discourse strictly so called], in such a way that these [non-sensible or non-spatio-temporal] thinglike-objects cannot therefore be absolutely (*schlechthin*) *denied*, while they also cannot be *affirmed* as thinglike-objects for *our* Understanding [or for the coherent Discourse], in the absence of a *determinate* notion [that is, one which is discursively developable, not to say 'definable' or 'deducible' ('de-monstrable'), to which it could 'correspond'], (seeing that no Category is usable to that end) [since their discursive utilisation cannot dispose of or 'transcend' the sphere of spatio-temporality].

Consequently, the [discursive or human] Understanding *limits* Sensation without thereby *extending* its own field [of application]; and insofar as it warns (*warnt*) Sensation in such a way that the latter may not aspire (*anmasse*) to reach for Things [considered] in themselves, but [reach] solely for Phenomena, it *thinks* itself a Thinglike-Object [taken] in itself, but only as a *transcendental* Object [to the extent that 'transcendental' is additionally in Kant an epithet applied to any notion that is not immediately derived from Perception, but without which (the coherent) Discourse (whose entire 'immanent' sense is derived from Perception) cannot understand itself, let alone 'deduce' or 'de-monstrate' itself qua *true* Discourse] which is THE CAUSE (*Ursache*) of the Phenomenon (thus not itself Phenomenon), and that cannot be thought of [that is, in this instance, developed *discursively*] either as Magnitude or as Reality or as Substance, ETC., since these notions [= Categories] always require *sensible* [that is, spatio-temporal] forms in which they *determine* (or 'define', or even 'deduce') a thinglike-Object [a transcendental Object], for which it is, therefore, absolutely *unknown* [in the sense of (true) *discursive* knowing], whether it can be encountered *within* or *outside us*, whether it would be overcome (*aufgehoben*) along with Sensation or whether it would still remain as a residue when the latter is eliminated. If we want to *call* (*nennen*) this [transcendental] Object 'Noumenon' because its representation (*Vorstellung*) is not *sensible* (that is, spatio-temporal), we are free to do so. But since *we* cannot apply (*anwenden*) to this Object any of *our* Notions-of-the-Understanding [=

Categories], this representation still remains, for *us*, empty and serves nothing [else] but to draw the *limits* of *our sensible* [that is, spatio-temporal] Cognition [of which, we can therefore say, without contra-dicting ourselves, that it is discursively *developable*] and leave open a *vacant space* [*Raum ubrig zu lassen*] that *we* can *fill up* [discursively] neither through possible [spatio-temporal] Experience [transformed into Discourse] nor through the pure Understanding [since the latter can be *discursive* only if it develops its notions or Categories within the spatio-temporal frame]. (III, 230, 30–231, 19)

It would be both futile and puerile to bring to Kant's attention the fact that, had he developed this ETC. in the cited text, he would have noticed that, according to him, the 'transcendental Object' cannot be 'thought' of as a CAUSE either (to the extent that the latter is one of the Categories that he began to enumerate), even though, two lines earlier, he said that this Object is the 'CAUSE of the Phenomenon'. It would be futile because that is what Kant himself says a few pages later (III, 279, 19–21), and it would be puerile because, in this case, the question pertains to a mere semblance of contra-diction born from a purely verbal slip (Kant says *Ursache* although he meant to say *Grunde*). What Kant intended to say in the cited passage is perfectly clear and coherent, even though what he actually says there is in no way *unavoidable*, as he wrongly thinks and claims to be the case.

Kant is just saying that, in *his* System or in the (coherent, in the sense of non-contra-dictory) *total* Discourse, which is not, nor is intended to be *circular* (that is, truly unique and *one*), the *negation* of all Transcendence with reference to Spatio-temporality cannot be 'de-monstrated' (or 'deduced'). That cannot be done because Discourse properly so called does not effectively become contra-dictory from the mere fact of implying the notion of such Transcendence, provided that the notion in question is either identified with the notion of strict *Silence*, that is, giving up, once and for all, any attempt to develop it *discursively* (and particularly to 'define' it) in some way or other, or developed (discursively) only in *the mode of* '*As-if*', in such a way that one is able to tell the difference between this 'singular' development and Discourse properly so called, which thus remains intrinsically 'open' without it being possible to say that the 'As-if' 'supplement', through which it appears 'as-if' it was closed or circular, is either in agreement or in contra-diction with Discourse itself properly so called. [If Discourse remains 'open', it cannot be identified with the Truth, to the extent that the latter is, by definition, *one* and unique or *closed* in upon itself and cannot thus coincide with any *open* Discourse whatever. If Discourse is closed by an 'As-if', it can be accepted and used *as if* it were true, but it cannot be said that it is true in the proper sense of the term since, by definition, it involves an element which is valid only in the mode of 'As-if'.] However, when a given proposition included in Discourse with the aim of rendering it *total* renders it contradictory instead, it becomes necessary to include the proposition in question under its negative form, that is, qua Error, by prefacing it with the words: 'it is not true to say that . . .'. Kant is therefore right in saying that *his* System does not require the 'absolute disavowal' (*schlechten ableugnen*) of Transcendence with reference to Spatio-temporality. But, in the last cited passage, he is both perceptive and honest enough to say (albeit implicitly) that in no way does this same System require the *affirmation* of this Transcendence [because if one can say (without contra-dicting oneself) that the Transcendence in question does not exist 'outside of us', that is, outside of the Discourse of which it speaks, one cannot say that this Discourse *must* imply that notion of Transcendence, seeing that, by definition, it does not become contra-dictory from the mere fact of its inclusion].

One may and should, then, wonder *why* Kant preferred to uphold the notion of Transcendence instead of dispensing with it altogether, even though he himself says that he is not bound to its upholding by the development of his Discourse, and despite his realisation that this upholding would oblige him to either render Discourse contra-dictory, to always leave it open, or to complete it only in the 'As-if' mode. For, contrary to what has often been put forth, it is not enough to say that the Sceptic who deliberately opts for an endlessly open System 'contradicts' themselves just as little as the Hegelian Sage does when, despite being in possession of the circular uni-total Discourse, they would want, from time to time, to taste the pleasures and joys of, say, erotic or even 'mystical' Silence. Being the true Philosopher that he was, Kant neither did nor could resign himself to Scepticism, since he insisted on *completing* (albeit only in the As-if mode) his, in principle, total Discourse so as to make it quasi 'circular' or *one* and unique, and he did not want to become a 'Hegelian' Sage either, by allowing his own Discourse properly so called to close in upon itself (which was possible, seeing that the

Discourse in question will be effectively closed under Hegel's pen). Kant deliberately opted for the solution of the 'closed' Discourse solely by means of a constituent-element, discursively developed in the mode of As-if, even though such a deliberately non-homogeneous Discourse (and thus 'incoherent' in the strongest sense of the word) may not fully *satisfy* him as a Philosopher, by definition, aspiring to Wisdom, but merely *content* him with its absence of contra-diction.

Kant's mental attitude is plain to see in several passages across his works, as for instance in the one from the *Prolegomena*, which expends on the one I have already cited, and where 'critical' Philosophy is reduced to anti-Platonic Aristotelianism. The passage in question can be translated as follows:

> It is in this manner that our previous proposition [statement], which is the result of the entire Critique, is upheld, [and which says]: 'that *our* Reason, through all its a priori Principles, never teaches us about anything more than thinglike-Objects of possible [spatio-temporal] Experience alone, and [teaches] of these, nothing more than what can be cognised [discursively] in Experience'. But this *limitation* DOES NOT PREVENT Reason from carrying us up to the objective *limit* of Experience, namely, to the relation (*Beziehung*) to Something that cannot itself be a thinglike-Object of Experience [and is, thus, situated outside Spatio-temporality], but which must nonetheless be the highest *Ground* (*Grund*) of all Experience; without, however, teaching *us* anything [valid] in itself about this Ground [which is transcendent with reference to Spatio-temporality], but only in relation to its own utilisation (*Gebrauch*); *it must complete* and *orient towards the highest Ends*, in the field of possible Experience. Now, this is also all the benefit (*Nutzen*) that can *reasonably* even be wished for here, and with which there is cause (*Ursache*) to be *contented* (*zufrieden*). (*Prolegomena* §59, last paragraph)

The tone of the passage clearly shows that Kant is 'contented' (*zufrieden*) with this solution without being truly satisfied (*befriedigt*) therewith. And, once again, he is not saying that 'Reason', that is, the total coherent Discourse, *requires* the introduction or the upholding of the notion of Transcendence (which, even on this occasion, he plainly presents as discursively undevelopable [otherwise than in the As-if mode, which, besides, he omits to say here]), rather that it merely does *not preclude* doing so. In these conditions, one may and should, then, wonder why he does it.

Now, the cited passage seems to suggest that the Kantian behaviour is underpinned by *three explanations or 'justifications'* [even though we will eventually retain only one of them].

Firstly, Kant seems to be saying that the notion of Transcendence with reference to Spatio-temporality or the notion of the 'Thing-in-itself' (if one is to definitively go no further than this designation) is 'unavoidable' because it is necessarily presupposed by the very notion of the 'Phenomenon', to the extent that spatio-temporal 'Experience' would not subsist without a transcendent 'Ground'. To be sure, this interpretation may find validation in the (already cited) passage from the first edition of the *Critique of Pure Reason*, where Kant says that 'it follows naturally from the notion of the [spatio-temporal] Phenomenon in general that something must correspond to it which is not in itself Phenomenon' (IV, 164, 19–21). But the fact remains that this Kantian proposition is, pure and simple, an error in reasoning. If it is, indeed, obvious or undeniable that something cannot 'reveal' itself or 'appear' (thus enabling a discursively developable notion that is supposed to be *true*) unless this something is also capable of subsisting independently from its 'appearance' or without being 'revealed', this does not mean that this something must be transcendent with reference to Spatio-temporality, that is, be a Thing-in-itself in the Kantian sense of this term. A falling star is a falling star even if no one is there to see it, but even qua unseen, its 'falling' happens in time and in space. And it seems that Kant came to realise his error by himself, since he struck the passage containing the erroneous proposition in question out of the second edition. As for the cited passage from the *Prolegomena*, he in no way says there that accepting the notion of the Phenomenon or that of Experience *requires* the acceptance of the Thing-in-itself.

One must, therefore, consider whether the *second* apparent *'justification'* in support of this notion of Transcendence has any merit. Kant seems to say that it must be introduced with a view to the *'complete utilisation'* (*vollständiger Gebrauch*) of 'Reason'. This may be interpreted in the sense that Discourse cannot be *total* unless it entails the notion of the Thing-in-itself [which, in any case, would be discursively developable only in the 'As-if' mode]. But we know, thanks to Hegel, that the Kantian Discourse properly so called can be developed thoroughly in such a way as to render it total, that is, circular, not only without introducing or upholding the notion of the Thing-in-itself; rather, Discourse can be rendered circular or total only when this notion is eliminated therefrom. Surely, Kant could have been wrong on this question. But insofar as he realised that the closure of his Discourse through the discursive development of the notion of the Thing-in-itself can be carried out only in the 'As-if' mode, which he knew was hardly 'satisfactory', it is difficult to accept that he introduced the notion in question *in view of* 'closing' his Discourse in this manner, without even trying (as did, during Kant's lifetime and beyond, Reinhold, Fichte, and Schelling) to close it qua Discourse properly so called (or qua true Discourse in the strong and proper sense of the term). Kant did not introduce the notion of the Thing-in-itself *in order to* close his Discourse in the mode of As-if; he did so *because* he did not want to remove the notion of the Thing-in-itself from his Discourse and could not close his Discourse otherwise without said notion being removed therefrom.

We are then left with the *third and last* possible '*justification*': Kant introduced or upheld the notion of the Thing-in-itself in view of the 'utilisation' of the 'Reason' oriented towards 'the highest Ends' (*höchsten Zwecke*) because he knew that the elimination of the notion of the Thing-in-itself would necessarily eliminate these 'Ends' themselves, and because he did not want, at any cost, to eliminate them. He thus behaved in his Philosophy exactly as Plato did, with this one and enormous difference that, unlike Plato, he did not want to render his Discourse contra-dictory by discursively developing therein the notion of Transcendence, that is, 'as if' it were a discourse strictly so called, true in the proper and strong sense of the term; he rather went about this in a different manner, that is, by coming to the self-realisation, and by openly saying, that it was a question of an acceptable discursive development in the total Discourse solely in the mode of 'As-if'.

The likelihood {*vraisemblance*} of this interpretation of Kant's System is confirmed when one refers to the 'transcendental Methodology' of the *Critique of Pure Reason*, without which the System would be difficult to understand, but which is nonetheless very little read, rarely commented on, and almost never interpreted. It is, therefore, of interest to briefly summarise at least part of what one finds therein.

The notion of the 'transcendental Methodology' is, on this occasion and from the outset, indissolubly linked to that of the complete System of pure Reason, that is, to the notion of the uni-total Discourse, because this is what Kant says there: 'By the transcendental Methodology, therefore, I understand the determination of the formal conditions of a *complete System* of pure Reason' (III, 465, 20–2). Here, Kant subsequently de-monstrates (I, 1) that the (philosophical) System of Knowledge is necessarily *discursive*; he then shows that Mathematics, which *constructs* its spatio-temporal notions, without referring to the empirical-existence of extended-duration, stands in opposition to the philosophical *Discourse*; the latter *develops* its irreducible notions (the Categories) discursively on the basis of Spatio-temporal Experience or Perception (cf. III, 472, 32–475, 35). In addition, he distinguishes the 'Critique' from 'transcendental Philosophy' strictly so called, which is the 'System' in the proper sense of the word (cf. III, 483, 18–32).

After that (I, 2), Kant opposes Philosophy to Scepticism, in a section titled 'On the impossibility of a sceptical *satisfaction* (*Befriedigung*) of pure Reason that is *divided* against itself' (III, 495, 15–16), which means that Philosophy must never eliminate contra-diction from its Discourse, thus rendering it (or in view of such an elimination), irremediably 'open', even in its intention.

There, he first describes the situation by saying the following:

> The ensemble (*Inbegriff*) of all thinglike-Objects [that exist] for our Cognition appears (*scheint*) to us to be a flat surface, which has its apparent (*scheinbaren*) horizon, namely that which comprehends the *entire* extent (*Umfang*) of this Cognition [or of these thinglike-Objects] and [that] which was called by us the rational-notion (*Vernunftbegrieff*) of *unconditioned* (*unbedingten*) *Totality*. It is impossible to attain this horizon *empirically*, and all attempts to determine it a priori in accordance with a given *Principle* whatsoever (*gewissen*) have been in vain. But still, all questions of our pure Reason pertain to that which might lie *outside/out of* this horizon or in any case also *within* its border-line. (III, 496, 14–22)

While commenting on this passage, Kant says that Scepticism (which is, for him, Hume's), is obnubilated by the necessarily *indefinite* character of *empirical* Cognition (which is *developed as long as* Discourse shall last), and resigns itself, prematurely and wrongly, to the notion of the 'open-ended' System (which precisely for this reason is not a *System* and cannot be interpreted as being the Truth). But Scepticism is right when it does not accept 'Dogmatism', which tries, in vain, to *limit* the System by particular or isolated 'Principles' wrongly considered as 'irreducible' or 'undeducible' or even self-'evident' or 'revealed' as such. What must be opposed to Scepticism (and thus to Dogmatism) is the 'rational notion' of the *Totality* of Discourse or of the *System* of Knowledge. The *total* Discourse is, by definition, 'limited' in the sense that there is nothing *outside* of it (except Non-discourse or Silence, as well as Contra-diction): it is therefore one and unique, that is, *uni*-total. But this Totality is 'unconditioned' to the extent that its 'limit' is merely self-imposed: Discourse, which is *one* in its own self, is 'limited' only because it is *total* (in the same way that it can be said to be *total* only if and because it is *one* in its own self, that is, coherent or non-contra-dictory). The 'limits' of the uni-total System are, therefore, neither vague like those of the *open-ended* Discourses of Scepticism, nor non-discursive, like those of the 'Discourses' of Dogmatism. The uni-total System 'limits' itself by itself only through a *complete* self-development: its 'limits' are thus given from its beginning because they involve *all* that is discursively *possible* (without contra-diction) and exclude only that which is discursively undevelopable (without contra-diction). The 'limits' of the uni-total Discourse are nothing other than the limitations set upon its 'possibilities'. Now, these limitations can be 'derived', with *absolute certainty*, from the very fact of Discourse, even *before* ('a priori') it has been (completely) developed. And this 'unconditioned' 'a priori' 'limitation' set upon the System of Knowledge is the work of the 'Critique', which excludes from Discourse all that cannot be included therein without rendering it contra-dictory, ensuring thereby the *unity* (coherence) of *totality*, that is, the unicity or uni-totality of the discursive System of Knowledge, which, once completely developed (at least virtually), could and should be accepted as the one and unique Truth.

For us, and for Hegel, this Kantian conception of the System is equivalent to the affirmation of the *circularity* of the Discourse through which it is constituted: the System can set a limitation upon itself by itself and be thus uni-total or true only if the culminating point of its discursive (or 'dialectical') development coincides with its starting point, because only then can we have the *absolute certainty* that there is *nothing* outside of it (except Silence and Contra-diction). Surely, this Hegelian conception of the System is not to be found, in black and white, in Kant. But the passage which concludes the commentary on the one that has just been cited is equivalent, in itself and for us, to the formula that Hegel himself uses to express the conception in question.

In fact, this is what Kant says there:

> Our Reason is not something like an *indefinitely* far extended *plane* surface/a plane (*Ebene*) the limits of which one can *vaguely* cognise only in general (*nur so* überhaupt) [as Scepticism wrongly thinks], but must rather be compared with a *sphere*, the diameter/radius of which can be found out from the curvature of the segment [of the greater drawn circle] on its surface from ([that is, starting with] the nature of synthetic a priori propositions), from which can also be indicated with *certainty* its *content* [in the sense of 'capacity' (*Inhalt*)] and its *limitation* (*Begrenzung*). *Outside* this sphere ([which is] the field of [spatio-temporal] Experience), *nothing* is *for it* [for Reason] an object. (III, 497, 27–33)

This would be perfect and perfectly Hegelian or even 'Aristotelian' (in the sense of anti-Platonic) or atheistic if it could be taken literally. It would then be possible to say that, already for Kant, the System of Knowledge or the (discursive) Truth is nothing other than the (coherent) Discourse which is uni-total because circular or closed in upon itself, that is, leaving nothing outside of itself other than Contra-diction and strict and definitive Silence. But taking this text literally would be synonymous with doing violence to Kant's thought.

For, here, Kant commits to Silence or Contra-diction only that which is *outside* the 'sphere' of the coherent Discourse. But, in the previously cited passage, he was also referring to that which is found *in* or *on* the Border-line of the said Discourse, suggesting that it is this to which all questions of 'pure Reason' ultimately pertain. Now, we know that the Border-line that 'closes' Discourse or the properly Kantian System is constituted by a pseudo-discourse that 'develops' the notion of Transcendence or the non-spatio-temporal Thing-in-itself, which is developable only in the As-if mode.

We thus encounter the notion of the Thing-in-itself wherever Kant speaks of the System as a whole. But by interpreting the above-cited passage from the *Prolegomena*, we have seen that, for it to be coherent, the discursive development of the Kantian System does not require the introduction of this notion [which is, therefore, and contrary to what

Kant sometimes says, well and truly 'Transcendent' (in regard to the System and to Discourse) and not 'transcendental' (that is, necessarily included in the Discourse that wants to close in upon itself, that is, become uni-total by [discursively] accounting [at the *end*] for itself by itself [and therefore for its *beginning*])]. We have also seen that Kant introduces this notion to 'close' Discourse and to thus render the System uni-total, since, in fact and on Kant's own admission, the System can be closed without it and cannot be 'closed' with it except in the mode of As-if. We have thus been able to note that Kant introduces, or rather upholds, the notion of Transcendence (with reference to the Spatio-temporality to which he reduces Discourse properly so called, or true discourse in the strong sense of the word) because, without it, 'Reason', that is, Human beings as such, cannot 'justify' (that is, account discursively for their contra-dictions, albeit only in the As-if mode) the 'highest Ends' which, according to Kant, {Reason} neither can nor should neglect. IN SHORT, the notion of the Thing-in-itself is present in the System of Kant so that the latter may speak, albeit only in the mode of As-if, of that which is, for Kant, the 'supreme End' of the specifically human in the Human being.

Now, Kant 'defines' this notion of 'supreme End' (that is, he develops it discursively by making its content specific and explicit) in the second section of the 'transcendental Methodology' titled 'The Canon of Pure Reason', whose first Subdivision is precisely titled: 'On the *ultimate End (letzten Zweckes)* of the pure utilisation (*Gebrauches*) of our Reason'. And what is said therein is so essential to the comprehension of Kantianism to such an extent that it is worth translating in large extracts with a view to its submission to a philosophical interpretation.

This is what Kant says there:

Reason [that is, the non-contra-dictory Discourse] is driven by a propensity (*Hang*) of its nature to go *beyond* its experimental [that is, spatio-temporal]/use in-Experience, to venture, in a pure use [that is, beyond Spatio-temporality] and by means of Ideas which are but mere (*blosser*) Ideas [or 'Notions' devoid of any spatio-temporal 'content' or 'significance'], to the outermost limits of all [discursive, and therefore spatio-temporal] Cognition, and to find *repose* only in the *completion* (*Vollendung*) of its *circle*, in a self-subsisting/self-maintaining (*für sich bestehenden*) systematic Whole. Is this propensity [belonging to Reason] grounded merely in its *speculative* [that is, theoretical or discursive] interest, or rather uniquely and exclusively in its practical [that is, active or acting] interest?

I want to set aside, for the time being, the Happiness [that is, the Joy] procured (*macht*) by pure Reason [when utilised] in a speculative regard and ask only about those tasks whose solution constitutes its highest/ultimate End (*letzten Zweck*), and it matters little [besides] whether it may reach this or not, in respect to which all other ends have merely the value of means. These highest Ends must, once again, in accordance with the nature of Reason, have *unity*, to *jointly* advance that interest of humanity which is subordinated to no higher interest.

The final-intention (*Endabsicht*) to which the speculation of Reason in its transcendental use [in the sense of 'transcendent' with reference to Spatio-temporality] ultimately leads, concerns three thinglike-Objects: the *Freedom* of the Will, the *Immortality* of the Soul, and the existence of *God*. With regard to all three, the purely *speculative* [that is, discursive] interest of Reason is but very weak (*gering*). These three propositions always remain *transcendent* for *speculative* [discursive] Reason and they absolutely have no *immanent* use, that is, permissible for thinglike-Objects of [*spatio-temporal*] Experience and therefore useful (*nützliche*) *for us* in some way (*auf einige Art*); but are rather, considered in themselves, entirely idle and extremely difficult/painful efforts of our Reason.

If, then, these three fundamental/cardinal (*Cardinalsätze*) propositions are not at all *necessary* for [*discursive*] *Knowledge* [and accordingly, for *discursive* Truth], and yet are insistently recommended to us by our Reason [insofar as the latter wrongly wants to *speak* of Transcendence], it follows that their importance, properly speaking [that is, from the standpoint of the Kantian System], must concern only the practical-Sphere [*das praktische*, that is, the domain of free Action, which according to this passage, seems able, or even destined, to forgo all Discourse, and must resign itself, if it wants to speak, to ultimately speak only in the mode of As-if].

Everything is 'practical' that is possible through *Freedom* or free Action ... Thus the entire armament of Reason, in the undertaking that one can call pure Philosophy [or System of Knowledge], is in fact oriented only towards the three problems that have been mentioned. These themselves, however, have in turn their/one more remote intention: namely, *what is to be done IF* the Will is *free*, [and] IF there is a *God*, and *a future World* [to be understood as post-mortal]. Now, since this concerns our conduct with reference to the highest End, the ultimate intention of Nature [that is, of God] which provides for us wisely, in the arrangement of our Reason is properly focused on/oriented towards Morality alone [*aufs Moralische*]. (III, 518, 15–33; 519, 28–520, I, 520, 17–24)

It cannot be said any more clearly that the notion of the Thing-in-itself is far from being an 'unavoidable' *exigency* of the uni-total Discourse or of the System of Knowledge (cf. *Zum Wissen garnicht nötig*; III, 519, 34–5), and that it is, on the contrary, incorporated therein as a foreign body, which is useless because unusable [since this notion can be developed discursively only in the mode of As-if] and, for that reason, it is cumbersome or even dangerous [because the introduction of a thorough discursive development of this notion in Discourse would render it contradictory]. One cannot express more forcefully or with further clarity the idea that this notion must be introduced or maintained [qua discursively developed in the mode of As-if] in Discourse and in the System solely and exclusively for 'practical ends', that is, with a view to free Action, to the extent that the latter is *the* 'highest End' of *all* that is truly human in the human being.

Every so often, passages of a similar kind to the one we have just cited, which can be found almost everywhere in Kant's writings, are generally referred to as instances of Kantian 'moralism'. This general manner of speaking is certainly not 'false'. However, because the meaning of the word 'Morality' is vague and ambiguous, the question is to flesh it out so that one knows what can and must be said when one speaks of the 'moralism' *of Kant*. Now, the cited passage is essential for the comprehension of Kantian 'moralism'.

Kant says, it is true (in the last cited subparagraph), that, ultimately, Philosophy and therefore the (discursive) System of Knowledge or the uni-total Discourse are there only for the purpose of addressing the problem of knowing what *must (or ought to) be done*. However, what is generally overlooked is the fact that this question, and thus the answer thereto, are, not 'absolute' or 'categorical' (contrary to what Kant himself says elsewhere), but essentially 'hypothetical' or 'conditional', not to say 'conditioned'. Indeed, Kant formulates his 'supreme' question as follows: 'what we ought to do, IF the Will is *free* [and] IF there is a God and a *future World*' (II, 520, 20-1). And the entire bulk of Kant's philosophy shows that these two (or three) IFs are no less than a verbal slip {*lapsus*}.

The 'condition' or the 'if' relative to Freedom is trivial. One cannot effectively speak of 'Morality' without speaking of 'Freedom', and Common Sense would be scandalised by a 'commandment' addressed to someone materially incapable of complying with it, or even *willing* to observe or reject it. And, yet, the history of Philosophy shows us that here, too, there is a 'problem'. Indeed, on the one hand, the Philosophers who wanted to discursively 'justify' (that is, discursively 'develop', in the sense of 'define' and 'deduce') a certain particular or general 'Morality', understood as a set of 'commandments' whose content is immutable in time and unlimited in space, have either been forced to explicitly deny the notion of Freedom (as, for instance, Spinoza did), or to realise that they cannot 'justify' it discursively, unless 'Morality' is interpreted as a '*divine* commandment', even at the risk of denying God's almightiness, or concede (as Saint Paul did) that, for reasons unknown to them, God renounces the use of his power so that human beings, to whom those commandments were apparently given so that they are *not* disobeyed, can also be permitted to disobey them, imperative as they are. On the other hand, the Philosophy which was willing and able to discursively account for Freedom, and which has reached its culmination in Hegel (via, among others, Descartes and the same Kant), was eventually forced to 'dialectically overcome' the 'classical' notion of 'Morality', no longer seeing in it anything other than the general forms or the temporary and spatially limited 'categories' of the free Action of the human beings who create History, even if they must admit that at the end of that History these forms, in their last avatar, take a definitive character, that is, a permanent and spatially 'universal' one. But we do not have to concern ourselves here with *this* 'problem' because Kant deliberately rules it out from the context we are interpreting. He contents himself with calling upon introspection to establish the *empirical fact* of Freedom, making only a brief allusion to the 'problem' arising from '*transcendental* Freedom' [which he addresses elsewhere], and which he defines [in anticipation of the Hegelian notion of Negativity] as autonomy vis-à-vis theoretical Reason, and thus vis-à-vis Nature itself; to then add that it 'seems to be *contrary* (*zuwider zu sein scheint*) to the Law-of-Nature and, therefore, to all possible spatio-temporal Experience' (III, 521, 26-522, 14).

* * *

Conversely, we should interpret the meaning and scope of the two other IFs or 'conditions' of any 'Morality', namely the existence of 'God' and the 'future World'.

One might as well, so it seems, dismiss these two new 'conditions' by calling upon the widespread opinion (adopted, for example, by Dostoyevsky) which says that the meaning and scope of 'Morality' rests solely upon the supposition that it is controlled and sanctioned by God, even though it is not promulgated by Him in person, and that, accordingly, it depends on the supposition that Human beings are endowed with an *immortal* soul, which alone may not only place them under the presence of an *eternal* God, but also prevents them from evading (as for instance through suicide) His 'judgement' and his 'sanctions'. But this opinion, as widespread as it is, has consistently been refuted by Common Sense which, when it comes to establishing or upholding a certain 'Morality', would rely less on the direct or 'immediate' intervention of God, and more on the 'mediated' action of the Police (the latter often acts, it is true, 'in the name of God', but may also come to realise that it is, in fact, imposing the respect of purely human-made laws without thereby diminishing their efficacy). It would therefore be insulting to Kant to presume that he is of the same opinion, albeit avant la lettre, of a certain Ivan Karamazov [That 'if there is no God, all is permitted': yes, but only within the limits tolerated by the Police force in place].

Let us then attempt to uncover and interpret the authentic motives of the two 'conditions' underpinning Kantian 'Morality', starting, first, with the '*condition of the future World*'.

Here, once again, if this expression was taken 'literally', one might say that the question pertains to a trivial matter, albeit one which is, on this occasion, agreeable with Common Sense [and, besides, introduced as such in the Hegelian System of Knowledge]. In this case, a 'moral commandment' would be devoid of meaning and effect unless it is addressed to a man with *a future* {*avenir*} ahead of him. Indeed, what is the significance of 'Morality' to someone condemned to death at the very instant preceding, let's say by 0.01 second, the moment when the blade of the guillotine will touch his neck? If 'Morality' refers to Action (and the so-called intentional 'Morality' likewise refers to an intention *to act*, even when, in conformity with 'Morality', the said intention is not *realised*), it must well be the case that, in this instance, Morality refers to the moment when the Action in question exists in the Present only in the form of a Project, which precisely signifies that Morality would be devoid of meaning and effect unless there is (at least virtually) a *'future* World' to which the Project of the Action, to which Morality can and should presumably be applicable, refers. Notwithstanding, if the projected Action is presumably *free* (that is, not entirely *determined* by the given *present* World), it must be admitted that, when carried out, it may *transform* the 'future' World that has become 'present' at the moment when an efficacious Action takes place, in such a way that it is rendered other than what it was supposed to be when it was still a future World and different from the past one which was present at the moment of the projected Action. And there is no guarantee then that the Morality of the 'future World' will approve or disapprove of the Action, which, qua Project, was disapproved or approved by today's Moral standards. However, it goes without saying that Kant would not admit this 'Moral' 'relativism' or 'historicism' (even while admitting that History has an end, with reference to which 'relativistic' Morals have an 'absolute' value, to the extent that the Morality which *ultimately stems* from History is, by definition, valid everywhere and always).

It remains to be established *why* this would be inadmissible to Kant. Now, let me say straight away that it is not *because* Kant wanted to avoid moral 'relativism' that he considered the *'future* World' as that which lies *Beyond* death, that is, beyond Spatio-temporality, that is, as a form of Transcendence or, put differently, of the Thing-in-itself. Rather, it is *because* he considered the *'future* World' to be *transcendent* that he denied himself the right to accept 'historical relativism' in the field of Morality and opted, instead, for an 'imperative' and 'categorical' Morality, that is, 'a priori' as he would say, or in fact, supposedly valid everywhere and always when a human being wants to be human, and not only at the *end* of History but from its first *beginning*.

To validate this point, one needs to begin with the question of what the desire to be *human*, and by implication, the fact of being or not being human, in fact means. According to Greek, ancient or pagan (scientific and philosophical) Anthropology, the answer is simple. To be *human* is to behave in such a way that I am able to gain awareness of the fact that my empirical existence (revealed through Perception) conforms (absolutely or relatively) to my Essence (which is also the Sense attributed to the word 'I' and which is revealed by what may be called an 'Intellect', to the extent that the latter may operate either inside Perception [Aristotle], or outside of it [Plato]); this Essence that is mine is the same in all human beings (there is, perhaps, only one essence whose unity is, in addition to that, a numbering number and not a numbered unity) and it does not change over time. If I notice a (more or less 'perfect') coincidence between that ('universal') Essence and my ('personal') existence, I am (more or less) *satisfied*. Being satisfied with what I *am*, I would no longer want to *become* other, and I would remain until my death what I *should* be everywhere and always, or even 'necessarily', namely an Existence in conformity with its Essence. In this respect, the Human being does not differ, indeed, in any way from the Animal and other 'natural' entities, which are likewise in conformity with their respective Essences, unless they are 'sick' and therefore sooner or later eliminated from the real World, where only Existence in conformity with Essence may subsist permanently, without causing it to malfunction.

But, for (mythological or philosophical) Judeo-Christian Anthropology, the situation is far more complicated. Jewish Mythology could not admit that the Human being has an Essence in the Greek sense of the word, since, in its view, one cannot be human unless one is born 'under the Law' or at least undergoes certain rites of passage (circumcision). As for Christian Mythology (initiated by Saint Paul), it was even less able to apply the Greek notion of the Essence to the Human being, seeing that it is entirely founded on the idea of Conversion, which would trans-form a merely anthropomorphic being into a truly/authentically human one, without even having to take a Jew as its starting point. However, at a given point in History, the very Law which made a Jew into a *human* being had lost, in the eyes of Christians, its humanising value, in such a way that conforming to that Law became 'inhuman', whereas previously, from the Christian point of view itself, one could be humanised only by conforming to it. In other words, a Judeo-Christian Human being did not have an Essence *determined* in a univocal way on account of the place (*topos*) they occupied in the natural World (*Cosmos*); they could become everywhere and always *essentially* other than what they were (to the extent that they alone among natural beings are the ones who conserve in themselves the Mana that magical Mythology attributed to all things). But what then does it mean 'to be *human*'?

The answer given by (religion-informed and theist-oriented) Judeo-Christian Mythology comes down to saying that being *human* signifies being in conformity *with God* or 'resembling' him, which allows the

Human being to *essentially* change their humanity if God changes or if they change Gods. As a result, Morality would consist in the 'imitation' of God, to the extent that the model to imitate is either God himself (as soon as he makes himself into a Human being to render that imitation possible), or an appropriate scheme, verbal or otherwise, that God sets up and with which he provides the Human being, for the purpose of this imitation. As for Human beings per se, they are, if we wish, 'satisfied' in and by that imitation of God, but solely because they imitate a *God* who could and should presumably make them *happy after* their death if their imitation is successful (at God's whim). Imitation, in and for itself, does not satisfy them, nor does it procure happiness for them: on the contrary, it is supposed to go against what they would have wished to do 'spontaneously' or 'naturally'. For the (indemonstrable) basic hypothesis underpinning any Religion is the absolute impossibility of being *satisfied*, in the proper and strong sense of the word, down Here-below, that is, by leading a purely 'natural' life, in conformity with what the pagans call the Human Essence and which, in the eyes of the Judeo-Christians, is merely animal 'nature' in opposition to their human life.

If, by contrast, a Judeo-Christian ceases to be religious and accepts the ideal-idea of satisfaction down Here-below, as in pagan philosophy, their position becomes difficult and complex and it is only late in the day, in and through Hegelianism, that they will find a definitive appeasement in the satisfaction that they can at long last effectively obtain at the end of History, after having pursued it in vain in the course of that History. For the Judeo-Christian *atheistic* and unreligious person would not be truly *satisfied*, that is, *happy* with the awareness of being *worthy* of happiness, unless their dignity is *recognised* by *everyone*, or at least by those who are capable of so doing. Indeed, being 'self-satisfied' when *everyone* disapproves of you is the most certain objective sign of Madness or 'mental *illness*'. And no one is so lacking in ambition to such an extent that they are truly self-satisfied with a *definitively partial* recognition, be it familial, amicable, social, national, or otherwise. Therefore, the atheistic, unreligious Judeo-Christian could and should admit terrestrial satisfaction, which they will effectively attain, albeit only at the end of History, that is, within the universal and homogeneous State.[5] Just as

---

5   On the face of it, this State can only guarantee the constituent element of 'dignity' (that is, of 'universal recognition') but not 'happiness', which is, nonetheless, essential in

well, their definitive Morality can only be that of the good citizen of that State. Until then, only their *Faith* or their subjectively *certain Hope* in that future State will be able to preserve them from Religion, that is, from the Human being's definitive renunciation of any satisfaction on earth, which threatens with such a frightening despair that one would be tempted to mitigate it with the idea of a transcendent satisfaction of an immortal soul 'recognised' by God.

But let us go back to Kant. In the second Subdivision of the 'Canon' he, himself, summarises the whole of his Moral philosophy (which is, for him, the supreme End of the Human being) in the following 'commandment': 'do [all] that through which you will become *worthy* of being *happy*' (III, 525, 12–13). Immediately after that, he asks the following question: If I behave so as not to be *unworthy* of Happiness, am I entitled to *hope* thereby to partake of it [effectively]?' (III, 525, 14–16). But what does this question mean for Kant?

First, it should be noted that this question makes no sense to the unreligious Pagan, regardless of whether they are atheist or theist. They will tell you that the issue here is not about Hope or Faith, rather it concerns Certainty or Knowledge. For, if someone is *worthy* of being happy, it is because their existence conforms to their Essence (which they can perfectly see for themselves); now, every Essence is determined by the place it occupies in the harmonious (because permanent) and immutable (because harmonious) World, and is, by definition, 'in conformity' with that place; to conform to one's Essence is, therefore, by definition, to have an existence that conforms to the 'natural' place it 'must' occupy in the World; and this conformity (= physical and moral 'health') *is* precisely Happiness: to be *worthy* of being happy (that is, to *know* it) and to *be* happy are therefore one and the same thing, and this Happiness (= Satisfaction) is the only true Happiness, because it alone

---

securing satisfaction. But this is only an illusion. Indeed, in this State, only rational or reasonable behaviour can be universally recognised. However, by definition, this rules out unhappiness, thereby securing the minimum of happiness essential for Satisfaction. The only apparent exception being the suffering caused by illness. But on the one hand, the capability of medical science to alleviate pain has increasingly grown, and on the other hand, if the suffering caused by illness becomes 'intolerable' to such an extent that it cancels happiness or the 'joie de vivre', it can be eliminated through suicide. As for death, in accord with Epicurus' view, it cannot disturb happiness because a dead person is no longer alive and the living one, who alone can be happy, is never dead.

can guarantee its own permanence and thus the absence of any desire to change; it is, for instance, the Happiness of the stoic Sage. Consequently, if Kant poses the question of Hope, he thereby implicitly accepts the Judeo-Christian Anthropology (of Negativity) and rejects the Greek or pagan Anthropology (of Identity).

But what answer would the Judeo-Christian give to the Kantian question? If they are unreligious (and thus atheistic because the unreligious Judeo-Christian is necessarily atheistic [at least if they are slightly inclined towards Philosophy] since, as we will see, coherent and discursive, [non-mythological], that is, 'Platonic' or 'pagan', theism contra-dicts the Judeo-Christian Anthropology with which it may cohabit only in the incoherence of Myth. One may seek to preserve Myth solely on religious grounds, at least as soon as one begins to take notice of its incoherence, which a Philosopher should not fail to do), they would give the following answer: the Happiness one is made *worthy* thereof is nothing else but Satisfaction, which has two inextricable constituent-elements: Happiness (or the Joie de vivre) derived, in certain conditions, from the realisation of self-consciousness [which is nothing else but the Happiness of the ancient Sage], and the Recognition of one's realised self-conscious by all those who are capable of recognising it by realising the consciousness thereof [which is, if we like, the secularised form of being recognised by God]; now, the realisation of self-consciousness can procure Happiness only *if* that of which we thus become self-conscious is at the same time 'recognised' by everyone. Kant wonders whether the opposite is true as well, that is, if the fact of being *recognised by everyone* suffices to guarantee Happiness. The unreligious and atheistic Judeo-Christian would answer in the affirmative, saying that a self-conscious life *can be* happy (in a permanent way) only if it is rational or reasonable (such as it was already envisioned by the Greeks); now, such a life can be recognised by *everyone* only in a rational or reasonable State (that is, one which is universal and homogeneous, in the image of the uni-total Discourse, that is, the Truth); but, in such a State, a reasonable life *is* necessarily happy; consequently, one may *know* that when one is *worthy* of being happy, in this sense that one is enjoying *universal* recognition, one *is* effectively *happy*.

And, yet, the Judeo-Christian, even when unreligious and atheistic, fully admits (contrary to the atheistic or the unreligious theistic Pagan) that Kant may have spoken of Hope {*Espoir*} and not of Knowledge {*Savoir*}. Indeed, the reasoning that has just been given (in line with the reasoning given by the ancient Sage), which was *false* in Kant's time, can validly be set forth only at the *end* of History. The point is that, by definition, a *reasonable* life cannot be *universally* recognised before the end of History, for the simple reason that, until then, the human World itself is not reasonable (otherwise, on the contrary supposition, it would not change and would be the last one instead). Before the end of History, 'reasonable' life is necessarily at *odds* with the human World (it is everywhere and always 'revolutionary') and, therefore, always and everywhere more or less unhappy and never and nowhere is it able to procure a full-fledged satisfaction, if only by dint of the fact that it cannot be *universally* recognised (because even when, before the end of History, life can only be *relatively* reasonable, it is relatively *reasonable* only to the extent that it is *more* reasonable than the life of the World where it is lived and where it cannot thus enjoy a universal recognition). Therefore, for as long as History shall last, perfect Satisfaction (which necessarily involves Happiness, because it is predicated on *universal* recognition) can be no more than a mere Hope rather than a *knowable* reality. That Hope can be associated with a subjective Certainty and valued accordingly as Faith (or as the certainty of hope, in accord with Saint Paul's definition) if it is permitted to say in a coherent discourse that sooner or later the universal and homogeneous State will be realised, which will complete History and thus validate the reasoning set forth above, transforming the Faith in question into discursive Knowledge or into Truth.[6]

---

6   On the face of it, there seems to be a contra-diction here. If Hope manifests itself in the Judeo-Christian only because, for them, Human beings are *free*, how then can they *foresee* the end of History and say that there will come a day when it *necessarily* happens? Because their 'foresight' is nothing else but the Project of *free* Action: *if* the Human being acts *freely* (that is, qua Negator), History will achieve its end through the universal and homogeneous State. However, Human beings *are* Freedom. They will, therefore, either cease to be human (until the realisation of their Project, which is designed as such and by us since the very first anthropogenic Struggle), or History will achieve its absolute end. Ceasing to be human is to no longer develop self-awareness; the realisation of consciousness, that is, Philosophy, is, therefore, if we wish, a Postulate (the Postulate of Truth), which can one day cease to correspond to reality. Be that as it may, at the end of History, Human beings cease to be free (= historical) since they cease to be negators of the (historical) given. But there is no contra-diction here, since Freedom is Action or the Primacy of the Future {*Avenir*}, that is, an essentially temporal or even temporary phenomenon. Human beings are born free in this sense that the anthropogenic Struggle is an Act of freedom. But they are free only insofar as they are Negators of the given, that is, of Natural or Animal reality. For, as long as Nature (in and outside of the Human being) can be actively negated, History will last, and the Human being

Morality would then consist in acting so as to accelerate this historical process, or at least, so as to preclude its slowing down. And, although this Morality does not guarantee absolute Satisfaction (or Happiness), since the one who practises it dies before seeing its result (unless one is living on the eve of the end of History), experience shows that if it cannot always make life happy, it can at least make it passionate and impassioned, that is, 'joyful' and therefore truly worthy of being lived, that is, all things considered, satisfying. In other words, when unable to live like a Sage before the end of History, one can always and everywhere live like a Philosopher aspiring to and having Faith in Wisdom.

But what answer would the Religious person, be they pagan or Judeo-Christian, give to the Kantian question? They would tell you that never and nowhere can Satisfaction, or even Happiness, be realised on earth, due to the fundamental and irremediable imperfection of Human beings and of the World in which they live. Accordingly, if one does not want to sink deep into the night of 'the Unhappy Consciousness', that is, into mindless and mind-numbing Despair (which is the worst of all possible sins, far worse than pride itself), one must accept a beyond that can be accessed via a soul, where blissful Satisfaction would be obtainable as a reward (if not necessary, at least possible) for a certain 'moral' terrestrial life. Surely, discursive Knowledge does not have access to that beyond, which is an object of Hope and not an object of Cognition. But, if that *Hope* is subjectively *certain*, it is a Faith that can be as solid as a rock. And even if discursive Knowledge will not ensure that certainty, it may

---

will remain free. But, since Nature is a given, that is, definite or finite, its negation cannot be prolonged indefinitely. Thus, there will come a day when Human beings will have negated all that is natural in them, and at that point they will create the universal and homogeneous State. But then, they will no longer be able to negate themselves, and will, therefore, no longer be free, and history will stop. All things considered, human beings are only free to no longer be animal life but cease to be free to no longer be god the day when they will become that god. And they will have no wish to no longer be god, since they will be perfectly satisfied. Now, no one acts *freely* unless they wish to do so. Therefore, there is no contradiction here. On the contrary, it is the necessarily *infinite* progress that would place a limit on human freedom, which is not only the freedom to act, but also the freedom to rest if one wishes to do so (like God after the creation of the World, but without the surprise of Adam's fall).

If they will not be taken by surprise by the unexpected fall of Adam, it will not be to their disadvantage: this will simply mean that *their* World is more rational or reasonable than the World that God had created, even though they invested in that world, it is true, much more time and perhaps more effort.

at least not bring about its demise, and to the extent that it may do so, one can and must deal with it, even when one is fortunate enough to have a non-discursive certainty, if only to eliminate the discourses that weaken Faith by attacking the discursive certainty of Hope.

Undoubtedly, the denial of the possibility of Satisfaction on earth cannot be discursively de-monstrated, for it presupposes the absolute inefficacy of human Action, that is, its incapacity to transform the World which, in its current state, does not satisfy Human beings in a World prone to satisfying them one day.

Thus, what is at stake here is the adoption of an indemonstrable and indisputable position, that is, an irrational 'existential attitude', which is discursively expressed by what is known as 'Dogma' or an 'article of faith'. The latter underpins every religious or 'theological' discursive development: it is necessarily admitted as an Axiom or Postulate by every 'Theologian', by every *speaking* Religious person, and that admission suffices to turn the discourse in which it is developed into a 'theological' or religious discourse.

Now, Kant's response to the question he posed shows that there was an essentially and authentically religious attitude underpinning his entire philosophy, which does not convey an impatience at being happy with any external conditions and without recognition from others (that would bring pseudo-religiosity and madness into a close proximity), rather it betrays his profound conviction that Human beings and the World in which they live cannot, *under any circumstances*, procure Satisfaction, which entails the Happiness one is deserving thereof. Indeed, Kant believed that the notion of a transcendent 'future World' can be deduced from his moral commandment because the realisation of his Morality in that World (which is equivalent to Satisfaction or to the Happiness one deserves) appeared to him absolutely, that is, everywhere and always, *impossible*. He was driven by this conviction because (as a Protestant) he admitted Judeo-Christian Anthropology and (as a Philosopher more radical than Descartes) defined Freedom, which is the very being of the Judeo-Christian, in terms of Negativity. In other words, Freedom is, for him, *necessarily* at odds or in conflict with Nature (= Identity), in such a way that the harmony between Duty and Reality (presupposed in Satisfaction) is achievable only beyond that natural, that is, for him, spatio-temporal, World (cf. III, 525, 27–531, 23). But this 'deduction' is valid only if one admits (as Kant tacitly does) that human Action (even if 'moral') is strictly *inefficacious*, that is, fundamentally incapable of transforming the World (through Struggle and Work) in such a way that it conforms to Human beings and to their freely conceived and executed Projects, unless one admits otherwise that the given World will everywhere and always remain the *same* and will always and everywhere prevent them from doing what they wish to do, since their desires are not *determined* by that World itself. We can thus say that Kant appears less as a Moralist (admitting that generally speaking this word makes sense) than as a Religious person: his 'Morality' is less concerned with commanding a free person (= Citizen) to do their Duty than with the avoidance of Sin which necessarily impinges upon them, insofar as they are, by definition, Creatures incapable of self-satisfaction. This is why, ultimately, for Kant as for any Religious person, Morality and Action in general make sense and have value only on condition that they refer to the Beyond. Kant's 'certainty of hope', which he himself calls 'moral Faith', is nothing else but *religious* Faith and, more specifically, a *Judeo-Christian* one.[7]

---

7   On the face of it, this interpretation seems to disagree with what Kant says on this subject in the third Section of the 'Analytic of Pure Practical Reason' (Book I of the *Critique of Practical Reason*) (cf. summary, V, 78, 20–79, 35) where he speaks of the 'Incentive' (*Triebfeder*) to free (= moral) Action and defines it as a 'Feeling' (*Gefühl*) (cf. V, 73, 2–5). In our terminology, the 'Feeling' that plays the role of an 'Incentive' {*Mobile*} is called *Desire*. Desire of what? Kant defines the 'Feeling' in question as the feeling of 'Esteem' (*Achtung*), or even of the 'highest Esteem' (*Grössten Achtung*) (cf. V, 73, 27–34). Thus, one can say, in our terminology, that the incentive to free Action is the *Desire for Recognition*. We thus have the impression that we are right at the heart of (unreligious and atheistic) Hegelianism. But this is only an illusion. For Kant defines 'Esteem' as 'Esteem *for the moral Law*' (cf. V, 73, 34–7). Thus, what is at stake is the Recognition of the 'moral Law' *in general* and not of a flesh-and-blood human being who acts (freely, that is, as a function of the *Desire for Recognition* alone) down Here-below. As for this human being, 'Esteem for the moral Law' 'provokes' ('reveals' itself) *in them* (taken qua 'revealed', or even self-conscious, Phenomenon or empirical-Existence) the feeling of 'Pain' (*Schmerz*) (cf. V, 73, 2–8). Consequently, acting in function of the *Desire for Recognition necessarily* (that is, everywhere and always) amounts to living in Pain, not to say in Unhappiness. This is already sufficiently religious (or to be more exact: Christian). But this does not yet contra-dict Hegelianism, because the latter neither affirms that free Action, that is, the one carried out as a function of the *Desire for Recognition* alone, *necessarily* (that is, everywhere and always) leads to *Happiness*, nor that *Unhappiness* is incompatible with the *Satisfaction* that Recognition (necessarily) procures. But Kant goes further and defines the 'Pain' in question as 'Humiliation' (*Demütigung*; a word which I do not have the slightest intention to translate as 'Humility', which is nothing else but a 'hypocritical' euphemism) (cf. V, 74, 23–30). Definitely, as far as the 'worldly'

This is shown with all due clarity in the following passage from the third Subdivision of the 'Canon' where Kant says this:

> It is entirely otherwise in the case of moral Faith [as opposed to dogmatic Faith]. For there it is absolutely necessary that something must happen, namely, that I fulfil the moral Law in all parts (*in allen Stücken*). The End/the goal here is unavoidably (*unumgängliche*) fixed that one cannot separate one's self from it; and according to all my conviction/what I can see (*nach aller meiner Einsicht*), there is possible *only* a single condition under which this [moral] end is in connexion with *all* Ends together [including those of the natural World] and thereby has *practical validity*, namely, that there be a God and a future World. I also know with complete *certainty*, that *no one* knows of any other conditions that lead to the same *unity* of Ends under the moral Law. Now, since *the* moral prescription is (thus) at the same time *my* maxim (as *the* Reason commands that it ought to be), I will

---

Human being is concerned, 'the moral Feeling' (= Desire for Recognition) is both *self-Humiliation* and *Esteem for the Law* (cf. V, 75, 6–19). Now, this is, in fact, religious (or even theistic or Christian) and diametrically opposed to Hegelian unreligious atheism ('the path to Salvation' 'Morality'). For this means that a Human being can live in the natural World as a *human* being only on condition of living in Unhappiness *and in Humiliation* coupled with Esteem *for the Law*. But what is this 'Law'? The 'naive' Religious Christian will tell you: it is the 'divine ('revealed' or *given*) Law'. Kant would say that it is the freely self-*given* Human Law ('*Gewissen*'). But the difference between these two answers is only apparent. Because, for Kant, the Law-*giver* (= pure practical Reason = pure Will) is not the *same* one as he or she to whom this Law is *given* (= empirical Subject = sensible Soul): in fact, it is the immortal Soul that gives the Law to the Human-being-in-the-World (who remains *unable* to implement it as long as they *live* in the World, hence their Pain and Humiliation). Now, saying '*immortal*' (that is, *non*-spatio-temporal) 'Soul' comes down to saying, in the Kantian terminology in the mode of Truth: 'Thing-in-itself', and in its counterpart in the mode of As-if: 'future World' and 'God'. Now, a 'subtle' (or a Kant-like 'cunning') Religious Christian will also say that a God-*given* Law must be *freely accepted* by the Human being (for it to be *efficacious* in the 'future World', by procuring therein the Satisfaction called Blessedness), which comes down to saying that (qua *immortal* Soul) Human beings give this to *themselves* by *themselves* (qua *mortal*, that is, spatio-temporal Creature). The *difference* between these two claims is illusory because they both share a *common* background, to wit, the absolute impossibility for the Human being to find self-*satisfaction* in the spatio-temporal World through *free* Agency, on account of the latter's fundamental *inefficacy*; hence the feeling of Humiliation or *self-Contempt* which can only be mitigated by religious Faith, that is, by the subjective Certainty of the Hope in being satisfied (blessed) after death in a non-spatio-temporal future World subjected to the Law of God.

unavoidably/unfailingly (*unausbleiblich*) *believe* in the existence of God and a future Life and I am *sure* that nothing can make this *Faith* unstable, since/otherwise [in the opposite case] *my moral principles themselves*, which I cannot renounce without becoming contemptible (*verabschenungswürdig*) *in my own eyes, would thereby be subverted.* (III, 536, 12–26)

Undoubtedly, Kant *begins* this passage with the claim that the End at issue in the moral Law is posed in an *unconditional* and unshakeable way, but he *ends up* saying that he does not want to renounce his moral principles *because*, were he to do so, he would *become contemptible* in his *own* eyes. But, on the one hand, the *moral* End would visibly make neither sense nor have value unless Morality has a 'practical validity' (*Praktische Gültigteit*). Now, Kant says openly, that this 'practical validity' *necessarily presupposes* the existence of 'God' and a 'future World'. It is, therefore, undeniable that, for him, and contrary to what he seems to say in the first instance, the 'moral End' and the 'moral Law' per se make sense and have value, or even a 'reality', only to the extent that there is a transcendent World with reference to the spatio-temporal one. On the other hand, if, according to Kant, one *must* follow the moral Law to avoid becoming '*contemptible* in one's own eyes', it does not follow therefrom that it is *sufficient* to obey this law to be *satisfied* (that is, in Kant's terminology: to be *happy* while being *worthy* of so being). For, between the mere *absence* of self-*contempt* and the *presence* of self-*satisfaction* there is, clearly, an enormous distance, and Kant's obstinate refusal to overcome this distance attests to the fact that he is aware of it. Indeed, no sensible human being (even the 'romantic' kind) would be *satisfied* with the (mere) fact of 'applying' (if one may say so!) a Morality lacking in 'practical validity', that is, one which is precisely 'inapplicable'! Now, once again, the 'practical validity' of Kantian Morality depends uniquely and exclusively (*eine einzige Bedinung*) on the existence of a 'future World'. Thus, Kant's view of 'satisfaction' depends entirely on this 'future World' and is not realisable in the *present* (that is, the spatio-temporal) one, whatever its Present may be. And this is what Kant himself openly admits, since, for him, Satisfaction is nothing else but an 'eternal' *Hope* or, to the extent that this Hope is (subjectively) *certain*, a *Faith*, namely the famous 'moral Faith'. Now, the nature of the (subjective) certainty and the 'Hope' that constitutes this Faith are quite clear in the cited passage, which is written precisely to *define* 'moral Faith' (in opposition to the 'dogmatic Faith' of the common or 'mythological' Religion). 'Hope' is the hope for *Satisfaction* in and through a *'future* Life' [to the extent that the possibility of Satisfaction down Here-below, even for someone *else*, in a distant *future* {*avenir*}, is excluded in a 'dogmatic' way, that is, without any 'de-monstration' or 'discussion', only on the (disavowed) basis of the Postulate proper to every Religion, to wit, the affirmation of the fundamental and irremediable *imperfection* of *all* 'Creatures', that is, of all that exists in the spatio-temporal World]; and the 'unshakable' 'Certainty' is ultimately the refusal of self-*contempt* [to the extent that all Religious persons must *necessarily despise* themselves qua 'Creatures' and can escape this self-contempt only by admitting in themselves something which is not a 'Creature' (a Soul-Image of God, for instance), which thus *transcends* every 'Creature', and, to arrive at self-Satisfaction, they must transcend the 'Creature' both 'materially' by 'leaving the World' for good in Death, and 'morally' by also 'leaving the world' in life]. Indeed, Kant says, word for word, that his Faith (in 'God' and the 'future' World) is *certain* (*sicher*) only *because*, were he to abandon it, he would be *compelled* to abandon Morality, which would *necessarily* lead to self-*contempt*. Kant would thus be perfectly capable (like any man with a religious temperament, for that matter) of *forsaking* his Faith if the price he was prepared to pay for so doing was the *contempt* he would then feel towards himself. Now, the idea of being prone to self-*contempt* must have appeared so monstrous to Kant [as it would have appeared, for that matter, to any man with a religious temperament who is consciously and deliberately Religious, that is, someone who accepts the servitudes of any Religion whatever in exchange for the possibility to not (to no longer) feel self-*contempt* and to have a subjectively certain Hope, that is, Faith in his 'Salvation', that is, in the (at least *possible*) Satisfaction outside of the spatio-temporal World, to accept all the more easily the 'miseries' of 'religious' life since he is profoundly convinced (albeit without any evidence whatsoever) of the *impossibility* of being *satisfied* or even of simply being happy in this world], to such an extent that he 'naively' rejects it (that is, without even invoking that idea or without taking any notice of it), thus betraying (perhaps for the one and only instance throughout his entire discursive life as a Philosopher) such an (anti-philosophical) absence of self-consciousness and of consciousness tout court, to such an extent that he does not even notice the precariousness of the Faith he claims is 'absolutely certain' (*sicher*), or even 'unshakable' (*nichts wankend machen könne*).[8]

---

8   The reader might be led to believe that, on the face of it, everything that has been said so far is irrelevant to Kantian Cosmo-logy, but in fact, we have long since been right in the middle of Cosmo-logy, which is, by definition, concerned with objective-Reality. Now, in Kant, objective-Reality is nothing else but (the) Thing(s)-in-itself/themselves (while everything else is 'Phenomenon'). We, therefore, simply wanted to see *what* it is that Kant considered to be 'objectively-real', and we have seen that it is not the 'physical' World of Newton (which is merely a Phenomenon), rather it is what he calls the 'intelligible', that is, the non-spatio-temporal World, namely the *free-immortal*-Soul (that is, an 'eternally-*changing-identical*-Entity'; first notion of the type 'square-Circle'), a '*future*-Life' (that is, the Future-that-*never*-becomes-present' = '*Life*-after-*death*'; second notion of the type 'square-Circle'), and a '*God*-who-*exists*' (that is, a '*lasting-non-temporal*-Being'; third notion of the type 'square-Circle'). We have also looked at how, according to Kant, one can *speak* of objective-Reality only in the mode of As-if and that the discourse referring thereto is thus an expression of Faith rather than of Knowledge, that is, of Hope grounded in purely subjective Certainty. (As for Being, in Kant, it is conflated with objective-Reality and opposed to empirical-Existence alone). However, we will see that if one simply eliminates the notion of the Thing-in-itself (introduced or maintained, as we have just seen, for purely and exclusively *religious* reasons) without touching anything else, one can find, in Kant, a Cosmo-logy that is almost identical to the one which we will present as ours and which is a Hegelian Cosmo-logy. We thus see that every Philosophy gravitates around its Cosmo-logy, which ultimately determines its whole content and overall structure. In any case, drawing on the interpretation of a *Kantian* text to analyse an existential religious attitude has the utmost intrinsic value, because Kant, like every great Philosopher, does not only have a heightened sense of self-consciousness (even when, as in the interpreted text, its development is articulated only in *implicit* and probably *unconscious* statements [which is not an absurd thing to do!]), but, on a personal level, he is also endowed with a good share of Common sense and absolutely exempt of any 'hysterical exaltation' (*Schwärmerei*), religious or otherwise, to which he is, besides, resolutely hostile. Now, the Kantian text clearly shows that the religious attitude (in addition to being presented here in its 'pure state', that is, without any concrete 'mythological' cladding) ultimately rests on the refusal of self-*contempt*, that is, on the Desire for Recognition, or even on Pride or Vanity. In other words, the religious attitude is essentially and specifically *human* (in the Hegelian sense of the word), even though it is not human in an *authentic* way because, by definition, it cannot acknowledge its self-grounding (the Religious person insofar as they are Religious cannot therefore be a Sage, that is, a fully *self-conscious* human being *satisfied* through the self-realisation of consciousness). Furthermore, this attitude is irreducibly ambiguous. On the one hand, one can say that the Religious person is *less* proud or vain than the 'man of the world', because their ambition does not go further than the desire to avoid self-*contempt* (Satisfaction [Blessedness] cannot, by definition, be *desired* by them, in addition to being, even as a mere possibility, relegated to an *indefinite future* {*avenir*} and its procurement is thus in no way *guaranteed*). But, on the other hand, one can say that the Religious person is *more* vain or has more pride than the 'man of the world', because the idea of 'falling short of expectations' and of 'being reproved', that is, the fear of being

In any case, the essentially *religious* nature of Kant's 'Morality' seems to be clear: it is not the 'Morality' that defines the *Duty* of (*free*) Human beings, which they must and can *fulfil* (that is, *realise*) in the World in which they *live* in such a way that they can be *happy* and *recognised* in that World, that is, *satisfied* with the realisation of their *own*

---

compelled to *despise* oneself, is so unbearable that they are prepared to 'sacrifice everything' for the sake of being at least 'subjectively certain' that they will not run this risk ('everything' does not only refer to the numerous and various 'troubles' {*ennuis*} of religious life, but also to the compulsion to contra-dict themselves as soon as they *speak* [which they would rather avoid, sometimes by taking refuge in Silence]). In this second interpretation, the religious attitude is an extreme form of 'inferiority complex'; while in the first, it is the attitude of a 'shrinking violet' [but 'Timidity' is perhaps merely an avatar of that famous 'complex' which is just the pathologically exacerbated form of a 'normal' human and anthropogenic Pride]. Be that as it may, it is that pride or that vanity, in either one of these interpretations, that the Religious person calls 'Humility'. {To the extent that} one acknowledges that Kant's 'moralism' is an essentially (existential) *religious* attitude, the famous 'paradox' of his Morality (which shocked the Common sense of many unreligious persons, starting with Schiller) says that action ceases to be 'moral' solely on account of being accomplished out of [*natural*] 'Inclination' (*Neigung*) instead of being accomplished as a function of 'Duty' (*Pflich*) alone (which is, *by definition*, somehow radically *opposed to* or *at odds with* Inclination). Indeed, this is the unavoidable *consequence* of the fundamental religious *Postulate* that Satisfaction is *impossible* in the *natural* (that is, the spatio-temporal) World. Indeed, if I do my 'duty' out of 'inclination', I can be *happy* (by so doing) while being *worthy* of being happy, which is to say precisely that I can be *satisfied* with and by what I do down Here-below. Admitting that this is impossible, Kant simply explains why this is the case (by 'developing' the Postulate): I can never be *satisfied* because if I do not do my 'duty' I am not 'worthy' (in my own eyes) of being happy, and if I do it, I am not *happy*, since 'unhappiness' is merely the realised self-consciousness of an action (or a state) at odds with one's 'inclination'. Surely, Kant's 'paradox' is also a 'consequence' of the Judeo-Christian identification (→ 'Hegelian') of the Human being and Negativity, to wit, Human beings are human (= free = historical = person) only insofar as they (actively) *negate* the given, including the given which they themselves are (including their 'inclinations'). But in fact, if negating Action *presupposes* 'unhappiness' or at the very least *unsatisfaction*, it leads to Satisfaction and to 'happiness' when it is successfully *accomplished* (that is, when it trans-forms what it negates). This cannot be contested unless one does not admit that Action can be successfully *accomplished*. Now, that is precisely what no religious person can bring themselves to admit, Kant included.

[It is altogether natural that this was all rather *shocking* to a certain Schiller. For the Poet is an Artist and the opposite or antipode of the Religious person. Indeed, the latter assigns a *negative* value to the given (spatio-temporal) World whatever it may be and whatever is *done* therein, while the Artist attributes a *positive* value to the World whatever it may be and whatever is done therein: for instance, a gruesome supplication, even of a Saint martyr, can be 'beautiful' and can give rise to a 'nice' painting or a 'sublime' poem.]

self-consciousness; rather, it is an 'internal Discipline' that ensures (*servile*) Human beings (at least in cases where they recognise a Master as their own) against the risk of self-*contempt*, which is *unavoidable* if Human beings are contented with *living* in *their* World without referring to a 'future World' as *theirs* (in the sense that *self*-satisfaction is for them *possible* in that world, albeit, generally, in no way *certain*), only insofar as they attribute to themselves (on account of their birth or following certain 'magical Rites' which can be anything we want except *their* Action) a constituent-element (the Mana-Soul) which participates (ever since it *is* {*depuis qu'il* est}) in the 'future World' because it is *irreducibly opposed* to that which *lives*, and, similarly, the 'future World' itself is *irreducibly opposed* to the World of the *present* moment, whatever this Present may be.[9]

---

9   On this occasion, I would like to quote one particularly revealing text from *the Critique of Practical Reason*, even though it is well and widely known. This text concludes the passage starting with the famous tirade on 'Duty' and refers to Man who lives in accordance with this 'Duty' alone (this man being obviously Kant himself). Kant admits that this man is fatally *unhappy* in this world, but he argues the fact that he also manages to evade *self-contempt* (which is inevitably triggered by the failing of one's 'Duty' [= religious Discipline]) and accordingly enjoys an 'inner Tranquillity'. 'This inner Tranquillity (*Beruhigung*) is therefore merely *negative* in regard to *all* that may make life *agreeable*; namely, it is [uniquely] the conjuration/ distancing [*Abhaltung*] of the danger of sinking in *personal* worth after he had entirely forsaken the worth of his own state (*Zustandes*) [in the world]. This Tranquillity is the action of an [expressed] Esteem for *something wholly other* (*ganz anderes* [cf. R. Otto!]) than *life*, in comparison and *opposition* to which life, with *all* its agreeableness (*Annehmlichkeit*) has, rather, *no* worth *at all*. He is still living only out of *duty* [= in view of securing, as far as possible, the *happiness deserved* in the Beyond, that is, his Salvation through the application of religious Discipline, itself also (wrongly) called 'Morality' or 'Duty'] and not because he has the *slightest* taste for life' (V, 88, 13–20). With the few precisions I have introduced between brackets, this text can do without commentary, because its authentically *religious* character is plainly distinguishable to the eye prepared to see. And this text clearly shows that Kant resigned himself to subordinating his *entire life* to the mere conjuration of the 'mortal' danger of seeing himself *despising* himself. If conversely, he wanted or wished to have *positive* 'hopes', he will have to necessarily relate them to the Beyond, that is, to what might happen *after* his death. At first glance, what seems to contradict this interpretation (which is, to tell the truth, merely a 'literal' commentary), is the solution to the 'Antinomy' of practical Reason, which is found in the 'Dialectic' of the second *Critique* (Section II, Subdivision II). This 'Antinomy' is about the fatal incompatibility of 'Duty' [= religious Discipline] and ['worldly'] 'Happiness'. Kant resolves it by introducing the notion of 'self-Satisfaction' or more precisely, 'self-Contentment' (*Selbst-zufriedenheit*), which is as compatible with 'Unhappiness' as it is with 'Duty'. This is, obviously, the ideal of the ancient Sage [taken up again by Hegel] and Kant effectively cites on this occasion

All in all, like any religious man, Kant is able to 'deduce' the notion of a 'future World' from his 'Morality' only because, on the one hand, he negates the very *possibility* of Satisfaction in the spatio-temporal Present, and because, on the other hand, he does not want to renounce all *hope* of obtaining Satisfaction [this total and definitive renunciation should necessarily be translated, in fact, as self-*contempt*, which is literally 'unbearable' or non 'viable' because it leads, in fact, to Suicide or Madness].

We note, however, that Kant does not only 'deduce' from his 'Morality' the 'future World' but also the existence of 'God'. This is hardly surprising insofar as Kant identifies the 'future World' with the 'future *Life*', that is, insofar as his (discursive) 'Morality' necessarily involves (even at the risk of thus being contra-dictory) the notion of the '*immortal* Soul'. Indeed, in the same way Human beings qua *living* and [even freely] *acting* organism are inconceivable without the notion of the World in which they live and act, the immortal (that is, the non-spatio-temporal) Soul is not conceivable (even by means of a contra-dictory notion of the type 'square-Circle') without the notion of a '*future* World' where it supposedly subsists (if not necessarily in *tranquillity*, at least without any form of *action* other than the one being *endured*). Now, this 'World' (= the 'Beyond' in the common theistic terminology) is, by definition, 'divine' (= the 'Wholly-other-thing' in the terminology of Rudolf Otto), to the extent that the 'divine' or 'God' is the 'receptacle' of 'immortal Souls' in the same way the natural or spatio-temporal World (= the down 'Here-below', in the common theistic terminology) is the 'receptacle' of all that *lives* and *acts*. Now, the 'God' of Kant's 'moral Faith' is

---

Epicurus and the Stoics. But Kant introduces that *notion* only to resolve the so-called *logical* contra-diction ('Antinomy') without affirming for that matter that this 'Contentment' can effectively be *reached* or *realised* on earth. Moreover, he hastens to distinguish that 'Contentment' from the 'Autarky' or 'self-Sufficiency' (*Selbstgenugsamheit*) of the ancient Sage (while acknowledging their 'analogy'), which he wants to ascribe, being the good theist that he is, only to the 'supreme Being' (cf. V, 118, 24–37). In any case, after giving this ('somewhat 'hypocritical') hats-off to authentic Philosophy (which is, by definition, the 'Love of *Wisdom*'), Kant is eager to establish the 'Primacy' {*Primat*} of practical Reason vis-à-vis theoretical Reason (Subdiv. III) so that he can establish his 'Postulate' of the Immortality of the soul and the existence of God (Subdiv. IV and V), which emphatically shows, as far as *he* is concerned, that secular and atheistic 'Contentment' does not fulfil his wishes and is in no way destined to *replace* his subjective certainty of hope in *Salvation*, that is, his (Christian) *Faith*.

effectively nothing else but the 'Manager' of the 'future World', which is kept entirely 'under his dominion' and managed in such a way that he guarantees the 'happiness' of the Souls that are 'worthy' thereof.

That being said, a Western person tends to believe that every (discursive) Religiosity is necessarily *theistic* and that, accordingly, the mere notice of the *religiously* informed aspect of the Kantian System is sufficient ground to 'explain' why Kant brought the [contra-dictory] notion 'God' into it (without 'developing' it otherwise than in the As-if mode), which is ultimately *identical*, as far as its [contra-dictory] *sense* is concerned, to the notion of a 'future World'. But the fact of Buddhism shows that this is not the case, because Buddhism is unquestionably a radically *atheistic* authentic *Religion*.[10] And a discursive interpretation of Buddhism shows that this situation is not in the least 'paradoxical'. To understand this, it suffices to notice that the religious Buddhist (like every Religious atheist in general) departs from an Axiom diametrically opposed to the one from which the religious Judeo-Christian departs (like any Religious theist in general). For the Buddhist, *natural* life is *eternal* (or at least co-eternal with Time); it suffices to *do* anything (to act in accordance with Desire; Karman) to be re-*born* and thus to *live* indefinitely. Conversely, in order to *annihilate oneself* (Nirvana) after one's natural death, one must do something special, namely (cognise a 'Dogma' [Dharma] and) 'apply' the 'Discipline' (Vinaya), which consists moreover in *doing nothing* or doing 'nothing' (e.g., the Taoist *Wei wu-wei*: 'to do

---

10   This is obvious for primitive Buddhism (Hinayana): a 'Buddha' is a *man* like all others who, following several anterior *lives* in conformity with their respective 'Morals' (Karman), can apply an 'internal Discipline' (Vinaya) (first promulgated and applied in the actual World by Gautama Buddha), which ensures his total *annihilation* (Nirvana) *after his* (natural) *death*. But it is also true for the Mahayana, which differs (from a 'dogmatic' standpoint) from the Hinayana only insofar as it introduces the notion of the 'Bodhisattva'. Now, the Bodhisattva, too, is a *man* like all other men; but, out of love for his 'neighbours' or, if we wish, out of 'charity', he nevertheless renounces the post-mortuary annihilation of which he is 'worthy' and is *reborn* as Bodhisattva, to the extent that the '*acting* love' is an Action (Karman) and thus a cause of a new *life*. The Bodhisattva avows to only self-annihilate last, after *all* else has been annihilated; but then he *will annihilate himself* 'like everyone else' {*tout le monde*}. The fact that (because of his 'morally' commendable *Action*), in his Bodhisattva's *life*, he possesses Wisdom and Power that theists habitually would only attribute to their *Gods*, does not change anything in this case. The Bodhisattva, like the Buddha, is a *man* in the proper and strong sense of the term, and not a 'God'.

non-doing'), that is, overcoming the 'Desire' (Ràga) that will necessarily lead to the Action (Karman) which determines (even if 'moral') a future *life*. Now, qua Religious person, the Buddhist admits the impossibility of Satisfaction in and through 'worldly' *life*. Religious 'Satisfaction' or 'Salvation' can thus consist, for that person, only in Annihilation (since, even if he is reborn as Brahma or the supreme God, which is possible if one observes a certain 'morality', he continues to *live* a 'worldly' life and therefore does not obtain religious Satisfaction as the only true thing of the greatest value for him. [What is truly remarkable is that the Buddha advises against the supreme 'morality' that 'divinises' the human being because, having become God, that is, being perfectly *happy* or 'blessed', one can no longer be aware of the *unworthy* character of that 'blessedness', in such a way that the very idea of true Satisfaction (= *happiness* of which one is *worthy*) becomes forever inaccessible to one, and one is thus condemned to *eternal* life (or co-eternal with Time)]. To be sure, Satisfaction is only 'lived' *during* the *life* of the Buddha, that is, of the 'accomplished' Buddhist, and it is, in the final analysis, nothing else but *Faith* in the sense of a subjective *certainty* of the *hope* to die at some point (close for the Buddha and deliberately distant, or even indefinite, for the Bodhisattva) once and for all. Since the Beyond of the Buddhist Religion is thus *Nothingness*, one cannot refrain from saying that it is *atheistic*, if one does not want to call 'Theism' the denial of all kinds of any transmundane Divine existence whatever it may be.

Basically, the Buddhist (whether religious or otherwise) is thus atheistic because they take the homogeneity or the absolute unity and unicity of Being qua different from (mere) Nothingness rather seriously. The *unreligious* Buddhist notices that Being (and thus *all* that *is* in whichever way) is necessarily spatio-temporal or Becoming (Samsara) *without being moved by it*. The *religious* Buddhist is moved by it to the point of horror, and to avoid this 'panic' {*affolement*} he imposes on himself a severe 'Discipline'. Ultimately, he prefers the absolute and immutable Identity of Nothingness to Difference or the Negation of any Becoming whatever: perhaps because, in fact, Difference, which is the Negation of Spatio-temporality in Being and the Negative of Space-Time in objective-Reality, 'reveals' itself or 'appears' to Human beings in the empirical-Existence of extended-duration as, among other things, their own Negativity which they, moreover, call Freedom or creative Action, or sometimes, Crime and Sin.

As for Theists of all kinds, they all are ultimately 'dualists' or 'Manicheans', in the sense that, while admitting (implicitly or explicitly) that there is something common to all that one speaks thereof, namely Being, they are eager to introduce into that Being an irreducible-Opposition which, if they are unreligious, does not 'alarm' {*affole*} them, but rather incites them to Action (Struggle and Work) and efficacious discourse, and sometimes to the discursive description called Cosmology, but if they are religious, it provides them with the possibility to talk (and contra-dict themselves) about a Beyond, which *is* only insofar as the down Here-below (of which one also speaks) *is not*, with all that it entails, including Becoming and Action. Thus, if the atheistic religious Buddhist shuns Action per se, the theistic Judeo-Christian dodges only the responsibility and the effort of the *efficacious* Action. For, if the (spatio-temporal) down Here-below is *merely* 'phenomenal', that is, basically, if the 'subjective *illusion*' of which 'idealist' Theism speaks (and which was called Maya in Hindu idealistic theism) *conceals* much more than it 'reveals' objective-Reality, and if objective-*Reality* can only be found *beyond* Spatio-temporality, that is, if in order to speak the common language of religious Theism, then the spatio-temporal World where one lives and acts (and how can one *act* where neither time nor space exist?!) is 'futile' {*vain*} and 'conceited' {*vaniteux*}. Action (which makes sense and has value only where there is space and time) is perhaps *possible* and may, if need be, contribute to the weaving or creation of the 'veil of illusion', but it might never be *efficacious* with respect to *objective-Reality*, which is *irreducibly-opposed* to any Spatio-temporality whatever.

By interpreting atheistic religious Buddhism accordingly, in opposition to theistic Religion, one can see that it presents multiple advantages from the point of view of Common sense and therefore, from the point of view of Philosophy, or even Wisdom. Firstly, it suffices to convince a religious Buddhist that they will be fatally annihilated after their death, whatever their life may be, in order for them to no longer be 'Religious' (assuming that they would want to be and remain self-*consistent*, which, it must be admitted, is rare among Religious persons who are, more often than not, no strangers to contradiction) while being able to remain Buddhist: for they would then know that they *are* 'Buddha' (like everyone else, for that matter) without having the need to submit themselves beforehand to the Buddhist religious 'Discipline', nor indeed to any other discipline. [Which means that, if they remain *religious*, that is, if they continue not to be satisfied by *any* 'worldly pleasure', they would be able to do *anything* and say accordingly that *they* are 'permitted' everything, and, in *their* eyes, a serious crime which may result in a death sentence will only accelerate their 'Salvation'; to wit, only an authentic Religious person can believe that 'everything is permitted' if they stop believing in God or, which is the same thing, if they recognise themselves as *really mortal*]. Secondly, if religious Discipline consists in the *overcoming* of every Action, it can and even should be carried out *in silence* (since Discourse is, in the final analysis, born from or generates Action), Gautama having effectively become Buddha only through solitary and *silent* Meditation; to wit, religious Buddhists (who are self-consistent) can and should thus *remain silent* without doing anything, which is always possible since this will not bother anyone [except the doctor who must attend the 'sick' who are literally starving themselves to death, since to consciously *want* to eat or to eat *willingly* is an Action or a Karman incompatible with the absolute quietude that Religion prescribes to self-consistent Buddhists (unless they are sufficiently cunning to say that *wanting not* to eat is a more authentic Action, because it is more 'negating', than wanting to *eat*)]. Thirdly, if the Buddhist, even when Religious, is also a Philosopher (and they can be so, because Religion is incompatible only with Wisdom), they can *speak* with the intention to tell *true* {*dire* vrai} without having to contradict themselves (which goes against that same intention). For Atheism does not *oblige* one to contra-diction, since it affirms the absolute and ultimate *homogeneity* of (spatio-temporal) Being, and therefore, the homogeneity of all that *is*, without being obliged to deny in an immediate way the fact that Objective-Reality or the irreducible-Opposition (which, for it, is situated *inside* of Being or the Spatio-temporality which *is*) involves an Inter-action between two Terms, which *are* both necessarily in *one and the same manner*, and that is what any Theist whoever they may be will have to deny, because for them the *objectively-real* (non-spatio-temporal) Beyond, or that which is *irreducibly-opposed* to the (spatio-temporal) 'phenomenal' down Here-below, *is* 'wholly *otherwise*' than what its empirical-existence *is* (while for the Atheist, 'phenomenal' empirical-Existence is nothing else but the 'revealed' Existence of the one and unique Being as such).

As someone endowed with Common sense and as an authentic Philosopher (even while denying the possibility of Wisdom, seeing that, as a religious person, he would not admit the Satisfaction obtained through the realisation of self-consciousness alone to the extent that he is a human being who lives in the 'phenomenal' World in which his actions are carried out), Kant would thus have certainly been a (religious) Buddhist . . . had he lived in Buddhist Asia. But he was religious in an exclusively Judeo-Christian world. And this is the only acceptable or 'plausible' way to 'explain' (or 'justify') his Theism.

Undoubtedly, the Judeo-Christian Anthropology (dear to Kant and *true*, since it is developable and developed without contra-diction in the sense of the circular Discourse) is perfectly at home with Atheism since it essentially coincides with the Buddhist or Taoist atheistic Anthropology. And we shall see that the Discourse which involves this Anthropology is not contra-dictory only *if* it is entirely atheistic (by identifying Being with Spatio-temporality) [in the same way that only the *atheistic* Discourse is circular, that is, truly *true* or self-de-monstrated as such]. But, in fact (and this fact could be 'understandable'), Judeo-Christian Anthropology strictly so called, which is the only one Kant knew, was bound up with a *theistic* Mythology. And it would be truly unfair to Kant to reproach him with failing to see that one can develop an *atheistic Philosophy* even without ceasing to be *religious* (if one remains self-consistent, that is, *remains* religious without ceasing to be a Philosopher [in which case, one should only 'love' and 'seek' Wisdom without harbouring the slightest hope to obtain it]). Had Kant been able to see it, he, himself, would have almost certainly announced, at least 'in theory', the Hegelian System of Knowledge (while rejecting it on 'religious' grounds since this System necessarily involves the idea of Wisdom, being the Knowledge of the Sage per se). But one must not forget that the man who effectively announced (and admitted) it was (like Aristotle) profoundly *unreligious*.

Since he was a Philosopher in addition to being religious, Kant could neither confine {*cantonner*} himself in (religious or 'mystical') Silence, nor content himself with the 'incoherence' of the Judeo-Christian Mythology, which moreover belonged to the Religion into which he was born (even though that 'incoherence' was such a perfect camouflage for the contra-diction of Theism that the clairvoyance of Kant was needed for it to be noticed). As a Philosopher, he aspired to *discursive Truth* and for that reason he was able to elaborate a *System* of Philosophy whose

Anthropology was both *theistic* and Judeo-Christian. Now, the elaboration of that System ultimately brought him back to Plato again, because, according to this hypothesis, there is no other outcome than the path towards Plato, even though Kant should not even *find* Plato *again* since he *knew* him already, if only under the name of Aristotle, and in any case, in and through the so-called 'scholastic' or 'modern' or even 'secular' or 'philosophical' Christian Theology, such as the one attributed to a certain Descartes, a Spinoza or a Leibniz.

All of the above shows, for sure, that the historical 'tradition' exerted an extraordinary influence even over a 'revolutionary' of Kant's rank. But it also shows that nobody is in the least bothered by Contradiction, not only when it is implicit (that is, unconscious) or (more or less consciously) 'camouflaged' (by the 'incoherence' of a Myth, Platonic or otherwise), but even when it is explicit and expressed (especially when someone is 'erotic' or 'religious' or even a 'mathematician' or an 'artist', that is, all those who are basically devoted to Silence, which, if it fails to 'satisfy' them, can alone at least provide them with 'happiness' or the 'joie de vivre'). In this regard, even the Philosopher is no exception (and who was more of a Philosopher than Kant?!), because only the Sage will no longer have a reason to be if they contra-dict themselves. Only those who speak the Language of *Accomplishment*, or who want to express *Recognition* verbally (regardless of whether it is Flattery, Contempt, or mutual Esteem), must avoid contra-diction if they do not want to 'miss their influence' {*rater leur effet*}. But these people do not interest us here since they do not discuss the True-semblance of what they are saying, considering that they do not speak with the *intention* to tell *true*.

Be that as it may, Kant believed himself obliged to accept Theism (which, under its discursive form, is necessarily Platonic or at least Platonising, that is, Greek, ancient or 'pagan') while wishing to uphold the Judeo-Christian Anthropology (which, in fact, contra-dicts any form of Theism whatever it may be). For this reason, he must be considered as an essentially and specifically *Christian* Philosopher, for (ever since Saint Paul) Christianism is nothing else but the attempt to reconcile the irreconcilable (according to the same Saint Paul, to wit, 'madness for the Greeks'), namely, to reconcile [the implicitly atheistic] Judaic ('moral') Anthropology of *Freedom* (Negativity) with the discursive

Theism (Identity) of a Greek or 'pagan' origin [which excludes, in fact, Human Freedom, and is thus always contra-dictory, since only that notion of Freedom can be developed discursively in such a way that it accounts (in and through a circular Discourse) for the Discourse which this development itself is].

It can, nevertheless, be said that Kant was more of a Philosopher than any of his theistic predecessors (and thus surpassing them all in his closeness to Wisdom [which, *for us*, can only be Hegelian]) because he did not want to *admit* (as even Plato did) a contra-diction immanent to his System along with its other constituent-elements. Indeed, the discursive development *strictly so called* (that is, supposed to be truly *true*) of the Kantian System is not contra-dictory even though it seems to be 'open' [the only apparent 'contra-diction' resides in the affirmation of the *truth* of an *open* System; but this is only an apparent contra-diction, since, in itself and for us, as it was for Hegel, this System was already closed or closes itself by itself as soon as the 'theistic' notion of the Thing-in-itself is eliminated therefrom]. Theism (with a religious basis) appears discursively in this System only in the mode of As-if, and what is presented 'as if' it were true cannot contra-dict that which is presented as true in the proper and strong sense of the term (even though Kant himself thinks that his System may be closed, and thus de-monstrated as true, only through the constituent-element which is discursively developed in the mode of As-if).

Consequently, Kant's System presents the optimum level of Philosophy compatible with the Christian Religion (reduced, moreover, to its simplest expression, that is, to the affirmation of Human Freedom, as far as the impossibility for the Human being to attain Satisfaction on earth goes). And it is for this reason that it must be said that Kant is the Christian Philosopher par excellence.[11]

---

11   If the case of Buddhism shows that an authentic *Religion* can be rigorously atheistic, the example of the 'young' Platonising Aristotle proves that an incontestably *theistic* Philosophy can be enunciated as true (or true-semblant) by someone who is not in the slightest bit *religious*. It seems to me that the mutual 'independence' of the notions of 'Religion' and 'Theism' is thus sufficiently established. But one can contest my discursive development of these two notions, so it would seem, using the example/case of pre-prophetic Judaism, which is believed to have produced a theistic Mythology that denies *immortality*, and which is supposedly *religious* while admitting the possibility of *Satisfaction down Here-below*. I admit, nonetheless, that this objection, which sounds plausible at first glance, does not seem to me convincing. Indeed, the Judaism in

Let us now see how the (religiously informed) Theism of Kant determines the structure, and therefore the content (or, if we want, for it is the same thing: the content and therefore the structure), of the Kantian philosophical *System*.

*   *   *

question (which *predates* the 'Greek miracle') reflects a magico-mythological or 'primitive' mentality that must be compared not to Christianism or Islam (both of which *have their source* in this mentality and *posterior* to the 'Greek miracle') but to other 'magical Mythologies' that can be found, for instance, in the Veda as in various 'Primitives'. Which means that this 'Judaism' is at once the 'origin' of Magic and Science, Religion and Art, Philosophy and 'Politics'. The Bible is as much a 'sacred history' as it is a 'natural history' and 'history' tout court, in which we can thus find anything we want, and it is impossible to oppose it *en bloc* to whichever theory of Religion or Theism. [A curious thing, the current text even involves a (later and Hellenic, it is true) visibly atheistic *and* unreligious writing, attributed (derisively, one might add) to King Solomon, who built the Temple, a unique hub of Judaic religious Theism.] As for the Theism of 'primitive' Judaism, it must not be forgotten that its conception of what will later evolve into the idea of the 'immortal Soul' was still limited to the idea of 'Mana'. However, if the Human Mana is 'Wholly-other-thing' with reference to (even human) empirical existence, it is unquestionably the strict homologue and analogue of the divine Mana. Hence, as the latter was being 'defined' (probably as a function of the 'Greek miracle') in terms of the 'eternal' or *trans-worldly* (in the sense of non-spatio-temporal) Theos (which was certainly not the 'primitive' Yahweh), the human Mana was being defined in terms of an '*immortal*', in the sense of non-spatio-temporal, Soul (thus identified more or less with the eternally self-*identical* Platonic Psyche). Moreover, even Abraham, who was authentically theistic [and religious], was enormously preoccupied with his sepulchre, which would almost be inconceivable for a man who would not have seen in his dead body anything else but a decomposing corpse without any relation whatever to 'Immortal' or at least temporal 'Survival'. In short, I do not think that the *theistic* Mythology imagined by the 'primitive' Jews was associated, in their minds, with a 'materialistic' anthropological Mythology. Be that as it may, its subsequent development has, *always and everywhere*, involved the Myth of some form of 'Survival' for a certain human 'Soul', which de-monstrates that this is how it must *necessarily* be, all the more so that no one knows of a Mythology with an *immortal* 'Soul' without some sort of 'God'. If one does not admit that the 'Divine' in the sense of the 'Wholly-other-thing' *exists* empirically, a Hegelian Philosopher will have to admit that the *Sense* of the word 'God' (even when contradictory) must be derived from 'natural' Perception. Now, I do not see what can be inferred from such an endeavour other than the 'phenomenon' of Death. Since Death is effectively 'wholly-other-thing' than Life, it suffices to prolong (through discursive 'extrapolation') Life *after* Death while taking the latter into account to get the (contradictory, that is, the 'square-Circle' type) Notion of 'Survival' and, therefore, of a 'future World', that is, of 'God'. As for 'primitive' Judaic Religion, one must refrain from seeing a 'Religious' person in *every* 'Primitive' person and believing that *every* Mythology is always 'religious'. When modern ethnographers began to distance themselves from this

In the second Subdivision of the 'Canon' Kant says what follows:

All Interest of my Reason (the speculative Interest as well as the practical Interest) is integrated/gathered (*vereinigt sich*) in the following *three* questions: What *can I know*? What *should I do*? What *may I hope*? (III, 522, 30–40)

---

error, they began to see in 'primitive' societies, exactly as in ours, Religious persons and Statesmen, Scientists and Artists, or even, Theologians and Philosophers (even though these types are more clearly distinguished from one another or discursively 'defined' and 'definable' only in societies which have benefited from the 'Greek miracle'). There is no doubt that some authors of 'primitive' Biblical texts admitted Satisfaction down Here-below and knew no other form of Satisfaction. But were they *religious*? We have as few reasons to suppose so as counter-reasons to believe in the *religiosity* of an Islamic conqueror who derives his satisfaction from his warlike activities and who sees the Beyond merely as an extension of 'worldly' *happiness*, of which he believes himself to be *worthy* on account of the very *actions* he undertakes. Inversely, nothing proves that from the very beginning there have been *religious* Jews who did not admit the possibility of self-satisfaction in and through a purely and exclusively 'worldly' life. There were certainly many such people in the Prophetic epochs. Now, surely (and contrary to what they claim), these Prophets did not 'fall from the sky' and must have had 'precursors' [although some Jewish 'Prophets' acted less as Religious persons and more like Statesmen]. Furthermore, the Biblical 'promised Land' is valued more highly as an After-life, or a 'Paradise', which is 'wholly-other-thing', even when 'terrestrial', rather than as a geographical region of the 'natural' world. And after all, Judaic religious 'Discipline' is not, for that matter, only and uniquely preoccupied with the procurement of petty pleasures in everyday life. In short, it seems to me that the primitive Judaic *Religious person* was as inept at finding self-satisfaction in any 'worldly' life whatever as any other authentic Religious person *anywhere* and *always*, to the extent that one may say that things are *necessarily* so. Furthermore, even in a phenomenon as evolved as the 'Christian Religion', authentically religious elements accommodate, for better or worse, undeniably 'secular' (albeit theistic) elements, presented under the title of 'Morality'. Certainly, Saint Paul was able to see and say that the so-called Judaic 'moral' Law was promulgated (by God) in such a way that it may *not* be fulfilled by the Human being, who thereby becomes a Sinner, thus making Redemption and Incarnation possible (if not 'necessary'). It is, therefore, clear that it is not by *acting* (in conformity with 'Morality') down Here-below that the (Pauline =) Christian can be *satisfied*, that is, be *happy* (or 'blessed') while knowing that they are *worthy* of being so. And Saint Paul, like Kant later, knew already ('Grecianised' as he was) that Satisfaction was not the *Knowledge* actually possessed by the Sage in their lifetime, but a mere *Hope* which, when endowed with (subjective) *Certainty*, was an 'unshakable' *Faith*, namely, the *Christian* Faith in an ('incarnated') God who would *guarantee* (just like Kant's God) the 'felicity' of the 'righteous'. As for those 'righteous' ones, they were not in any way 'justified' by their *Acts*, even when (per impossible! Saint Paul would say) in conformity with the 'moral' Law. They are justified by their *Faith* alone (*sola fide*), that is, precisely, by the 'unshakable' conviction that one can*not* be *satisfied* down Here-below, no matter what one *does* therein.

Given that *all* the 'Interest' of 'Reason' is condensed in these three questions, it is obvious that their given answer encompasses *all* that can be 'sensibly' said: this threefold answer is therefore nothing else but the *unitotal Discourse*, that is, the *ensemble* of what can be *said* (or expressed with *sense*-endowed words) with the intention to tell *true* and thus without wishing to *contra-dict* oneself; in other words, the answer given to the 'last' or 'primordial' three questions is the *System of Knowledge* (or at least *of Philosophy*, since, according to Kant, this System does not *close*

Except that, as the Statesman that he *also* was, Saint Paul was neither able nor willing to remain self-consistent (by showing us thus, in attaining consciousness thereof by himself, that he was not a Philosopher), and insofar as it was and remained a *social* or a *political* phenomenon, the Christianism he founded followed him down this same path of inconsistency. Indeed, Saint Paul declared that his view of Faith was 'dead without Acts' and this allowed him to uphold the Judaic 'Morality' (by bringing it into line with the 'circumstances' of the Roman world) insofar as it might contribute to the foundation and upholding of a State (= Church). If Christian or Pauline 'Morality' was a 'morality' in the proper sense of the word, that is, rules of conduct to guarantee (at least in principle) *satisfaction* in the given natural and social, or even historical, world where it was 'orthodox', that is, where it could be applied without having to radically trans-form that world, it would not be *religious* at all. But the Christians have never gone so far as saying such a thing. Their 'morality' remained *religious* in this sense that it was not supposed to render possible (rather than guarantee) Satisfaction (in the Beyond) unless it was coupled with *Faith* (which, precisely, presupposes the inefficacy of all Morality conducive only to Action down Here-below). The hybrid, half-religious half-secular character of this Christian 'Morality' is manifested in and through the notion of 'Charity': the Christian is 'justified' not because they *do* this or that, but solely because they do (almost anything) 'out of Charity' or 'out of Love', which is, in a certain measure (and a rather weak one, for that matter), a 'love' of the 'neighbour' (who is, moreover, 'close' and 'brother' only in and through the 'communion in Christ'), but which is ultimately the love of 'God', in such a way that every Christian action is 'justified' and 'justifying' only insofar as it is carried out 'in the name of *God*' and to 'God's glory', and not in the name of he or she who executes it (to the extent that the discursive development of this notion results in the negation of the very possibility for the human being to act in the proper and strong sense of the term, which overcomes, of course, Freedom and therefore Judeo-Christian Anthropology in its entirety). And it is for this reason that Christianism was not able to create a State properly so called, but only a Church, which would have disappeared a long time ago as a social or political, or even historical (and not 'private') phenomenon if it had not benefited (even in our times) from the support of the 'secular arm' which *acts* for good {*pour de bon*}, and basically is in contradiction with the so-called Christian 'Morality'. A similar inconsistency can be found in Buddhism insofar as it is a Church. But, in its purely discursive development, it alone was able to account for the irreducible opposition between every Morality of Action whose aim is to procure Satisfaction down Here-below, and whichever religious 'Discipline' aimed at earning 'Salvation' in the Beyond.

in upon itself and to the extent that it is not truly *circular* but only 'tied together' {*bouclé*} in the mode of As-if, it is not [discursive] *Truth* in the proper and strong sense of the word, forever inaccessible to Human beings, at least in their lifetime).

At first sight, this System appears to entail *more* than is necessary, since the *second* question seems to incite the Language of Accomplishment/the efficacious Discourse and not Discussion/the theoretical Discourse of the True-semblant in view of (discursive) Truth.

However, in fact, Kant's System entails nothing of the sort. The second question does not mean: What should I do *to achieve* something (in a *given* natural or historical World with a view to *trans-forming* it through my very Action [of struggle or Work])? Rather, it means: How should I *act* in the World where I live so as to be able to *speak* of my own Action, that is, of myself as *acting* [freely], with the intention to tell *true* and without having to *contra-dict* myself when I would speak, with the same intention, of this World itself, and of myself as *speaking* thereof [in the mode of Truth]? In other words, the answer given to this *second* Question is philosophical Anthropology [Judeo-Christian, for Kant], that is, in our terminology, the anthropo-graphic Phenomeno-logy which Kant himself calls 'Metaphysics of Morals' (*Metaphysik der Sitten*) and which he identifies with what he calls 'Morality'.

As for the *first* Question, it can be fleshed out in such a manner that it means this: what *truth* can I *say* about the World in which I live and of which I speak, and which thus comprises, among other things, my discourse and myself qua *speaking* in view of telling the *truth* about the World in which I speak, but which does *not speak* per se? To put it otherwise, the answer given to this first Question brings (or should bring) together the ensemble of what we have called 'Onto-logy', 'Cosmo-logy' and the non-*anthropo*-graphic part of Phenomeno-logy (since, as we will see later, Kant excludes from this arrangement *bio*-graphical Phenomeno-logy, which he brings to bear on his answer to the third Question, following a rather curious reasoning, albeit one that is perfectly understandable in the sense that it is 'deduced' from his System as a whole).

The answer given to the *third* Question, which is a 'final' answer, should not be *part* of the (Hegelian) System of Knowledge strictly so called, where it is permitted, in and through its (closed and circular) *ensemble*, to he or she who conceives or understands it, to give the following answer to the third Kantian Question: There is no *Hope* at all, neither for myself nor for anyone, as far as the Beyond is concerned, since I am a *living* and, therefore, a *mortal* being, that is, limited to my empirical-existence in the extended-duration; but, insofar as the Discourse that I transmit/pronounce or assimilate/comprehend closes in upon itself, I *know* (in the mode of discursive *Truth*) that (being *free*) I should be able to act in such a way that I can be fully *satisfied* only through the perfect realisation of my self-consciousness as acting in that manner in the World wherein I live and where *everyone* 'recognises' my 'personal' value in function of this mine own (free) self-conscious action. Thus, the third *Question* does not so much pertain to the System itself as to the existential attitude taken by the Sage in reference to and in function of themselves, and the *Answer* to this third question is precisely the *ensemble* of the System of Knowledge of the Sage.

But we have seen that such is not the situation in Kant, who knows that he is and wants to be a Philosopher and not a Sage (on account of asserting that Wisdom is impossible, at least *in the course of* Human *life*). His 'final' Answer to that 'last' Question (which is from an 'existential' point of view the 'first' Question or *the* Question tout court), is, as we have seen, the following: According to what I may *know* (in the discursive mode of Truth), I have the right to *hope* that by *doing what* I *should do*, I might (eternally) enjoy the *happiness* of which I am *worthy* (in my *own* eyes and *in them alone*) in a 'future World' (which has an *objective-reality* while being non-spatio-temporal, that is, 'transcendent' in reference to the 'divine' or the Spatio-temporality which *is*, that is, to speak like Kant himself, an 'intelligible World' which is a 'Thing-in-itself'). In other words, which are, for that matter, Kantian as well, the Answer to the 'last' Question is *Faith*, which Kant calls 'morality' and which is, in fact, the religious Faith of the Christian. For Kant answers this question (in and through the *ensemble* of his System) by saying that it is 'permitted' to say without contra-dicting oneself that one is subjectively *certain* of the *hope* to be satisfied in the Beyond after one's death (on condition that one conforms to the 'Morality' which is, in fact, a religious 'Discipline', inactive, or even quietist, or *inefficacious down Here-below*). Now, according to Saint Paul, who should know a thing or two about that, the *certainty of hope* is nothing else but *Faith*. And this is how we can say that, in and through his 'last' or 'first' intention ('Interest'), the authentically Kantian System is the authentic System of *Christian* Philosophy.

In *this* interpretation, the one provided by Kant himself in the 'Canon' of the 'transcendental Methodology', which concludes the *Critique of Pure Reason*, the Answer given to the *third* Question is (as in Hegelian Knowledge) the System *itself* (that is, the 'combined', that is, non contra-dictory, Answer to the first and second questions) and not one of its integral *Parts* (which are, therefore, only *two*). But the (religious) nature of the Answer Kant provides is such that he was unable to interpret it as we have just done, after Hegel, without ceasing to be the *Philosopher* he wanted to be while wishing to be and remain a (religious) Christian. And it was in order to be able to be a *Philosopher* (with a Christian religious foundation) that he conceived (*after* having written the 'Methodology' in question) a *third* 'Critique' which is the philosophical or (non-contra-dictory) discursive Answer to his *third* (existential) Question [which is, in fact and for us, as it is for Hegel and already for Schelling, his *bio*-graphical Phenomeno-logy].

Saint Paul, who wanted to be a (religious) Christian without wishing to be a *Philosopher*, was able to content himself with the Answer he gave to the third Kantian Question, an answer with which all Christians without philosophical intentions or ambitions {*velleités*} were, everywhere and always, contented. This Christian and religious, but essentially *aphilosophical* Pauline Answer being the 'revelation' of Jesus-Christ, which Saint Paul himself had in and through a *sui generis* Perception (the 'Encounter on the road to Damascus'), but which the majority of Christians are supposed to admit or believe 'at his word' (ultimately, at the word of Saint Paul himself and at the word of those who had the same 'experience' he had). Saint Paul *saw* Jesus, whom he *knew* was *dead* in 'worldly' ignominy, *resuscitated* for a trans-worldly (eternal) *life in Glory* [and to confirm that 'vision', he would avidly search again for the *empty* Tomb and for the 'eye' Witnesses of the Resurrection]. Now, that 'vision' gave him, as would do any Perception, the 'subjective certainty' of the 'fact' that Human beings can *live* down Here-below in such a way that their Satisfaction is not rendered *impossible* (or their 'deserved blessedness', that is, the '*blessed* life' of which they are 'worthy' [in their *own* eyes, *because* and *only* because they are 'worthy' of it in the eyes of God, who *alone* is capable of effectively 'blessing' those and those *alone* whom *he* considers 'worthy' of being blessed; *his* 'Judgement' might, moreover, be 'arbitrary' or 'free' or even 'irrational', that is, not everywhere and always (therefore 'necessarily') *the same*, in the sense that it might be founded not on Reason, but on Love]). That 'Vision' does not *guarantee effective* Satisfaction, but only its *possibility*, and it is for this reason that it gives rise merely to the 'certainty of *hope*', that is, *Faith*. But this *Faith* is amply sufficient for the Religious person who is, by definition, contented with a form of insurance against the risk of self-*contempt*. If, by becoming *Human* and by living and *dying as such*, God was able to resuscitate or be re-born qua God in the ('recognised') Glory of his ('blessed') Felicity (for it is a serious 'heresy' to believe that he lived and died qua *God*), Human beings *may*, if they 'imitate' the Man-God in their lifetime (to the extent that this 'Imitation' of Jesus-Christ is the essence of the Christian religious 'Discipline'), have after their death a life that 'imitates' the life of God in the sense that it, too, will be 'eternal', 'glorious' and 'blessed'. And the 'unshakable' Faith of the Christian is nothing else but the 'certainty of hope' in that, if not 'divine', at least 'divinised', life.

But a Philosopher, and Kant wanted to be one, cannot be contented with the 'subjective certainty' given by a 'Perception' in the *rough*, that is, non-*verbalised*, even when it is a *sui generis* Perception, that is, a specific 'sensible experience', so-called 'mystical'. A person/the Human being becomes a Philosopher only if and because they want to *speak* with the intention to tell *true*. Now, to do so, they must transform Perceptions (the Perception 'revealing' to them explicitly [through its 'content'] empirical-Existence which, when 'revealed' as such, is 'Phenomenon', and, implicitly [through Tonal Sensation and the Feeling of Well- or Ill-being] objective-Reality and given-Being) into Notions, by 'detaching' them from their respective *hic et nunc* (that is, by transforming the Essences that these Notions 'reveal' into the Meaning of their ['arbitrarily'] assigned Phenomena). Now, Kant knows that he did not have the (*sui generis*) Perception in question (that Saint Paul purports to have had). And had he had it, he would not have wished, *qua Philosopher*, to make use of the [contradictory] Notion [(*mortal*) Human being–(*immortal*) God] stemming from the ('arbitrary') phonemic incarnation of the Meaning that the corresponding Essence would become as a result of its detachment from its *hic et nunc* [which is, in fact and for us, following Hegel, if not for Kant himself, an Act of human Freedom, anchored in the anthropogenic Action of Struggle → Work]. For Kant knew perfectly well that *this* Notion would be contra-dictory and that it would contra-dict the rest of his System.

Just as well, Kant started by saying (in the *Critique of Pure Reason* and even in the *Critique of Practical Reason*) that the 'subjective *certainty*' of Hope came only and exclusively from the 'subjective certainty' of 'moral Duty' (*Pflichtbewusstsein*). But we have seen that, in Kant, this was in no way the case, for 'moral' Duty would make sense, for him, only IF there was a 'future World' in such a way that wishing to lay the foundations of the certainty of hope in a 'future World' on the certainty of the feeling of Duty would come down to committing a *vicious* circle (and not a 'dialectical' one).[12] And Kant ultimately makes this realisation by himself. Now, having made that realisation, he should have looked for another thing, lest he either forsakes his Faith (which he is neither able nor willing to do, on account of his *religious* 'nature') or renounce accounting for it discursively in a philosophical System.

Kant believed at a later stage that he had found that 'other thing' in the Perception of the Beautiful and the Living [to the extent that the Beautiful (like the Good {*Bien*} / Right {*Bon*} and the True) are 'variations' on the Feeling of Well-being, which Perception sometimes implies and is at the basis of Onto-logy when it 'reveals' the Meaning of a Phoneme (by giving rise to the Notion of given-Being), and at the basis of ('secular') Eroticism or (religious) Mysticism (as the 'silently revealed *Good*'), ('pure') Mathematics (as the 'silently revealed ['secular'] Truth'), and Art (including the art of Poetry) (as the 'silently revealed Beautiful'), which he transforms into a Notion and develops discursively in the *Critique of Judgement*, to thus provide the (discursive) Answer to his third and last Question. In other words, what 'Christology' is for the religious Christian Saint Paul, the *Critique of Judgement* is for the religious Christian *Philosopher* Kant.

* * *

---

12   The (discursive) 'Circle' would be 'dialectical' and not 'vicious' if the 'Feeling of Duty' was truly an 'immediate' (that is, 'irreducible') 'given of consciousness'. However, in fact, for Hegel and for us, this is not the case. The 'behaviourist' experiment and introspection show that this 'Feeling' is everywhere and always (that is, 'necessarily') 'mediated' by the social or historical World in which the human being to whom this 'Feeling' belongs lives and acts. Now, obviously, Faith in the (non-spatio-temporal) *Beyond* cannot be deduced from that 'Feeling' which is essentially a 'worldly' (indeed, spatio-temporal) phenomenon.

To understand what has just been said, one must recall the *structure* of the Kantian System as it was set forth by Kant in the third (non-subdivided) Section of his 'Methodology', which he called 'the Architectonic of Pure Reason'. What he says therein is of paramount philosophical importance to such an extent that it is indispensable to translate it in large excerpts right here (especially considering that nowadays, in France at least, this essential part of the *Critique of Pure Reason* is very little studied and poorly read).

This is what Kant says:

> By an Architectonic I understand the art of *Systems*. Since *systematic unity* is that which in the first instance (*allererst*) transforms ordinary cognition into *Science* [or *Knowledge*], that is, makes a System out of a mere aggregate of such cognitions, Architectonic is the doctrine (*Lehre*) of that which is *Scientific* in our Cognition as such (*überhaupt*) and therefore necessarily belongs to Methodology.
>
> Under the government of Reason, our Cognitions in general are not entitled to be a Rhapsody, but must constitute a *System*, within which alone they can support and advance essential Ends of Reason. Now, I understand by a System the *unity* of the [true and, therefore, non-contra-dictory] *manifold* Cognitions [established] under [the sway of] one *Idea* [the latter being, therefore, the *Totality* of Cognition, and insofar as it is *developed discursively*, either the uni-total Discourse, which is the System per se, or *the* (discursive) Truth]. This is the rational-notion of the form of a Whole [= Totality], insofar as through this notion the *extent* (*Umfang*) of the Manifold [of the true Cognition] as well as the reciprocal/mutual *place* of the Parts are determined a priori. The *scientific* rational-notion thus contains the *End* and the *Form* of the *Whole*, the latter being congruent with that End. *The unity* of the End to which *all* Parts are referred, and by also being referred to each other in the [discursive uni-total] Idea of the End, allows the lack of *any* Part to be noticed [that is, it would be noticed if it were effectively missing] when one gains cognition of the rest [of the Parts] and there can be no *fortuitous addition*, that is, no *undetermined* magnitude of *complete-perfection* (*Vollkommenheit*) that would not have its *limit* determined a priori. The *Whole* is therefore *articulated* (*articulatio*) and not heaped together (*coacervatio*); it can, to be sure, grow *internally* (*per intussusceptionem*), but not

externally (*per appositionem*), [which means that this Whole can grow only] like an animal body whose growth *does not add* a limb, but, without any alteration of *proportion*, rather makes each limb stronger and more efficient (*tüchtiger*) for its End. (III, 538, 20–539, 11)

This text is so clear and precise that it speaks for itself, without a commentary or interpretation. It suffices to underscore in its regard that Kant's System, which is, for him, *the* discursive Truth, is a *uni-total* Discourse, because, on the one hand, it is *one* in itself and *unique* in its genre (which is the genre of Truth), and because, on the other hand, it involves (at least virtually) *all* that can be *said*, without contra-dicting itself, with the intention to tell *true*: the System can be 'developed' *internally* through the discursive development of the notions it *entails* (to the extent that this development of its constituent-elements is nothing else but the discursive development of the discursive uni-total 'Idea' which is one and the same thing as this system itself), but *outside* of which there is no discourse strictly so called (that is, non-contradictory in itself and uttered with the intention to tell true) which could have been *added* to it *somewhere* in space, at a random *moment* in time.

But a commentary on the cited passage, if one still wants one, can be found further on in Kant's own text, and this is what it says (while articulating a very 'Hegelian' conception of the History of Philosophy[13]):

---

13   One point I would like to mention on this occasion, even though, unfortunately, I cannot here dwell at length upon it, is the fourth and last Section of the {doctrine of} 'Method' (subdivided into three paragraphs, with an introduction) titled: 'The *History* of Pure Reason' (which, by the way, covers only two and a half pages). On Kant's own admission, this is only a brief overview, which solely designates a place left open for future development in the completed System. But what matters to us is that Kant had already seen what Hegel will subsequently say, namely the fact that the (discursive) *System* of Knowledge necessarily involves the *History* (the historical evolution) of the uni-total Discourse (which is this System), that is (for Hegel), History tout court, in such a way that the System of Knowledge might also be set forth in the form of the History of Philosophy, which would in fact bring about its advent {*avènement*}. Furthermore (despite his great and notorious ignorance of facts in the History of Philosophy), Kant's very brief remarks suffice nonetheless to show how well he grasped the meaning and scope of the history of Philosophy that preceded science, thus demonstrating his awareness of its historical place. To make this clear, I would simply translate the second paragraph dealing with the historical evolution of Philosophy. 'With regard to the origin of pure rational-Cognitions, [in view of knowing] whether they are deduced from [spatio-temporal] Experience or whether they have, independently of it, their [purportedly non-spatio-temporal] source in [the supposedly non-spatio-temporal] Reason', Kant

[Philosophical] Systems seem to have been constituted by mutilated forms at first but complete in time, like maggots (*Gewürme*) by a *generatio aequivoca* from the mere confluence of [randomly] aggregated notions, although in reality they all without exception had their schema, as the primordial seed, in the mere self-development of Reason [in the literal sense of 'unwrapping'; *auswickeln*], and on that account are not

---

says what follows (III, 551, 15–20): 'Aristotle can be regarded as the head of the Empiricists, Plato by contrast that of the Noologists. Locke, who, in recent times, followed the former, and Leibniz, who followed the latter (although with sufficient distance from his *mystical* [in the sense of "mythological"] System, have nevertheless not been able to bring this *discussion* (*Streite*) to any *decision*. But at least [one can say that] Epicurus, on his part, proceeded more *consistently* in accord with his *sensualist* System (for in his inferences [or Syllogisms; *Schlüssen*], he never exceeded the limits of [spatio-temporal] Experience) as Aristotle and Locke did (*especially*, however, the latter), who after he had deduced *all* Notions and *all* Principles from *Experience* [alone], goes so far in their use as to assert that it would be possible to *demonstrate* (*beweisen*) the existence of God and the *immortality* of the Soul (though both these thinglike-objects lie entirely *outside* of the limits of possible Experience) in a [discursive] manner which is just as *evident* [that is, as "indisputable" or "irrefutable"] as any mathematical theorem [which Kant wrongly believed to be part of *Discourse* strictly so called rather than of *Calculus*].' This short passage highlights many questions of the utmost importance. Firstly, Kant opposes clearly and in a radical way Aristotle to Plato, siding resolutely with the former (for he claims, without saying so in so many words here, that he *settled* the 'Discussion' once and for all in favour of Aristotelianism in and through his *Critique of Pure Reason*). He subsequently reproaches Plato for his 'philosophical Myths' (in which the 'As-if' is often presented 'as if' it were a Discourse properly so called, that is, *true* or at least *true-*semblant, while Kant himself would never tolerate such a confusion, not to say such a 'camouflage', in his own System), and in this context it clearly transpires that these Platonic 'Myths' essentially pertain to 'God' and the 'immortal Soul'. As for Aristotelianism, it is in Epicurus that he found its most consistent representative, even though for Kant's contemporaries, the Epicurean System was the very epitome of the *atheistic* philosophical System, and despite the fact that Kant himself says, between parentheses, that Epicurus was 'consistent' (that is, non-contra-dictory) precisely because he never *spoke* of the non-spatio-temporal. Finally, Kant reproaches not only the 'historical' Aristotle, who was for him the 'Platonic' Aristotle, but *even more so* Aristotle's successors (thus demonstrating a great philosophical perspicacity in a man who basically knew Aristotle only via the Scholasticism which drew on Aristotle only insofar as he was considered to be a *theist*, that is, *Platonic*), designating Locke as their representative (yet another sign of Kant's great perspicacity), for *speaking* of 'God' and the 'Immortality of the soul' (without saying it and without taking notice of it) *as if* this part of their discourse was also *true* in the proper and strong sense of the term, even though their own well-understood Systems were saying (albeit implicitly) that such discourses could only be made in the deliberate mode of As-if, that is, in such a way that they can be unambiguously used in life and even in Discourse *as if* they were true, without ever being able to say that they were 'truthfully' true.

merely *each articulated for themselves* in accordance with a [uni-total] Idea, but are rather *all* teleologically (*zweckmässig*) *gathered together with each other*, once again as members of an [organic] *Whole* in *one* [single] *System* of human Cognition [that is, of the true discursive Knowledge], and [thus] allowing an Architectonic to *all* human Knowledge [that is, discursive or true in the proper sense of the word], which at the present time, since so much material has already been collected or can be obtained near the ruins of collapsed ancient edifices, would not merely be possible but would not even be very difficult. (III, 540, 12-23)

Let us now look at the *structure* of Kant's own philosophical System according to the 'Architectonic' as it was set forth in (the first and second editions of) the *Critique of Pure Reason*, where Kant says what follows:

> The legislation of human [that is, discursive] Reason (Philosophy [qua uni-total Discourse]) has *two* objects: *Nature* and *Freedom*, and thus contains the natural Law as well as the moral Law, initially in *two* particular/specific (*besonderen*) Systems, but ultimately in a *single* philosophical System. The Philosophy of Nature pertains to *all* that *is*; that of Morals only to that which *should* be.
>
> Now, all Philosophy is either Cognition from pure Reason or rational-Cognition from empirical Principles. The former is called *pure* Philosophy, the latter *empirical*.
>
> The Philosophy of *pure* Reason is either Propaedeutic (Pre-exercise), which investigates a priori the faculty of Reason in regard to *all* pure Cognition and is called *Critique* [of pure (theoretical) Reason and of pure practical Reason], or, second, the *System* of pure Reason (*Science*), [that is,] the *whole* (*true* as well as *illusory* [*scheinbare*]) philosophical Cognition from pure Reason [expounded] in a systematic context, and is [therefore] called *Metaphysics* . . .
>
> Metaphysics is divided into the metaphysics of the *speculative* [that is, discursive] and the *practical* use of pure reason [that is, active or acting (but in the *System*, it can only be of course a question of the *discursive* development of the notion of 'the practical use of Reason' or of 'Freedom', indeed, 'Morals')] and is therefore either *Metaphysics of Nature* or *Metaphysics of Morals* . . . Now . . . the Metaphysics of *speculative* Reason is that which has customarily been called *Metaphysics* in the narrower sense [of the term]; . . .

Metaphysics in this narrower sense [that is, the *Metaphysics of Nature*] consists of *transcendental Philosophy* and the *Physiology* of pure Reason. The former considers only the Understanding and Reason themselves in *one* System of *all* notions and principles that pertain to thinglike-Objects in general (*überhaupt*), without assuming (*annehmen*) Objects that would be *given* [in and through Intuition] (*Ontologia*); the latter considers [the] *Nature*, that is, *the sum total* of [all] *given* thinglike-Objects (whether they are given to the Senses [that is, to the spatio-temporal Intuition or Perception, in which case they can give rise to knowledge, that is, a true discursive cognition] or, if one will, [referring to something that, if one cannot *speak* of it at all, one can at least speak of it without contra-dicting oneself], to another kind of Intuition [so-called 'intellectual']) and is therefore *Physiology* (though only rationalised). Now, the use of Reason in this rational consideration of Nature is either physical or hyperphysical, or, better, either *immanent* or *transcendent*. The former [use of Reason] pertains to Nature insofar as its cognition can be applied *in* [spatio-temporal] *Experience* (*in concreto*); the latter [pertains] to the connection/conjunction (*Verknüpfung*) of the thinglike-Objects of Experience, which *transcends* (*übersteigt*) all [spatio-temporal] Experience. Hence this transcendent Physiology [which cannot be developed discursively without contra-dicting itself and which is consequently the aforementioned '*illusory* philosophical Cognition'] has, in a similar way to its ['illusory'] thinglike-Object, either an *inner* or an *outer* connection/conjunction, both of which, however, *go beyond* possible Experience [that is, to the extent that Perception is able to give rise to Notions that can be developed discursively without contra-diction]; the former is the Physiology of Nature taken in-its-entirety (*gesammte*), that is, the transcendental *Cognition of-the-World* [in the sense of transcendent (?) which Kant will call, half a page later: 'rational Cosmology'], the latter [is the Physiology] of the connection (*Zusammenhangen*) of Nature taken in-its-entirety to a Being *beyond* (*über*) Nature, that is, the transcendental Cognition-of-God [in the sense of transcendent (?) which Kant will call in the place previously indicated: 'rational Theology'].

Conversely, [discursive and true] *immanent Physiology* considers Nature as the *ensemble* (*Inbegriff*) of all thinglike-Objects of the Senses [that is, of Perception], thus considers it as it is *given* to *us* [indeed, as

'Phenomenon'], but only in accordance with a priori conditions, under which it can be given to us in general [since we are still talking about *'pure'* and not 'empirical Philosophy']. There are, however, only *two* types (*Zweierlei*) of thinglike-Objects of *this* Nature: 1. Those of outer Senses, thus the *ensemble* of these, *corporeal Nature*; 2. The thinglike-Object of inner Sense, the Soul, and, in accordance with the fundamental principles of this, *thinking* [that is, discursive] *Nature* as such. The Metaphysics [or, to be more precise, the immanent Physiology] of corporeal Nature is called *Physics*, but since it is to contain only the principles of its a priori cognition, [it must be called] *rational* Physics. The Metaphysics [that is, the immanent Physiology] of thinking Nature is called *Psychology*, and for the reason that has just been indicated, only the *rational* cognition of this Nature is meant here [that is, in *'pure* Philosophy']. (III, 543, 18–544, 9–11; 544, 19–20; 546, 16–547, 10)

To facilitate the comprehension of this long citation, one can summarise its content in Table 1.

In interpreting this table, let us start with the elimination of 'empirical Philosophy'. What is at stake here, in and for Kant, is 'Science' in the common sense of the word, that is, for us, the ensemble of discourses (in a broad sense, but not contra-dictory) which neither takes nor gives any account of the very fact of the empirical existence of Discourse in extended-duration: this is where the ensemble of what we call '-graphy' (or '-metries') is situated.

Let us note *in passim* that Kant excludes from any Philosophy whatever it may be Mathematics in its entirety (and all Sciences which have a mathematical basis, such as Newtonian Physics for example). He, indeed, says very clearly (in a Note) that the *Metaphysics* of Nature is *entirely* different from Mathematics (III, 547, 30) in the same way it is different from *physica generalis* (III, 547, 28–37). This is because, according to Kant, 'every rational Cognition is either the one [derived] from Notions or [the one derived] from the *construction* of Notions; the former is called *philosophical*, the latter *mathematical*' (III, 541, 18–20). Unable to provide an interpretation of this citation here (III, 468, 26–476, 27), we will only say that Kant opposes *philosophical* 'rational-Cognition' (*Vernunfterkenntnis*) to *mathematical* 'rational-Activity' (*Vernunftgeschäfte*) because the former is *discursive* while the latter is *constructive*.

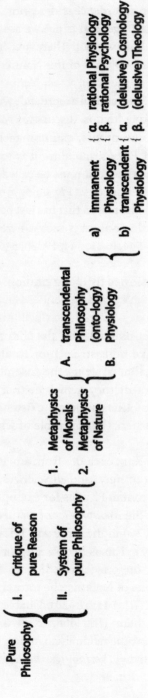

Table 1.

As for the *Critique*, it is most likely that when Kant published the first edition of the *Critique of Pure Reason* (1781), he knew *only* one 'Critique' which he envisaged as some sort of a (systematic) Introduction to the System. By the time the second edition was published (1787) he was probably already familiar with the *Critique of Practical Reason* (published in 1788), even though the text of the second edition of the first *Critique* does not in any way take into consideration the fact that its 'Methodology' had barely changed. Be that as it may, it is sure that in 1788 Kant was not yet familiar with the *Critique of the Power of Judgement* (published in 1790). But we will have the opportunity to talk about this a little further down.

It now remains to interpret the structure of the *System* strictly so called. What is first striking is the radical and extreme *dualism* that this structure reveals. One can say that here the *Metaphysics of Nature* and the *Metaphysics of Morals* stand against one another like a Yes and a No, and such a formula would in no way be an exaggeration. Indeed, according to Kant, human Freedom is defined as that which *sets itself against* human Nature in an irreducible manner, and he defines Nature tout court, that is, 'possible Experience', as that which is irreducibly *opposed* to Freedom whatever it may be, for the specific character of Nature and the Experience through which it is revealed consist in absolute and total Causality or *Necessity*. If the two Parts of the System were to overlap when brought to bear on one and the same object, they would, therefore, necessarily *contradict* one another, which would be the case if the Human being was at the same time and in the same way a *natural* being and a *free* agent, or if *free* Action ('Freedom') were to have tangible effects in the *natural* World ('Nature'). And Kant was fully aware of all this, as may be inferred from numerous passages in his writings, from which we could indicatively cite, a bit at random, this one (from the 'Canon'):

> Transcendental Freedom requires an *independence* of this [practical, that is, pertaining to free Will] Reason itself (with regard to *its* Causality [which consists in the fact of] *initiating* a series of Phenomena [but this intrinsically spontaneous initiation is not *determined* in any way whatsoever through preceding series of Phenomena]) from *all* determining Causes of the sensible World and [this Freedom] thus seems to be *opposed* (*zuwider*) to the Law of *Nature*, and consequently to *all* possible Experience, and [it] therefore remains a [theoretical] *Problem*. (III, 522, 1–5)

Without a doubt, this Kantian 'Problem' is one of the many forms of the famous conflict between 'Athens' and 'Jerusalem'. For this 'Problem' arises only if we conceive of Human beings (or of their human specificity) in accordance with Judeo-Christian Anthropology (Soul = Mana = Negativity), which does not admit that Human beings are *necessarily*, that is, everywhere and always, *identical* to themselves, this self-*identity* being their 'Essence' or 'Nature', in every way similar to other natural beings, and, *at the same time*, conceive Nature (including 'natural' Human beings) to be in accordance with ancient or pagan Cosmology (Soul = Essence = Identity), which knows only Identity alone, this requiring, among other things, under the title of Causality or Legality, that the apparent changes in natural things leave their 'basic substance' {*fond essentiel*} intact or eternally the same. The Kantian 'Problem', therefore, arises necessarily for every truly Christian Philosophy. And it arose, obviously, for Descartes, who admitted in his *Cogitationes privatae* that 'Freedom is a *mystery*'.

But what is specifically Kantian is that the conflict in question is not situated, as in Descartes and others, between Human beings and Nature, but within the former themselves. Indeed, the passage that has just been cited opposes *practical Reason*, that is, the free Will, to the Ensemble of *possible Experience*, which, in Kant, is in the major part the work {*oeuvre*} of *theoretical* (or 'pure') *Reason*, which *imposes*, among other things, on ('phenomenal') Nature the category of Causality even though the latter *contra-dicts* (Human) Freedom (in the 'phenomenal' World). The conflict is, therefore, well and truly situated *within* Human beings and is a conflict or an irreducible opposition between *their* practical Reason and *their* theoretical Reason, indeed, between their *Will* and their (discursive) *Thought*. Now, if Descartes *differentiates* the Will (which is 'infinite') from Thought in the narrow sense (which is 'finite') insofar as he admits a certain *tension* between the former and the latter (to the extent that the Will is able to mislead Thought into error as it might reject the errors of Thought), he, nonetheless, incorporates them both in 'Thought' in the broad sense; and far from *opposing* one to the other in an irreducible way, he, on the contrary, *identifies* them with one another, since 'Thought', in the broad sense, is *all* that is Non-extended and since the Will is not more 'extended' than Thought itself in the narrow sense.

This allows us, moreover, to determine the position of the Kantian System with reference to Descartes'. It has been often said that in the former, Cartesian 'Extension' was absorbed by Cartesian 'Thought' (in the narrow sense), since *spatio*-temporal 'Intuition' is, according to Kant, one of the constituent-elements of one and the same 'Subjectivity' whose other element is rational or discursive Thought, that is, the 'pure Reason' that 'gathers together' the 'Manifold' ('given' in 'Intuition') in accordance with its own 'Categories'. But we now see that the *opposite* is true. In fact, it is Cartesian 'Extension' that, in Kant, absorbed 'Thought' (in the narrow sense). For not only is '[theoretical] pure Reason' rigorously *limited* by the spatio-temporal frame, without ever being able to go beyond it (as Cartesian 'Thought' was able to do), but it is also *opposed* (qua constitutive for Experience or Nature) to '[pure] practical Reason' (= the Will) in the same manner Extension (qua Nature) is opposed, in Descartes, to Thought in the broad sense (and notably to free Will which is part of it). That being so is because, for Kant, contrary to all his great philosophical predecessors, Human beings are thus *natural* beings in the 'Greek' sense of this word (that is, *essentially* self-*identical* beings or *determined* in a *univocal* and *permanent* way by the 'nature' which is 'theirs', owing to the fact that the latter is 'innate' or 'co-eternal' with its own duration), not only as Animal or 'Body' but also as (discursive) Thought or as Discourse (Logos) [which, for Kant, is moreover as *spatio-temporal* as Cartesian 'Extension' (but not Cartesian 'Thought')]; it is uniquely (as in Rousseau) qua 'Free agent' or 'Will' that the Human being is radically different from the Animal and from any 'Nature' whatever, be it mute or endowed with the ability to speak {*parlante*}.

Be that as it may, from the outset, Kant has acknowledged that his System involved a latent *conflict* and an apparent *contra-diction* between the *Metaphysics of Morals*, which says that (only) the Human being is absolutely *free*, and the *Metaphysics of Nature* which *contra-dicts* it by affirming that the Human being (like all things) is absolutely *determined*, and he himself saw in this a 'problem'. The way in which Kant overcomes that contra-diction is well known: the Human being is *free* qua (non-spatio-temporal) *Thing-in-itself* and *determined* qua (spatio-temporal) *Phenomenon*. Indeed, there would be a contra-diction if one asserted that one and the same thing is *at the same time* in different *locations* or that, *in the same location*, something is at once what it is and what it is not (that is, A and non-A, or even B). Now, Kant does not say that the Human being (qua Phenomenon) is *at the same time* in a given location of the determined World and *elsewhere* (qua Thing-in-itself), for, not being temporal, the Thing-in-itself cannot be situated *within the same time* as the Phenomenon, and to the extent that it is not spatial, it cannot be *elsewhere* than the latter. Similarly, Human beings are not said to be at once free and not free (determined) *at the same place/location*, since, as free or Thing-in-itself, they are not in any *place/location* at all.

But, if Kant thus manages to eliminate the contra-diction from his System, he does not overcome the 'conflict' that he acknowledges and neither does he resolve the 'problem' that he, himself, poses.

The 'conflict' remains because, visibly, human beings do not content themselves with saying that they *are* free qua non-spatio-temporal Things-in-themselves. Their 'Will', which they say they themselves are (and, according to Kant, say so with reason), also wants to *act* freely, and they cannot, visibly, say that they may do so otherwise than in some *place* at any given *moment*. Now, their own 'Reason' (at least according to Kant) *obliges* them to say that all that is or is done *somewhere* at a given *moment* is necessarily, that is, everywhere and always, determined and not free. As for the 'problem', rather than being *resolved*, it is, on the contrary, *specified*, or even *doubled up* by the Kantian overcoming of the contra-diction that gave rise to it. Indeed, Kant overcomes the contra-diction by introducing the notion of the Thing-in-itself. Now, he, himself, acknowledges that this notion is far from being a 'theoretical necessity', not even a 'transcendental' one, that is, 'deducible' as *sine qua non* condition of the possibility of (discursive) Experience, not to say, of the coherent Discourse in general. Rather, he says that this notion 'imposes' itself on Reason only as *sine qua non* condition of 'Morality', that is, precisely, of Freedom, and that *this*, if one wishes, 'transcendental', condition is the 'existence of God' and the 'future World'. The non-spatio-temporal Thing-in-itself is, therefore, necessarily not only *human* free Will, but also 'God' and a 'divine' World. Thus the 'Problem' becomes both more *precise* and *twofold*: on the one hand, the 'natural' World must be 'reconciled' with the 'divine' one, and on the other hand, human Freedom must be 'harmonised' with God's existence.

That said, let us not forget that, for Kant, this double 'conciliation' can only be an 'article of Faith', since it is only a discursive development of the *subjective certainty* of *Hope*. The discursive solution of the 'Problem' cannot, therefore, be a (discursive) Truth in the proper sense of the term: at best, one can take it into consideration and behave in its regard and with respect to it *as if* it were true (which is something entirely different from saying, with Plato, that it is *true*-semblant). But even in this As-if mode, the solution is neither convenient nor 'satisfactory' for the spirit, and it is even less so for the flesh-and-blood human being.

As for the 'conciliation' of the 'natural' World (in which Human beings are *determined*) with the 'divine' World (in which these Human beings are *free*, since it is only in function of *their* Act of *freedom* that they can be *worthy* of *happiness* in the 'future Life'), the affirmation that both worlds have been 'created' by one and the same God (who thus created both natural Human beings, including their theoretical Reason, and free Human beings, that is, their Volition or practical Reason) is of no use at all, because the Spinozist–Leibnizian 'solution' of 'complementarism' or a 'pre-established harmony' cancels Freedom out, no less than the occasionalism of Malebranche [to the extent that both solutions are, besides, expressly rejected by Kant, who justifiably says that they cancel out the '*necessary* character' of the Categories, thus opening the path to Scepticism (cf. III, 128, 24–129, 22)]. The only imaginable 'solution', which is the one that Kant proposes by repeating word for word (perhaps unknowingly) Plato's famous 'Myth', consists in saying that human beings make the (free) choice of their (determined) life *before* they are born and that it is this prenatal (free) choice that constitutes an object of 'recognition' or a post-mortuary divine 'reprobation' *after* their death (that is, after their *life*, which is entirely *determined* both by the Laws of the natural World and by their free choice): this solution, while being implicitly contra-dictory, will certainly not 'satisfy' Common sense, the latter being never able to figure out the sense and value that might be attributed to the (predetermined) 'worldly' comedy played out by Human beings before their God *after* the (free) choice that already fixes 'the last judgement' has been made.

As for the other aspect of the 'Problem', it is yet to find a 'satisfactory' solution from any standpoint whatever, not even from the standpoint of the imagination, which would be less contra-dictory than the preceding 'solution'. For if it is not 'absurd' to say that a divine, free and omnipotent Being abstains from action because such is his 'good pleasure', and therefore, among other things, allows human beings to act as they please (while admitting that the notion of an *action* carried out outside time and space may not be contradictory in itself, even while being so in reality), one cannot see why that which is granted to the human being in this manner would be called 'freedom': for, otherwise, the convict who can wander 'as they please' around the courtroom for half an hour might as well be called 'free' just like a child who can do 'whatever they want' in the paternal home at their birthday party. Inversely, one cannot convincingly see why one must call 'God' a being who is either unable or unwilling to prevent his 'beloved children' from enduring 'endless' sufferings following a 'passing gluttony' (all the more so, one which is 'tolerated' for some unknown reason), or what purpose this God serves if human beings can effectively do what they want without thereby enduring anything other than what they, themselves, *wanted*, unless God has the same 'use' as the bottom of a torrent when someone falls, deliberately or inadvertently, into a precipice where 'perchance' this torrent flows.

But all of this has been said so often before Kant, and as far as his knowledge went, for it to make sense to say it again to him or to his followers (be they conscious or not of their origin). All that might be validly said to Kant is that which he himself must have told himself while writing the *Critique of Pure Reason*, namely, that the very notions of 'free-acting prenatal Action' and a 'free-acting God' are contradictory per se, like any notion of the type 'square-Circle'. For if the notion '*free* Action' is endowed with any sense whatever, it refers to the transformation of a concrete (objectively-unreal) *future* {*avenir*} Project into a *present* objective-reality, which is not *necessarily*, that is, *everywhere* and *always*, wholly derived from the *past*. Consequently, the notion 'free Action' cannot exclude the notion of 'Temporality', or even that of 'Spatio-temporality' in general, and since it additionally refers to objective-Reality, the Spatio-temporality it entails is (as we will see later) Space-time. The notions 'free God' or 'free Soul' are, therefore, synonymous with the explicitly contra-dictory notion '*non*-spatio-temporal-Being-*in*-space-time' or 'objectively-*real*-Being-who-*is*-not'.

Now, Kant must have said all this to himself, since he never wanted to *speak* of the *free action* of God and the Soul other than in the mode of As-if, even though his *religious* temperament (*theistic* on account of its tradition) had, undoubtedly, made him do so, no less than Plato. Kant resigned himself to the As-if of his theology only because he knew that any discourse on God and the Soul (purportedly) developed in the mode of Truth, being contra-dictory per se, would inevitably introduce Contradiction in the System, that is, contra-dict its non-theological Part, which is intrinsically non-contra-dictory per se. For it is only in this manner that he managed to avoid the said Contra-diction (which was ruinous for the System), given that the discursive *As-if*-it-were-true (but not the discursive True-semblant) is unable to contra-dict the discourse about That-which-*is*-true.

But there is yet another aspect of the 'Problem' in question that interests us at this point. To the extent that the notion of the 'intelligible World' (= eternal free God + acting immortal Soul + 'profane' Thing-in-itself) is supposedly endowed with *Sense*, one must indicate its *source*, that is, the way in which this 'World' is *given* or *revealed* to a Human-being-who-speaks-thereof. Now, all of Kant's 'critical' oeuvre was meant to prevent him from admitting that any Sense whatever could be *given* in 'divine Revelation' (*Offenbaruung*) or through any 'non-sensible-Proof' (*intellektuelle Anschauung*). In agreement with Aristotle, this oeuvre had demonstrated (or presupposed as 'indisputable' basis) that *every* Sense whatever it may be could only be derived from (spatio-temporal or 'sensible') 'Experience', that is, in our terminology, from Perception. Now, Kant did not admit *sui generis* 'experiences' ('mystical visions') like the ones Saint Paul claims to have had on the road to Damascus. For the Sense that may be extricated (through the detachment from the *hic et nunc*) from a similar 'Perception', by definition if not necessarily 'unique of its kind', at least everywhere and always reserved for just the rare few 'elect' ones, could not have this 'universally valid' (*allgemein gültig*) character, that is, to be 'reproducible' *everywhere* and *always* by *everyone*, without which Sense would never be a Truth (by integrating itself, without contradiction and even as an indispensable constituent-element, in the uni-total discursive System). It is therefore only in Perception, which is 'ordinary' or accessible to *everyone*, that Kant would find the ultimate source of the Sense of the notion 'intelligible World'. Now, given the way in which Experience was presented in the *Critique of Pure Reason* and even in the *whole* of the System, whose outlines were sketched out in that *Critique*, there was no means to even search therein the source of the Sense in question.

This Sense could not be found in the *Metaphysics of Morals* (founded on the [future] *Critique of Practical Reason*) because the only specific *given* it is cognisant thereof is the Consciousness-of-Duty (*Pflichtgewusstsein*) which, according to Kant, has no *theoretical* content (to the extent that it is an incentive {*mobile*} for Action rather than a source of *Cognition*). As for the *Metaphysics of Nature* (founded on the *Critique of Pure Reason*), which integrates the ensemble of (theoretical) Cognition, it could not provide this source either.

To validate these claims, let us see what was and what should have been, over the period of the second edition of the *Critique* (1787), the theoretical Part of Kant's System.

Concerning this issue, here is what Kant himself has to say in the 'Architectonic':

> Accordingly, the completed (*ganze*) System of Metaphysics [in the narrow sense, that is, Metaphysics of Nature, which constitutes the *theoretical* part of the Kantian System] consists of four main Parts. 1. Ontology. 2. [*Immanent*] rational Physiology. 3. Rational Cosmology. 4. Rational Theology [Cosmology and Theology constituting the two Sections of *transcendent* Physiology]. The second Part, namely the *natural* theory (*Naturlehre*) of pure Reason, contains two Sections: *physica rationalis* and *psychologia rationalis*. (III, 547, 11–15)

Kant never elaborated on his *Ontology*. But, in its gist, this Kantian Ontology appears in the 'Transcendental Analytic' of the *Critique of Pure Reason* (which deals with 'Categories' and 'Principles'), as Kant himself says very clearly: 'the proud name of an Ontology, ... must give way to the modest one of a mere Analytic of the pure Understanding' (III, 207, 18–22; see also: III, 94, 36–7). Consequently, the origin of the Meaning {*Sens*} of the notions God and the future World cannot be found in Kant's Ontology, since the latter is entirely limited to the domain of 'sensible Intuition', that is, to spatio-temporality.

Conversely, Kant outlined 'immanent Physiology' under the title of *Metaphysical Foundations of Natural Science* (1786). In the Preface, he first distinguishes *empirical* ('historical') Science from *rational* Science (focusing exclusively on the latter) and indicates that, from a systematic standpoint, the 'Natural Science' is divided into two Sections whose respective objects he defines as follows:

> Now, Nature, ... in accordance with the principal distinction of our Senses, has two major Parts, one of which contains the thinglike-objects of the *outer* Senses and the other the thinglike-Object of *inner* Sense, in such a way that as far as Nature is concerned, a twofold natural Doctrine (*Naturlehre*) is possible, [namely] the Doctrine of Bodies and the Doctrine of the Soul, where the first

takes into consideration *extended Nature*, the second *thinking Nature*. (IV, 467, 12-17)

The book itself, as is known, contains only the first elements (of Newtonian influence) of the Doctrine of Bodies (to the extent that the Doctrine of the Soul is the object of the *Anthropology* of 1798). But the few words cited above suffice to show that, for Kant, the Doctrine of the Soul is a purely *natural* Science, which, just like the Doctrine of Bodies, does not in any way imply an escape route towards the Beyond. This passage confirms, besides, what we have said above about Kant's relationship to Descartes, for it clearly shows that Kant associates Cartesian 'Thought' with 'Extension' and considers it as a purely *natural*, not to say spatio-temporal, entity, reducing the *non-natural* in the Human being solely to a 'Freedom' radically opposed to all 'Nature' (cf. IV, 458, 2: the human Ego {*Moi*} properly so-called, *that is*, the human Will).

As for 'transcendent Physiology', Kant relegates it, as we have seen, to the domain of 'illusion' (*scheinbare philosophische Erkenntnis*, cf. III, 544, 1 and 546, 29-35), that is, to the domain of discourse, which would in no way aspire to the dignity of (discursive) *Truth*. As for 'rational Theology', in Kant, it is reduced to what he calls 'moral Faith', of which he speaks in the 'Canon' and then sets forth in more detail in the *Critique of Practical Reason* (1788), as well as in *Religion Within the Limits of Reason Alone* (1793), where moral Freedom, that is, Duty, is radically opposed to all that is Nature, including the 'given' Nature of the Human being per se, even when taken as Volition, like the Good in opposition to 'radical Evil'. Now, we have seen that the feeling of Duty cannot be considered as the source whence that Meaning {*Sens*} of the notion of Transcendence is derived, because Duty itself, according to Kant, makes sense only IF 'God' and the 'future World' are admitted beforehand (cf. III, 520, 17-24). In, if not for Kant, Duty is, in fact, born from the refusal of self-Contempt, but to the extent that the Action that flows therefrom is, according to the fundamental Postulate of every Religion, inefficacious, and therefore incapable of procuring Satisfaction down Here-below, Duty engenders only *Hope* for Satisfaction in the divine Beyond. Now, for that Hope to become *Faith*, that is, for it to be operative and engender Action in function of Duty, there must be a subjective *certainty*, which practical Philosophy ('Metaphysics of Morals'), itself exclusively founded on the notion of Duty, cannot, by definition, procure. But, as we have just seen, theoretical Philosophy ('Metaphysics of Nature'), that is, 'Ontology' and 'immanent Physiology', cannot procure this satisfaction either. For even though 'subjective', this *Certainty* of Satisfaction as a function of free (moral) Action cannot be given in the Theoretical, that is, ultimately in Perception, unless Perception reveals an *agreement* or a *harmony* between Duty (= Freedom = Volition) and Nature (= Necessity = Thought). Now, conversely, Nature revealed through Perception is, for Kant, at least in 1787, *radically and irreducibly opposed* to Freedom, to the extent that it is *defined* as the Non-free or the Necessary, while Freedom is *defined* as the Non-natural, that is, as the Non-perceptible or as the non-spatio-temporal 'Thing-in-itself' in opposition to the spatio-temporal 'Phenomenon' which is Nature alone.

The subjective Certainty in question could not, therefore, be drawn from a theoretical Philosophy based on Perception unless that Philosophy implied 'rational Cosmology', which Kant defines as Physiology of Nature *taken in its totality* (*der gesammten Natur*). But he hastens to say that *this* (completed) *totality* of Nature surpasses [sensible or spatio-temporal] possible Experience (III, 546, 34–31). Now, only this natural *Totality*, which, according to Kant, pertains to a Being beyond Nature (*Wessen über die Natur*) or to God, could also 'refer' to that 'Being beyond Nature' which is the Human being qua free Agent, and this 'reference', were it perceptible, could and should ensure the *Certainty* of Hope of the Agent in question, and, therefore, the *Faith* that makes them act, even *against* Nature, which is this agent's own nature as well.

But if Kant, in 1787, admits Theology in his System, albeit qua 'moral Faith', that is, qua discourse [which is, besides, contra-dictory] developed in the mode of As-if, he categorically denies himself the possibility of introducing in that system the 'Cosmology' in question, even though he already seems to have realised that, without this 'Cosmology', the Hope in which practical Philosophy culminates remains without subjective (theoretical, or even 'perceptible') *Certainty*, in such a way that his 'moral Faith' is less a *Faith* in the strong sense of the term than it is a 'Myth', which is perhaps *possible* [if one wrongly admits that it is not contra-dictory], but in no way *certain*, even in the sense of a purely *subjective* Certainty. In other words, this 'Myth' is neither *true* [by definition], nor even *true*-semblant, and the very 'As-if' of its discursive development is without any *foundation*, not even a *theoretical* one.

This Kantian System circa 1787 can be represented graphically by the diagram on the left-hand side in Figure 3.

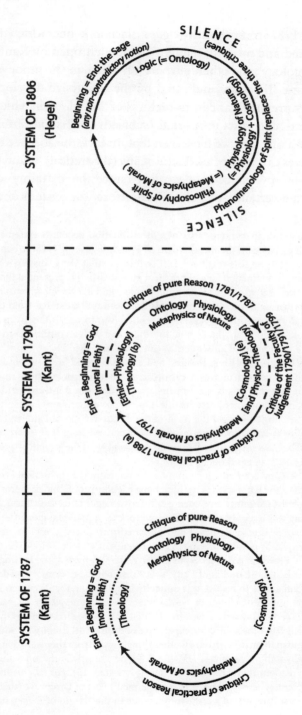

(a) Introduction to the *Critique*: *Groundwork for the Metaphysics of Morals* (1785)
(b) Systematic exposition: *Religion within the Boundaries of Mere Reason* (1793)
(c) Stand-alone exposition: *Critique of Pure Reason* (1781/1787)
(d) Exposition in the *Metaphysical Foundations of Natural Science* (1786) and *Anthropology {from a Pragmatic Point of View}* (1798/1800)
(e) Stand-alone exposition: *Critique of Judgment* (1790)

Figure 3

The System of 1787 comprises two *gaps* {*lacunes*}: one which is consciously admitted and avowed, namely the one left open by Kant's non-existent 'Cosmology'; the other, purportedly filled, in the mode of As-if, through 'moral Theology', indicated by the discursive development [not explicitly presented as contra-dictory] of 'Moral *Faith*', which is supposedly able to derive its purported (subjective) *Certainty* from the feeling of Duty alone. But we have seen that, in fact, the absence of 'Cosmology' deprives this purported 'Faith' of any (theoretical) 'foundation' and thereby of any subjective *Certainty* (since the 'certainty' of Duty *depends* on the certainty of Faith).[14] Therefore, the System does

---

14   From the standpoint that interests us here, the situation becomes extremely muddled and absolutely untenable in the *Critique of Practical Reason* (1788), but it would take too long to interpret this text here. Suffice it to say that Duty (discursively developed in the famous 'fundamental Law of practical pure Reason') is presented there (cf. §7 and Note) as a '*Fact* of Reason', that is, as an *immediate* and *irreducible* 'given', and as 'the *sole* Fact of pure Reason'. More specifically, this 'Fact' cannot be derived from the Consciousness of Freedom, since this is not antecedently *given* to us [to the given of Duty]', because this would require an 'intellectual Intuition' and such an intuition is not, by definition, available to Humans. Consequently, this 'Fact' is a theoretical 'Proof' of the Platonic-Cartesian type, which Kant, besides, had always rejected [and rightly so], but to which he nonetheless resorts, on this occasion, in a somewhat apologetic manner while underscoring the fact that this is the *only* instance he does so. But this (besides, understated) 'apology' is certainly neither a 'justification', *in our eyes*, nor, in fact, in the eyes of Kant himself. Seeking *to ground* the As-if of the discursive moral Faith in that 'Proof' is impossible. For if Theology was grounded in or derived from that *theoretical* Proof (and it must well be *theoretical*, since it *precedes* and *conditions* the 'practical' proof of Freedom), it would be a *Truth* and not an *As-if.*

Consequently, if Theology is a *Faith*, it cannot be *derived* from the theoretical Proof in question. Either that or the latter itself is nothing but a pseudo-proof, that is, a proposition without the slightest Certainty, not even a subjective one. Let us see what Kant himself says concerning this issue. In the 1785 *Groundwork for a Metaphysics of Morals* (which, three years earlier, thus anticipated and prepared/introduced the *Critique of Practical Reason*), he explicitly admits to being in the presence of a 'vicious circle': on the one hand, the notion of Freedom is *derived* from the (irreducible) *given* of the Feeling of Duty, but, on the other hand, the notion of Duty is *derived from* the notion of Freedom (cf. IV, 450, 18–29). Kant seems to resolve this difficulty by admitting that Freedom is a *given* (from which the notion of Duty can be *derived* without *presupposing* it). More exactly, the notion of Freedom is itself *derived* from a Fact or from the irreducible Given of Introspection, namely from the subjective experience of the a priori Faculty 'by which Human beings distinguish themselves from all other things, even from themselves insofar as they are *affected* by thinglike-Objects' (IV, 452, 7–9): no a priori Cognition without Freedom, and when Freedom then Duty, etc. (cf. IV, 452, 9–453, 15). *For us*, this indicates the instance, *in Kant*, where he appeals to the ('defined') Fact of Discourse (that is, the raw Fact of Discourse, postulated as *true* in reference to the Axiom of *Error*); now,

indeed give rise to two *interruptions*, and is, therefore, anything but uni-total or circular. In other words, it is a *sceptical* 'System', that is, a [so-called non-contra-dictory] Discourse which is incapable of coming back to its starting point, thus presenting itself as a Discourse with a Beginning, but without an End. Now, regarding the 'cosmological' gap, it is openly acknowledged by Kant himself, since according to him, the

---

this would be an authentically Hegelian, indeed atheistic, 'Beginning', from which there is no means at all to 'derive' a notion of the Beyond ('God' and 'Immortality'), for the 'future World' is thus the *human* World that completes History: no (true) Discourse without Freedom, and when Freedom then (negating or creative) Action of Struggle and Work, that is, the History which culminates in the universal and homogeneous State, where the Citizen-Sage utters {*émet*} the uni-total or circular Discourse which *is* the discursive Truth. Now, for *religious* motives, Kant did not want to follow *this* reasoning and renounced it altogether in the 1788 *Critique of Practical Reason*. There, the Feeling of Duty (in regard to the 'moral Law') is the *irreducible* Given from which the notion of Freedom is *derived*. For us, this is a Kantian *error*: on the one hand, Introspection contains, in fact, the famous 'moral Law' (formulated in §7 of the *Critique*) not as an irreducible Given (to the extent that the latter is [positively] the 'Desire of desire' [real-ised as Struggle → Work] and [negatively] 'Boredom'), but as a very *derivative* notion [of the Desire of Desire and appearing, besides, only towards the end of History, precisely in Kant]; on the other hand, by admitting this 'Law' qua *theoretical* irreducible Given, that is, qua 'Proof' of the Platonic-Cartesian type, the System that discursively develops this purported 'Given' is rendered contra-dictory (ultimately: theistic or 'theological' because the '*Gewissen*' is non-discursive; thus, the 'System' in which it is involved cannot be self-deduced, that is, self-de-monstrable). Indeed, if the 'moral Law' is a theoretical 'Proof', it must be discursively developed in such a way that it provides a *Definition* of Human beings qua beings that act in such a way that *their* Project of action is a '*universal* Law'; the Sense of that Definition corresponds to the Human *Essence* (in the 'Greek' sense of the word), which is by definition everywhere and always, that is, *necessarily*, identical to itself; that is, Human beings are not *free*, and what they claim to be *their* 'moral Law' (their 'Project') is in reality nothing other than a *natural* 'universal Law'; now, as Kant himself envisaged it, Discourse *presupposes* Freedom; therefore, it is contra-dictory to *say* that the 'moral Law' is an irreducible (theoretical) Given (for, if that were the case, one would be unable to *speak* and, in particular, unable to formulate this [in fact *natural*] 'Law' *discursively*). If one wants to 'transform' that Kantian error into truth (which is proven as such through its inclusion in the uni-total Discourse in a non-contra-dictory way), the situation must be 'reversed' to *derive* the notion of the 'moral Law' from the *irreducible* Given of Freedom (more exactly: from the *irreducible* Given of the Desire of desire realised by the Action of Struggle → Work, from which the notion of Freedom = Negativity is, in turn, *derived*). But then one is once again right at the heart of Hegelianism, or even atheism: derived accordingly, the 'moral Law' should be inter-preted differently from the way Kant interpreted it, and a proper interpretation of that 'Law' excludes every possibility of deriving the notion of Transcendence (and therefore of 'God' and 'Immortality') therefrom. Indeed (as we envisage to de-monstrate, albeit summarily, in and through the ensemble of our exposition of the Hegelian *System of*

Metaphysics of Nature is 'open' in this sense that it involves an 'indefinite' discursive development (the famous 'infinite Task'), just like the Metaphysics of Morals, which, moreover, discursively develops the notion of a Duty which can never and nowhere be *fulfilled* by an Action carried out in Spatio-temporality [cf. V, 122, 9–12: The complete adequacy (*Angemessenheit*) of the Will to the moral Law is Holiness,

---

Knowledge), Freedom or Negativity is not pure Nothingness only insofar as it exists-empirically as negating or creative Action of Struggle → Work, which is developed in the extended-Duration as universal History in such a way that the very notion of discursive Truth makes sense only when that creative History has an end and can thus 'resume' {*résumer*} in and through, or as, uni-*total* or circular Discourse, which is nothing other or more than the (non-contra-dictory) discursive development of the notion of Freedom, which sets the Human being against Nature *in an irreducible way*, and derives its Sense from the irreducible Given of the Desire-of-desire, which exists-empirically as Action of Struggle → Work, that Action giving rise to any Discourse whatever (which can thus be discursively *derived* therefrom and which *defines* the notion of Freedom), such that when this Discourse closes in upon itself, it is (in its sum total, that is, in its result) the discursive de-monstration of Freedom which has ultimately given rise to it. This discursive development of the notion of Freedom (defined *at the beginning*, in and through a Definition-project, qua Project of Action) may be, *at its end, summed up* {*résumé*}, if one will, as Kant did in his 'fundamental Law of the pure practical Reason [= Freedom]': 'So act that the Maxim of *your* Will [that is, the Project of *your* Action] could *always* be *at the same time* valid as [guiding] Principle of a [spatially] *universal* Legislation' (V, 30, 38–9). However, the meaning attributed to this 'Law' by the Hegelian *interpretation* will be radically different to the one attributed thereto by Kant himself. In this 'accurate' interpretation (that is, one which does not lead to Contra-diction, or even to Theology), the 'fundamental Law' means: Govern the universal and homogeneous State [coeternal and co-extended with the extended-Duration] in such a way that it remains identical to itself, or at least do not act in such a way that you perturb it, when it exists-empirically, and if it does not exist yet or if it does not exist everywhere (but only somewhere, that is, as a 'seed-bud' {*germe*}), act in such a way that you accelerate its advent or, at least, in such a way that you do not impede, that is, either delay in Duration or limit in Extension, its access to empirical-Existence. Why? Because your Freedom is revealed to you (as a Project of an Action) only as Desire of desire, which is a Desire for Recognition and exists-empirically for you and for others (as accomplished Oeuvre) only in and by Struggle → Work, which will not cease to *create* History (= historical, human, 'artificial' World) through the *negation* of Nature (= the Given) until the Desire for Recognition is fully *satisfied*, which is achievable only in and through the universal and homogeneous State. Now, if the accomplished Oeuvre in the said State *satisfies* the anthropo-genic Desire, Human beings are capable of not despising themselves without having the need to *hope* for anything whatsoever beyond that State (to the extent that their only discursively 'justifiable' Hope is, *before* the advent of that State, the *subjective Certainty* of that *hoped for* event, that is, Faith in the *future* universal and homogeneous State). Consequently, the Faith engendered by the non-contra-dictory discursive development of the notion of Freedom is Faith in the historical or *human* 'future World', and [which is] a Perfection (*Volkommenheit*) of which no rational Being in the sensible World is capable at any moment of their existence]. And, although Kant believes or purports to have realised the 'agreement' between the Metaphysics of Nature and the Metaphysics of Freedom through the theological discourse, which he develops in the mode of As-if, it is easy for the Sceptic (in a conscious and deliberate way) to

---

by becoming itself discursive, it cannot therefore involve any notion of Transcendence, in such a way that it is impossible to *derive* therefrom, without contra-dicting oneself, the notions 'God' and 'Immortality', as Kant wanted to do. Moreover, Kant seems to have already realised this in the *Critique of Reason* itself. For this is what he says there: 'But Freedom is nonetheless the *only* one among all the Ideas of *speculative* [that is, *theoretical*] Reason whose Possibility we *know* (*wissen*) a priori, though without *comprehending* it (*einzusehen*), because it is the *condition* (*Bedingung* [in the sense of *ratio essendi*]) of the moral Law, which we *do know* [and which is the *ratio cognoscendi* of Freedom]. Now, the Ideas of God and Immortality are not conditions of the moral Law, but conditions . . . only of the purely *practical* use of our pure Reason; consequently, we cannot claim to *cognise* and *comprehend* (*einzusehen*) either, I am not saying merely [objective] Reality, but even the possibility of these Ideas. But [these Ideas] are nonetheless conditions for *the application* of the morally determined Will . . . Consequently, their Possibility can and must be *admitted* (*angenommen*) in this *practical* regard, without however *cognising* or *comprehending* it *theoretically*. For this latter demand (*Forderung*), it suffices, for the *practical* aim, that these Ideas contain no intrinsic *Impossibility* (Contradiction)' (V, 4, 7–21). Regarding this last point, Kant is simply wrong, for 'God' and 'Immortality' are, in fact, contra-dictory notions of the type 'square-Circle'. But that matters little, for now. What matters is that Kant acknowledges that these two notions (which, for us, are but one) cannot be *derived* from the (*theoretical*) notion of the 'moral Law', not even as merely 'possible' (in our terminology: as that which *is* without being *objectively-real*) [nor, by definition, exist-empirically]. In the *Critique of Practical Reason*, Kant tries to 'derive' these notions from the *practical application* of the 'moral Law', but it is easy to see that there, the 'deduction' is in no way 'indisputable'. In fact, he can *deduce* them (correctly) only by *supposing* (as *irreducible* Given) the *inefficaciousness* of a Human Action carried out down Here-below as a function of the 'moral' Law (cf. V, 122, 4–25) and hence the *impossibility of Satisfaction* down Here-below (cf. V, 124, 7–20). Now, this ('gratuitous') supposition is nothing else but the fundamental Postulate of every Religion (which presupposes, in fact, qua *human* phenomenon, the anthropogenic Desire for Recognition, merely qua refusal of self-Contempt), which has nothing to do with 'Theory' or 'Morality' or, therefore, Philosophy in general. We thus fall back into the situation we have encountered in the 'Canon' of the *Critique of Pure Reason*, where it was said that the very notion of 'Duty' (= 'moral Law') does not make sense unless one *presupposes* the notions 'God' and the 'future World' (= Immortality) (cf. III, 520, 17–24) [which, for us, can only be *deduced* from the religious Postulate]. Now, Kant seems to have come to this realisation by himself, for two years after the *Critique of Practical Reason*, he says in the *Critique of Judgement*: 'But *speculative* [that is, theoretical] Reason has no *insight* whatever (*sicht ein*) into the possibility to execute (*Ausführbarkeit*) the latter [that is, Duty] (neither as far as our own physical ability nor

show that this purported As-if does not rest on any theoretical *foundation* and therefore has no *certainty* at all, not even a subjective one. Now, as soon as this Kantian As-if Theology is overcome, his System becomes irremediably fragmented, that is, according to Kant himself, it ceases to be a System that may claim to be the discursive development (by definition, not contra-dictory) of the *Truth*.

---

as far as the collaboration [*Mitwirkung*] of Nature is concerned); quite the contrary, insofar as we are capable of making reasonable judgements, it *must* (*muss*) obtain, [if it departs] from *such* [merely natural] causes, *such* a *success* from our good moral conduct (*Wohlverhaltens*), [that is, a success obtained] from Nature alone (within and outside us) [and] *without taking God and Immortality*, albeit well intentioned, for a baseless (*ungegründete*) and futile (*nichtigen*) expectation (*Erwartung*; the counterpart of Hope, *Hoffung*), and, IF it could obtain from [its] judgement complete *certainty* (*Gewissheit*), {speculative reason} would have to regard the moral Law itself as a mere *illusion* (*Täuschung*) of our Reason in a practical respect (*Rücksicht*)' (V, 471, 21–8). Kant goes on to say that to the extent that the notions God and Immortality are not *contra-dictory*, Reason, even when theoretical, must admit them (and *deduce* from them the efficaciousness of the 'moral Law') to avoid falling into *contradiction* with itself, which it would do if it denied them, since it, in turn, accepts this 'Law' as theoretical 'Proof' (cf. V, 471, 28–33). It matters little to us, for the time being, that the notions in question are, in fact, contra-dictory and that, by introducing them, Contradiction becomes thus unavoidable in the System. What matters is, on the one hand, the fact that Kant explicitly admits an irreducible *conflict* between 'speculative' (= philosophical) 'Reason' and the 'moral Faith' in God and Immortality. For he says that IF Reason was absolutely *certain* of itself, 'Duty' and therefore the 'Faith' that flows therefrom, would be 'futile' and 'baseless', that is, purely 'illusory'. To save 'Faith', Kant must therefore renounce the very idea of a *purely theoretical* discursive Truth and thus surrender to (theistic or theological) *Scepticism*, which can be perfectly explained by the fact that Kant's System involves a *gap* as soon as one eliminates its theology (in which only 'moral Faith' is developed discursively); now, a 'moral Scepticism' synonymous with 'moral Faith' contra-dicts the entire bulk of the *Critique of Pure Reason*, where the Categories have laid the foundations for a *confident* {*certaine*} cognitive faculty that can stand up to Scepticism whatever it may be. What matters, on the other hand, is the fact that for theoretical Reason (= Philosophy), as Kant already said in the *Critique of Pure Reason* (cf. III, 520, 17–24), the notion of Duty and, therefore, that of Freedom (which, in fact for us, as for Kant, are meaningless if Freedom is inoperative or inefficacious and if Duty is unachievable) make sense (and have a practical value) only if the notions God and Immortality are associated therewith (which, for us, are conflated with the notion of Transcendence, that is, the Beyond of given-Being or Spatio-temporality). According to Kant, these notions must be taken/given/posited accordingly and comprehended *en bloc*. Now, for us, this 'bloc' can be admitted or 'deduced', or even 'de-monstrated' only if one *postulates* the inefficaciousness of Action down Here-below while making common cause {*se solidariser*} with the Desire for recognition, which can only come to the mind of a human being with a *religious* temperament, and which would fatally lead to contra-diction, if the Religious person elaborates a discursive *Theology* (even though it is possible, as Buddhism proves,

It still seems as though Kant must have come to this realisation by himself and thus felt the need to seek the *foundation* of the subjective certainty of his Hope (that is, the origin of the Sense from which the notion of Transcendence is derived) only where, according to him, it might be found, namely in the Metaphysics of Nature, ultimately based on Perception, and, more exactly, on that 'Cosmology' which dealt with Nature *in its sum total* and therefore in its *reference* to that which is not nature and which he initially wanted to *exclude* completely from his System.

It is this 'Cosmology', defined since 1781 but rejected again in 1787, that Kant develops in 1790 under the title of *Critique of Judgement*, a title which is justified in the sense that, in fact, in Kant (but perhaps not for him), that Cosmology is the source and foundation of ('moral') *Theology* in the same way the other two *Critiques* are, respectively, the source and foundation of the two *Metaphysics* of Nature and Morals. This analogy is, nonetheless, far from suggesting an identity, for, on the one hand, the third *Critique* does not ground Theology *directly*, but only by means of the other two *Metaphysics* (hence the graphic representation in the second diagram of Figure 3 above), and, on the other hand, it does not 'justify' it as *Faith*, that is, as a *Certainty* of *Hope*, which is itself valid, according to Kant, only in the discursive mode of As-if. And that is what Kant himself indicates, by saying that there are indeed *three Critiques*,

---

to be both Religious and Atheistic, on condition of seeking the supposedly impossible Satisfaction down Here-below and the Beyond in total Annihilation: Nirvana), for the notion God = Immortality *excludes* the notion of Freedom, while, without the latter, one cannot 'deduce' the fact of Discourse, in such a way that one must either fall into *silence* or speak while contra-dicting oneself, since one would then have to *say* that it is impossible to *speak* (which is, generally, expressed implicitly when *speaking* of a God who is, by definition, *ineffable*). Kant must have harboured doubts about this since, in the *Critique of Practical Reason*, he rejects the possibility of deriving the discursive content of 'moral Faith' from the (theoretical) *notion* of the 'moral Law' alone (and calls upon, in fact, the religious Postulate of the impossibility of its *execution* in the extended-Duration of empirical-Existence, not even from Spatio-temporality as such or from given-Being, not to mention objective-Reality). He deduces from this notion only the notion of Freedom (cf. V, 4, 7–13). Moreover, he recognises therein the 'vicious circle' of that deduction. In other words, he admits, at least for us, that the notions of the 'moral Law' and 'Freedom' are ultimately endowed with one and the same *Sense* [which, for us, derives its ultimate source from the realised awareness of the Desire of Desire, that is, of the Desire for Recognition and Boredom]: these two notions [which, for us, are but one] must also be taken/given/posited and comprehended *en bloc*.

but only *two* Parts of the *System* strictly so called, namely the two *Metaphysics*. The content of the *Critique of Judgement* is too well known to warrant summary or commentary here. But its 'systematic' *interpretation*, albeit only in a perfunctory way, seems to me indispensable.

Kant says on several occasions that the third *Critique* aims to establish the *unity* (and therefore the uni-*totality* or unicity) of his System, serving as a hyphen {*trait d'union*} between the two preceding *Critiques*. But he himself admits that he succeeded only imperfectly, since the *three Critiques* have in front of them only *two* Parts of the *System* strictly so called, standing in an *irreducible opposition* to one another insofar as there, Freedom remains *irreducibly opposed* to Nature. That is what Kant expresses implicitly when he develops the third *Critique* in the mode of As-if, which entails the necessity to 'connect' for better or worse the two Parts of the System by means of a 'moral Theology' also developed in the mode of As-if, bearing in mind that this Theology is 'founded' on the third *Critique* in the same way the two Parts of the *System* are respectively 'founded' on the first two *Critiques*, developed in the mode of discourse strictly so called, that is, supposedly *true*. It is this 'dissymmetrical' and in fact pseudo-uni-total System that Kant wants to pass for the discursive *Truth* that may stand up to any form of Scepticism whatever. And it is this discursively developed pseudo 'Truth' in this *dualist* pseudo 'System', associated to a *triple* 'Critique', that we must now look at more closely.

In line with the tenets of Psychology in his time (which he seemingly drew upon mostly via Tetens), Kant distinguishes *three* Human 'mental Faculties': a Cognitive Faculty, the Feeling of Pleasure and Displeasure, and the Faculty of Desire (*Begehrungsvermögen*), respectively called Understanding, Judgement, and Reason. The 'Understanding' and 'Reason' were analysed (their notions discursively developed, in principle without contra-diction and in a complete, that is, 'circular' way) in the *Critique of Pure Reason* [= 'Understanding'] and in the *Critique of Practical Reason* [= Reason]. It now remains to analyse the faculty of 'Feeling', and this task will be carried out in the *Critique of Judgement* (cf. V, 168, 6–22).

Now, already in the Preface, Kant cautions that this third *Critique* will not have, in view, a third Part of the *System* strictly so called. This is, indeed, what he says there:

A *Critique* of pure Reason [in the broad sense of a complete Introduction to the System of Knowledge, analysing *all* the 'Faculties' that come into play during its *discursive* development], that is, of our Faculty to judge according to a priori Principles, would have been incomplete if the Critique of Judgement . . . was not treated as a *special Part* (*besonderer*) of that *Critique* [in the broad sense]; even if these Principles may (*dürfen*) not constitute, in a *System* of pure Philosophy [or a priori, which is not the same thing as empirical Philosophy, that is, in fact, Science in the common sense of the term], a *special Part* [situated] *between* [the Part constituted by] [pure] theoretical Philosophy and [the one constituted by] [pure] practical Philosophy, but *if need be* (*im Notfalle*) it could *occasionally* (*gelegentlich*) be connected (*angeschlossen*) with either of these *two* (*jedem von beiden*) Parts [this passage appears to suggest that the connection can be made interchangeably with *either* one of these two Parts without it being said that the adjunction establishes *ipso facto* a 'connection' or allows a 'gap' to subsist between these two Parts themselves]. For if such a *System* is to be achieved some day under the general name Metaphysics [which is *possible* and, for the use of Reason, highly important in every regard to accomplish (*bewerkstelligen*) in an *absolutely complete* way (*ganz vollständig*)], the *Critique* must already have explored the terrain supporting this edifice, to the depth at which lies the first basis (*Grundlage*) of the Faculty of Principles independent of [sensible/sensual] Experience, so that no part of the edifice may give way, which would irremediably result in the collapse of the whole. (V, 168, 23–37)

To put it crudely, on the first read, this strange text 'puts a bug in our ears'. Not only do we find the expressions 'if need be' and 'occasionally' surprising from the pen of Kant; not only does it seem surprising that Kant admits the possibility for something to be added indiscriminately to either one or the other Parts of the System, or perhaps to both at once, without telling us what implications such an adjunction might have for the System as a whole; but what is most striking is the apparent ease with which Kant abandons here the rule of symmetry, for which he otherwise had such an unhealthy fondness that he sometimes applied it against the tenets of Common sense (of which he is anything but bereft). Something unconscious or 'unspeakable' seems to have determined Kant's attitude towards the question to which we now turn our attention. And we will see that in effect his refusal to introduce a *third* Part in his *System*, in view of the third *Critique*, determines the difference between his (dualist, or even theistic) System and the (trinitarian, or even atheistic) Hegelian System. We must now speak of the motives and consequences underpinning that refusal, and to that end, interpret the passage I have just cited accordingly.

First, it should be noted that Kant reaffirms once again the principle of the *uni-total* Discourse (put forward by Parmenides and upheld by Hegel), which alone is assimilable to (discursive) Truth and thus prone to successfully facing up to Scepticism. He says that the *Critique* (which is, if one will, a constitutive part of the System qua its *systematic* 'Introduction' [analogous to the *Phenomenology of Spirit* for Hegel]) must guarantee the solidity of this System, and that it can do so only if the first two *Critiques* are completed by a *third* one. This third *Critique*, Kant says, is there 'so that no *part* of the edifice may give way (which would result in the collapse of the whole)'. But *which* Part? The first two *Critiques* are respectively supposed to guarantee *by themselves* the foundations and therefore the 'unshakable' solidity of the 'Metaphysics of Nature' and the 'Metaphysics of Morals', since Kant was able to *complete* these two *Critiques* without even envisaging the idea of a third one. Now, if we go back to the 'Canon' (cf. III, 547, 11–15), apart from the 'Metaphysics of Morals' (completely 'grounded' in and through the *Critique of Practical Reason*), there are only *four* Parts in the 'Metaphysics of Nature', *two* of which, namely the 'Ontology' and '*immanent* Physiology', are entirely 'grounded' in and through the *Critique of Pure Reason*. Only '*transcendent* Physiology', which is subdivided into 'Cosmology' and 'Theology', may therefore need, in view of securing its solidity, a *third* 'Critique' to guarantee its deep foundations. Now, it is obvious that the 'Cosmology' that Kant had in mind was meant to only provide a detailed development for the content of the teleological Part of the *Critique of Judgement* without adding anything essentially new thereto, in the same way the 'Ontology', had Kant written it, would have only developed the content of the 'transcendental Logic' of the *Critique of Pure Reason* without adding anything of substance thereto (cf. III, 94, 32–95, 10). The third *Critique* can, therefore, guarantee the foundations of something essentially *other* than itself only if it guarantees the foundations at the basis of 'Theology'.

In fact, this 'Theology' appears in the third *Critique* (§§79–91) under the general title: 'Methodology of Teleological Judgement', but with the modest designation: *Appendix* (*Anhang*) (we find no such designation in the first two *Critiques* where the 'Methodology' is presented as a 'second *Part*'). And, there, we can encounter once again all the content of 'moral Theology' that we have encountered in the preceding two *Critiques*. One can therefore admit that the third *Critique* is essential to the 'solidity' of the *System* insofar as the latter involves a 'Theology'.

This is easily admissible, even more so since Kant himself almost admitted it in the concluding passage of the *Critique of Judgement* where he says what follows (after setting forth once again the 'moral Faith' that was already developed in the two other *Critiques*):

An *ethical Theology* (*Ethikotheologie*) [= a moral Theology developing in a discursive way the content of moral Faith] is indeed possible; for Morality, it is true, can subsist without Theology as far as its Rule is concerned [that is, the moral Law], but it cannot do so as far as its final Goal (*Endabsicht*) is concerned ... But a *theological Ethics* (of pure Reason) is impossible; for the Laws that are not originally (*ursprünglich*) given by Reason *itself*, and whose execution (*Befolgung*) it does not impose (*bewirkt*) [by itself] as a pure practical Faculty, cannot be *moral*. Similarly, a *theological Physics* would be impossible (*Unding*), for it would not inculcate natural laws, but the dispositions (*Anordnungen*) of a supreme [that is, divine] Will; conversely, a *physical* (or properly speaking, *physico-teleological*) *Theology* [as outlined in the *Critique of Judgement*] can at least serve as a *Propaedeutic* to Theology proper [to the extent that the Philosophy of pure Reason is either a System called Metaphysics, which Theology is part of, or a Propaedeutic called Critique (cf. III, 543, 27–30)]: insofar as, through the consideration of natural Ends, of which it presents a wealth of material, it initiates (*Anlass giebt*) the Idea of a supreme End (*Endzweckes*) that Nature cannot set up/erect (*aufstellen*); thus, rendering, it is true, sensible (*fühlbar*) the *need* for a Theology ... even though it cannot produce (*hervorbringen*) and have *an adequate basis for it* (*zulänglich gründen*) in its own [critical] apparatus of *proofs*. (V, 485, 4–19)

We will not interpret here what Kant says regarding 'ethical Theology', otherwise we would have to repeat once more what has been said previously, time and time again. We only note that Kant is fully aware of the contra-dictory character of that [of every] Theology, since, in essence, he says, while dismissing the possibility of 'theological Ethics', that the notion of God (prescribing Morality and making sure that it is obeyed by the Human being) is incompatible with the notion of Freedom. It is for this reason that Theology cannot be presented, strictly speaking, as a (discursive) *Truth*, but may only be developed (discursively) in the mode of As-if. It is for this same reason that Kant denies the possibility of a 'theological Physics' (which would contra-dict what was said in the *Critique of Pure Reason*). Now, the *Critique of Judgement* would be nothing other than such a 'theological Physics' had it not been developed only in the mode of As-if. As it stands, that *Critique* is mere 'physical Theology', which is, by definition, just like 'ethical Theology', not a (discursive) *Truth*, but merely a discourse (in principle non-contra-dictory) developed only in the mode of As-if.

That said, discursive Kantian 'Theology' (developed in the mode of As-if) no longer has 'moral Faith' for its one and unique foundation [which, as we have seen, is anything but 'solid', even from Kant's point of view], that is, the subjective Certainty of Hope to obtain Satisfaction in the Beyond. Henceforth, it is also founded on and by the *Teleology* of the third *Critique*. Just like 'moral Faith', this 'Teleology' is a mere subjective *Certainty* and not a *Truth*. But it has the enormous advantage of being able to derive its Sense and therefore its 'proof' from everyday sensible Experience, that is, in our terminology, from Perception. And this is how the third *Critique* makes up for the gap that we have identified in the first outline of the Kantian system and of which Kant must have ultimately taken notice by himself.

Kant could have, therefore, now dropped the rather 'dubious' subjective Certainty, which transforms Hope for Satisfaction (in the Beyond) into a (purportedly 'unshakable') *Faith* that can be discursively developed (purportedly without contra-dictions) into a Theology. For this Theology can now be founded on *theoretical*, that is, ultimately *experiential*, or *sensible* (subjective) Certainty, updated or engendered by and through the *Critique of Judgement*. This new Certainty is constituted by the *Fact* that (natural) Human beings find themselves in a (natural)

World which *appears to be* beautiful or sublime, also by the Fact that they produce therein works of art that *seem to be* beautiful or sublime, and finally by the Fact that this World *appears* to those Human beings, if not as a living Being, at least as populated with living beings including the (natural) Human beings that they themselves are. Kant could therefore have said that Human beings have a 'moral *Faith*', that is, a (subjective) *Certainty* of Hope to obtain Satisfaction in the Beyond, BECAUSE they are (subjectively) *certain* of the Fact that the World down Here-below *appears* to them, on the one hand, as *beautiful* and *sublime*, and on the other hand, as populated with works of *art* and *living* beings.[15]

Now, from a systematic standpoint, the purpose of Kant's Theology is to unify his System, for it serves as a hyphen between the Metaphysics of Nature (= Causality or Necessity) and the Metaphysics of Morals. To the extent that Freedom or free Will is in fact included [erroneously and contrary to Judeo-Christian Anthropology] by Kant, regardless of what he himself says on the subject, within his System not qua acting and creative, or even efficacious Negativity, but qua Identity or Essence or qua the 'Platonic' Idea of the Human being (or even 'Nature' in the ancient or 'pagan' sense of the word), while being [rightly and in agreement with Judeo-Christian Anthropology] *irreducibly opposed* to Nature, which is transfixed [justifiably and in line with the 'Greek' conception of the Cosmos] in its identical Essence, he was able to avoid the contra-diction between the two Parts of the System dealing, respectively, with Nature and Freedom conceived accordingly, only by distinguishing the Phenomenon from the Thing-in-itself, through the discursive development of the notion of the Thing-in-itself [in fact contra-dictory, since the Thing-in-itself is, by definition, and according to Kant himself, *ineffable*] into the Theology of the God-creator of the (spatio-temporal) natural World and the (non-spatio-temporal) immortal Soul of the Human being, which have both been created in such a way that there may not be an inherent irreducible opposition between them and, therefore, no contra-diction between the two Parts where they are dealt with in the System.

---

15 It is interesting to note that in the Kantian epoch of the Enlightenment, the notion of the *Unum-Verum-Bonum* of the scholastic epoch tends to be replaced by that of the *Unum-Verum-Bonum-Pulchrum*. Moreover, for Plato as well, the *Beauty* of the Cosmos was one of the fundamental principles of Theology, besides the fact, 'obvious' for him, of *natural* Teleology (see above our comments on the *Timaeus*).

Consequently, if the third *Critique* is to provide a 'foundation' for Theology, it must serve as a hyphen (albeit in the mode of As-if) between the two Parts of the *System* and their corresponding two *Critiques*. Now, this is what it does indeed, at least according to Kant, since he calls the third Section of the Introduction: 'On the *Critique of Judgement as* a means to unite (*Verbindungsmittel*) the two Parts of Philosophy into one [single] *Whole*' (V, 176, 17–18), and the ninth Section: 'On the *coupling* (*Verknüpfung*) of the [theoretical] legislations of the Understanding and of [practical] Reason [= free Will] by the Judgement' (V, 195, 2–3). The way this 'coupling' {*liaison*} takes place, according to Kant, is so well known that it is hardly worth the trouble to sum it up or comment thereon. We need only be reminded that Kant interprets the Beautiful and the Sublime (in nature or in art) qua 'Teleology without [an explicit] Telos' (conscious and willed in the case of Art), and the Living qua involuntary and unconscious Teleology. Now, Teleology *is opposed*, on the one hand, to (natural) Causality; but, on the other hand, it is carried out *in* the (natural) World and is, therefore, *compatible* with Causality; however, qua Teleology, it is analogous to 'Causality through Freedom', which Duty or the free Will needs in order for it to be 'objectively real'/'realised' and therefore 'revealed' qua 'Phenomenon' to the Human being, otherwise it would be irreducibly opposed to Nature, thus giving rise to contra-diction between the Metaphysics of the former and the latter (cf. V. 195–7).

Now, in these conditions, one is increasingly less inclined to understand why Kant did not want to incorporate the Teleology (= 'Cosmology') of the third *Critique* within the body of the *System* proper (in the same manner he handled the 'Ontology' elicited from the first *Critique*) as a 'particular' third Part (*besonderer Teil*), or, to put it differently, why he believed he had to develop his Teleology only in the mode of *As-if*. Just as well, Kant's successors, Schelling in the first place, were puzzled by his reasoning on that particular point of his doctrine, and never wanted to follow him down that path. Indeed, taken as 'immediate' or 'psychological data', the beauty and 'vitality' of the World are neither more nor less 'evident' or 'questionable' than its extended-duration or its 'legality' (which Kant calls Causality), and they differ in nothing, regarding their mode of presentation, from the famous Feeling of Duty. And if one would want to say that the *Teleology* or the *Cosmology* of the third *Critique* is an As-if because it refers to Phenomena rather than to the Thing-in-itself, then the first *Critique* [and, in fact, the second one], as well as its corresponding *Metaphysics of Nature* [and, in fact, the Metaphysics of Morals], should also be developed in the mode of As-if, which leaves only Theology to lay claim to a development in the mode of Truth. Now, quite the contrary, it was *Theology* alone (and its corresponding third *Critique*) that Kant expounded in the mode of As-if, while he developed the rest of his System (including the first two *Critiques*) in the mode of Truth. Despite the 'coupling' established by the *Critique of Judgement*, Kant's System, therefore, remains indeed *heterogeneous* (that is, not genuinely *uni*-total) in this sense that only one Part of the *System*, together with its corresponding *Critique* (or, because Kant does not want to consider this Part as a genuine Part *of the System*, that *Critique* alone), is (discursively) developed in the mode of As-if, while the rest is (discursively) developed in the mode of Truth. And Kant's successors did not understand *why* this was the case, when it would have been easier to establish the homogeneity of the System and, thus the uni-totality of the philosophical Discourse by admitting, notably, just as Schelling did, that the third *Critique*, too, is developed only in the mode of Truth. If we want to *understand* Kant's reasoning on this point of his doctrine (without nonetheless wanting to *follow* him), we must try to see what would happen to his *System* when introducing therein a third Part founded on the third *Critique*, which would be developed, to that end, in the mode of Truth.

All depends, of course, on the content of that third *Critique*, which would necessarily determine the content of the third Part of the *System*.

Even though Kant undertakes the third *Critique* in view of looking for a hyphen between the *given* natural World and the Human being qua holder of a *free Will*, it does not even cross his mind (nor, for that matter, the minds of any of Hegel's predecessors) to engage a 'critique' of the Action of Struggle and Work, which is nonetheless even more 'striking' than human artistic activity. The third *Critique* analyses the 'Faculty of Judgement' which, at first glance, seems capable of *noticing* only that which *is* without *trans-forming* it in any way whatsoever, lest it utters a 'false' judgement. Now, oddly enough, Kant presents things differently. On the one hand, the Faculty of Judgement is, it is true, *passive* and does not *create* anything by itself. But, on the other hand, it 'judges' the given World as being beautiful and living *in and by itself*, while the 'Critique' de-monstrates that this is not the case and that the 'judgement' in question is valid only in the mode of As-if. This means that the Faculty of Judgement is an *active* Faculty, which *engenders* the notions of the Beautiful and the Living, since without it, the World, which *in itself* is neither beautiful nor living, *would* not even *appear* as such. Therefore, the As-if of the third *Critique* corresponds to some sort of a specifically human activity which, in contrast with the activity of theoretical pure Reason (= the Understanding), does not impose its law on Nature, as Kant says, or, as we would say, does not (discursively) reveal the structure of Being, of the *given* objective-Reality and empirical-Existence. The exercise of the Faculty of Judgement is therefore a creative pseudo-*action* which engenders a purely 'subjective' pseudo-World, that is, one which is essentially *different* from the natural *given* World (to the Understanding, through Intuition, in and by Sensibility [= Perception]). It is, therefore, no coincidence that Kant talks about *Art* in the third *Critique*. Even though he does not say that it is the Faculty of Judgement that *produces* works of art, the fact remains that a product of human *Work* (because one must *work* to produce a work of art) cannot be *beautiful*, that is, 'artistic', unless and only insofar as the *Faculty of Judgement* 'judges' it to be such. Therefore, the Faculty of Judgement is, in fact and for us, a pseudo-*Action*, some sort of substitute if not for Struggle, at least for Work. But not for Kant (nor for Schelling, who drew inspiration from the third *Critique* from start to finish throughout his 'hectic' philosophical career). For the As-if character that Kant attributes to the (aesthetic and teleological) 'judgements' of the Faculty of Judgement clearly shows that he does not intend to attribute to that 'Faculty' the *efficaciousness* needed for an *objective* or *real* trans-formation of the given World (which Hegel was the *first* to attribute to *Work* as a form of Action). In short, according to the Kantian third *Critique*, the Human being is not (as in Hegel) a being who *struggles* and *works* while thus *really* transforming the *given* social and natural World, but a being contented with making 'value judgements' about the *natural* World, which have no *real* basis and as such are not adequately reflective of what the natural World *really* is, but which have this particular feature, in that they leave this World 'undisturbed' and, *in reality*, as it is *given*, that is, as *natural* World (whereas Work *trans-forms* this World in its *objective-reality* and makes a 'technical' or *human* World out of it). That is why the 'Critique' of the Faculty of Judgement can admit the validity of its 'judgements' only in the As-if mode: they are only *as if* they were true because they are not truly true, considering that nothing in objective-reality corresponds to them (nor even in the empirical existence revealed by the experience that does not involve the 'judgement' in question, that is, the Experience that the first two *Critiques* had in view, which is also true for a *Project* of work at the origin of the not yet existing *arte-fact*), but they nonetheless are *as if* they were true, for this is not 'refuted' by objective reality, which does not oppose any 'resistance' to them either (even though it would not shy from so doing as soon as one seeks to really trans-form it through Work).

Surely, all this is strictly applicable only to aesthetic and teleological 'judgements' concerning the *given* natural World, rather than to *Works* of art. For the Artist produces objectively *real* things, which are, nevertheless, produced by a Human being and not by Nature. But it is interesting to note that Kant skates over this aspect of the question: his 'critique' does not touch upon the *production* of the work of art, rather it deals with the 'judgement' made on the already existing one. We are thus left with the impression that the Human beings produce their artworks in the same way plants 'produce' their flowers and birds their songs. This impression is, moreover, confirmed by the fact that Kant defines (natural *and* artistic) Beauty as a 'Teleology *without* a Telos'. And it is quite astonishing (unless one is not afraid of a 'Marxist' explanation of the history of Philosophy) that Kant (although he does not seem to have had a particularly 'artistic' temperament) provides a detailed analysis of the products of Human (*and* Natural) *artistic* activity, whose Telos is, according to him, *absent*, without even touching upon the Action of Struggle and Work (by which he is, nevertheless, surrounded from dawn till dusk, and in which he is not merely 'interested', but unquestionably 'takes an interest'), where the *presence* of the Telos is, however, truly 'unquestionable'. (As for Schelling, he contents himself with putting the emphasis on Human artistic *activity*, but like Kant, he entirely overlooks the existence of Work: for him, the Human being is a creative Agent [or negator of the given] only qua Artist).

This most curious content in the third *Critique* delineates the object of the third Part of the *System* which it would have engendered had it been developed in the mode of Truth. That third Part would have dealt uniquely with: the Human being as creator of *really* (objectively) beautiful Works of art; Nature's (objective) *real* Beauty; and the (objective) *real* teleological structure of living Organisms. This is to say that the object of that third *Part* would have been identical to the object of Schellingian Philosophy of the 'first epoch'. Now, it is easy to see that this 'Schellingian' triple object is nothing other than the Human being and the World of which Plato speaks, namely in the 'teleological', that is, the *true* or *true-semblant*, discourse of the *Timaeus* (and not in his 'mathematical' or 'causal' discourse which is, according to Plato, *erroneous*): the World (Cosmos) is *really* (objectively) beautiful and living, and Human beings are human insofar as they 'judge' this World (as beautiful and living) and produce artworks (but not insofar as they *struggle* against the social *given* or *trans-form* the natural *given* through their *work*). Developing the third *Critique* in the mode of Truth would therefore necessarily amount to advancing as far as Schelling or, which is the same thing, moving backward all the way down to Plato.

Now, Plato stands for philosophical or even pagan Theism (effectively recovered by Schelling with such a disconcerting 'polytheistic' and 'mythological' enthusiasm). Indeed, Plato, like Kant for that matter (but not always like Schelling), had enough common sense to see that stones (which Kant, moreover, excluded from *his* Teleology), plants, and animals could not 'arrange' themselves in function of a Telos of their own, nor produce their own 'beauty' in function of an artistic project which they may have set up by themselves. As far as artists are concerned, both Kant and Plato (cf. for instance his *Ion*) agreed with one another and with Common sense when they said that their 'projects' were as little 'conscious and voluntary' as was the Telos that makes natural things beautiful and living. Hence the necessity (established by the 'Critique' of aesthetic and teleological 'judgements', regardless of whether they are true or uttered in the mode of As-if) to consider the Telos of the Beautiful and the Living qua *transcendent* in respect to Nature and even to the Human-Artist. In other words, when developed in the mode of Truth, the third *Critique* would necessarily result in a 'Platonic' Theology properly so called which would likewise be endowed with a Truth value (something that Schelling would accept in his last days, after passing through a period of 'pre-Socratic paganism', during which he 'anthropomorphised' or 'divinised' the living Organism by attributing to it an *immanent* Telos, while 'divinising' only the Artist, but not the military General or the Engineer).

Now, Kant did not want to introduce Theology into his System other than in the mode of As-if and that is why he did not want to develop his third *Critique* otherwise than in that mode, even though he did not have nor would he cite any specific valid reason to justify his aversion to attributing a Truth value to his Aesthetics and to his Teleology. By limiting (most likely, in an unconscious way) his Teleology to natural and artistic Beauty and to organic Life [even though it has no business being there, as we shall see later], and by excluding therefrom the sphere of the human Action of Struggle and Work, he was able, just like Plato, to 'deduce' from that teleology a 'physico-teleological *Theology*' (cf. V, 485, 12– 19). But this *Theology* did not rise above the value of the As-if mode proper to the *Critique* that served as its basis.

Why, then, was Kant against the introduction of Theology in the System in the capacity of a third Part deemed to be as true as the other two? Because he understood that, by so doing, his System would become contra-dictory while thus ceasing to be truly 'systematic', that is, *uni*-total or true. It is true that Kant was probably not yet able to see what is now within our grasp thanks to Hegel, namely that any Theo*logy* whatever is contradictory because 'God' qua non-spatiotemporal entity (and that is what 'God' is for Kant) is not a *notion* strictly speaking, that is, discursively developable without contradiction, but a contra-dictory pseudo-notion of the type 'square-Circle' [the graphic inscription GOD can be considered, obviously without *contra*-diction, since it is without *diction*, as a 'Symbol' devoid of discursive *Sense* and having no *Value* other than in and for (religious) Silence]. But Kant perfectly realised the contra-diction between the notion 'God' (even when discursively camouflaged in such a way that it does not allow its inner contradiction to be evident) and that of the 'Human being' developed discursively (without contra-diction) in agreement with the meaning {*sens*} of Judeo-Christian mythological Anthropology. Indeed, that is what he says at the end of the *Critique of the Faculty of Judgement*, in the aforecited passage (cf. V, 485, 7–10) where he states that a 'theological Ethic' is *impossible* [*unmöglich*; now, for Kant as for us, 'impossible' means 'contra-dictory'] because 'Laws' *originating in God* [and *all* ultimately originates in God in a 'consistent' Theology as '-graphy' or 'Science' (which ignores the fact that it is a *discourse*), even though it is contra-dictoy as '-*logy*' (having to, by definition, account for this fact) from the moment it negates itself as *discourse* on God, the latter supposedly *ineffable*] *can*not be (*sein können*) 'moral', that is, *free*, that is, exclusively anchored in the Human being as conceived in line with Judeo-Christian Anthropology. Now, qua Philosopher, Kant held on firmly to this Anthropology (in 'existential contradiction' with his *religious* attitude) which, to his mind, seemed to basically rest on 'proofs' that were more *certain* and more agreeable with Common sense than the notions 'God' and 'future World', or even 'Immortality'. Just as well, he preferred to discursively develop his notion of the Human being (= free Will) in the mode of Truth [which was doable since, effectively, as Hegel will later show, *this* discursive development can be *completed*, that is, come back to its starting point, without encountering on its path one single contra-diction], even at the expense of relegating to the mode of As-if the ensemble of his Theology, and therefore of his third *Critique* whose 'foundation' it was supposed to provide. And he thought he had thus avoided the contra-diction within his *System*, since Theology did not constitute one of its *parts*, or, to put it differently, because according to him, a notion that is developed discursively only in the mode of As-if cannot contra-dict the one whose discursive development is carried out only in the mode of Truth.

However, qua Philosopher, Kant must have paid a hefty price for this incontestably very 'cunning' expedient. The *System* strictly so called continued to comprise a *gap* {*lacune*} even after the adjunction to the first two *Critiques* of a third one. Now, a *lacunary* system is not a 'System' at all, even in Kant's eyes, and is basically nothing else but an ('indefinite') *sceptical* discourse. And Kant has only (again, in a very 'cunning' way) camouflaged this sceptical character of his Philosophy with a theoretical 'infinite Task' and with 'moral' or 'practical' 'infinite Progress'; we will have more to say about this.

But before then, let us ask ourselves what becomes of the Kantian System if the third *Critique* were to be developed in the mode of Truth while 'defining' or 'delineating' its basic notion, to wit, 'Teleology', otherwise and more 'accurately' than Kant himself did.

Broadly speaking, it is 'undeniable' that *Teleology*, that is, the 'determination' of the Present (which is determined by the Past) by the Future {*Avenir*}, is a *Phenomenon*, that is, an ineliminable constituent-element of empirical-Existence as revealed in and through Perception. But it is equally undeniable that this Phenomenon imposes itself not as living Organism or as Work of Art, or even as natural Beauty, but as the (negating or creative) Action of human Struggle and Work. It is, therefore, natural to devote the third *Critique* ('critical' in the sense of eliminating any element foreign to the developed notion) to the discursive development of that notional 'Action'.

Consequently, there is no shadow of a reason why this development should be presented in the As-if mode. Indeed, when it comes to natural Beauty, Art, or an Organism, Common sense warrants this mode, at least insofar as it conveys an *existential* attitude vis-à-vis the three phenomena in question. As far as living Organisms are concerned, it is certainly not absurd to speak of them and to act in their regard *as if* their structure and their behaviour were *willed* (by them or by the Gods) in the *human* sense of this term. But it would be puerile and often absurd, not to say dangerous, to eliminate this *as-if* in favour of an unconditional acceptance of the *truth* of that 'manner of speaking'. For instance, it would be puerile not to be contented with the ditch surrounding an area allocated to lions in a zoological garden, under the pretext that, should they want to escape therefrom, these beasts would one day build, with the stones at their disposal, a staircase allowing a way out. Similarly, it would be absurd to train cats in view of enabling them to replace travelling pigeons, relying on the hypothesis that they will end up developing the ability to fly if we manage to persuade them that they fancy doing so. Lastly, it would be dangerous to let cobras run loose about town while putting at their disposal an appropriate amount of food and overseeing their protection, under the pretext that they would no longer thus wish to attack people. As for natural Beauty, surely, nothing prevents us from saying that it is *willed* by Nature itself or by the God who created it. But no one endowed with common sense will ever think that it can spontaneously cease to be beautiful (unless it is 'disfigured' by human Work or Struggle). Finally, as far as Art is concerned, a teleological interpretation seems closer to the Truth. But Kant himself defines the Beautiful, even when Human-made, as a 'Teleology without a Telos', that is, as some sort of 'natural' production. And the phenomenon of the work of art, as well as the 'behaviour' of the artist, seem to confirm this way of seeing things. For no one has ever been able to develop *discursively* (even in a contradictory way) the so-called 'meaning' {*sens*} of the notion 'artwork', other than by saying that what is 'beautiful' and made (exclusively or otherwise) in view of being 'beautiful' is the product of human *Work*, without being able to discursively define the 'meaning' {*sens*} of that term [which leads us to say, precisely, that it is not a discursive *Meaning* {*Sens*}, but once again a 'Symbol' or a 'Value' revealed uniquely in and through an essentially *silent* contemplation]. We are therefore talking about an activity in function of an 'aim' that is impossible to define *discursively*, in the same way it is impossible to define the so-called 'aim' that a singing nightingale might be 'pursuing'.[16]

In short, while accepting the As-if in question, it is useful not to count too much on the presumed Telos and, in any case, to treat the Organism as a function of the Past rather than of the Future {*Avenir*}, that is, to interpret ('explain') its structure and its behaviour (in the mode of Truth) using the principle of Causality [which, according to us, does not apply to inorganic Nature, where Legality alone rules]. As for Beauty and Art, it is preferable to recognise their essentially *silent* character, and to speak of them only in the manner we may speak of (natural or human) Silence, by reserving the word Telos for discursively developable *notions*, serving as the starting point for an action that is *conscious* of its aim (Telos = Project of a conscious action).

Thus receiving a specific object of its own, the third *Critique* may reassign the analysis of the notion Life to 'immanent Physiology' [which is perfectly possible, according to Kant, since he says that the third *Critique* may be reattached to the theoretical Part of his System], which may, even when completed as such, continue to be developed in the mode of Truth and remain non-contra-dictory, provided that this notion is developed in the context of the category of Causality (while developing the notion of the 'Inanimate' in the context of the Category of Legality). As for the Beautiful and Art, they should be reassigned to Meta-physics (part of which is, in fact, the aesthetics that Kant developed in his third *Critique*), which *speaks* of references between (the non-contra-dictory) Discourse whatever it may be and all variants of (human) Silence.

---

16 Obviously, this does not mean that Bach's fugue and a nightingale's song are *identical* phenomena (as Kant, following Plato, seems to suggest). Undoubtedly, from a discursive standpoint, these two types of 'music' are 'voices of *Silence*'. But, on another note, Bach *can speak*, while the nightingale cannot. Art is therefore the Silence of those who are *endowed with the ability to speak*. Besides, the humanity of Artists is guaranteed by the fact that the products of their artistic activity still have for them, besides their Beauty Value, a Meaning {*Sens*} similar to the one implied by any other means to satisfy the (specifically human) Desire for Recognition: artists are always 'proud' of their work, while the nightingale is not proud of its song.

Reduced to the Teleology of the human Act of the Struggle and Work, the third *Critique* would thus coincide with Hegel's *Philosophy of Spirit*, serving as a 'critical Introduction' not to a theology, but to Judeo-Christian Anthropology, which is also that of the second *Critique* and therefore of the *Metaphysics of Morals* [and Kant admits the possibility of reattaching the third *Critique* to the practical Part of his System]. As a result, this practical Part of the System would really live up to its title. For instead of being a 'Morality' that is everywhere and always identical to itself, determining thus, in fact, an immutable Human 'nature' constrained to the fundamental conception of Judeo-Christian Anthropology, it would genuinely be a philosophical account (that is, discursive, non-contradictory and complete, that is, giving an account of itself qua discourse) of the 'Morals' {*Moeurs*} displayed by Human beings in the course of their historical becoming, departing from the anthropogenic Desire for Recognition, which is realised in the extended-duration of empirical-existence in and through Struggle and Work, *creating* thus the *human* phenomenon properly so called in opposition to its *natural* counterpart.

In short, in the envisaged hypothesis, Kant's System would necessarily be transformed into a Hegelian System [which closes in upon itself by entirely eliminating the theological pseudo-Part and by completing Ontology, raised to the rank of an autonomous (first) Part, with a (second) theoretical Part, called 'Philosophy of Nature' (which includes Kant's 'immanent Physiology' *and* the 'Cosmology' that Kant refuses to include in his System), and with a 'practical' (third) Part called 'Philosophy of Spirit' (which integrates the third *Critique*, turned teleological in the proper sense of the term, and 'the Metaphysics of Morals', turned into a non-contradictory discursive development of the notion of History)]. In other words, in this hypothesis, the (fundamentally religious) theistic Kantian System becomes a System of (unreligious) Atheism, which is based both on a *purely* 'Greek' notion of Nature and on a *purely* Judeo-Christian notion of the Human being.

It is, therefore, not at all surprising that Kant did not want to develop his third *Critique* in the mode of Truth, nor did he, above all, want to submit to critical analysis therein the only 'teleological' phenomenon strictly so called, which is the Human *efficacious* free (= negating) Action, namely, that of the *victorious* Struggle (undertaken in function of the Desire for Recognition) and of the *accomplished* Work (born of that Struggle). Kant was, wanted to be, and wanted to remain a *religious* man (or to be more exact: a 'protestant' Christian). Now, by definition, a Religious person does not admit (and cannot do so qua Human being) self-Contempt (at least as a *viable* existential attitude) and does not dare or is unwilling to admit (qua Religious person) the *efficacy* of the (free) human Action. Given that the absolute and irremediable feeling of the inefficacy of Action, that is, of the *impossibility* of self-satisfaction, necessarily leads to total self-contempt (or that Contempt is a constituent element of the phenomenon of Failure, in the same way Satisfaction is a constituent-element of the phenomenon of Accomplishment [but not of Failure camouflaged by Success]), this double refusal ['contradictory' from an 'existential' standpoint] inevitably leads to the Hope of Satisfaction beyond the World in which Action is deemed to be inefficacious and, if this Hope is subjectively *certain*, it leads to Faith in Satisfaction, which, in this case of transworldly or transcendent Satisfaction, can be called Salvation [this Faith, in the case of a correctly developed self-consciousness and, in the case of a coherent discursive development of this realised consciousness, bequeaths the *quietist* religious Discipline rendering Salvation dependent on total *inaction* and on an *atheistic* 'Theology' identifying Salvation with Annihilation (to the extent that this 'Theology' is *true* in this sense that total *inaction* effectively leads to death, and to the extent that the death obtained accordingly is a 'hoped for' death and a death 'in hope', in contradistinction with an act of Suicide stemming from (unreligious) self-Contempt)]. In the case of a *theistic* (necessarily contra-dictory) discursive development of this Faith, as in Kant's case, we have a Theology with one or several Gods and a divine World wherein immortal Souls subsist before they are born or after their death, to the extent that their destiny, that is, the Satisfaction (blessedness) or self-Contempt ('infernal' Suffering) that befalls them, depends on the *transcendent* efficacy (vis-à-vis God or the Gods) of their terrestrial Action (by definition, inefficacious in the sense that it cannot procure Satisfaction on Earth) which a religious ('Moral') Discipline can guarantee, either in an objective way, or qua subjective certainty of some Hope, that is, qua Faith in one or several 'just' Gods who grant Satisfaction (Blessedness) to all those who act down Here-below in conformity with the Discipline that they prescribed for them.

In short, like any other Human being and therefore like any other Philosopher, Kant was searching for Certainty. But qua Religious man, he did not want to find anything but the (subjective) Certainty of Hope, that is, Faith. Hence the necessity, on a philosophical front, to develop discursively the 'content' of the Certainty in question merely in the mode of As-if. The aim is, on the one hand, to prevent the substitution of the (philosophical) *Knowledge* of *Satisfaction* down Here-below (*possible*; or even effective, in and through Wisdom) for the religious (theistic, in Kant's case) *Faith* in *Salvation* in the Beyond. On the other hand, the aim is to avoid the contra-diction between Theology and Cosmology (developed in the mode of As-if, but [erroneously] deemed to be coherent in themselves) on one side, and the System strictly so called (developed in the mode of Truth), on the other.

Seen through this lens, the introduction of the As-if notion into Philosophy is undoubtedly a remarkable 'trick' {*astuce*}, worthy of the 'cunning {*astucieux*} old man' that Kant was according to the sayings of some (*der listige Alte*). But it is difficult for us not to think that this fundamentally religious philosophical 'trick' attests to the Hypocrisy entailed, to different degrees, in any religious existential attitude that does not immediately lead to death by 'inaction' (if nothing else, by starvation). This Hypocrisy is in no way manifested, as it is often said, in and through Sin, that is, by means of the Action or the Intention (= Project which is not supposed to be followed up by an Action in view of its realisation) *contrary* to the prescriptions of the religious Discipline in question, that is, *detrimental* to Salvation, or even automatically resulting in Damnation. For, in fact, the religious Postulate of the inefficacy of 'worldly' Action implies the impossibility to efficaciously resist the 'temptations of that world' [the existence of these 'temptations' may be explained, in a bi-theistic theology, by the competition God–Devil, and reconciled, in a strictly monotheistic Theology, through the notion of divine 'justice' if the latter is tempered with the notion of the 'goodness' of the God who 'pardons' the 'weaknesses of his creatures', even though he 'willed' them (for if he *alone* is *divine*, nothing nor anyone would be able to face up to his desire not to have to 'punish' and, therefore, to 'pardon' Sins born of Temptations)]. Religious Hypocrisy is revealed by the mere *Interest* that every (*living*) Religious person has in things, which, from the standpoint of the Discipline that they accept and apply, are strictly *irrelevant* {*indifférentes*} from the standpoint of Salvation, as are, for example, aesthetic values in Christianism, including those which concern dress. As far as Kant is concerned, this is the case in his indisputable interest, albeit one which is absolutely 'unwarranted' from the standpoint of his religious Discipline (which he calls 'Morality'), in questions of Physics, for instance, and in the solutions to those questions, from which he seems to derive the most vivid 'satisfaction' in his *published* writings.[17]

Whether it was a Trick or an expression of Hypocrisy, the fact remains that Kant was the first to introduce the As-if notion and the development in the As-if mode in Philosophy. We must, therefore, ask ourselves what this Kantian notion signifies *for us*.

---

17   When it comes to Hypocrisy, the representatives of the Christian Religion seem to have broken all records. This is not at all surprising if one acknowledges, with Hegel (reprised by Nietzsche), that Christianism is the quintessential ideology of the Bourgeois (that is, of the Slave-without-a-Master who purportedly *works* 'on his own account', but who in fact works to obtain Recognition which he cannot or does not want to obtain in and through a bloody Struggle for pure prestige). Now, it is indisputable that Christianism had conquered the world *after* being adopted by, and thereby adapted to, the Bourgeois of the Roman Empire. The Hypocrisy of the Bourgeois resides in pretending that they are treated like a Master while refusing to risk their lives to become one (while, in fact, the Master is Master only in and through this risk), and by justifying this refusal through the proclamation of the *innate* 'equality' of all human beings (which would effectively exclude the very possibility of any Struggle for pure prestige). As for Christian Hypocrisy, it essentially manifests itself through the prescription of a *negating* Discipline or 'Morality' in respect to the given (in line with the Judeo-Christian conception of the Human being qua free Agent) and the affirmation of the absolute *inefficacy* of any Action down Here-below. This allows the Christian Bourgeois to 'critique' everything and to even be 'revolted' by all sorts of 'absurd' or 'ignoble' things that take place in the bourgeois World where they live, without ever being moved to 'revolutionary' action in view of genuinely trans-forming that world, under the pretext that every action is inefficacious and that it is, therefore, the intention alone that counts. As for the Kantian 'trick' of the third *Critique*, it made its fortune in the modern bourgeois World, where it became standard practice to 'justify' the 'bullshit' that happens there by the fact that Artists can produce in that world *beautiful* things 'in total freedom'. (One can have Faith, that is, the subjective *Certainty*, in the 'Salvation' of this World [or in Satisfaction in this World] because it is *beautiful* [or, by developing this 'cultured' idea]). Saying that Kant has envisaged the As-if because he was a Bourgeois, is to see oneself accused of Marxist 'naivety' or 'vulgarity' by those who are nonetheless sufficiently 'naive' to declare themselves satisfied when they find the 'source' of a Kantian notion in one or the other of his 'predecessors' (as if Kant was not equal to the task of *not* accepting something that he might have found there). For the fans {*amateurs*} of subtlety, one might say (with Hegel) that Kant invented the As-if because he was Christian, even at the risk of showing (with Hegel and Marx) that Christianism could not manifest itself in the Palaeolithic era, rather it presupposes 'social conditions' which were realised within the Roman Empire.

For Kant, the As-if is neither *true* nor even *true*-semblant (like the Platonic myth for Plato), but it is not *false* or *un*-true-semblant, either. In fact, when Kant affirms something in the mode of As-if, he is trying to say that Human beings can *live humanly* in the World *as if* what they are affirming was *true*. To *live* humanly, one must live tout court. Life in function of an As-if must therefore be first compatible with the given (and immutable) conditions of biological existence. But to live *humanly* is either to *speak* or to *shut up* and *act* (freely). Kant does not openly mention Silence [even though he also speaks of Art and the Beautiful] and one can effectively exclude it from this context, since the As-if is, by definition, a *discursive* phenomenon. But one can speak either without contra-dicting oneself, or while contra-dicting oneself.[18] Kant, with no justification thereof, excludes contra-dictory utterances from the domain of the As-if while admitting that the As-if is not contra-dictory *in itself* (even though in fact his theistic Theology is intrinsically contradictory and even though he admits that the As-if, when erroneously admitted as Truth, would contra-dict discursive Truth strictly so called). Finally, Kant openly says that Human beings can and must *act*

---

18   Experience shows that one can *live* (more or less well) 'in contra-diction with oneself', that is, particularly, in accordance with a theory that is inherently contra-dictory and accepted *as if* it was *true*. A simple example allows us to understand how and why this is possible. Let us take the example of a theory that implies the contra-dictory notion 'square-Circle'. If a perpendicular line R [radius] is brought to a lower position from the centre of the square-Circle on its constituting curb, one must admit that its surface is at once equal to Π. If the difference (4 − 3,14 . . .) is in the margin of the diverse 'fluctuations' of the Organism that are compatible with its survival, that (human) Organism may *live* even if it (erroneously) admits that the theory involving the notion squared Circle is *true* and acts accordingly: this person would not be eliminated from the set of *living* Organisms merely as a result of this admission. Conversely, if a fluctuation of an action in accordance with the possible fluctuations *within* the 'theoretical' margin 0,86 *exceeds* the tolerable biological margin, the Organism would necessarily perish. This example shows why 'experiment' (a rather relatively 'rough' one, that is, one that does not allow us to conclude whether the measured area follows the 'law' of the Circle or that of the Square) does not always reveal the contra-dictory character of a theory whose ('complicated') discursive development disguises its underlying contra-diction. This is how one can *live* in accordance with a *theistic* religious Discipline, by definition, contra-dictory, seeing that its underlying notion, to wit, 'God', is in fact a notion of the type 'square-Circle'. For the 'strictest' religious Discipline does not admit any fluctuations (with respect to Truth or 'worldly' Morality, which is by definition *viable*) *incompatible* with the biologically tolerable margin (even though it can *decrease* the vitality of those who practise it). Every Discipline is, therefore, in fact viable, particularly when it is tempered with Sin and above all with Hypocrisy, which is always possible since *every* Discipline admits so-called 'irrelevant' actions in which one can therefore fully take 'interest' without the risk of Damnation.

'morally' *as if* it were *true* that their action was efficacious, even though, in the mode of (theoretical) Truth, he affirms the opposite.[19]

What should be *our* attitude vis-à-vis all this?

If a doctrine is in fact *true* (as is true, according to us, the Bio-logy of the third *Critique*, to the extent that 'Teleology without a Telos' is nothing else but Causality), there is no reason why it should not be included in the uni-total Discourse, that is, be developed in the mode of Truth, since, not being contra-dictory by definition, it cannot contra-dict the rest of the Discourse in which it is introduced. If, by contrast, this doctrine is inherently contra-dictory, then this must be said rather than camouflaged by a development in the mode of As-if. By *saying* that it is contra-dictory, it can be included, if one will, in the uni-total Discourse (even though this would be 'useless' in cases where no one admits it), for it is *true* to say that it is contra-dictory (in the same way it is *true* to say that an erroneous theory is false, which allows, if it is 'useful', its inclusion in the uni-total Discourse). It therefore seems, at first sight, that the As-if notion does not have any purpose whatsoever. However, on a closer look, one can see that this is not at all the case and that its (albeit inadequate) introduction in Philosophy is one of Kant's claims to fame.

Indeed, experience shows (and Judeo-Christian Anthropology requires, through its de-monstrating within the *System of Knowledge*) that Human beings may *live humanly* AS IF *a false* statement, not only in fact or for us but also for them, was *true*, provided that one *acts* so as to trans-form the given World in such a way that the statement that *was* false before this trans-formation *becomes* true in its aftermath. In other

---

19 In his 'Morals' (= Discipline) Kant is therefore a 'reverse' hypocrite: he *prescribes* Action even though it is, according to him, inefficacious 'in truth' and 'in reality'. But bourgeois Common sense would soon intervene to 'rectify' the position, by *forbidding* any 'moral' Action in the Kantian sense, that is, 'negating' or 'revolutionary', under the pretence of its inefficacy (concerning the 'true values', that is, people's 'moral intentions' and 'cultural values' [for which such an action is even detrimental]). As for Christian (or any religious) Discipline, (insofar as Religion in general wants to *uphold* itself in a *given* World, that is, to be a Church), it is conceived so that it does not prescribe any 'subversive' activities, that is, ones which are incompatible with the existence of the given social (as it happens: bourgeois) World. By and large, it is preferable (with the helping hand of Hypocrisy) to *act* in the strong sense of the term as little as possible when one wants to *live* in function of a contra-dictory doctrine (be it moral or otherwise).

words, the Kantian *As-if* would make sense and have value only as a *Project* of an efficacious negating (= creative or 'revolutionary') Action. And it is undeniable that it cannot be said that Human beings are *free* unless they formulate such *Projects*, that is, to speak with Kant, unless the *As-if* makes sense and has value for them. For acting in function of the Truth, that is, acting in accordance with empirical-Existence or objective-Reality (Action, by definition, pertains to the latter as well), is not to be *free* in reference to them, rather it is to be *determined* by them. But one can also see that the formulation of Projects (or the admission of an As-if) without the will to *act* in the indicated manner is wanting to live in function of Error, which is biologically possible if the 'variance' between Meaning {*Sens*} and the Essence is upheld within the fluctuation margins tolerated by Life, but it would not be *humanly* 'viable', since human beings can never be *satisfied* by Error while recognising it as such (as is the case in the Project or the As-if, since the As-if is not true by definition in the same way the Project presupposes the non-existence of that which is 'projected'[20]). The As-if-Project, which is supposed to be followed up by an efficacious Action, can be presented in the mode of the subjective Certainty of Hope for Achievement, that is, a Faith. But it would be Faith in the Human beings and, especially, the one they have in themselves when poised to act. As for the As-if which is not conceived qua Project of an Action, it can only give rise to Faith in transcendent Salvation and, eventually, in a positive or 'divine' Beyond. Lastly, an As-if which is conceived as an ongoing and never completed Project of

---

20   A 'contradictory' Project is, by definition, unrealisable if one admits the (discursive) Postulate of Truth. Indeed, Truth is possible only if given-Being as such is 'homogeneous': no Action can thus introduce contradiction (incompatible with homogeneity) into Being (which means that contra-diction is 'impossible'), nor therefore in objective-Reality or empirical-Existence (which means that Contra-diction is 'unrealisable' and 'inexistent'). The Action undertaken in accordance with Contra-diction is, therefore, pathological and is revealed as lack of Common sense (which may go as far as Madness) and will *fatally* result in Failure. The Action carried out in accordance with a coherent Project *can* also result in Failure due to the lack of sufficient Action, which can be either subjective or objective ('materially impossible' Action). The appreciation of the 'material possibility' of Action belongs to Common sense, which must therefore always temper the ('revolutionary') acting Faith. But without Faith, Common sense would admit only Actions which are possible in the *given* (natural or human) World and would thus eliminate any Action truly *free*, that is, negating with respect to this given, to wit, one which is 'creative' or 'revolutionary'. It is the balance between Faith (Imagination flanked by subjective Certainty) and Common sense that characterises the Human agent of (technical or political) action.

an Action, gives rise to a pathological 'Faith', which goes from the 'utopian Dream' of the neurotic to Insanity/Madness itself.

A simple example can illustrate what has just been said.

A person may go through life *as if* it was *true* that they could fly [or as if there was no King in an absolute monarchy]. If they say such a thing without ever trying it out, they are either a dreamer or a mad person (or even a hypocrite). If they try it out without having *done* anything to make it work, they will inevitably crash to the ground and perish [or be put to death for the crime of lèse-majesté]. If they work to achieve the aims of their Project, they are a great Technician [a great Revolutionary]. And what is true for one person is true for all humanity, that is, for this famous 'self-same individual who never ceases to learn'. If, while the Acheulean age was in full swing, a person had said that animal fur detaches itself from the skin of the animal, spins into threads, and comes to cover, by itself, a human body, they would have been treated as a 'liar', a 'utopian' or a 'mad' person. But there are those who, since then, made substantial contributions towards the realisation of this project, that is, transformed this erroneous As-if into a truth per se; these people (even though their names are unknown to us) rank among the greatest Technicians in human history.

In summary, we acknowledge with Kant (who was the first to acknowledge it, thereby paving the way for Hegel) that the *As-if* is an indispensable notion in Philosophy and that it is a necessary constituent-element of the System of Knowledge, without which the latter would not be able to close in upon itself by accounting for the fact that it is a Discourse. But we admit this notion only to the extent that it can be defined as 'a supposedly efficacious (that is, 'creative' or 'revolutionary') Project of a negating (= free, that is, conscious and voluntary) Action'. Now, Kant precisely excludes this definition of the As-if. For him, the As-if is ultimately an exclusively *discursive* or *theoretical* statement that does not give rise to any *efficacious* negating *Action*. It is not *true* because it cannot be 'verified by Experience', that is, in our terminology, because its Meaning {*Sens*} does not correspond to any phenomenal Essence (because, in fact, Kant wrongly believes that he can account for the *discursive* Truth or the true Discourse without resorting to the notion of the As-if). But it is not *false* either because, according to Kant, it is not inherently contra-dictory and because no Experience 'refutes' it (which, for us, comes down to the same thing, for its Meaning {*Sens*} is brought to bear on any Essence, be it phenomenal or objectively-real, and by definition, its discursive *development* cannot be in 'disagreement' with that Essence, in the same way the Sense of a *false* discursive development would be in 'disagreement' with the Essence it supposedly 'corresponds' thereto, insofar as it can be said that the Kantian discursive development of the As-if is false only if it is inherently contra-dictory[21]). This is to say that, ultimately, Kant's As-if does not refer to the necessarily spatio-temporal Phenomenon (in the Kantian sense of the word, that is, in our terminology, neither to given-Being, nor to objective-Reality, nor to empirical-Existence), but to the essentially non-spatio-temporal Thing-in-itself, which is, for religious and theistic Kantianism, the immortal Soul, the future World and God.

One can therefore say that the exclusion of the notion of the As-if = Project is equivalent to the inclusion in the philosophical System (albeit in the mode of As-if) of a *religious* or 'theological' (discursive) constituent-element. The inclusion of the ('positive') notion of the non-spatio-temporal Thing-in-itself (other than the 'negative' notion of the Nothingness-Nirvana) is equivalent to the inclusion of the (contra-dictory) notion God in this 'theological' discourse, thus rendering it a *Theology* per se (which, in turn, must be developed in the mode of As-if so as not to contra-dict the Judeo-Christian Anthropology admitted or postulated as true). Inversely, the exclusion of the notion of the

---

21 For us as well, the As-if = Project is neither true nor false, or, if we will, false at the start and true at the end. But this notion necessarily implies the notion of negating Action, without which the As-if would either be an Error or a Truth, depending on the moment at which one 'judges' the statement made in the mode of As-if. This is why, qua 'existential' phenomenon, the As-if belongs to the domain of the verbal Expression of Recognition or to the Language of Accomplishment, and not to that of the Discussion of True-semblance, which is the proper domain of pure 'theory'. As for the System of Knowledge (= discursive Truth), the As-if intervenes therein only as 'Project of negating Action *that was* efficacious', that is, as the notion of '*achieved* History', which is a constituent-element of discursive Truth when developed in a discursive way. The As-ifs of *aborted* Projects are included therein (if applicable) only as Errors. Generally speaking, Error is a discursive statement which can be inserted in the uni-total Discourse that accounts for itself as Discourse, only on condition of being preceded with the words: 'it is *false* to say that . . .', everything else can be preceded with the words: 'it is *true* to say that . . .' As for the purported As-if which consists in *speaking* of the Ineffable as-if something could be *said* thereof, it cannot feature in the System unless it is preceded by the words: 'it is contra-dictory to say that . . .'

Thing-in-itself from the System is equivalent to discursive Atheism, which becomes unreligious as soon as the notion of the As-if = Project is introduced therein.

In other words, the mere exclusion of the notion of the Thing-in-itself, together with the inclusion of the notion of the Project, transforms the Kantian System of Philosophy (of 1790) into the Hegelian System of 1806, as illustrated in the two diagrams on the right hand-side of Figure 3 above.

Indeed, the exclusion of the positive *notion* of the non-spatio-temporal Thing-in-itself throws into Silence, that is, outside of the uni-*total* Discourse, all that pertains to Transcendence with reference to Spatio-temporality (of which one can only *say* that it does not exist empirically, that it is not objectively real, and that it *is* not at all qua any datum that may 'correspond' to any discourse, to the extent that the only remaining adequate [negative] *notion* of Transcendence is that of Nothingness). Thus, the 'theological' pseudo-Part, developed in the mode of As-if, disappears completely from the Kantian System. As for the 'cosmological' pseudo-Part, likewise developable solely in the As-if mode, it becomes a properly so called constituent-element of the System, by merging with immanent Physiology, to form, under the name of 'Philosophy of Nature', the second Part, which is added naturally to the first one, called 'Logic', in turn constituted by 'critical' Kantian Ontology, turned into *Onto*-logy properly so called owing to the fact that Being as such has been 'spatio-temporalised'. Lastly, a Teleology of the Project merges with Kant's 'Metaphysics of Morals', to form the third and last Part of the System of Knowledge, titled 'Philosophy of Spirit', which is ultimately a 'Philosophy of *History*', that is, of the 'implemented Project' (within 'Nature' which is the objective-reality and the empirical existence of the given-Being discursively described in and through the Onto-logy included in the 'Logic'). As for the three *Critiques*, they merge with one another, after being extended to the notion of the As-if = Project and after being rearranged in a way that excludes the Thing-in-itself from the domain of Discourse, thus providing the only 'critique' that serves as an Introduction to the System of Knowledge under the title 'Philosophy of Spirit'.

In that respect, the Kantian System of 1790 is transformed quasi automatically into the Hegelian System of 1806 by the mere fact of excluding the notion of the Thing-in-itself, which was preventing the inclusion of the notion of the As-if = Project in the body of the System and even in its 'critical' Introduction. And this trans-formation is reflected in the fact that the System closes in upon itself without leaving any 'gap' susceptible of 'justifying' any Scepticism whatsoever, whereas, in Kant, it was 'closed' only by a Cosmology and a Theology developed in the mode of *As-if*, unable to stand up to the sceptical negation of the notion of *Truth* and giving rise to Scepticism in its theological part, on account of its rather contra-dictory character. In the Kantian system, it is the ('supreme' *End* of Human beings, which is transcendent with reference to their life in the World) that coincides with the Beginning of Philosophy and thus with the so-called uni-total (but in fact open) Discourse that constitutes the System. Conversely, in Hegel, it is the *Beginning* (of Philosophy, that is, of the virtually uni-total Discourse developed in the mode of Truth [and, at the origin, of Error]), that coincides with the ('supreme') End (of Human beings, which is the realisable and realised Wisdom in the course of their lifetime); this Beginning can be any notion *whatsoever* that is discursively developable without contradiction and ultimately deriving all its Sense from Perception, that is, from the Phenomenon.

Let us now see how the notion of the Thing-in-itself 'deforms' the very content of the System of Kantian Philosophy and how that content is automatically trans-formed in such a way that it becomes identical to the Hegelian System of Knowledge, which is also ours. This 'automatic' trans-formation is, moreover, possible only because Kant had the immense merit of formulating the 'transcendent' element in his System in an explicit way, making it thus easily 'accessible', by condensing it in the *explicitly* non-spatio-temporal notion of the Thing-in-itself alone and thereby making the latter easily 'removable' from this System by developing it only in the mode of *As-if*, which allowed him to develop in fact 'correctly' (the few 'deformations' of which we will speak notwithstanding) the System strictly so called, which is supposed to be valid in the mode of Truth.

Insofar as the Kantian System admits the Thing-in-itself, it can, ultimately, admit only one irreducible-Opposition, namely the one between this non-spatio-temporal Thing-in-itself and the spatio-temporal Phenomenon. In other words, it is the Thing-itself that is objective-Reality, in an irreducible opposition to the Phenomenon, whose empirical-existence is admitted ipso facto. But, given that the Concept and therefore the Kantian Discourse 'refer' only to Spatio-temporality in such a manner that the Thing-in-itself is strictly ineffable (to the extent that this pseudo-notion, discursively undevelopable, at least in the mode of Truth, is in fact just a 'Symbol' devoid of sense, for which Kant himself had chosen the algorithm = X), one cannot say whether it is a question of objective-Reality in opposition to Being or Being itself, since the non-spatio-temporal Being is just as little 'given' to Discourse as the equally non-spatio-temporal objective-Reality. Therefore, one cannot tell whether Being is One, Two, or Three in Kant, in the same way one cannot tell *what* objective-Reality is, for him. However, the notion of the Thing-in-itself is 'slightly' contra-dictory because it is 'defined' by its irreducible-opposition to the notion of the Phenomenon and to that extent it is discursively developable, even though this should not have been the case, according to Kant himself, since it pertains to that which is transcendent with reference to Spatio-temporality. Indeed, being 'derived' from the notion of the irreducible-Opposition, the notion of the Thing-in-itself coincides with that of objective-Reality in the sense that the latter is essentially *dyadic*. One might therefore *say* that the Thing-in-itself is essentially *Two*. Now, this is what Kant effectively *says*, at least implicitly, since that notion, for him and in his System, would neither make sense nor have any value if it did not imply the notion of the irreducible-Opposition of the Human being (= immortal Soul) and God (= future World). And since Kant cannot effectively *say* anything as far as Being is concerned, and therefore say nothing which would be different from what he says as far as objective-Reality is concerned, one can say that for him, Being as such is Two. We can thus see that, ultimately, the Kantian System is based on the Platonic dualist Onto-logy, which is not in the least astonishing, insofar as it is the (contradictory) 'Ontology' of any theistic Theology of whatever kind.

By contrast, if one eliminates the pseudo-notion of the Thing-in-itself from the Kantian System, which limits the (true) Discourse to Spatio-temporality, his 'Phenomeno-logy' can be immediately broken down into Onto-logy, Energo-logy, and Phenomeno-logy strictly speaking, in the Hegelian sense of these terms, without substantially modifying its content. But before doing so, we must quickly see what this content looks like while the notion of the Thing-in-itself is upheld therein, that is, the notion of the irreducible-Opposition between the spatio-temporal Phenomenon and a Transcendent with reference to Spatio-temporality.

Now, although familiar to everyone, this content is, at first sight, so complex and chaotic, not to say incoherent, that it may be useful to somewhat untangle things by reference to a graphical schematic representation (besides, rather simplified), reproduced in Figure 4.

The notion of the Thing-in-itself is at the centre and the basis of Kant's philosophical System as it was published in 1790. Seen from the standpoint of the *Metaphysics of Nature* (grounded on the *Critique of Pure Reason*) the Thing-in-itself is strictly ineffable: nothing can be *said* thereof (in the mode of ['theoretical'] Truth), not even that it *is*, and even less so that it is one and unique or multiple and varied; what 'corresponds' to it is not a *discursively* developable *Notion*, but a *Symbol* devoid of *sense* (for which Kant has chosen the algorithm = X [which, according to us, can be 'developed' or 'defined', or even 'diversified' {*varié*}, only in and through or qua *Silence*]). But, in the mode of As-if, *moral Theology* (grounded on the *Critique of the Faculty of Judgement*) 'defines' or 'develops' the [pseudo] 'notion' of the Thing-in-itself by *saying* that it is ['free'] 'immortal Soul', 'future World', and 'God' (to the extent that 'God' and the 'future World' are, so it seems, each *unique* and *one* in themselves, while the 'immortal Soul' is *multiple* and in [at least possible] *conflict* with itself [Freedom = Negativity]). As for the *Metaphysics of Morals* (grounded on the *Critique of Practical Reason*), it defines and develops the Thing-in-itself in a *discursive* way (in the mode of ['practical'] Truth) qua 'pure Will' (or, more exactly, qua ensemble of 'freely' inter-acting 'pure Wills' [without specifying the nature of their inter-action with each other, on the one hand, and with 'God' and the 'future World', on the other, not to mention that the interaction between the 'future World' and 'God' is likewise left vague]). Moreover, the discursive notion of the 'pure Will' of which one speaks in the mode of ('practical') Truth is not identical to the pseudo-notion 'immortal Soul'; the latter is a Thing-in-itself properly so called, of which one can *speak* only in the As-if mode. I shall come back to this later, but for the moment, I will limit myself to noting that Human beings could have *spoken* of the Thing-in-itself, and, in particular, of their immortal Soul, in the mode of *Truth* if the

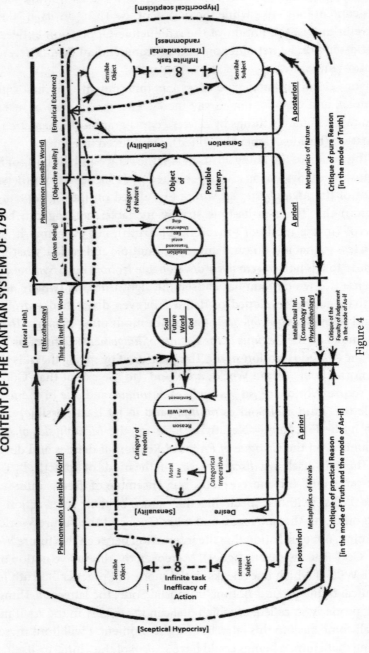

Figure 4

faculty of an 'intelligible', that is, non-spatio-temporal 'Intuition' was available to them; but since it is not, they cannot *say* anything truly valid or *true* on the subject of the Thing-in-itself, because the *totality* of their *coherent* Discourse (that is, *one* in itself), which is by definition *unique* of its kind (since it is both *one* and *total*), is determined by the 'Categories' which make *Sense* only within Spatio-temporality.[22]

Let us now see what *we* can *say* of the Thing-in-itself in the context of the Kantian *Metaphysics of Nature*.

If that *Metaphysics* was absolutely *coherent*, we would not have been able to *say* anything at all, because from the standpoint of a 'theoretical' Discourse developed in the mode of Truth, the Thing-in-itself is supposed to be *ineffable*. But Kant's *Metaphysics of Nature* is contradictory in this sense that it does *speak* of the Thing-in-itself, if not explicitly, at least *implicitly*. And this allows *us* to make the *discursive implications* of that *Metaphysics explicit* in a *discursive way* and see the extent to which the implicit discourse 'deforms' the explicit one in that context.

To begin with, the Thing-in-itself 'conditions' and 'determines' in a certain manner the Phenomenon, which is the object of the (supposedly true) explicit discourse of the *Metaphysics of Nature*. Surely, Kant is diligent enough to tell us that this 'conditioning' has nothing to do with 'Causality' and that, by and large, nothing can be *said* (in the mode of Truth and in an *explicit* manner) of the 'connection' {*rapport*} between the Phenomenon and its 'corresponding' 'Thing-in-itself'. But, in fact, Kant admits these 'connections', 'correspondence', 'conditioning', and

---

[22] The Categories are nonetheless supposed to have a non-spatio-temporal 'Significance' or 'Importance', or even a 'Value' (*Bedeutung*), allowing their utilisation when the Thing-in-itself is 'given' in the mode of As-if (in and by the aesthetic and biological 'Teleology' of the third *Critique* or 'moral Faith'), in which a 'discourse' is given in this same mode ('Cosmology' and 'Theology') (cf. V, 136, 9–35 and 141, 15–25). However, Kant also often says that the 'intelligible Intuition', to the extent that it is, by definition, non-spatio-temporal, would not use *any* 'Category' whatsoever and would not be therefore *discursive*. 'Our' Categories are 'valid' only for any '*sensible* Intuition' (assuming, as Kant does, [in the unlikely event, we would say] that one can envisage the *possibility* of an Intuition that would be *sensible* without being *spatio-temporal*), but not for an *intelligible* Intuition, which alone can 'give' or 'reveal' the Thing-in-itself, by definition non-spatio-temporal and non-'sensible' (if there is such a thing as a non-spatio-temporal 'sensible'). (See, on this complex, albeit secondary, question the following passages: III, 70, 25–71, 2; 118, 2–37; 213, 22–36; 229, 30–232, 2; IV, 160, 19–168, 11; V, 65, 5–67, 23; 136, 9–35).

'determination'. He thus *speaks* thereof, albeit in an *implicit* way. And that is, whatever he may say in its regard, a *contra-diction*, *implicit* for sure, but a contra-diction all the same, which sometimes 'deforms' what is being said in an explicit way.

Thus, although one cannot *say* that the Thing-in-itself is *one*, in the sense of *non*-multiple, Kant admits that the Manifold (*Mannigfaltigkeit*) is 'given' to ('theoretical') Discourse only as *spatio-temporal* Manifold, while affirming that the Thing-in-itself is *not* spatio-temporal. Hence the notion of the *subjective* (= spatio-temporal) 'sensible Intuition' and the affirmation of an irreducible-Opposition between the Phenomenon and the Thing-in-itself, which alone is *objectively*-real.

Whence comes that 'Intuition' and the screen of Spatio-temporality, which, even though semi-transparent, 'conceals' more than it 'reveals' the Thing-in-itself? Impenetrable mystery, for we cannot truly *speak* of that which lies beyond Spatio-temporality. Who is in possession of that Intuition or, put differently, who is wearing the semi-transparent spatio-temporal glasses? It must be said that it is the 'transcendental Ego'. But this Ego is also the (active) 'subject' of the (true) Discourse determined by the 'Categories', in which capacity it is called, first, '[theoretical] pure Reason', and then, '[pure] Understanding'. Now, the spatio-temporal Intuition is not situated in Reason [= Understanding] per se, rather it must be taken {*prise*} from (*hergenommen*) *elsewhere* (*anderwärts*), namely from Sensibility (*Sinnlichkeit*) (V, 65, 36–66, I). The Ego is therefore both Intuition and Understanding, even though the latter is essentially something other than the former (to the extent that their coincidence is precisely the [divine] intelligible Intuition that Human beings do not have). Qua Intuition, the Ego passively *receives* (*Receptivität*) the *multiple* datum (which is, so it seems, nothing else but the light emitted by the Thing-in-itself qua 'diffused' and 'refracted' [in an 'undefinable' or even *ineffable* manner] by the 'semi-transparent prism' of Spatio-temporality). Qua 'transcendental Synthesis of the Apperception', this same [?] Ego actively *creates* (*Spontaneität*) [in Spatio-temporality?] the *unity* of the Manifold (*Einteil der Mannigfaltigkeit*) *given* in the spatio-temporal Intuition. Lastly, qua 'Understanding' (*reiner Verstand*), this same Ego 'defines' or 'determines' the Unity-of-the-Manifold (or 'Totality') in accordance with certain 'rules of synthesis', called 'Categories of Nature' (to the extent that the notion of the 'Category' is defined and developed in a discursive way in the 'Analytic of Concepts' [*Begriffe*]), which Kant himself fixed once and for all (*outside* Spatio-temporality, since they are 'valid' for the Non-spatio-temporal). This is the only way a coherent ('theoretical') Discourse developable in the mode of Truth becomes and is *possible*.

The spatio-temporal Manifold *as such*, unified, in accordance with the Categories, in and through Time (= *the transcendental Schema*) [without being attached to Space in this context], constitutes the 'thinglike-Object of possible Experience' (*Gegenstand möglicher Erfahrung*), to the extent that this constitution is, as Kant says, *a priori*, that is, 'necessary' or valid *everywhere and always*, 'come' what may. Thus, the discursive development of the notion of that 'Object' can be said to be *true* in this sense that it remains everywhere and always, that is, 'necessarily', identical to itself, or even 'irrefutable', even though it is certain that the said (spatio-temporal) notion does not exactly 'correspond' to the (non-spatio-temporal) Thing-in-itself, without it being possible to *tell* what the discrepancy or inadequacy between that *Notion* and the *Thing-in-itself*, alone *objectively*-real, consists of. [The notion of that 'Object' is discursively defined and developed in the 'Analytic of Principles' (*Grundsätz*).]

Now comes a second semi-transparent and deforming screen of unknown origin and provenance, of which it cannot truly be said that it 'falls *from the sky*' and that it cannot be located anywhere or attributed to anyone (especially not to the transcendental Ego). This is the famous 'Sensibility' (*Sinnlichkeit*), which is involved in Spatio-temporality, but 'deforms' the latter insofar as it is 'pure' or 'a priori'. Kant defines this second screen as 'Sensation' (*Empfindung*; = Perception in our terminology). It is after being 'diffused' and 'refracted' by this 'empirical' screen that the thinglike-Object of *possible* Experience becomes a multiplicity of thinglike-Objects of *effective* ('= sensible') Experience. The screen of Sensibility separates the domain of *a priori* (true) discursive Cognition from the domain of *a posteriori* discursive Cognition, and we must see in what sense, and to what extent, the latter can be said to be *true*.

After passing through that screen to become the Object of sensible Experience, the Object of possible Experience *divides into* {*se dédouble*} a multiplicity of sensible *Objects* [= Bodies = Descartes's Extension] and a multiplicity of sensible *Subjects* (= Souls = Descartes's Thought). If the (transcendental) Ego wants to attain self-consciousness in an *effective way* (that is, in and through Sensation [= Perception]), it can do so only by becoming conscious of a *sensible* Subject (of which many things can be *said* except that it is the (transcendental) Ego, which was supposed to become conscious *of itself* by becoming conscious *of the sensible subject*). And when this Ego wants to *effectively* become conscious of the Object of *possible* Experience, it in fact becomes conscious of a *sensible* Object (of which, once again, many things can be *said* except that it is *identical* to the 'possible' Object in question, considering that this Object has been 'deformed' by the screen of 'Sensibility'). But it is not qua *transcendental* Ego that it becomes conscious of the *sensible* Object; it can do so only qua *sensible* Subject. Now, this Subject is *passive* in the sense that it accepts as it stands {*tel quel*} the sensible Object that 'gives' or 'reveals' itself to it (through Perception), without being able to re-*act* upon it in any way whatsoever.

In other words, the Discourse 'referring' to sensible Objects [that is, in *our* terminology, to Phenomena or to the empirical-Existence 'revealed' through Perception] can be said to be *true* only if it 'reflects' the 'light' that these Objects (or even the *sui generis* 'Object' which is the sensible Subject per se, that is, the 'sensible Soul') project onto it, without any 'deformation' or 'omission'.

This *empirical* (= *a posteriori*) discursive Cognition, even if coherent (= non-contra-dictory), is therefore not *true* in the strong sense of the word, since it is not commensurate with the Thing-in-itself, which alone is *objectively-real*. Conversely, it is *true* in the sense that it can never and nowhere be 'refuted' (replaced by another one), but it is so only insofar as it refers to the Object of *possible* Experience. Surely, the Object of *affective* (= sensible) Experience cannot be in 'disagreement' with the Object of possible experience, for otherwise it would be 'impossible' and *would* therefore not *be* at all. But it is and may be everywhere and always 'richer' than this 'possible' Object because it represents any of the 'variations' of empirical-existence compatible with its 'possibility', while Possibility, by definition, excludes *all* these 'variations' from its empirical-existence. Empirical discursive Cognition *as such* could not therefore be said to be *true* in the proper sense of the term unless it *wholly* and adequately 'corresponds' (without deformation or omission) to *all* the *variations* or *varieties* of empirical-Existence taken in its extended-duration as a *whole*.

Now, at that point, two difficulties presented themselves to Kant's mind. Firstly, the screen of Sensibility is, on the one hand, absolutely heterogeneous with reference not only to the non-spatio-temporal Thing-in-itself, but also to the Categories, even though the latter are placed in the same spatio-temporal frame as the said screen itself; on the other hand, to the extent that the nature of the 'deformations' undergone by the 'possible' Object while passing through that screen are totally unknown, nothing says that the 'deformations' which give rise, respectively, to the sensible *Subject* and the sensible *Object*, are not important and divergent enough to render the 'commensurability' of the former to the latter, that is, *true* empirical Cognition, *in fact* impossible. Secondly, inasmuch as 'sensible variations' *can* be made within the frame of Spatio-temporality, they can take place *everywhere* and *always*, that is, be *infinite* in the sense of coextended with space and coeternal with time. Consequently, the commensurability of the sensible Subject to the sensible Object, and the Discourse which accordingly refers thereto, is or at least may be an *infinite* process, bearing in mind that Discourse remains subject to *change* in the course of time as long as Time shall last.

Kant honestly admits these two difficulties inherent to his System and speaks explicitly of a 'transcendental Randomness (*Zufälligkeit*)' and an 'infinite Task' (*Unendliche Aufgabe*). In other words, he renounces, on the one hand, the task of accounting for the discursive Truth (by 'deducing' or 'justifying' it) in and through his philosophical Discourse, overtly appealing to the notion of 'Randomness', that is, to the 'unpredictable' or the 'undeducible', or even the 'indemonstrable' or the 'unjustifiable'. On the other hand, he admits that the supposedly *true* Discourse is never in fact *completed*, rather it is developed 'without end', that is, *indefinitely*. In other words, the supposedly uni-*total* discourse, *in fact* always comprises a *gap*, which is narrowed down throughout the entire duration of Discourse without ever being definitively filled within that Discourse itself.

Now, admitting in the (purported) 'System' a 'gap' that can *never* be *filled* is to be given over {*se vouer*} to Scepticism. Surely, Kant affirms that the 'infinite Task' of (true) discursive Cognition is an 'infinite *Progress*'. In other words, the circle of the uni-total Discourse (= discursive Truth) is *in principle* closed, even though it is not *in fact* closed (on the side of the *Metaphysics of Nature*) other than by a 'dotted line' which shrinks indefinitely without ever disappearing altogether. This means that any adjunction to the System can only be a *supplement* thereto, without ever being able to *contra-dict* what is already contained therein.

But, on the one hand, this is valid only insofar as the System (in its 'theoretical' Part) is limited to the Discourse that Kant calls *a priori* (= Intuition + Categories + Principles), in such a way that it cannot be said to be true in its *totality* (since it still involves a Discourse *a posteriori*). On the other hand, the notion of that Progress is conceivable ('justified' or 'deduced', or even 'de-monstrated') only if one postulates the famous 'transcendental Randomness', that is, if one admits Progress itself as a Postulate, that is, merely as Hope. Now, when Kant tries to establish a discursive (subjective) Certainty of this ('theoretical') Hope, he must resort (in the third *Critique*) to the development (in the mode of As-if) of the [pseudo] notion of the 'intelligible World', that is, of the immortal Soul, the future World, and God. Thus, the subjective Certainty of Hope in theoretical Progress is not a *theoretical* Faith, rather it is the famous '*moral* Faith' that we have recognised as the religious Faith of the Christian.

In short, Kant can only *camouflage* the Scepticism inherent to his System (which, therefore, is not one) by dissimulating it under the *mask* of religious Faith, which in turn *masks* only the gaps in this System, 'filling' them up with a discursive development in the mode of *As-if*. On the 'theoretical' front, Kant is, therefore, a *hypocritical Sceptic* who is trying to live humanly, that is, to speak and act, *as if* he was not doing so.

Let us now move on to the 'practical' front, where the situation becomes even more confused, complex, and implicitly contra-dictory.

Just like the *Metaphysics of Nature*, the *Metaphysics of Morals* (grounded on the second *Critique*) can *speak* of the non-spatio-temporal Thing-in-itself, discursively 'defined' as immortal Soul, future World and God, only in the mode of *As-if* (within the frame of a 'moral Theology' grounded on the 'moral Faith' gleaned from the second *Critique*). It cannot *speak* of it in the mode of *Truth* because, to the extent that Human beings (even qua Freedom or free Will) are not endowed with an intelligible Intuition, they are confined to *discursive* cognition, which is, by definition, *spatio-temporal*. Moreover, the content of the As-if as developed discursively within the frame of the *Metaphysics of Morals* (by the second *Critique*) coincides absolutely with the content of the As-if developed discursively within the frame of the *Metaphysics of Nature* (by the third *Critique*).

Let us now see what the content of the 'practical' Part of the System developed in the mode of Truth consists of in comparison with its counterpart in the 'theoretical' Part, insofar as the latter is developed in the same mode.

The Thing-in-itself qua 'immortal *Soul*' is said to maintain with the nexus 'free Will' and 'moral Law' 'connections' analogous to those that the Thing-in-itself qua 'intelligible *World*' is supposed to maintain with the homologous nexus 'transcendental Ego' and 'possible Object'. Except that Kant is now talking *explicitly* about the *Causality* of the Soul (cf. V, 55, 11–56, II; 65, 5–66, 15; 67, I–II), even at the expense of developing this notion discursively (in the As-if mode) by resorting to the Platonic Myth of the Soul's *prenatal* free act of choice {*décision*} that determines the entire *life* of its 'corresponding' 'sensible Subject' and bears its fruits *after death* (cf. V, 97, 21–98, 12).

As for the relationship that exists between the two nexuses in question, it is complex, confused, ambiguous, and difficult to establish. Is it one and the same 'transcendental Ego' that is at once 'Synthesis of the Apperception' and 'pure Will'? It seems to be the case, and Kant says so sometimes explicitly (cf. V, 121, 4–6). For, on the one hand, in both instances, the question pertains to a 'spontaneous' rather than a 'receptive' Ego, in such a way that one would be tempted to say that it *freely* establishes the Categories to which it submits itself (insofar as it is discursive) in the same way it prescribes for itself the (moral) Law it is supposed to follow (?) or follows necessarily (?) (insofar as it is 'practical'). On the other hand, Intuition and the Categories of the transcendental Ego are certainly valid for the pure Will (insofar as it is *discursive*), for the latter cannot (discursively) promulgate its moral Law otherwise than within the frame of Spatio-temporality and in line with the 'Categories of Nature' (to the extent that the 'moral Law' is sometimes assimilated by Kant, in the mode of As-if, it is true, to a 'Law of Nature'). However, if the transcendental Ego thus imposes 'its will' upon the pure Will, the latter cannot impose anything on it in return: qua free Agent, the Human being cannot even *have the will* to modify the spatio-temporal character of Intuition or the categorial structure of Discourse (= Thought). Therefore, the Ego *acts* upon the Will, but there is no *inter*action between them. By contrast, the transcendental Ego, as 'spontaneous' as it is, can neither have any influence over the Thing-in-itself nor act upon it, since the screen of Spatio-temporality that separates them is a semi-transparent mirror, which not only allows the 'light' emanating from the Thing to pass through (by 'diffusing' and 'diffracting' it and partly perhaps 'absorbing' it), but also blocks the 'lights' of the Understanding and reflects them back towards their source, while the Will seems to be *acting*, or even *efficacious*, vis-à-vis the Soul and therefore in the future World and consequently in regard to God (even though all of this can be *said* only in the mode of As-if). It therefore would appear that there is *inter*-action between the Will and the Thing, but only *action* of the Thing upon the Ego, without a possible re-action on the part of the latter. This question is nevertheless obscure, and I would have to say more on this. But one thing sure and certain is that the nexus 'Will', even if it integrally involves that of the 'Ego', is much 'richer' than the latter. For in addition to the spatio-temporal screen, there is still the (homologous) screen of 'Feeling' (*Gefühl*), which is absent from the Thing-in-itself (at least insofar as it is God and World): it is the famous feeling of 'Esteem for the moral Law' which necessarily goes hand in hand with the feeling of 'self-Humiliation' (*Demütigung*). These two 'practical' Feelings are just as 'interdependent' and 'indissociable' as are the space and time of the 'theoretical' Intuition, and they play vis-à-vis the Will and ('practical') Reason a role analogous to the one these play vis-à-vis the Ego (= Synthesis of the Apperception) and the Understanding (= 'theoretical' Reason). Human beings may live and *speak* only within the frame of Spatio-temporality; while they can live and *act* 'morally' (= freely) [even though in fact, in Kant, they do not act] only within the frame of the twofold Feeling in question, without ever being able to go beyond it (in their lifetime) (cf. V, 72, 28–76, 15).

As for the ('pure') Will properly so called, it is the counterpart of the ('transcendental') Ego properly so called. In the same way that the Ego, departing from the 'data' of the (dyadic) Intuition (which is formed integrally with it {*fait corps*}), spontaneously constitutes its self-imposed 'possible Object' through the mediation {*truchement*} of the Categories (of Nature) which it establishes by itself (qua Understanding), the Will, departing from the 'data' of the (dyadic) Feeling (which is formed integrally with it), spontaneously constitutes its self-imposed 'moral Law' through the mediation of the Categories (of Freedom) which it establishes by itself (qua Reason). One may say that Feeling is the *driving spring* {*mobile*} (*elater animi*, says Kant; Desire, as we would call it) of the Will in the same way that Intuition is the *driving spring* of the Ego, which can exercise its synthetic *action* only in the Manifold 'given' in

Intuition (cf. V, 71, 28–72, II). As for the Categories of Freedom (established by Reason), Kant says, it is true, that they are just *modi* of the Category of *Causality* alone (as established by the Understanding). But given that they are (also) applied to the 'data' of Feeling, and not (uniquely) to spatio-temporal 'data', they nonetheless have a specific content that is not found in the Categories of Nature (to the extent that these are integrally valid for the Will itself) (e.g., V, 65, 5–67, 23). Be that as it may, it is by means of those Categories of Freedom that the Will, qua ('practical', but *discursive*) Reason, *synthesises* the Manifold of 'data' at stake in the Feeling of Esteem-Humiliation, thus constituting the 'moral Law', which, while being analogous to its (homologous) 'possible Object', nonetheless essentially differs from it. For the 'Law' thus constituted by Reason (on the basis of Feeling = Desire) imposes itself upon the Will qua the '*categorical* Imperative' of ('moral') *Action* (which, to the extent that it is free, that is, conscious, *may* give rise to discourse), while the 'Object' constituted by the Understanding (on the basis of Intuition) imposes itself upon the Ego qua '*possible* Object' of a true *Cognition* which is, to the extent that it is 'sensible', that is, spatio-temporal, *necessarily* discursive. In any case, if the Object is integrally involved in the Law (which otherwise could not be formulated discursively), the Law remains completely foreign to the Object.

It now remains to see what fate lays in store for the 'Law' of Reason in comparison to the one awaiting the 'Object' of the Understanding.

In the same way the Object necessarily passes through the diffusing and deforming semi-transparent screen of *Sensibility*, which Kant assimilates in the 'theoretical' context to 'Sensation' (*Empfindung*) [= Perception], the Law cannot be prevented from passing through the equally diffusing and deforming semi-transparent screen of *Sensuality*, which is, in the 'practical' context, assimilated to the 'Faculty of Desire' (*Begerungsvermögen*). [I take the liberty of introducing this terminological innovation because the word *Sinnlichkeit* can signify both 'Sensibility' (in the Kantian sense of the term) and Sensuality in the current sense of the term.] The relation of Sensibility to Sensuality (both terms being indisputably homologous) seems to be analogous to the relation of the Intuition to Feeling, or even of the Categories of Nature (of the Understanding) to those of Freedom (of Reason), or of the Ego to the Will. Sensibility is integrally involved in Sensuality, which would not subsist without it or outside of it. But the opposite is not true, for Sensuality is something purely 'subjective', the 'sensible *Object*' not being affected by it in any way: the '*sensual* Object' is thus strictly identical to the 'sensible Object' [and appears separately in Figure 4 above only for reasons of expediency]. Thus the 'sensual' screen 'deforms' only the 'sensible *Subject*' by trans-forming it into '*sensual* Subject'. There is not, moreover, a shadow of a doubt that the '*sensible* Subject' and the '*sensual* Subject' are but one and the same 'Subject' ('sensible *and* sensual' in opposition to the '*sensible* Object') [and again, it is for reasons of mere expediency that the 'two' Subjects have been represented separately in Figure 4 above], so that, even though Kant does not say so explicitly, the screen of Sensuality participates in the incommensurability of the 'sensible Subject' to the 'sensible Object', which already originates from the screen of Sensibility.

It is, moreover, impossible to tell where the screen of Sensuality comes from and where it is situated, in the same way it was impossible to say where the screen of Sensibility comes from and where it is situated. One thing is sure, both screens separate the domain of the A priori from the domain of the A posteriori (in the same way the one or many screens of the Intuition and Feeling separate the domain of the Thing-in-itself and that of the Phenomenon). One would therefore be tempted to say that it is one and the same screen (as, indeed, in the case of the Intuition and Feeling) if it were not for the fact that the screen of Sensibility deforms the 'possible Object' into 'sensible Object' *and* 'sensible *Subject*', while the screen of Sensuality affects only the 'Subject'. Be that as it may, it is by passing through the (deforming and absorbing, albeit diffusing) screen of Sensuality that the 'moral Law' exists-empirically and 'reveals' itself qua Phenomenon in the form of a multiplicity of 'sensible and sensual Subjects' which find themselves facing a multiplicity of 'sensible Objects' (originating in the passage of the 'possible Object' through the, equally deforming and absorbing, albeit diffusing, screen of Sensibility).

What happens then? We have seen that, qua 'sensible' or 'theoretical', the (supposedly 'cognising') Subject finds itself in the presence of an 'infinite Task' that only (religious) *Faith* is able to define discursively (in the mode of As-if) as (indefinite) *Progress*, in such a way that this Kantian 'cognising Subject' may only be, *in our eyes*, a 'hypocritical Sceptic' who *believes* in that which they cannot de-monstrate or who lives (humanly), that is, speaks and acts, AS IF the (discursive) Truth was accessible to them, while *knowing* that it is not (at least in their lifetime). Let us now see in which situation is found, in fact and *in our eyes*, (this time the supposedly 'active') Subject qua 'sensual' or 'practical'.

Well then, being more than a counterpart to the 'cognising Subject', the 'acting Subject' finds itself in a strictly similar, albeit worse, situation. Indeed, if there is no (discursive) *reason* (developable in the mode of Truth) to affirm the commensurability of the (sensible =) 'cognising Subject' to the (sensible =) 'Object to be cognised', seeing that both are the result of the passage through the *same deforming* double screen of Intuition-Sensibility (without it being possible to tell whether the 'deformation' was the *same* in both cases), there is even less reason to admit the commensurability of the (*sensible* =) 'Object to act upon' to the (*sensual* =) 'acting Subject', seeing that in this case (unlike the 'Object') the 'Subject' must have undergone an *additional* deformation because of its passage through the *deforming* double screen of Feeling-Sensuality. In other words, if the 'theoretical' Ego, (involved in whichever manner [moreover, left vague] in the 'sensible Subject') manages to act, by acting qua Understanding based on the Intuition mediated by the 'possible Object', through the screen of Sensibility, on the 'sensible Object', albeit 'negatively' by at least eliminating the Impossible, the Will (involved in as 'vague' a manner in the 'sensual Subject' which is at one {*fait corps*} with the 'sensible Subject') does not have the slightest impact {*action*} on the 'sensible Object'. For the semi-transparent screen of Sensuality completely halts any (direct or 'immediate') action of the ('pure') Will upon the 'sensible Object' whatever it may be, allowing to pass through (at least partially, while defusing and deforming it) only its action upon the 'sensible Subject', rendered 'sensual' by this same screen. Thus, the so-called 'theoretical' Reason is, in fact, 'objectively' more efficacious than the purportedly 'practical' one, derisively called 'Will' (with the qualifier 'pure', which one would like to know whether it was meant ironically), which, moreover, is not difficult, given that the (direct) 'objective' efficacy of that purported 'Will' is strictly void. What might then be the odds for the 'sensual Subject', being left only with a weak reflection of the 'pure Will' and which it can only deform on account of its 'sensuality', to be efficacious vis-à-vis the 'sensible Object' over which the 'pure Will' itself has no control at all? A far lower chance, for sure, than the one available to the 'sensible Object' to act efficaciously upon the 'sensible Subject' in order to produce in it (or in the transcendental Ego involved in it) an adequate or true (= a posteriori) empirical Cognition. Therefore, if the 'pure Will' fails completely in its attempt (if attempt there is, even though it seems that the noun 'Will' should indicate that it exists) to act *directly* or 'immediately' upon the 'sensible Object', why would it fare better when acting qua involved in the 'sensual Subject', which can only 'diminish' and 'attenuate' its 'categorical and imperative' character?

Kant was well aware of this, since his answer to our question, which is, besides, purely rhetorical, is frankly negative: not only (as in the case of Cognition) is there no *reason* at all to affirm the commensurability of the Object (upon which one supposedly acts) to the (supposedly 'acting') Subject, but 'theoretical' *Reason* (= Understanding), which is, moreover, in full agreement with 'practical' *Reason* (= *discursive* 'pure Will'), affirms 'categorically' that such a commensurability is 'imperatively' *impossible*. For the 'pure Will' would be able to act (upon the Object) in and through the 'sensual Subject' only by *denying* the latter qua 'sensual' (cf. for instance: V, 74, 23–30). Now, the 'sensual (and sensible) Subject' is everywhere and always, that is, necessarily, *determined* by its *causal* inter-action with the World of 'sensible Objects', in such a way that its implied 'pure Will' would neither be able to *radically* modify (that is, 'deny') by itself, nor modify, in anything whatsoever, qua intermediary (nor, for that matter, in an 'immediate' or direct way), the 'sensible' World, which it can actively 'determine' only while being (on account of its causal *inter*-action with it, where action is *equal* to the re-action) at the same time passively 'determined' by it. In short, the 'Will' remains everywhere and always *pure* in this sense that it will never and nowhere become efficacious *Action*. There is therefore, within the *Metaphysics of Morals*, a *gaping lacuna* between the 'categorical Imperative' of the 'moral Law' (counterpart of the 'possible Object') and the 'sensual Subject' (counterpart of the 'sensible Subject', if not identical to it) to which it supposedly conforms without ever being able to do so effectively, seeing the total inefficacy of its negating or free action (that is, in 'line' with the 'Law') in and over the sensible World, which it *must* nonetheless modify *radically* if it wants itself (as it should) to *radically* change, since it is 'determined' by it and thus can trans-form itself only by trans-forming the given World [through the negating anthropogenic Action of Struggle → Work carried out in function of the Desire for Recognition, as Hegel would say].

On account of this *gap*, Kant's attitude in the 'practical' Part of his Philosophy is, in fact and for us, as *sceptical* as it is in the 'theoretical' Part. But in the former it is infinitely more *hypocritical* than it is in the latter. But both here and there, he seeks to camouflage the gap in the circle of the purportedly uni-total Discourse by filling it with a dotted line and speaks once again of an *'infinite* ('moral') Task' or even of an 'indefinite ('moral') *Progress*'. But if in the domain of 'Theory' his entitlement to do so was dubious, it is strictly void in the 'Practical' domain. For he is no longer entitled to speak of 'transcendental Randomness' there where the commensurability at issue (which 'would close' the circle) is not 'improbable' even though it is 'possible', but rather strictly 'impossible' on account of the 'iron law' of Causality.

To be sure, in both cases, Kant fills the gap only through the (discursive) development, in the *As-if* mode, of the subjective Certainty of Hope, which is, in fact, a (Christian) theistic *religious* Faith. But, 'in theory' at least, this discursive Faith was not contra-dicted by the (discursive theoretical) Truth, since nothing was *opposed* 'a priori' to the 'immediate' commensurability of the '(sensible) cognising Subject' to the '(sensible) cognised (or to be cognised) Object', while, 'in practice', the 'a priori' law of Causality absolutely *excludes* any Action that is efficacious *free* or 'negating', or even 'creative' of the sensible given in the World that exists empirically. Saying that this Action is an 'infinite *Task*' in 'indefinite *progress*' is therefore talking as *Hypocrites* who hide their total lack of Faith in themselves under the mask of Scepticism, which purports to discover in the *Metaphysics of Morals* a purported *gap* in a sensible World committed {*voué*} to Causality, and which can be filled, in the As-if mode, by the discursive development of a purported subjective Certainty of the Hope to succeed {*réussir*} 'one day', there where one has everywhere and always, that is, *necessarily*, failed. A Certainty which, on Kant's own admission, does not rest on anything other than the 'perceptible' fact (which, for us, has nothing to do with the question) that Human beings are *alive* and that they live in a *beautiful* World while *creating* there . . . beautiful Works of art (which bother nothing and no one, seeing that they are beautiful and 'artistic', not in an 'objective' or 'real' way, but only in, through and for the purely 'subjective' ('regulative' rather than 'constitutive') 'judgement' of those who *contemplate* them when they have nothing to *do*).

Kant is for that matter nothing less than fooled by the purported philosophical value of his 'hypocritical' developments. When he speaks in the mode of Truth, that is, qua authentic Philosopher, he explicitly acknowledges that a *free* Action is strictly *impossible* in the *spatio-temporal* World, which is, according to him, irremediably committed to Causality, that is, to 'Necessity', to the extent that the notions of 'Freedom' and 'Necessity' are (regardless of what Spinoza says in their regard) effectively contra-dictory (cf. V; 97, 24–5: . . . the Necessity of Nature, that cannot coexist with the Freedom of the Subject). It is therefore not the Action of the sensual Subject upon the sensible Object that can be free, considering that the inter-action of both is committed to causal Necessity. If there is *efficacious* free Action, it can take place only beyond Spatio-temporality, that is, between Things-in-themselves. One should therefore admit an efficacious free Action of the pure 'Will' upon the Thing-in-itself, which is, as we know, immortal Soul(s), future World, and God. But to be able to act upon the Thing-in-itself, the Will would have to rid itself of the screen of Feeling with which it is associated and would not therefore be able to make use of its ('practical') discursive Reason. Now, when rid of Feeling and Reason, the Will is itself an authentic Thing-in-itself, that is, immortal Soul. It must therefore be admitted that inside the Thing-in-itself, the Soul might act freely with efficacy in and upon the intelligible World and vis-à-vis God, as upon the other Souls (by supposing that the latter are multiple, which is neither more nor less discursively 'justifiable' than the affirmation of the Soul's unicity, nor of the plurality of the Gods and the intelligible Worlds, or of the unicity of the Worlds and God). And this is what Kant effectively admits, mostly in an implicit way, but sometimes even word for word (while availing himself, occasionally, of the phenomenon of the moral 'Conscience') (cf. for instance: V, 97, 21–98, 14). But we must acknowledge that Kant is wrong to do so, even from his own point of view. For if the efficacious free Action of the sensual Subject upon the sensible Object is, according to him, strictly impossible (in such a way that affirming it would be a discursive *Error*), the efficacious free Action of the immortal Soul upon other Things-in-themselves (Souls, World or God) is absolutely *incomprehensible* or 'inconceivable' from the Kantian standpoint, seeing that, according to this view, the Thing-in-itself is beyond Discourse or *ineffable*. Even a discursive development in the mode of As-if would not be appropriate here, and when Kant says that the 'Categories', when they are applied to a thinglike-Object *given* [?!]

through pure practical Reason [!] (and not in the spatio-temporal Intuition), serve for a determinate [discursive?!] Thinking of the *Supra-sensible* [that is, of the non-spatio-temporal], although only insofar as this Supra-sensible is determined merely through predicates belonging necessarily to the a priori given practical *Intention* and to the possibility thereof (V, 141, 21–5), one cannot truly take him seriously. And one would have to take him even less seriously if one wanted to follow him down this path where it would be absolutely impossible to *say what* an Action in general is, what an *efficacious* Action in particular is, and more specifically what a *free* Action is, there where there is neither space nor time, and therefore no possibility at all to tell the future {*avenir*}, the present, and the past apart.

Indeed, and no matter what Kant himself says in its regard, the Kantian System thus involves *two* irreducible gaps, camouflaged more than they are filled by two discursive developments in the mode of As-if: one, 'theoretical', by the (coherent only in appearance) discourse of *hypocritical Scepticism* (fundamentally religious and theistic), which says that one can live in a human way, that is, speak and act, AS IF the discursive Truth was accessible; the other, 'practical', by *sceptical Hypocrisy* (having the same religious theistic basis, which is, in fact, Christian or bourgeois), which says that one can speak and act AS IF the efficacious and free Action was possible. But had Kant consented to speak solely in the mode of Truth, he would have had to say that this Action is *impossible* and this Truth *inaccessible*, and by so doing he would have found it impossible to discursively account for the so-called *Truth* of this negative, or even sceptical, or 'disillusioned' proposition.

Be that as it may, if the 'sensual Subject' qua constituent-element of the Kantian System wants to reflect on itself and develop an awareness of itself, it would only 'discover' itself as a sceptical Hypocrite, and were it capable of 'describing' itself discursively in a 'Critique' of its 'practical Reason', it would have to insert somewhere therein the following passage, which would attest both to the broad range of its hypocrisy and ('moral') scepticism as to the unprecedented virtuosity of its artifice:

> This is how it happens that, considering that in *all* the commandments (*Vorschriften*) of pure practical Reason the concern is *only* with the determinations of the *Will* [that is, of Intention alone] and not with the

natural conditions [that is, existing-empirically and objectively-real] (of the practical Faculty) for *carrying out* (*Ausführung*) its Intention (*Absicht*), the practical a priori Concepts [that is, the Categories of Freedom], *immediately* become *Cognitions* in reference to the supreme Principle of Freedom [= pure Will (?) or immortal Soul (?) or moral Law (?)] and are not permitted (*dürfen*) to *wait* for [sensible] Intuitions to acquire Significance (or Importance; *Bedeutung*), and this happens for the noteworthy (or odd, *merkwürdigen*) reason that they [the Concepts-Categories] themselves *produce* (*hervorbringen*) the OBJECTIVE-REALITY (Wirklichkeit) [*sic*!] of that to which they refer (*beziehen*) [namely] the volitive-CONVICTION/the ORIENTATION of the Will (*Willens-GESINNUNG*), which is not at all the business of *theoretical* Concepts [that is, of the Categories of Nature]. (V, 66, 3–11)

Thus summarised, using his own words (in the second *Critique*), Kant's *Metaphysics of Morals*, and therefore the entire System, appears to be extremely 'disappointing', given {*vu*} its 'cunningly' camouflaged 'hypo-critical' and 'sceptical' character by discursive developments in the mode of As-if, and its content, in fact, contra-dictory, being moreover extraordinarily complex and confused.

But such an impression would be profoundly unfair and historically inaccurate. As I have said several times, Kant had, on the one hand, the enormous personal and historical merit of *elucidating*, for the first time in Western Philosophy, the (theological theistic or contra-dictory) 'notion' of Transcendence with reference to Spatio-temporality, by narrowing it down to the pseudo-notion (unique, if not uni-total) of the Thing-in-itself, and by affirming the absolute impossibility of its *discursive* development (at least in the mode of Truth); on the other hand, and thanks to the artifice of the *As-if*, he developed (also for the first time in Western Philosophy) the System strictly so called (supposedly *true*) almost without bringing this contra-dictory pseudo-'notion' of Transcendence into it, that is, without introducing an 'immanent' contra-diction therein. This is certainly not to say, as we have just seen, that Kant's System per se is exempt from contradiction in the part developed in the mode of Truth. But there, contradiction pertains only to the implicit presence of the notion of the Thing-in-itself and is eliminated by itself as soon as this implication is overcome. Now, owing to the fact that, furthermore, the pseudo-notion of the Thing-in-itself was elaborated by Kant in an explicit manner, and somehow in isolation from the rest of the System, it became too easy, on the one hand, to note both the internal contra-diction of the 'notion' of the Thing-in-itself and the contra-diction between this (contra-dictory) pseudo-notion and the rest of the System (which is the System strictly so called, developed in the mode of Truth) where it does *not* feature, at least *explicitly*, and on the other hand, to eliminate the (inherently contra-dictory) explicit pseudo-notion of the Thing-in-itself from the philosophical System (through its relegation to Silence or to contra-dictory discursive theistic Theology).

This is so straightforward that even a Reinhold was able to do it soon after the publication of Kant's seminal works. As for the elimination of the *implicit* presence of the pseudo-notion in question from Kant's System, it was far more difficult and it was only thanks to the intervention of Philosophers of the rank of a Fichte and a Schelling that it was properly initiated, while awaiting a Hegel to get it fully over and done with.

But, thanks to Hegel, *we* can see that the elimination of the Transcendence *implicit* in the Kantian System somehow happens 'automatically' as soon as its *explicit* counterpart, that is, the pseudo-notion of the Thing-in-itself, is eliminated therefrom. Once the latter is removed, the System sets itself, by itself, into a 'dialectical movement', whose intermediary stages present themselves to us in the forms of the different 'Systems' elaborated successively by Fichte and Schelling, and whose end-result is the Hegelian System of Knowledge, which is also ours.

Before we leave Kant behind, we should then try and see how his System is 'auto-matically' trans-formed into a Hegelian System (thanks to the elimination of this *implicit* transcendence) as soon as the *explicit* pseudo-notion of the Thing-in-itself is overcome.

Whether we want it or not (and Fichte, for example, certainly did not *want* it), the elimination of the notion of the Thing-in-itself transforms the Kantian (pseudo-theistic) System into a strictly *atheistic* one. Indeed, since Kant concentrated *all* that is 'transcendent' (with reference to Spatio-temporality) in this 'limit-notion' (*Grenzbegriff*), its expulsion *outside* of the (albeit imprecise) frontiers of the *discursive* System forbids any systematic, that is, philosophical or 'scientific', Discourse to speak of

'God', the 'future World', or the Beyond and the 'immortal Soul'. Henceforth, one can *speak* (without contra-dicting oneself) of 'God' only when considered qua 'Phenomenon' in the Kantian sense of the word, that is, as that which is situated *within* Spatio-temporality (objectively-real qua Space-time and existing-empirically qua extended-Duration). But it would obviously be inappropriate to apply the notion of the 'Divine' to anything Kant calls 'Phenomenon'. Consequently, the very notion of 'theo-logy' (qua *explicitly* contra-dictory) must now be eliminated from the System, not so much for the 'Theos' as for the '-logy'. For, while it certainly cannot be said that the overcoming of the notion of the Thing-in-itself overcomes *God*, or even the *notion* 'God', it must necessarily be acknowledged that this overcoming now makes that notion *contra-dictory*, seeing that there is no longer any means to *speak* of God within the uni-total Discourse, which encompasses (at least implicitly) *all* that can be said *without contra-dicting itself*. In other words, the 'Symbol' GOD is henceforth committed (qua 'Symbol of Faith') either to contra-dictory ('theo-logical') Utterances, or to Silence whatever it may be (and, particularly, to 'mystical' Silence).

As for Anthropology, which, in Kant, is the subject matter of the 'practical' Part of the System, it undergoes substantial modifications following the elimination of the notion of the Thing-in-itself. But far from overcoming this Kantian Anthropology, those modifications, on the contrary, make it truly consistent with Judeo-Christian 'magico-mythological' anthropological conceptions (rid of their '*theo*logical' cladding) which are its ultimate source (both in fact and for us, as for Kant himself).

Inasmuch as the 'immortal Soul' is overcome (since it is Thing-in-itself), 'Freedom' (= 'pure' or 'free Will') is no longer anchored in a transcendent 'thing' with reference to Spatio-temporality and thus to objective-Reality and to empirical-Existence. It is a 'Phenomenon' like all Phenomena, in the sense that it exists-empirically *in* (or *qua*) the *limited* extended-Duration, that is, it has its 'limits' *in* (the) Spatio-temporality (of Being) which *is*, but which 'extends beyond' this 'free Will', and being thus limited in the extended-duration of its empirical-existence, it is the *ultimate* source of all that is authentically human (= 'moral') in Human beings, in general, and therefore, in they who discursively attain consciousness thereof.

Accordingly, the 'Feeling' of 'Esteem-Humiliation' [= Contempt], which is the 'incentive' {*mobile*} behind this free will, is no longer something falling from who knows where to disfigure and conceal {*voiler*} the 'immortal Soul'. This (authentically human) 'Feeling' is one with {*fait corps*} free Will, the latter being nothing other than the [dialectical] 'movement' to which it gives rise, and which is carried out in accordance with it. As for 'Feeling' per se, no longer able to refer to anything *other* than itself, that is, to a '*thing in-itself*', it can only refer to itself or, which is the same thing, to the 'movement' to which it gives rise (*ex nihilo*) as 'free Will' ['free' of any 'support' other than itself]. In other words, the anthropogenic 'Feeling' in question cannot be anything other than '*self*-Esteem' or 'self-Contempt', and insofar as it gives rise to the 'movement' of the Will (to the extent that the latter is nothing outside of this 'movement', that is, being this very 'movement'), it is '*Desire*-for-Recognition' or '*Refusal-of-self*-Contempt'. Now, the 'voluntary' Movement born of Desire or Refusal is called 'Action'. The free 'Will' is therefore nothing other than free 'Action'. 'Freedom' is an *Action* carried out in function of the Desire for self-Recognition alone, or, which is the same thing negatively put, in function of the Refusal of self-Contempt alone.

What then becomes of 'practical Reason'? Kant clearly says that, regardless, it is always *one and the same* Reason that judges according to Principles a priori, be it [qua Understanding] in theoretical intent (*Absicht*), or [qua Reason strictly speaking] in practical intent (V, 121, 4–6). We will therefore have to talk about 'Reason' [= 'Understanding'] when we examine the transformations of the theoretical Part of the Kantian System after the elimination of the notion of the Thing-in-itself. But we can already say that the (essentially *discursive*) 'Categories' of that 'Reason' will henceforth refer *solely* to spatio-temporal 'Phenomena'. Furthermore, Kant says that, overall, the 'Categories of Freedom' are nothing but modalities of only one Category [of Nature], to wit, of Causality (V, 65, 11–12), and that, generally speaking, the Categories that *discursive* practical Reason utilises are identical to the Categories of the Understanding (cf. V, 136, 9–35). However if, by means of these Categories, the Understanding speaks of *Nature* (which implies the 'natural' Human being) 'given' or 'revealed' in Perception, Reason utilises them only to speak of the Human being conceived as 'pure Will' or 'Freedom', which *now* means that Reason speaks of the *Action* carried out in function of the Desire for Recognition in and by the 'natural'

Human being who lives in the natural World, of which the Understanding speaks.

The 'moral Law', in whose statement the Discourse of (practical) Reason culminates, thus becomes, while remaining a 'categorical Imperative', a *Project of Action* in view of achieving Recognition. Both that Action and its supposed resulting Recognition would, by definition, take place only in the extended-Duration of the World that constitutes the Discourse of theoretical Reason or the Understanding.

Thus, the 'screen' of 'Sensuality', interposed, in Kant, between the 'pure Will' and the 'empirical' Subject having to 'exercise' this will, ceases to be a diffusing and deforming semi-transparent screen. The 'sensual Subject' is no longer a 'deformation' (one knows not how or by whom it was brought about) of the 'pure Will' or 'Freedom', rather it is the empirical-existence, in the extended-Duration, of that very Will or Freedom. This 'sensual Subject', at one with the 'sensible Subject' (which is the 'Subject' of 'Sensation' or Perception) that the discourse of the Understanding is concerned therewith, is the flesh-and-blood Human being, outside of whom there is neither 'Freedom' nor 'Feeling' of Esteem or Contempt, neither 'practical Reason' nor 'moral Law', that is, a discursively articulated Action-Project in function of the Desire for Recognition alone, that is, one which is articulated with full and total 'Freedom' vis-à-vis all that is 'given' as Nature, or, put differently, this Desire is Desire *of Desire* which, as such, *is* certain and exists-empirically, but which has no *objective-reality* at all, being on the contrary the 'revealed' *absence* of that Reality 'given' as such.

It is these *free* flesh-and-blood Human beings who are (self-)summoned to freely *implement* the freely conceived Project of the free Action that they themselves *are*, insofar as they exist-empirically while *differing* or while *distinguishing* themselves (actively, that is, freely) from Nature which *is* and *exists* only insofar as it is also *objectively-real* (which these Human beings are not, qua Human beings, that is, qua free Agents).

These free flesh-and-blood Human beings must act *in* but also *against* Nature (including their own nature) to therein *realise* their Desire for self-Recognition or their Refusal of self-Contempt. They must *act* with *efficacy*, for only efficacious Action can *satisfy* a Desire unfulfilled by that which is *given* to it without any intervention on its part. Now, the Desire of *a Desire* cannot, by definition, be fulfilled by the *Given* whatever it may be. Nature being wholly 'given', the Desire of Desire, which cannot be fulfilled by Nature, must act *against* it, since Nature does not fulfil the Desire which must *act* to satisfy itself. Since the fulfilment of *this* Desire cannot come from the maintaining of the Nature *given* in *identity* with itself, the 'satisfying' Action can only consist in the *negation* of that identity, indeed, of *Identity* in general: it is *negating* Action or *Negativity*. But since it is not Nature, this Action, which *is* and *exists-empirically* (qua Desire [for Recognition]–Project [of action in view of its achievement]), has no *objective-reality* at all, for (as we will see right away) only the Nature of which the Understanding speaks has an objective-Reality in addition, in some way, to its empirical (or 'phenomenal')-Existence and its given-Being. Now, a Desire whatever it may be, if it is not *realised* (by an active Will or a willed Action), cannot be *satisfied*. The *result* of the free Action must therefore have an *objective-reality*, that is, a 'natural' one: that which was *accomplished* by Action must be *given* in Desire in the way all that is Nature is *given* to it. For a Desire can be *fulfilled* only through what is *given* to it in the way 'natural *things*' are *given* to it.

The *Desire* for Recognition, having become the *Will* to act in function of a *Project*, can therefore be satisfied only by the creation of a 'thing', by definition, 'non-natural' (since nothing of what constitutes *given* Nature can satisfy it), that is, by the production of an *Arte-fact*. In other words, 'Freedom', which is a specifically human attribute, is nothing other and nothing more than the negating or creative efficacious Action of Work [born in function of the Desire for Recognition, initially *objectively-realised* qua Desire of *Desire* in and through (or qua) bloody *Struggle* for this very Recognition, to the extent that this Struggle is, in the 'physical' ('material') or 'natural' manifestation of its victory, that is, of its success, the *objective-realisation* of this *self*-Desire, or of its own Desire, which is the primordial (anthropogenic) Desire for self-Recognition or the Refusal of self-Contempt, which, according to Kant, ultimately *differentiates* the empirical-existence of the Human being from the empirical-existence of Nature].

Therefore, the free flesh-and-blood Human beings (that is, Kant's 'sensible-sensual Subject') actively *trans-form* the natural World where they live (that is, the Kantian 'sensible-Object') in such a way that they are able to therein satisfy their Desire (through which they become Human) to 'experience' {*ressentir*} self-*Esteem* instead of the Contempt they would have 'felt' {*éprouvait*} (to the extent that they might be human) towards themselves if they did not do anything, and contented themselves with *living their* 'natural' Animal *life*.

The Desire of Desire, which runs 'counter to nature', is an irreducible datum of self-Consciousness (which is nothing else but this very Desire) and therefore of the discursive development of the latter, which, insofar as it is not contra-dictory, culminates in the exposition of the 'practical Part' of the Kantian System (from which we have eliminated the notion of the Thing-in-itself). It can now be said that the entire of Kantian anthropology (which became Hegelian) is nothing else but a discursive development of the notion of the 'Desire for Recognition', and this Desire, to the extent that it is discursive, is nothing else but Kant's 'practical Reason' or 'pure Will', indeed, 'Freedom': distant albeit authentic offshoots of the 'Soul-Mana' of the Judeo-Christian magico-mythological Anthropology.

Now, in accordance with this Anthropology (and in accordance with its very content), Kant affirms the 'Primacy' of practical Reason over theoretical Reason or the Understanding. If this notion of 'Primacy' {*Primat*} is upheld (and the elimination of the notion of the Thing-in-itself in no way requires that it is renounced, as we will see later on), it can be developed discursively by saying that the (coherent) Discourse on Nature (including the natural Human being), that is, the theoretical Part of the System, must in no way contra-dict the Axiom [which, as we will see in and by the exposition of the *System of Knowledge* that de-monstrates it, is identical to the Axiom of Error or to its corollary, which is the Postulate of (discursive) Truth] of the *efficacy* of *free* Action, that is, the one carried out in function of the Desire for Recognition *alone*, which is, as we have just seen, the negating or creative Action of the bloody Struggle and of 'physical' Work, which must, by definition, *succeed* {*résussir*} in the *natural* World where the Human being *lives* (= 'worldly' success {*résussite*} because {it consists in the} Spatio-temporal {success} of the Action of the 'sensible-sensual Subject' over the 'sensible-Object' in function of the 'categorical Imperative' of the 'pure Will', which is discursively articulated by 'practical Reason' on the basis *of a* 'Feeling' of 'Esteem' for that very 'Imperative').

So far, we have merely gone back over the content of the second *Critique* while eliminating therefrom the notion of the Thing-in-itself. But a similar readjustment has shown that this *Critique* must be supplemented with a 'critical' analysis of the notion of the Efficacy of the free Action, which has just been posited as an Axiom (in light of the 'Primacy' of practical Reason). In other words, a 'teleological Critique' of human Struggle and

Work (developed in the mode of Truth) must be incorporated in the *Critique of Practical Reason*, thus filling the unjustified gap of Kant's third *Critique*, which neglects both human Action properly so called, and its Efficacy [to the extent that the content of this third *Critique*, to be incorporated, concerning its 'theoretical' or 'logical' second Part, in the mode of Truth, in the *Metaphysics of Nature*, has to be substantially readjusted in such a way that what is excluded therefrom is the very idea of the Telos, that is, of the *presence* of the Future {*Avenir*} in the World; for that Presence is nothing else but the presence of the Human being, while the Living (including the Human 'animal') live in function of the Past, that is, in the realm of what Kant calls 'Causality', to the extent that the World of inanimate Things is governed by 'Legality' alone, which reveals the 'primacy' of the Present in that World; (as for the 'aesthetic' first Part of that third *Critique*, it belongs to a *theory of Silence*, which represents the extreme 'limit' *of the System of Knowledge*)].

Being founded on this *second* [*and last*] *Critique*, the practical Part of the System becomes effectively consistent with its Kantian name. It is now really a question of a *Metaphysics of Morals* (*der Sitten*), that is, an Anthropo-*logy* which *says* (in a coherent and comprehensive way) what Human beings *succeed* {*réussit*} *in doing*, in function of their Desire for Recognition alone, in the extended (but limited) duration of their empirical-existence within the natural or 'phenomenal' World, as 'revealed' to them in and through Perception. And if Philosophy comes to realise that this Desire has been in the end *fully satisfied*, the said Human beings can *say* (without contra-dicting themselves) that their *Metaphysics of Morals* (which no longer has a theological 'extension' in the mode of As-if) is completed and perfect (even if it has been set forth only by speaking of the 'ideological' or even 'moral' 'superstructure' of 'accomplished Projects') and that it is therefore no longer part of a *philosophical* System, but rather it is part of the one and unique, indeed, necessary *System of Knowledge*, since from then onward it will never be 'refuted' anywhere nor even be 'up for discussion', a System which is by dint of that fact *objectively* 'sure and certain' but not qua 'Faith' or '*subjective certainty*' in what was, previously, effectively only a 'Hope'.

Let us now move on to the *theoretical Part* of Kant's System, and likewise eliminate therefrom the notion of Transcendence, condensed in that of the Thing-in-itself.

Seeing that the two 'Reasons' are but one, it is difficult, even for Kant himself, to dissociate the 'transcendental Ego' from the 'pure Will', and it is now impossible to consider it with reference to a Thing-in-itself or an 'immortal-Soul'. In Kant, this 'Ego' is the *origin* of the Discourse dominated by the Categories of the Understanding. Now, since these 'Categories of Nature' do not differ from those of 'Freedom' (seeing that Freedom *is* and 'reveals' itself as empirically existing only in the *natural* World, where it is objectively-realised as the *result* of the *efficacious* Action of Struggle and Work while not being objectively-real in itself), and, since the 'practical Reason' that utilises them does nothing other than translate into Discourse (in the form of discursive Project) the Will to satisfy the Desire for Recognition, it can be admitted that theoretical Reason, that utilises the Categories of Nature, is, likewise, a discursive translation of that Will, that is, more exactly, the 'theoretical' supplement to the discursive Project of free Action. For a Project of action *against* Nature cannot be formulated discursively unless one may *say* what Nature *is*, by speaking of its objective-reality and its empirical-existence (which must necessarily be 'revealed' or 'phenomenal' for one to be able to *speak* thereof by means of *sense*-endowed words). And, for an Action carried out *against* Nature to be *efficacious*, the Discourse on Nature (including the natural Human being) must be *true*. In other words, it should be admitted that Human beings begin to *speak* and (finally) tell *true*, as a function of the same anthropogenic Desire that makes them act (freely) *in* but also *against* Nature (including their own 'nature'): Human beings take words {*prend la parole*} (besides, from nowhere else other than themselves) only to articulate discursively a *project* of a (free) action or to give a discursive account of that which they *succeed* {*réussi*} in *doing* (freely).

Surely, to accomplish a 'particular' or rather 'isolated' project, one does not have to know *everything*, nor even be able to speak *in truth* {*en vérité*}. It suffices to have an 'accurate opinion' on the Data at issue, that is, a 'good hypothesis of *Work* [or one of struggle]', which is neither true nor false, but one whose 'accuracy' is 'verified' (*bewährt*) by the very success of the enterprise in question, that is, by the *accomplishment* of the conceived project. But the active *negation* of the natural Given can be 'limited' only by the limits of the extended-Duration of that Given itself. The Project of a free Action will therefore, sooner or later (if Human beings remain *alive* long enough), inevitably seek the trans-formation of the natural World *in its entirety*. Now, the *accomplishment* of *that* Project will de-monstrate that the efficacious or 'useful' 'work hypothesis' is not a 'personal opinion' which is valid here and now in certain given circumstances and for them alone, but a Discourse (coherent by definition, since 'incoherent' Projects or the ones that are self-'contra-dictory' fail *necessarily*, that is, everywhere and always) which says about the natural World *all* that can be said in view of acting freely and efficaciously therein. In other words, there will be left only *one* 'orthodox opinion' (*one* in itself) about the natural Given whatever it may be, and *such* an 'Opinion' ('verified' by the *accomplishment* of the uni-total Project of Human domination over Nature, that is, to speak the language of the 'Scientists', one that is 'verified' by the one and only 'Experiment') resembles very closely the Truth and can therefore be said to be true-semblant.

Now, the objective-realisation of the uni-total Project is, by definition, nothing other than the full and entire Satisfaction of the anthropogenic Desire [which, qua Desire or (free) Will, or even qua Project (not yet carried out), *is* and *exists-empirically* even though it never and nowhere has an *objective-reality*] which is at the very origin of human Discourse. The moment when Human beings will have the ability to discursively give an account (to themselves) of the complete Accomplishment of their 'universal' Project, they will have therefore said *all* there is to say, not only about the natural World where they live [concerning the *given being* of this World, as well as its *objective-reality* and its (phenomenal) *empirical-existence*] but also about their own *life* per se, that is, among other things, about the 'revealed' ('phenomenal') empirical-existence of their *being* human (given by themselves to themselves), which is reduced to anthropogenic *Desire* and, as such, has no *objective-reality*. In other words, Human beings would *exhaust* the Discourse to which their free Action had given rise in the World. They will have nothing left {to do} other than to arrange into one *single* (coherent) Discourse *all* that they had to say and said, in order effectively (explicitly or implicitly) to be able to *say*, by finishing this uni-total Discourse, that it *is* the discursive Truth that exists-empirically (without nonetheless being objectively-real *per se*). And it is insofar as the 'theoretical' Discourse about the natural World may be included, without contra-dictions, in this uni-total Discourse, that it may likewise be said to be *true* in the proper and strong sense of the term [to the extent that all discourses that have subsequently become false are included in the uni-total Discourse with the typical opening words: 'it is false to say that . . .', and contra-dictory Utterances are abandoned to the sad fate of burying one another, not to say each one burying itself by itself, to the extent that the sum total of Discourse, contra-dictory and coherent, takes place against the great background of Human Silence, which, not being Concept or thus Spatio-temporality, is everywhere and always, that is, necessarily, *identical* to itself, or even reduced to the 'geometrical Point' which *is* only insofar as it *distinguishes* itself from itself (to *extend* and *endure*) and which, in 'absolute' Identity, is nothing else but pure Nothingness, that is, nothing at all].

But let us come back to the 'transcendental Ego' that we have identified with the 'pure Will'. It passively 'receives' the spatio-temporal 'multiplicity' which is 'given' to it in Intuition, while it 'spontaneously' *creates* by itself, out of this Manifold, a discursively developable notional 'Unity'. To this end, it can then *speak* of this 'Unity of the multiple' 'using' the twelve 'Categories' that constitute its own discursive/discoursing, somehow innate, nature, by 'applying' them to the Unity in question either separately, in groups, or in their totality. Lastly, by using the 'Schema' of Time, which is available to it qua Intuition, it can, through its discursive, that is, categorial, Understanding, give a [spatio-] temporal content to the Categories themselves and thus constitute the 'thinglike-Objects of a possible Experience'. The entire process is carried out 'a priori' without any appeal to 'Sensation' or Perception, and it is the first *Critique* that describes the ensemble of these various aprioristic operations of the transcendental Ego (in the *Analytic of Concepts* and the *Analytic of Principles*, which constitute the *Transcendental Logic*, to the extent that the *Transcendental Dialectic* demonstrates that it is impossible to *speak* [without contra-dicting oneself] of that which is not 'given' in Intuition, that is, of that which is not spatio-temporal).

Given that now there is no longer a Thing-in-itself, it makes no sense, nor is there any reason, to oppose to the Categories of the Understanding ('valid' for the Thing-in-itself, even though discursively 'inapplicable' to them) the Space-time of Intuition (valid solely for the 'Phenomenon' or, more exactly, constitutive thereof). Accordingly, the Intuition and the Understanding can be dissolved into a single whole, which is the discursive aspect of the transcendental Ego oriented towards the spatio-temporal (or 'natural') Given [to the extent that this Ego itself is the free will, which is self-conscious by definition, since it is born of a *Desire*, insofar as, by conceiving (qua Reason) its Project of an action *against* Nature, {this free will} turns discursively *towards* {Nature}, as towards the point of departure or application of the negating or creative Action that it projects].

From a discursive standpoint, Spatiality 'given' in the purported 'Intuition' is nothing else but the *difference* of *identical* 'Units' that the Ego (or the self-conscious Will) 'constitutes' by referring the World as a whole back to it, whose consciousness it attains by attaining consciousness of itself qua Desire (unsatisfied in and by this World) and by 'detaching' the content of its consciousness (unified in and by the unity of the self-conscious Desire) from the situation or the 'topos' (the *hic et nunc*) that it assigns to itself within this very content. As for Temporality, it is the *identity* of these *different* 'Units', which are re-united in and through the unity of the desiring and voluntary self-consciousness. It is this differentiation of the identical which coincidences with the identification of the different, which translates discursively into the 'fundamental' {*premières*} notions (= 'Categories') of {'Quantity'}, being those of 'Unity', 'Plurality' and 'Totality' [which can be called: 'given-Being'].

But, to the extent that self-Consciousness (= 'transcendental Ego'), which involves the Consciousness-of-the-external-world (= 'Intuition'), is the consciousness of a Desire, it is also the consciousness of the Action which should supposedly satisfy it. Now, this Action is directed *against* Nature. [Self] consciousness thus involves the [external] consciousness of an irreducible-Opposition (qua *given*) between the content of the Consciousness of the external (given) and self-Consciousness (to the extent that the 'Self' is creative Action), and it can then be *said* that Totality (or given-Being) is an Objective-Reality, which is expressed through the Categories of 'Quality', being those of 'Reality' [of the given], the [active] 'Negative', and the 'Limitation' of Reality by Negation [or the active or 'laborious' trans-formation of the objectively-real natural Given by the objectively self-realised negating Action, insofar as it is 'inscribed' in the natural Given by assigning to it its own 'limit' or 'form'].

The consciousness at stake in self-Consciousness thus reveals a fundamental 'Relation' (which is the third triadic Category of the Kantian Table): the relation of Form to its Content, to the extent that the latter may be trans-formed by the negating or free Action, which is equal to (freely) assigning a new Content to a given Form. This relation is either that of 'Inherence and Subsistence (*substantia et accidens*)' [which is the 'Law of the eternal Present' that unites a given Form or the Essence with an Existence everywhere and always, that is, necessarily, identical to itself], or that 'of Causality or Dependence (Cause and Effect)' [which allows the Past to 'determine' the Future {*Avenir*} through the intermediation of the ('legal') Present, in such a way that Consciousness can (discursively) fore-see that which will not satisfy the Desire that gives rise to the acting self-Consciousness], or, lastly, that 'of Community (Inter-action between the Agent and the Patient)' [which allows the (free) Agent to trans-form the ('legal' and 'determined' by the Past) Present in function of the Future {*Avenir*}, that is, of the (freely conceived) Project of the negating Action that is conscious of itself and therefore of that over which it acts, by also developing awareness of its impact on it], to the extent that the ensemble of these three Categories of 'Relation' describes discursively what can be called 'empirical-Existence'.

Lastly, by attaining an awareness of its Accomplishment or its Failure, self-conscious Action realises the consciousness of the 'Modalities' of given-Being, objective-Reality, and empirical-Existence, to the extent that given-Being differentiates itself qua 'Possibility' (of Reality and Existence) from the 'Impossibility' of Nothingness, objective-Reality opposes itself irreducibly qua 'Presence' (*Dasein*) to the 'Absence' (*Nicht [da] sein*) of the Unreal, and empirical-Existence distinguishes itself qua 'Necessity' (of that which exists *everywhere and always*, that is, of that which exists wherever it exists and endures throughout the whole duration of its existence) from the 'Contingency' of the Inexistent (which can effectively be anything whatsoever provided that it might be, that is, provided that it is not 'impossible').

It is the ensemble of these discursive, that is, spatio-temporal, Categories which constitutes (through their discursive development) the (non-contra-dictory) totality of the uni-total Discourse referring to the 'thinglike-Object of possible Experience'. On the one hand, one can indeed de-monstrate that these Categories are (implicitly) *utilised* as soon as one *says* something (the pronounced words being supposedly endowed with *Sense*) in such a way that nothing can be *said* without utilising them. On the other hand, the first *Critique* has made it clear that they must (and it suffices for them to) be *made explicit* to account discursively (by making use of them) for Discourse itself, taken as such (to the extent that their further elaboration as a constituent-element of Discourse as such is Kant's *Transcendental Logic* or *Hegel's Science of Logic*).

But the Experience that is merely *possible* (which 'gives' the *Sense* of employed words and therefore of the Categories they involve) merely *is*, without existing-empirically (to the extent that empirical-Existence is *necessary*). Now, it is in (the necessary) empirical-Existence that (free) Action is carried out, accomplished or failed. Discourse is endowed with Value, and therefore makes Sense for the Human being (who *is* the free empirically-existing Action, albeit one deprived of objective-reality) only insofar as it refers to empirical-Existence, which exists for Human beings only insofar as it is 'Phenomenal', that is, 'revealed' to them in and through 'Sensation' (= Perception [whose 'Degree' (*Grad*) (= 'Tonus']) 'reveals' to what extent empirical-Existence is objectively-real or unreal, indeed, 'illusory' (that is, 'deceptive/disappointing' {*décevante*} for the Action that wants to satisfy Desire, even though it is discursively expressible insofar as it is 'revealed' or 'given' in and through Perception). Thus, when the Human being *speaks*, 'Sensibility' (= Perception) necessarily, that is, everywhere and always, forms a block with the discursive, that is, spatio-temporal, Categories, some of which are also 'valid', when taken in isolation, for given-Being or objective-Reality, 'abstractly' separated from their empirical-existence as extended-Duration. The *real-Object* of discursive experience (where the 'given' Perception of the Meaning {*Sens*} of the Concept is developed into discursive Categories) therefore *is*, only insofar as it *exists-empirically*, on equal terms with the 'sensible-sensual Subject' which attains self-consciousness through its becoming conscious of the anthropogenic Desire which is from the outset revealed as its own, but which is present to the Consciousness that this self-Consciousness involves (and without which it is not *self-Consciousness*, being no longer Consciousness at all) only to the extent that it actively trans-forms the 'sensible-Object' 'revealed' in and through Perception (which is precisely the Consciousness in question).

The *concrete* uni-total Discourse (which alone is able to transmit a Sense [it receives, qua 'sensual-sensible Subject', from Perception] to the *abstract* Discourses resulting from it following the transformation of some of these explicit constituent-elements into mere 'implications' [deducible or substantiable, or even 'explicable']) thus and in the final analysis refers back, everywhere and always, that is, necessarily or insofar as it exists-empirically, to the 'sensible-Object', that is, to the natural World where the Human being *lives* or to the Human being who *lives* in that world. *This* is the Discourse that now constitutes the Kantian *Metaphysics of Nature*, the latter dealing (in a manner and in the mode of Truth) not only with the World of inanimate-Things, as in Kant, but also with the World of living Organisms (of which Kant did not want to speak except in the mode of 'As-if' in his third *Critique* and of which Hegel tries to speak 'in truth' within his *Philosophy of Nature*).

Now, to the extent that the (speaking) 'sensible Subject' is no longer in any manner 'immortal Soul' or Thing-in-itself, it makes no sense nor is there any reason to say that (true) discursive Cognition is an 'infinite Task'. If Discourse is born of negating Action in the 'natural' World, nothing of that which is actively trans-formable in that World can be subtracted from it [nor, even less so, from what is *done* there in function of human discursive Projects]. That which does not give rise to Action is, surely, ineffable.[23] But this *Ineffable* cannot contra-dict the *discursive*

---

23 If the 'Divine' is defined as that which *acts* upon the Human being without the latter being able to *re-act* against that Agent, one could, so it seems, *say* something about God. (The Stars have lost their 'divinity' for us from the moment we have admitted that their action upon us is strictly equal to our reaction against them.) But this 'theological' discourse would still be contra-dictory. For we can *speak* only in function of the Action which is necessarily an Inter-action, as evidenced by the realisation that the irreducible-Opposition that constitutes objective-Reality may be (discursively) defined (without contra-diction) only qua Inter-action of Opposites where the (destructive) action of the one strictly counterbalances the (conservative) re-action of the other (which I will try to show in my exposition of the *System of Knowledge*). Consequently, the notion 'objectively real God' (that is, 'God-of-which-one-*speaks*-by-saying-he-is-objectively real') is contra-dictory in the sense that what is objectively-real with reference to us, that is, to our 'body', is necessarily in *inter*-action with it, while the Sense of the (contra-dictory) notion 'God' excludes (among other things [to the extent that this exclusion is possible, since a 'square-Circle' can be said (without any new contradiction) not to be 'triangular']) the possibility for the Human being to act upon God with the same strenuous force that God acts upon the Human being. Thus, the notion 'God' is not contra-dictory solely if its meaning {*sens*} excludes the notion of objective-Reality: one can *speak* (without contra-dicting oneself) of 'God' only the way one speaks of the 'Unicorn' for example. Yes, the 'Unicorn' is supposed to be a 'phenomenon' with an extended-Duration, while God is said (while contra-dicting oneself) to be 'transcendent' even with reference to spatio-temporality. Now, we have seen that this transcendence is strictly *ineffable*. The notion of such a God is thus necessarily only the fact of it being a *Notion*, that is,

Truth, which alone is developed qua *System of Knowledge*. What matters, in order for Discourse to be *true*, is for it to be one and unique, that is, uni-total. Now, if it may be shown (through accomplishment) that the Discourse that begins with any (but not contra-dictory) Notion (= Sense-endowed Word) by developing it discursively (in a 'correct, that is, non-contra-dictory manner) *ends* up returning necessarily (that is, everywhere and always) to its starting point (while having a *limited* extended-duration and one that is congruent to the extended-duration of human *life*), the uni-total character of this 'circular' Discourse would be de-monstrated and it might be *said*, after having gone through it, that the discursive Truth in general had been exhausted accordingly.

To speak of this 'circularity' (that is, to say of Discourse that it is the discursive Truth), one must speak of Discourse itself or of its *Sense*, 'in abstraction' from its (arbitrary and thus variable) 'Phenomenon' and thus from the sum total of the 'natural' (or 'mute' and making *sense* only for the Human being who *speaks* thereof) World. And since the Discourse of which one may speak (like anything of which one *speaks*) ultimately has an empirical existence in the extended-Duration, to the extent that its own existence is nothing else but that of the Human being taken qua human being, to speak of Discourse comes down to speaking of the specifically human attribute in Human beings as a whole, that is, in the sum total of their empirically-existing extended-duration. Thus, the *Philosophy of Nature* is necessarily supplemented (in view of being able to say about itself that it is *true*) by what Hegel called *Philosophy of Spirit*, which is nothing else but the Kantian *Metaphysics of Morals* (rid of the notion of the Thing-in-itself) updated in such a way that it accounts discursively for *all* that Human beings *say* (without contra-dicting themselves) by speaking of *all* that they *do* (freely). And it is this *Philosophy of Spirit* that de-monstrates, by re-joining at the *end* the *beginning* of the Logic, which is necessarily transformed into a *Philosophy of Nature* establishing, as indispensable supplement to truth, this same *Philosophy of Spirit*, that Discourse closes in upon itself, which enables the one who understands it to see that anthropogenic Desire has been

---

something that is *discursively* developable. One may therefore *speak* (without contra-dicting oneself) of God only by depriving the word GOD of all its 'specific' Meaning, and by conveying to it the meaning of something similar to the one conveyed by words that refer to purely 'imaginary' entities, which are, moreover (qua 'possible'), *immanent* to Spatio-temporality.

fully and completely satisfied by the ensemble of human negating Action (which exists-empirically qua achieved or perfect universal History, or even qua its Resulting natural and human World), even if certain human beings are not happy with the sole fact of *knowing* that this is indeed the case (in anticipation of which they are never Philosophers and consequently deprive themselves of striving to 'understand' within themselves, by becoming thus Sages, the *System of Knowledge* 'understood' as Truth).

We have just seen how and why Kant's philosophical 'System' is 'automatically' transformed into a Hegelian *System of Knowledge* as soon as one eliminates therefrom the notion of Transcendence (with reference to Spatio-temporality) condensed in the (contradictory) notion of the Thing-in-itself.

In the history of Philosophy, this elimination seems to have been undertaken for the first time by a rather mediocre thinker by the name of Reinhold and was repeated several times by German thinkers, some of whom (such as Schulze 'Aenesidemus', and Maimon), having abandoned this 'eternal support' of the Concept, had let it drift away into 'temporal' variations and thus resigned themselves (sometimes with arrogance) to Scepticism, which, although it became 'critical', did not become more compatible with the very idea of the (discursive) Truth. But it was in the hands of Fichte and Schelling that the Kantian System started to trans-form itself in the direction of the Hegelian *System of Knowledge*.

It would take too long (and be pedagogically useless) to interpret in this Introduction the various stages of the 'Fichtean-Schellingian movement' that leads to Hegel's System. I preferred to 'burn' these stages and show the *continuous* movement that transforms the Kantian philosophical System into this *System of Knowledge* which I do not need to summarise here since it is my intention to set it forth (albeit summarily) within the actual body of this book.

Assuming that all of this is already known, I shall conclude this Introduction by saying a few words about the philosophical situation in the post-Hegelian World.

If the Kantian System is taken literally, one must say that it admits only one truly irreducible Opposition, which is the one between the

Phenomenon and the Thing-in-itself. It is the latter that must then be considered as the only *objective*-Reality. Kant's Energo-logy would therefore be the discourse that deals with Inter-action within the Thing-in-itself, that is, ultimately with the Inter-action (if *inter*-action there is) between the 'immortal Soul' and 'God', to the extent that this Inter-action constitutes the objectively real 'future World'.

But *this* 'Energo-logy' does not interest us in the present context. For Kant develops it (without, besides, saying much about it) only in the mode of As-if (without, however, avoiding internal contra-diction) within his 'practical Philosophy', whereas Hegelian Energo-logy is developed in the mode of Truth in the (first) 'theoretical' Part of the *System of Knowledge*, which Hegel calls, following Kant, *Logic* and which effectively corresponds to the 'transcendental Logic' of the *Critique of Pure Reason* or more precisely to the 'analytic' Part of this 'Logic' augmented with the 'transcendental Aesthetic'. Now, not only does this *Critique* omit to speak of the Thing-in-itself, but it also says explicitly that it is absolutely impossible to *speak* of it, at least in the mode of Truth. Nevertheless, *we* can distinguish there what *we* call Onto-logy, Energo-logy, and Phenomeno-logy. For if, following the Kantian *Critique*, we limit our discourse to Spatio-temporality, which is, for Kant, the 'Phenomenon' in the broadest sense of this term, Kant distinguishes in fact, implicitly, within the limits of the 'Phenomenon', the same given-Being, objective-Reality, and empirical-Existence that we distinguish explicitly when we discursively develop (in the exposition of this first Part of the *System of Knowledge*) the notion of the *Concept* in general, which is identified, for us, with Spatio-temporality.

In Kant, the *Concept* is discursively developed into four Categories each one of which is subdivided into three sub-categories. But these twelve Categories ('utilised' by what Kant calls the Understanding) are not truly discursive (that is, themselves discursively developable or 'definable') unless they have as 'content' (or 'sense') a *spatio-temporal* Manifold ('given' in what Kant calls Intuition). Furthermore, the Categories rendered discursive by their spatio-temporal 'content' cannot give rise to what Kant calls 'Cognition' (*Erkenntnis*), that is, to what we call discursive Knowledge or System of Knowledge, except on condition of being 'applied' to 'Phenomena' in the narrow sense of the word, that is, to what constitute for us the 'contents' of Perception (to the extent that these 'contents' are detached from the respective *hic et nunc* of their corresponding perceptions). This 'application' is carried out by the 'Schema' of Time; the 'schematisation' or temporalisation of the Categories (already equipped with a spatio-temporal 'content') transforms them into 'Principles' (*Grundsätze*), which one finds at the basis of any non-contra-dictory Discourse and thus also in the Discourse which is (discursive) Knowledge.

Kant *separates* the analysis of Spatio-temporality ('transcendental Aesthetics') from that of the Categories ('Analytic of Concepts') and the Principles ('Analytic of Principles') (the two 'Analytics', taken together, constitute the first Part of the 'transcendental Logic' set against the 'Aesthetics' [and supplemented by a purely negative 'transcendental Dialectic', with which we will not have to concern ourselves, for its only purpose is to de-monstrate that one cannot *speak*, without contra-dicting oneself, of that which is not *spatio-temporal* or 'phenomenal' in the Kantian sense of this word]). But this *separation* makes no sense unless one *sets* the Phenomenon, which is, by definition, spatio-temporal, *against* the Thing-in-itself, which is, also by definition, not spatio-temporal. This (irreducible) Opposition makes sense in Kant, who considers the Categories in 'reference' not only to the 'intuitive' *Time* (or Space-time), but also to the non-spatio-temporal Thing-in-itself, that is, to Eternity. Surely, Kant refuses to 'apply' the Categories discursively to the Thing-in-itself *in the mode of Truth*. But he reserves to himself the right (which he makes use of in the third *Critique* and in the 'practical Part' of his Philosophy) to 'apply' them there *in the mode of As-if*, believing that he can *speak* in that mode without contra-dicting himself. Now, following Hegel, we have become more Kantian than Kant himself and we refuse to *speak* of the Transcendent (with reference to Spatio-temporality) in any 'mode' whatever, having seen and de-monstrated that one cannot do so in any 'mode' without contra-dicting oneself. As a result, the Kantian *separation* between Intuition and Understanding and, within the latter, between Concepts (= Categories) and Principles, no longer makes any sense or serves any purpose. By *interpreting* Kantian Philosophy, that is, by putting it in the Hegelian light of day, we should try and see to what extent the *undivided set* of Kant's three '*critical*' or 'transcendental' analyses coincides with the content of Hegel's 'Logic', that is, with what *we* are saying in this first Part of the exposition of the *System of Knowledge*, where (contrary to Hegel) we *separate* onto-logy from Energo-logy and Phenomeno-logy.

To gain insight into this question, the easiest thing to do is to take the famous Table of the Categories as our point of departure.

The first Category is that of Quantity. One can *speak* of it, that is, it can be discursively developed in a 'dialectical' way or defined, only if its Sense is determined *first* as Unity (*Einheit*), *then* as Plurality (*Vielheit*), and *finally* as Totality (*Allheit*), to the extent that Unity, Plurality and Totality are the three sub-categories of the Category of Quantity. The *actual* necessity of this Tripartition (*Trichotomy*) and its *content* can be de-monstrated. Every 'analysis', that is, every definition or determination, necessarily proceeds by way of Negation (*quod libet ens est aut A, aut non-A*), that is, by means of Dichotomous terms [since one cannot say (in an explicit way) what Some-thing *is* without *saying* (in an implicit way) what this Some-thing *is not*]. But the *unity* of which one speaks, or its Identity with what is defined or discursively determined, can only be maintained in and through the *unification* (*Vereinigung*) of the 'antithetical' terms that were used to determine or define what was said. This is how the third [Sub-] Category arises (*entspringt*) everywhere and always (*allenthalben*) out of the combination {*liaison*} (*Verbindung*) of the second [Sub-category] with the first of its class. Hence, Totality is nothing else but Plurality considered as Unity (III, 96, 6–9). A Category is therefore everywhere and always, that is, necessarily, a set of *three* Sub-categories, wherein the second is the Negation of the 'absolute' Position of the first, while the third is the Synthesis of the Negation and the Position, to the extent that this Synthesis is nothing else but the (first) discursive development (that is, the first definition or determination) of the Thesis which was the Category itself *prior to* its development or, if we prefer, as 'absolute' Positing, that is, not yet brought to bear on the Antithesis of its Negation (cf. V, 197, note).

Hegelian *Logic* retained the Kantian 'Dialectic' of the Categories unaltered. We must therefore see whether its *content* and that of our own Dialectic correspond to one another.

Kantian Quantity is the *Beginning* of the entire Dialectic. Now, in Hegel, this Beginning is given-Being (*Sein*). Following Parmenides, Kant *begins* by *saying* that Quantity (= given-Being) is Unity (meaning: Unity-that-is; ἕν which is ὄν). But following Plato (aside from the fact that he does not appear to have had any direct knowledge of him), Kant realises that he cannot *say* so without thereby saying that Unity *is not*

Plurality. Thus, the notion of Quantity can only be developed or defined by the generation of the notions of Union *and* Plurality. Now, while anticipating Hegel and contrary to Plato, Kant does not exclude the *third part {tiers}* represented by the AND, which *re-unites* Plurality, 'deduced' from the Position of Unity through the Negation of the latter, with the 'primordial' Unity, absolutely *one* (or 'homogeneous') in itself, in and through the *differentiated* Unity, or the Unity implying a Plurality considered as Totality, that is, the 'discursively' developed 'dialectical' Union or Unity of the Category of Quantity (= given-Being).

Kantian Quantity is therefore indeed a Triad. There is then nothing to prevent its identification with the Hegelian 'Tri-nity' of given-Being (which is neither One, like Parmenides's *όν*, nor Two, like Plato's Being-Idea). But how can the *Spatio-temporality* of Hegelian given-Being be 'deduced' from Kant's triadic or trinitarian quantity?

To be sure, as soon as Kant *speaks* of given-Being (= Quantity) in the mode of Truth (and therefore without contra-dicting himself), he affirms its spatio-temporal character. But, for him, this Spatio-temporality is in some way *added* (thanks to an Intuition coming out of the blue and located who knows where) to given-Being, which is '*neither* spatial *nor* temporal per se' and yet the Category of Quantity 'refers' to it, even though it is discursively 'applicable' only to that which *is* spatial *and* temporal. Conversely, in Hegel, Spatio-temporality is nothing else but the Totality of given-Being which, qua Spatio-temporal, effectively implies *all* that *is {qui* est} (that is to say, all that of which one may *say* that *it is {que* c'est}).

Let us then take a closer look at what the Kantian Dialectic of Quantity or Being *signifies*, in fact and for us, independently of the way it was interpreted by Kant himself in his *Critique*.

Kant 'derived' Plurality *from Unity* and he could derive it from anything other than Unity because the latter is the *first* or 'primordial' Positing. Now, Unity being at the same time *unique* and *one* per se (or 'homogeneous'), it is nothing else but Positing in general or 'absolute' *Identity*. Kantian Plurality cannot therefore be anything else but the Plurality, that is, *Difference*, of Units each of which is not only *identical* to itself, but *identical* to every other one as well. Now, it is precisely this 'primordial' *Difference* of 'absolute' *Identity* that we have called *Spatiality*-of-given-Being or *Spatiality*-which-*is*.

Now, when Kant 'reflects' on his Categories (in the Appendix of his Analytic, titled 'On the Amphiboly of Reflexive Notions'), he says the exact same thing we have just said. Indeed, here is what one reads there:

> *Identity* (*Einerleiheit*) *and Difference* (*Verschiedenheit*). When a thing-like-Object is presented (*dargestellt*) to us *several* times, but each time with exactly the *same* inner (quality and quantity) Determinations (*Bestimmungen*), it is *always*, when it counts as a thinglike-Object of pure *Understanding* [which is not spatio-temporal] precisely the *same* and [it is therefore] not *many* Things, but *one* Thing only (*numerica identitas*); but if the thinglike-Object is a [spatio-temporal] Phenomenon, then the issue is not at all the comparison of Concepts, but rather that, however absolutely *identical* everything may be in regard to its *Quality* (*einerlei*), the *difference* of the *places* of this [identical] Phenomenon *at the same moment in Time* is still a *sufficient ground* (*Grund*) for the *numerical* [that is, quantitative] *Difference* of the thinglike-Object (of the Senses) itself [or of the Perception grounded in the spatio-temporal Intuition]. Thus, in the case of *two* drops of water, one can completely *disregard* all inner *Difference* (of Quality and Quantity), and it is enough that they be intuited *at the same time* in *different Places* for them to be considered as *numerically* [that is, quantitatively] *different*. (III, 217, 29–218, 4)

It matters little that Kant assigns Unity to the Understanding and calls it a Category, and the Manifold to Intuition while calling it Spatiality. The fact is that from a *discursive* standpoint, Spatiality is for him, as it is for us, nothing other or more than Difference of the Identical [Kant says: the plurality of Places (that is, precisely Spatiality) is the *sufficient ground* (*genügsamer Grund*) of this Difference], that is, the 'primordial' (or 'any') Plurality of 'absolute' Unity (that is, whatever it may be).

This text is clear without a commentary and does not even need to be *interpreted* for it to be aligned with our texts. We only note that, when *speaking* of the notion of Spatiality, Kant introduces (twice) that of Temporality, while saying that spatial Difference is 'simultaneous', that is, situated within one and the same 'instant', and that it is therefore necessarily situated in Temporality in general. Now let us see what Kant *says* elsewhere of the latter.

In a new paragraph (§5) of the second draft of the transcendental Aesthetic, Kant says:

> if this Representation (*Vorstellung*) of Change (*Veränderung*) were not a priori [an] (inner) [that is, *Temporal*] Intuition, no Concept, whatever it might be [and therefore no Category] could make conceivable (*begreiflich*) the possibility of a Change, that is, the *combination {liaison}* (*Verbindung*) of contradictorily opposed predicates in one and the same Object (as for instance the being in a place and the non-being in the same place of the very same thing). *Only in* time can *both contradictorily opposed* determinations *in one* [single] Thing be encountered, namely one *after* the other (*nach einander*). (III, 59, 7–14)

To be sure, Kant is only saying here that Difference (indeed, the Opposite or the Contrary) can be *identical* (or *one*) only *in* [or *through*] Time without *saying* that Temporality *is* the Identity (or the Identification) of the 'primordial' Difference, deduced, by way of the Negation, from the 'absolute' Positing, to the extent that this Identity *of the* Difference is nothing else but the (spatio-temporal) Totality of the differences of the identical. But, in fact, when he develops what he *said* in this text, he says (at least implicitly) nothing else but what we, ourselves, *are saying* in an explicit way.

Thus, for example, in the 'general Remark' added to the Aesthetic in its second draft (§8), Kant says this (in a sentence which is, besides, very badly written, and obscure in its German text):

> If the Faculty for becoming conscious of oneself (*sich bewusst zu werden*) is to seek out (apprehend) that which lies in the conscious Soul (*Gemüte*), what lies therein must affect (*officieren*) this Faculty [?] and *in such a way* [that is, by 'affecting' self-Consciousness], that it can only produce an Intuition of itself [that is, of that which 'lies' in the conscious Soul], whose *Form* (which [already] lies in the conscious-Soul *before* [self-Consciousness became 'affected' by that which otherwise 'lies' in the conscious-Soul]) determines, *in the Representation of Time*, the way in which the *Manifold* [or the Different] is gathered (*beisammen ist*) in the conscious Soul. (III, 70, 31–6)

The Unity of the Manifold (or of Plurality), that is, the Identity of the Different, is accordingly defined here as receiving its 'Form' from Time in general, or from Temporality. The latter is therefore the *only* (sufficient) ground of this famous 'Unity of the Manifold' (*Einheit der Mannigfaltigkeit*) that realises, according to Kant, the 'transcendental Synthesis of the Apperception', which is the one and only oeuvre proper of the 'Spontaneity' attributed to the 'transcendental Ego'.

In the first draft of the 'transcendental Deduction' of the Categories, Kant expresses himself, it is true, in an even more obscure, not to say confused, way. However, what he says there can be used to *interpret* (or comment on) the passage that has just been cited.

Let us start with the translation of a few passages:

> Our Representations may arise from wherever they want ... in any event (*doch*) they belong, as modifications of the conscious-Soul, to *inner* [that is, *temporal*] Sense, and as such [qua modifications], all of our [discursive] Cognitions are, in the final analysis, still subjected to the formal condition of inner Sense, namely *Time, in* which they must all be *ordered, gathered* (*verknüpft*) [despite their difference] and brought into *relations* ... Every [empirical] Intuition contains a *Manifold* in itself, which however would not be represented as *such* [that is, as *Manifold*] if the conscious-Soul did not distinguish the *Time* in the sequence of successive impressions: for as contained in *one* [single] Instant, no Representation can ever be anything other than *absolute Unity*. Now, for the *Unity* of [empirical] Intuition to be constituted (*werde*) from this *Manifold* (as for instance in the Representation of Space), it is necessary, first, to *run through* (*Durchlaufen*) [*temporally*], and then to *re-unite* (*Zusammenrechnung*) this Manifold, [which is] the action (*Handlung*) I call the Synthesis of Apprehension, because it is oriented directly towards the Intuition, which to be sure *presents* (*darbietet*) a *Manifold*, but can never *produce* (*bewirken*) this as *such* [that is, as *multiple*], namely as [a *multiple*] contained in *one* [single] Representation, without the occurrence (*vorkommende*) of a Synthesis on this occasion (*dabei*) ... (IV, 3–23)

There must therefore be something that itself makes *possible* this Reproduction of Phenomena [in the conscious-Soul], by being the a priori *ground* of a *necessary* synthetic unity thereof. Now, one soon comes upon [the discovery of] this something if one recalls that Phenomena are not Things [subsisting] in *themselves*, but rather the mere play of *our* Representations, which in the end come down to determinations of the [*temporal*] *inner* Sense . . . (IV, 78, 20–5)

[Now], without [a] consciousness of the fact that what we are *thinking* [of] [at this moment] is the very *same thing* as what we thought [of] a moment before [in {the activity of} 'thinking' which is thus *different* from actual 'thought'], all Reproduction in the series of Representations would be in vain/of no avail (*vergeblich*) . . . (IV, 79, 16–18)

[In summary,] we find qua a priori *ground* (*liegt zum Grunde*) of the totality of Perception, pure Intuition ([namely,] with regard to Perception [taken] as Representation, the Form of *inner* Intuition [that is], time); [as ground] of Association, the pure Synthesis of the Imagination, and [as ground] of empirical Consciousness, pure Apperception, that is, the permanent (*durchgängige*) *identity* of oneself/[which manifests itself] in (*bei*) all sorts of [*different*] Representations. (IV, 86, 28–33)

Now, whether or not Kant says so, the *identity* of self-Consciousness which manifests itself in and regardless of the *difference* of its 'contents' (or the 'contents' of the Consciousness-of-the-world) is nothing else but the continuity of its *temporal duration*, in such a way that Kant's 'pure Apperception', which guarantees the Identity of the Different is, in fact, also a Temporal (or Spatio-temporal) modality, in a similar manner to 'inner Intuition' which guarantees *the identity* of 'Representation' in and regardless of the *Differences* of its 'content'. Lastly, the 'Synthesis of the Imagination', which guarantees the *Identity* of the 'content' of 'thought' in and regardless of the *difference* of successive acts which constitute this very 'thought', *presupposes* in all likelihood the *temporality* (that is, the 'discursive' character) of 'Thought' as such and can therefore also be considered as a Temporal 'modality' per se. What Kant himself *says* while speaking of the 'Schematism' (in the first Section of the 'Analytic of Principles') confirms this *interpretation* of the first version of his 'transcendental Deduction' of the Categories.

The 'transcendental Schema' is the 'Third part' (*Drittes*) which, being 'analogous' (*in Gleichartigkeit stehen*[d]) both to the Categories and to [empirical] Phenomena, allows the 'application' (*Anwendung*) of the latter to the former and is, according to Kant, nothing else but Temporality (which he, himself, calls Time) (cf. III, 134, 22–7). Now, when speaking of Time in *this* context, Kant says this:

> If it is thus conceded that one must/it is necessary to go *beyond* a given Concept [= Notion] in order to compare it *synthetically* with another Concept [by definition *different*, because otherwise there would be nothing *Synthetic* in the 'Comparison'], then [it must be conceded that] a Third (*Drittes*) is needed, without which the Synthesis [that is, the *re-union* or the *identification*] of two [*different*] Concepts cannot arise on its own (*allein entstehen kann*). But what is this Third, [understood] as the Medium of all synthetic Judgements? It is only one *unified-ensemble* (*Inbegriff*) where *all* of our [different] Representations are contained, namely inner Sense and its a priori Form, [that is,] Time [= Synthesis of the Apperception]. [In addition,] the *Synthesis* of Representations [that is, the unity or *identity* of the 'content' which is 'differentiated' or inherently *different* from each 'Representation'] rests on the [Synthesis of the] Imagination [= 'Synthesis of the Reproduction'], [and] the *unity* [or the *identity*] of [*different*] Representations (which is necessary for Judgement), [rests] on the unity of Apperception [= 'Synthesis of Recognition']. Herein therefore [that is, in these *three* 'Syntheses'] is to be sought the *possibility* of synthetic Judgements, and, since all *three* contain the sources for a priori Representations, also the *possibility* of pure [that is, a priori] Judgements. (III, 144, 1–11)

It thus seems that *in fact*, at the very least, if not in an explicit way (even though we have seen him *say* that a 'Representation', insofar as it is contained in one single *Instant*, can never be anything else but *absolute Unity*), Kant assimilates to Temporality (= 'Time') *all* that is for him 'Synthesis', that is, unity or re-union, indeed, identification or *identity* of the separated multiple or the diverse, or even of the *different*.

By not saying so *explicitly*, that is, by not being fully conscious thereof, Kant is unable to 'deduce' all the consequences following therefrom and does not particularly see the links of absolute *solidarity* which unite Temporality and Spatiality into one and the same Spatio-temporality. Kant does not see that Temporality, which must be defined discursively qua *Identity* (or Identification) of that which is (or was) different, is not conceivable (in a discursive way and without contra-diction) unless this Different is the difference (or the differentiation) of that which is (or remains) *identical*, that is, Spatiality. And likewise, conversely, Spatiality, which must be discursively defined as the *difference* (or differentiation) of that which is (or remains) identical, is not conceivable (in a discursive way and without contra-diction) unless this Identical is the identity (or identification) of that which is (or was) *different*, that is, Temporality.

However, although Kant speaks sometimes of Space without speaking (explicitly) of Time, and of the latter without speaking (explicitly) of the former, more often than not he speaks of Intuition in general, which is, for him, neither Spatiality (= Space) alone, nor Temporality (= Time) alone, but necessarily, that is, everywhere and always, Spatio-temporality. And when he speaks explicitly of Time, he is at the same time speaking, in fact or implicitly, of Space.

From this standpoint, the following passage (excerpted from the third section of the 'Analytic of Principles', which deals with 'Phainomena and Noumena') is particularly important and typical. When he speaks of the absolute impossibility, in any discourse, of dispensing with the spatio-temporal 'Intuition' without which there would not be any (discursive) *Notion*, since 'words' would make no *sense* at all, this is what Kant says there:

> That this is also the case with all *Categories* and [thus not only] the *Principles* spun out from these Categories [by means of temporal 'Schematism'], becomes even more obvious from the fact that we cannot even really (*real*) *define* a single one of these Categories, that is, make the possibility of its Object comprehensible, without immediately descending to conditions of [*spatio-temporal*] Sensibility and thus to the [*spatio-temporal*] *Form* of Phenomena ... since, if one removes this [*spatio-temporal*] condition, all *Significance*, that is, all relation to the Object, disappears and one cannot make it conceivable (*fasslich*) for oneself through any example what sort of thing is really intended by Concepts [Categories or Principles] of that sort.
>
> [Thus, for example,] no one can explain the concept [or Principle] of Magnitude (*Grösse*) in general except by roughly saying something like this: that Magnitude is the determination of a thing through which it can be thought how many *times the One* (*wie vielmal Eines*)

is posited in this thing. Only this How-many-*times* is grounded on *successive* repetition, thus on *Time* and the *Synthesis* (of the homogeneous) (*des Gleichartigen*) *in* the latter. (III, 205, 14–28)

Undoubtedly, Kant is speaking here again of the Synthesis that is carried out *in* Time, without saying that it is carried out *through* or *qua* Time, nor even less so that this conceptual or discursive ('dialectical') Synthesis *is* Time, as Hegel will later say. But that does not matter. What interests us at this point is that Kant speaks explicitly of Time (=Temporality) *alone* while implying in what he says the notion of *Spatiality*. Indeed, he does not content himself with saying explicitly that the *Sense* of Categories, that is, what makes them constituent-elements of the unitotal *Concept*, disappears with the disappearance of *Spatio*-temporality. In the example of the notion of Magnitude, where he explicitly speaks only of Time, he implicitly invokes the notion of Space. For he says that the Synthesis that is carried out *in* 'Time' is Synthesis of the 'Homogeneous' (*der Gleichartigen*), which means that the Synthesis or the Unification, indeed, the Identification, in Time could not be carried out if there was not, *in* Time per se, a *different identical*, which moreover Kant himself defines as being essentially *spatial*. The Time that Kant has in mind cannot therefore play its conceptual or discursive role unless it is the Time where *Space* endures. Surely, Kant says in the same passage that it is the '*successive* repetition', that is, Time, that 'multiplies' the identical One. But it is easy to see that he is expressing himself incorrectly, even from his own point of view, for Magnitude is obviously the *Unity* of these multiple Ones and Kant himself says that it is *Time* that *re-unites* the Manifold that goes with it. Kant should have therefore said that the 'How-many-times' is neither spatial alone, nor temporal alone, but spatio-temporal, to the extent that the 'times' {*fois*}, that is, the multiplicity or the *difference* of the *identical* Ones, is the *spatial* Manifold that the 'How-many' re-unites or *identifies* in or regardless of the ('spatial') *difference* of its 'constituent-elements' (which are moreover *identical* with each other) as *temporal* Unity (or Totality).

The same inaccuracy, not to say inconsistent language, can be found again in Kant in another passage (in the exposition of the 'Schematism'), which clearly shows that such wavering is uniquely due to the fact that Kant *envisions*, without however *visualising* it clearly and distinctly, the genuine nature of Spatio-temporality, which renders Spatiality, defined as Difference of the identical, *indissociable* from Temporality, in turn defined as Identity of the different. Indeed, this is what one can read in the passage in question:

> Time, as the formal condition of the *Manifold* of inner Sense, [and] thus [qua condition] of the *connection* {*liaison*} (*Verknüpfung*) of *all* Representations [this *universality* rendering it 'homogeneous' with the Category], *contains* an a priori Manifold in pure Intuition . . . But, on the other hand, Time is homogeneous (*gleichartig*) with the Phenomenon insofar as Time is CONTAINED in *every* empirical Representation of the Manifold. (III, 134, 29–36)

Thus, Kant is saying that Time *contains* the Manifold and 'at the same time' that it is *contained* in the Manifold, which ceases to be contradictory only if one admits that Kant is speaking, in fact, not of Time, but of *Spatio*-temporality, whereby Temporality does indeed 'contain' the totality of the *spatial* Manifold, in this sense that the identical Different of Spatiality does not 'extend beyond' the *duration* of Temporality or its 'instantaneous' or 'momentary' *extension*, and whereby Spatiality 'contains' *temporal* Unity in this sense that the different (or the differentiated) Identity of Temporality does not 'surpass' the spatial Manifold, in such a way that it can be said that Temporality is 'contained' therein.

This interpretation is fully confirmed by the analysis of the first Kantian 'Principle' (*Grundsatz*), where the (triple) Category of Quantity is discursively developed into 'Axioms of Intuition' and its Principle' (*Prinzip*) formulated in the following terms: 'All Intuitions are *extensive* Magnitudes' (III, 148, 19–20). The 'Principles' are indeed deduced from their corresponding Categories by means of the 'Schema', which, following Kant's words, is exclusively *temporal*. Now, the temporalisation of the Category of Quantity (= given-Being) yields the notion of *extensive spatio*-temporal Magnitude, to use Kant's own words. Thus, the introduction of the Kantian 'Time' in his (first) 'Category' engenders therein . . . 'Space'. This shows clearly that this 'Space' was already there, that is, that the so-called 'Time' is, in fact, *Spatio*-temporality, to the extent that the latter is nothing else but the Category of 'Quantity' or the discursively developed given-Being. Now, Kant's discursive development of this very Category has already enabled him to define it qua Unity *and* Plurality, that is, Totality. Consequently, as Hegel has seen and shown, given-Being (*Sein*), or the *totality* of that which *is* (while being *different* from Nothingness), is nothing else but *Spatio-temporality* or 'Becoming' (*Werden*).

In short, it therefore suffices to eliminate the (contradictory) notion of the Thing-in-itself from Kant's 'transcendental Logic' for his 'Transcendental Aesthetic' to be identified with the discursive development of his first 'Category', this development being, besides, identical with the content of the constituent-element of Hegel's 'Science of Logic' that we have summarily set forth under the title: Onto-logy.

Let us now see if the discursive development of the second Category coincides with the content of our Hegelian Energo-logy, which should be the case if this Kantian Category was really *second* in a genuine ('dialectical') *System* of Categories.

Quality is Kant's second Category, and is developed into three sub-categories: *Reality, Negation, Limitation*. The term 'Quality' seems to be in disagreement with all that we have said so far about objective-Reality, which is the object of our Energo-logy, since (like Being) this Reality is at first sight a 'quantitative' rather than 'qualitative' notion [if 'Quality' is the defined 'Attribute' of 'Substance', which effectively makes sense only with reference to the 'Monad' or the *structured*-Unity, that is, to empirical-Existence ('revealed' qua 'Phenomenon')]. But we will see that it is only a question of terminology. Conversely, one is straightaway tempted to identify the Kantian term 'Reality' with our 'objective-Reality'. However, one should not be misled by a mere terminological coincidence. Before we make up our minds, we should see what Kant himself says about his triple Category of Quality.

Given that for Kant, as for us, the Meaning {*Sens*} of a Category is necessarily spatio-temporal and that, for us as for Hegel, objective-Reality can only be the objective-reality of given-Being, that is, of Spatio-temporality (that *is*), it may be expedient to see straight away what this (second) 'Principle' (*Grundsatz*) consists in, and which Kant deduces from his Category of Quality by applying thereto the temporal 'Schema', that is, in fact, by assigning to it a 'content' or a spatio-temporal Sense. It is a question of the 'Anticipations of Perception', whose 'Principle' (*Prinzip*) is the following: 'In all Phenomena, the *Real*, which is a thing-like-Object of the Sensation, has *intensive* Magnitude, that is, a *Degree*' (III, 151, 31–3). The Real is an *intensive* Magnitude (and not an *extensive* one, as is that of given-Being) because it is 'given' (in Sensation and not in Perception) in one single Instant (*erfüllt nur einen Augenblick*) and not as 'Synthesis' of successive 'data' (*successive Synthesis*) (Cf. III, 153, 11–16). Now, this immediately resonates with the 'Tonus' (or more exactly, 'Tonal' *variation*), which 'reveals' (within Perception) objective-Reality as such. Now, it is to this 'intensive *Magnitude*' that the Sense of the Kantian Sub-Category of 'Reality', and therefore of the Category of 'Quality' itself, is ultimately reduced. For Kant points out that 'we can recognise a priori [that is, as a Category strictly so called] in all *Qualities* (in the *Real* of the Phenomenon) nothing more than their intensive *Quantity*, namely that they have a *Degree*' (III, 158, 9–11).

Kantian 'Quality' is then a 'Degree', that is, a *quantitative* Quality or a qualitative *Quantity*, which fits in perfectly well with our (pre-) notion of objective-Reality, all the more so given that Kant insists on the *variable* character of the 'Degree' in question, which, starting at zero, can increase indefinitely (since this zero is precisely the *absence* of Reality or Negation). Consequently, Kant admits, as we do, that Reality is 'revealed' *in general* (or qua Category) through the *variation* of a 'sensible content' (*Empfindung*) [involved in Perception (*Wahrnehmung*)], besides being anything whatsoever, and not presenting any proper *structure* (Kant talks about an 'illuminated surface' reduced as much as one wants). In other words, the Sense of the Kantian Category of 'Quality' is ultimately the *same* as the one attributed to our notion of objective-Reality.

It is therefore not surprising that Kant's discursive development of this Category coincides with our development of our notion of objective-Reality. Kant defines 'Quality' *first* as 'Reality' (which is therefore the Position of Quality [in given-Being (= Quantity)]), to the extent that the *subsequent* Negation is called by Kant 'Negation' [and by us the Unreal]. Elsewhere, Kant defines 'Reality' as Being (in Time) and 'Negation' as Non-being (in Time), (III, 137, 12–14), or, respectively, as Something (*Etwas*) and Nothing (Nothingness; *Nichts*), namely the concept of the *lack* of a thinglike-Object, such as a shadow or cold (*nihil privativum*) (III, 232, 25–7). The example immediately resonates with Parmenides, who defined objective-Reality constitutively by the irreducible-Opposition of 'Light' and 'Darkness'. This example shows that, for Kant, as it was already for Parmenides and again for Hegel and for us, Negation = Non-being (in Time) = Nothing or Nothingness is nothing else but the 'contrary' of the 'Positive' that Kant calls Reality =

Being (in Time) = Some-thing, that is, the 'Negative'. Now, for us, there is an *irreducible*-Opposition between the Positive and the Negative, to the extent that this Opposition manifests itself qua Inter-action, where (destructive) Action, being strictly equal or equivalent to (conservative) Re-action, is absolutely 'neutralised' ('cancelled out') by the latter, in such a way that the antithetical 'Terms' remain everywhere and always (that is, necessarily) unaltered and are therefore 'unalterable', their Opposition thereby being 'irreducible'. Inter-action is thus the Synthesis of the Thesis of the Positive and the Antithesis of the Negative. Kant calls this Synthesis 'Limitation', while making it clear that 'Limitation (*Einschränkung*) is nothing else but [the] Reality linked (*verbunden*) to Negation' (III, 96, 9–10).

Now, Kant also says that this 'connection' {*liaison*} is an *Opposition* between Reality and Negation, and he makes it clear that the Opposition (*Entgegensetzung*) of both thus takes place (*geschieht*) in the differentiation of one and the same Time qua *filled* and *empty* Time (III, 137, 14–15; cf. also: III, 205, 28–206, 1). This leads us to Democritus' definition of the (objectively-real) irreducible Opposition, if one speaks of Space rather than of Time. But this definition is also ours, if instead of Space one speaks of Space-Time. Now, this substitution of terms is perfectly acceptable in the context of the Kantian System itself.

Indeed, we have seen that when Kant speaks of Time he, in fact, generally has Time and Space in mind, and it is obvious that in the cited passage he wants to speak of Time where a 'filled' or 'empty' *Space* endures. Now, this makes us see that, in the context of his second Category, Kant effectively speaks, and appropriately so, of what we call, in our Energo-logy, *Space-Time*, and no longer of 'onto-logical' Spatio-temporality. For one must say of Temporality either that it is always and everywhere 'full', in the sense that it is everywhere and always 'filled' by the Spatiality that endures in it, or that it is everywhere and always 'empty', in the sense that it is 'filled' only by the Spatiality that has no 'content' at all other than itself. To Speak of 'full' *or* 'empty' Time [where a Space endures] is therefore necessarily to speak of the *objectively-real* Space-time and not of Spatio-temporality which only *is*.

But there is more. Considered in its 'Essence', that is, taken in its Totality, objective-Reality is, for us, irreducible-Opposition, which, as the ground of empirical-Existence, 'reveals' itself in the Phenomenon as Inter-action. Now, for Kant as well, the 'Limitation' that 'totalises' the ('dialectical') discursive development of the Category of Quality (= objective-Reality) is 'Conflict', or '*active-or-acting*-Opposition' (*Widerstreit*), or even the Inter-action of 'negative' and 'positive Forces', which 'neutralise' one another by attaining a state of equilibrium or by 'cancelling' each other out, and therefore do not alter the antithetical 'Terms'.

Indeed, here is what Kant says on this subject (in the 'Amphiboly'):

If Reality is represented only through the pure [that is, non-spatio-temporal] Understanding (*realitas noumenon*), one cannot think/conceive (*sich denken*) any *active-Conflict* (*Widerstreit*) between Realities, that is, any Relation/Rapport (*Verhältnis*) such that when these Realities are bound together (*verbunden*) in one [single] subject, they reciprocally/mutually cancel out (*aufheben*) their effects (*Flogen*), as in [for example] 3 – 3 = 0. Conversely, the Real[s] in the Phenomenon (*realitas phaenomenon* [that is, the Real in Space-time]) can perfectly (*allerdings*) be in *active-Conflict* with each other and, [when they are] reunited in the same subject, one can, partly or wholly, *cancel* (*vernichten*) the effect of the other, like [for instance] two moving *forces* in the same straight line [would do], insofar as they either push or pull a point in opposite directions.[24] (III, 217, 19–28)

This passage is interesting because it clearly shows that, according to Kant himself, the Thing-in-itself, which is, if one will, 'objectively-real' by 'opposition' to the Phenomenon, cannot be the objective-Reality in the Kantian-Hegelian sense of the word. For Kant says that the Thing-in-itself per se does not involve any active *irreducible Opposition* in the sense that its constitutive '*positive*' and *negative* 'forces' would cancel each other out reciprocally in such a way that any alteration or overcoming of these very 'forces' or their corresponding 'agents', that is, of the objective-Reality that these 'agents' and these 'forces' constitute, is rendered impossible. Now such an *irreducible*-Opposition does exist in

---

24 Kant expresses himself with even more clarity in his *Metaphysical Foundations of Natural Science* (of 1786), where the Real in Space (otherwise called the Solid) is defined as the 'filling of Space through repulsive Force', while the *Negative* with reference to this *Real* is defined as an 'attractive Force', which would suppress the 'solid' if it acted alone; the 'Limitation of the first Force by the second' determines the 'Degree of filling of a Space' (cf. IV, 523, 6–17). Now, this '*Degree*' is nothing else but objective-Reality (= 'Quality' in general).

Space-time and it is precisely for that reason that there are constituent-elements or 'actions', or even 'forces' there, which because they are by definition *indestructible*, can accordingly be called objectively-*real*.

However, an attentive reading of the cited passage shows that it is even more unsatisfactory, from our point of view, than what we have just said in its regard. Let us not attach a great deal of importance to the fact that Kant is not saying there that active-Conflict (= irreducible-Opposition = 'well-balanced' Inter-action) *must* necessarily take place in the objectively-real Space-time; rather he only says that it *may* take place there. Apart from the fact that the wording of the sentence is not clear, mere 'possibility' suffices for the definition of the 'Essence' (= Category) of objective-Reality. However, the passage in question entails a more serious issue insofar as Kant seems to admit only the *partial* possibility of a 'neutralisation' or 'cancellation' of 'opposed' actions. For, if that was the case, it would no longer be possible to speak of the *irreducible* character of 'active-Conflict', that is, of the Opposition (of the Positive and the Negative), which precisely guarantees the *indestructible* nature of this Opposition as of, therefore, its 'Terms' or 'constituent-elements', which allows them to be called *objectively-real*. Indeed, to use Kant's example, if a 'positive' force, for instance, is not exhausted through the neutralisation of its 'negative' counterpart, that is, if it 'cancels' it out without 'cancelling' itself out, it acts alone on the 'point' that then *moves* along the straight line. And so, 'negative force' may be considered as a purely 'fictitious' one, to the extent that the positive force alone is 'real'. But 'in reality' its action will be lesser than the one assigned to it when the (fictitious) negative force was taken into consideration, and it will be impossible to say that it is the 'objective' magnitude of that 'real' force, since one can indiscriminately consider the 'fictitious' negative force as equal to zero or as any force whatever. As for the 'point', it will cease to be 'real' and 'objective' in Space-time and will become a mere 'geometrical point' (of Spatio-temporality) on the 'geometrical' straight line (which is the 'line' of the 'real' positive force), and its position on this straight line will be 'arbitrary', since it would be dependent on the 'choice' of 'origin'. Thus, if Inter-action is not *absolutely* 'equilibrated', that is, if the Opposition is *reduced* (or augmented), its Terms are immediately *altered* and, at most, *cancelled out* or caused to vanish, that is, cease to be *objectively real* (or, more exactly, revealed as if they have never been such), by being reduced to their *given-being* alone or to pure Possibility which, qua 'revealed' or phenomenal empirical-existence, is precisely called *Fiction* or '(discursive) Being-created-by-reason'.

One might, undoubtedly, say that not a great deal of importance must be attached to the three little words 'or in part' (*oder zum Teil*) in the cited passage, seeing that the two examples Kant brings up (the second being that of the 'balance' of pleasure and pain) pertain to *integral* 'neutralisation'. But, unfortunately, Kant himself clearly explains elsewhere the implicit consequence of these three fateful words (without of course keeping them in sight) and talks about a *continuous transition* from Reality to Negation, that is, the absence of reality.

This is indeed what he says (in the 'Schematism'):

> Now, every Sensation has a Degree or Magnitude, through which it can *more* or *less* fill the same Time, that is, the inner Sense with reference to the same representation of a thinglike-object. Hence there is a Relation/a Rapport (*Verhältnis*) and Connection (*Zusammenhang*) between, or rather a *Transition* from, Reality to Negation, that makes every Reality representable (*vorstellig*) as a *Quantum*: and the Schema of a Reality [comprehended] as the *Quantity* of Something (*Etwas*), insofar as this Some-thing *fills* Time, is precisely this CONTINUOUS AND UNIFORM *creation* (*Erzeugung*) of that Quantity [or Reality] in Time, [this 'creation' happening] as one descends, in Time, from the Sensation that has a certain [given] Degree to its disappearance or [when one] GRADUALLY (*allmählig*) ascends from Negation to the Magnitude of [given] Sensation. (III, 137, 22–9)

The same idea is expressed with the utmost clarity, as far as possible, in the 'Demonstration' of the 'Principle' of the 'Anticipations of Perception'; the said Principle condenses all of Kant's Energo-logy by summarising the triadic discursive development of the Category of Quality (= objective-Reality). Therein one, indeed, reads this:

> That which corresponds, in the empirical Intuition [= Perception], to the Sensation (*Empfindung*) is [the] Reality (*realitas phaenomenon*); that which corresponds to the absence of Sensation [is] Negation = 0. Now, every Sensation is capable of [having] a diminution in such a way that it can decrease and, thus, GRADUALLY (*allmählig*) disappear. Hence, between [the] Reality in the Phenomenon and [the]

Negation, there is a CONTINUOUS nexus (*Zusammenhang*) of many POSSIBLE intermediate Sensations, whose difference from one another is always smaller than the difference between the GIVEN Sensation and Zero or complete Negation [of Sensation and thereby of Reality]. That is: the Real in the [empirical] Phenomenon has a *Magnitude* at all Times (*jederzeit*); but this Magnitude which is[25] encountered in Apprehension [that is, in the becoming Conscious of Perception or Sensation] because said Apprehension takes place/ occurs by means of/through (*vermittelt*) Sensation alone, in *one* [single] instant and not through the successive synthesis of many Sensations and thus does not proceed from the parts to the whole; the Real therefore, it is true, has a *Magnitude*, but not an *extensive* one [it only has an *intensive* Magnitude, that is, a Degree]. (III, 153, 16–29)

A legitimate *interpretation* of the last sentence in the cited passage can render Kant's construal perfectly consistent with ours. 'The Real in the Phenomenon' signifies, in our terminology: 'the revealed *empirically-existent* objective-Reality in a Phenomenon (through Perception)'. Now, we will see later that, once it is 'revealed' or phenomenal, the *objectively real* (non-unreal) empirical-Existence provides the means for a 'metry' (= Physics) founded on 'Measurements' and therefore on *objectively-real* phenomenal (measurable) 'magnitudes'. But *measurable* magnitude is necessarily 'extensive', in Kant's terminology, since Measurement is a 'synthesis of *many* Sensations' and 'thus proceeds from the *parts* to the whole'. Now, Kant says that the Real *in general* is a *non-extensive* 'magnitude', which he calls 'intensive' or 'Degree' (*Grad*). According to Kant, the Real *in general* is 'revealed' by *one single* 'Sensation' which 'fills' *only one* 'Instant' and 'fills' it up *entirely* with a *homogeneous* 'content'. If the Real 'corresponds to Sensation', as Kant says [or as we ourselves would say, if objective-Reality is 'revealed' through a constituent-element of Perception (in fact: through its 'Tonus')], it accordingly follows that this Real is present in its entirety at every 'instant' of Time and that it is, qua *real*, absolutely *homogeneous* with or identical to itself. In other words, there exists *only one* Real, which is everywhere and always, that is,

---

25 I have deleted the word *nicht* in the 25th line, for it is an obvious typo (which has nonetheless escaped Kant's notice during the revision of the text for the second edition).

necessarily, *equal* to itself as far as its reality is concerned. To be sure, Kant admits differences in intensity or degree between *different* Sensations. But because he diligently says that the 'Real' is not [that which corresponds to] a (successive) 'synthesis' of *many* Sensations, but [to] a *single and unique* Sensation, thereupon, the Real is *real* [or is 'revealed' as *real*] independently from the 'degree' of the Sensation [to which it 'corresponds' or through which it is 'revealed']. And this conclusion agrees with Common sense, which considers something as either *real* or *not* (unreal) and which does not admit that something could be *more* or *less* real, or real *otherwise* than (an 'equally' real) something else. That is precisely why we have seen the 'revelation' of objective-Reality *in general*, not in the 'content' of Perception (which is, for Kant and for the Psychologist of his time, a sum of 'Sensations', and which is, for us and for the modern Psychologist, undivided unity), but rather in its Tonus, which, as such, has no 'qualitative content' at all. Obviously, we, too, admit that the Tonus can have different 'degrees'. But, for us, objective-Reality is revealed as *real* and *objective* solely through the *fact* of the *variation* (in the sense of augmentation) of the Tonus, which is everywhere and always the same (even though the 'degree' of variation could be different in accordance with different cases).

There is therefore a complete agreement between what we are saying and what Kant is saying in the sentence that we have just interpreted. Now, this interpretation is confirmed by what Kant himself says elsewhere on this subject:

> The Quality [or the 'content'] of Sensation is always merely empirical and cannot be represented a priori at all ... But the *Real*, which *corresponds* to Sensations in general (*überhaupt*) *in opposition* to the Negation = 0, only represents [a priori] something (*etwas*) whose *Concept in itself* contains a Being ... (III, 157, 30–4)

Hence, *One and the same* Real 'corresponds' to all 'Sensations' whatever they may be and this Real is 'defined' only by its *Opposition* to the Negation or the *total absence* of Reality: it is the 'Concept' or the Category (of 'Quality') whose Sense 'corresponds' to a (*sui generis*) 'being' which is 'conditioned' by nothing other than itself (cf. IV, 502, 31–3) and which is 'revealed' in its entirety by any 'sensation', independently from its 'content' [and therefore from its *quantitative* 'content', that is, from its 'intensity' or 'degree']. In short, [objective-] Reality is everywhere and always *real* [and objective] in one and the same way and is always and everywhere encountered [qua Positive] in [an irreducible] *opposition* to its 'Negation' [the Negative] or the Unreal.

The problem is, if this interpretation is satisfactory from every point of view, including Kant's own, the fact remains that it is contradicted by the sentences in the cited passage which precede the sentence that has been interpreted in this way. For there, Kant clearly says that there are 'degrees' of *reality* and a *continuous transition* from the Real to the Unreal. We must therefore admit that, in making this claim, Kant made an *error* and that he is wrong even from his own point of view.

The underlying causes, not to say motives, of this error are obvious. On the one hand, Kant is ostensibly very impressed by the success of infinitesimal calculus, and he wanted to entrench the principle of continuity in the very notion of objective-Reality, with a view to founding thereon or deducing therefrom a *Physics* of the continuous (while also clearly separating the Physical qua 'Science' from 'Ontology' qua Philosophy [cf. e.g., IV, 469, 21–5; 470, 13–35; III, 151, 3–28; 468, 25–483, 32; 541, 18; 542, 2; 547, note]). On the other hand, Kant uncritically accepts the error of the Psychology of his time, which admitted *continuous* variations of the intensity of 'Sensation' between zero and a given degree. But the decisive influence does not seem to come from this psychology or from Newtonian physics. For, in Kant's time, psychology was too rudimentary to be able to *determine* a philosophical doctrine. As for physics, Newton himself seems to be rather leaning towards a *corpuscular* conception of 'Matter', that is, of objective-Reality or 'Quality' in the Kantian sense of the term. The *determining* influence seems to come from Leibniz and his 'Monadology' with its 'infinitesimal Perceptions', which Kant was obviously well familiar with.

That said, we now know that 'Sensation' is anything but 'continuous'. In fact, it occurs only at a finite 'threshold' and has its own *finite* minimum intensity. In addition, its intensity increases or diminishes in saccades when the stimulus is increased or decreased in a practically 'continuous' way. The intensity or 'degree' of 'Sensation' is, therefore, a magnitude that is clearly 'quantified'. But this does not in any way prevent us from attaching the Sense of the notion 'objective-Reality' to the (discontinuous) variation of 'Sensation', or even to the sensation of the (discontinuous) variation of the 'Tonus'. For modern Physics clearly shows that continuity is anything but a *necessary* property of objective-Reality.

But what matters to us in the present context is the fact that Kant is wrong from his *own* point of view. Indeed, the cited passage (III, 153, 19–24) admits that the difference between zero and the intensity of a *given*, that is, effective, 'Sensation' is always *finite*. Infinitesimal 'Sensations' situated between the finite degree of a Sensation and zero are '*possible* intermediate Sensations', but not effective ones. The purely fictitious character of these 'intermediate Sensations' is all the more evident given that, according to Kant, an effective 'Sensation' 'fills only one instant', while, obviously, there is in each 'instant' an 'infinite' number, by definition, infinitesimal, of 'intermediate Sensations'. Now, if Kant defines [the Sense of] the notion of 'Quality' as the notion of that which 'corresponds to Sensation in *empirical* Intuition', he obviously has no right to deduce the purported continuity of that 'Quality' from the hypothesis (which is, moreover, gratuitous, and psychologically false) of the continuity of only *possible* or 'virtual' 'Sensations'. Kant admits that effective 'Sensation' has a *finite* minimum or an irreducible 'quantum'. He must then admit that what 'corresponds' to effective 'Sensation' must also be 'quantified' instead of admitting a *continuity* of 'degrees' linking zero to a given (finite) magnitude.

Generally speaking, Kant does not ostensibly think about matching one (objectively-real) 'degree' of objective-Reality with a given degree of the intensity of an effective 'Sensation'. He calls upon the 'degrees' of 'Sensation' only to deduce therefrom the 'intensive' character of objectively-real 'magnitudes', and he would deduce this character only to deduce therefrom the *continuity* of objective-Reality (which he believes he should postulate in order to account for the indisputable success of Newtonian physics, which was founded on the application of *infinitesimal* calculus to [the notion of] objective-Reality). Now, on the one hand, we know, thanks to quantum Physics, that infinitesimal calculus can perfectly accommodate the notion of a *discontinuous* objective-Reality. On the other hand, we have seen that Kant fails in his deduction attempt, since he must call upon the conspicuously contradictory notion (of Leibnizian origin) of a '*Sensation*' which would only be purely *possible* or *virtual*, that is, which would not precisely be a Sensation (which is necessarily effective otherwise it would not be a Sensation at all).

If Kant knew modern Physics (or if he was only a Newtonian *Physicist* and not a *Philosopher* desirous to take into account, in his Energo-logy, the fact of the existence and achievement of Newtonian Physics), he would certainly not have attempted such an unsatisfactory, not to say contra-dictory, 'deduction', and, generally speaking, he would not have wanted to deduce the notion of the *continuity* of objective-Reality. For, as defined by Kant, the notion of *continuous* objective-Reality per se is, in fact, a contra-dictory notion. Indeed, 'Continuity' is, according to the above cited passage, 'a [continuous] *transition* from Reality to Negation' (III, 137, 23). In other words, there would not be irreducible-Opposition between the Unreal (the Negation) and Reality, while the latter is moreover *defined* as that which *is* irreducible-Opposition or necessarily *entailing* such an Opposition.

This implicit contra-diction becomes a contradiction in terms when we refer to the following definition of [objective-] Reality (which substantiates the passage cited above [p. 158] where Kant *opposes* Reality and Negation as 'full Time' and 'empty Time'):

> Since Time is only the *Form* of Intuition and therefore of thinglike-Objects [taken] as *Phenomena*, that which corresponds in [an] these Phenomena to Sensation is the transcendental *Matter* of all thinglike-Objects, [taken] as *Things in themselves* (Thinghood [*Sachheit*], Reality). (III, 137, 15–18)

If 'that which corresponds to Sensation', that is, [objective-] Reality, is the 'Matter of all thinglike-Objects taken *as Things-in-themselves*', it is obvious that Reality can neither vanish, that is, be transformed in a continuous manner into Negation, nor have 'degrees' of intensity. For the Thing-in-itself, not being temporal, does not admit any change whatsoever and remains 'eternally' identical to itself. For Kant as for us, objective-Reality is therefore necessarily, that is, everywhere and always, identical to itself in this sense that it does not admit any *variation* in its reality or in its objectivity and that it maintains itself in *the same* irreducible Opposition to all that is not it, that is, to the Unreal whatever it may be.

For a long time (explicitly since Democritus, so it seems), this *irreducible* character of the Opposition that constitutes objective-Reality was discursively articulated in the guise of the 'Principle of *conservation*', which during Kant's time took the form of the Law of the conservation of Matter, that is, precisely of this 'transcendental Matter' with which Kant identifies [objective-] Reality in the passage that has just been cited.

In the *Metaphysical Foundations of Natural Science* Kant articulates this Law as follows:

> First Law of Mechanics: In all changes of corporeal Nature, the total quantity of Matter remains the same, [being] neither increased, nor diminished. (IV, 541, 28–30)

This formula clearly shows that, according to Kant, the ensemble of what is objectively-real in the proper and strong sense of this term, that is, everything which is 'Thinghood in itself', remains 'constant' or 'inalterable' (even quantitatively) in its irreducible Opposition to the Unreal, to the extent that this 'constancy' of the Opposition is the very definition of objective-Reality or the 'Thinghood' that 'corresponds' to Sensation or Perception as distinguished from the purely 'subjective' 'Phenomenon', that is, from Sensation or Perception themselves.[26]

In summary, Kant was wrong when he believed he could derive the notion of Continuity from his Category of 'Quality' and therefore define '[objective-] Reality' as a '*continuous* Magnitude' (which is, moreover, not *extensive* but only *intensive*). He was wrong, on the one hand, because like everyone else he was unable to avoid the (persistent) conflation (in Philosophy and in Physics) of objective-Reality (revealed by the *fact* of the 'Tonal' *variation* of Perception or 'Sensation') with 'empirical-Existence' (revealed by the *content* of Perception or 'Sensation'). On the other hand, Kant was wrong because, also like everyone else, he did not know how to draw a clear distinction between Physics and Philosophy,

---

26 The Principle of conservation strictly speaking is nothing else but the discursive development of the notion irreducible-Opposition, *which constitutes* objective-Reality. As for the notion of the irreducible-Opposition of the Positive and the Negative (= Interaction), which is *implied* in objective-Reality, it is formulated discursively into the Principle of the conservation of the Opposition. For example, the quantity of (negative) positive electricity can decrease (increase), but only on condition that the quantity of (positive) negative electricity decreases (increases) by the same amount. The same applies to Full ('Matter') and Empty ('Radiation'). But there is always something that is 'conserved' in the strong sense of the term (that is, even quantitatively), as for instance Energy. Objective-Reality in the proper sense is precisely identified with this 'absolute constant'.

to wit, Energo-logy, even though (following Plato and Aristotle) he was able to recognise an *essential* difference between the two (to the extent that Kant is the first to elucidate the fact that Physics, which is necessarily *mathematical*, is *thus* non-discursive, while the Truth that Philosophy seeks is by definition discursive).

But the error of Continuity set aside, Kant's Energo-logy is perfectly accurate from a Hegelian standpoint, which is ours. According to this Energology, objective-Reality is nothing other than the *irreducible*-Opposition between the Positive and the Negative, which are 'conserved' as such, and which can be defined only by saying that they constitute a pair of 'Contraries' (A and Non-A). The irreducible-Opposition between the objectively-real Positive and Negative is Inter-action, to the extent that the objective-Reality involving this Inter-action is nothing else but the objectively-real Space-time, which is ultimately an irreducible-Opposition between the Empty and the Full. As for the constituent-elements of objective-Reality, they are 'intensive Magnitudes' in the sense that they do not have a proper *structure* (or 'extension'), and therefore do not correspond to any ('qualitative') Perceptual 'content': as such, they are '*measurable* Magnitudes', but not discursively developable sense-endowed notions.

In short, if one *eliminates* from Kant's Energo-logy any explicit or implicit interference of the notion of the Thing-in-itself, and if it is *interpreted* correctly, that is, in such a manner that the *erroneous* deduction of the notion of Continuity (which is erroneous from the Kantian standpoint itself and in fact contra-dictory) is overcome therein, it may be said that it coincides entirely and perfectly with Hegelian Energo-logy, which we are preparing to set forth {*exposer*}.

Prior to proceeding with that exposition, it would be useful to see what Kant's last two Categories are.

If, following Kant's assertion, the Category of *Relation* is truly the *third* in a genuine (uni-total) categorial *System* (because it implies *all* the Categories according to a determinate ordered sequence, which is the *only* possible order of the 'deduction'), the said Kantian Category ought to coincide with our Hegelian notion of *empirical-Existence*.

Now, in the commentary on the Table of Categories, to which Kant appended some remarks in the second edition of the *Critique* (§11), one can read first this:

This Table can first be split into two Sections, the first of which [comprising the first two so-called *mathematical* Categories] concerns *thinglike-Objects* of Intuition (pure as well as empirical), while the second [constituted by the last two so-called *dynamic* categories] concerns the *Existence* (*Existenz*) of these thinglike-Objects (either in *Relation* to each other or in *Relation* to the Understanding). (III, 95, 25–9; cf. also: III, 159, 34–7)

It is completely obvious that the view of *Existence* that Kant has in mind here is nothing other than our *empirical-Existence*. Indeed, on the one hand, Kant clearly sets it apart from [objective-] Reality and defines it as the existence *of* Quality (= [objective-] Reality) *and* Quantity [= given-Being]. On the other hand, he identifies it, equally, with a *Relation* of Things to each other and of these Things to the 'Understanding'. Now, by definition, the latter is *discursive*, and according to Kant, one can *speak* only of that which is ultimately 'given' in Experience [= Perception]. In other words, Existence is also Appearance {*Phénomène*} in the narrow sense of the word, and in agreement with our use thereof: it is the empirical-existence of that which is (or may be) 'revealed' in any *hic et nunc* as Perceptual '*content*' (which, once 'detached' from its *hic et nunc* [through an Act of Freedom], constitutes the Concept of the 'Thing' in question, susceptible of being 'incarnated' in a Phenomenon while constituting its Sense, which 'corresponds' to the Essence of the Phenomenon in question, in turn, 'incarnated' in the Existence of the latter). As far as 'Relations of Things *to each other*' are concerned, they are, for Kant and in like manner for us, the basis of the discursive definitions of those Things: one can therefore, following Kant, define empirical-Existence per se (that is, the *Totality* of those 'Things' which are its constituent-elements) qua *Relation* in general.

Consequently, the discursive development of Kant's third Category is not expected to be anything else but our Hegelian Phenomeno-logy. We must quickly see if this is truly the case.

As first Positing [or thesis], Kant defines the third Category in terms of 'Relation of Inherence and Subsistence (*substantia et accidens*)'. The development of this definition into 'Principle' (through the application of the third Category to Time [or more exactly to Space-time]) allows a better grasp of its meaning and scope. This development is presented as follows:

ANALOGIES OF EXPERIENCE

[FIRST EDITION] – *Their general Principle (Grundsatz) is: All Phenomena are subjected, a priori, as regards their empirical-existence (Dasein), to* Rules *of the determination of their mutual* Relation *(Verhältnisse) in one* Time. (IV, 121, 22–4)

[SECOND EDITION] – *Their Principle (Prinzip) is: Experience is possible only through the representation of a* necessary Conjunction *{Liaison} (Verknüpfung) of Perceptions.* (III, 159, 15–17)

These [three] Principles [that is, the 'Analogies'] have the peculiarity that they consider (*erwägen*) not the Phenomena and the Synthesis of their empirical Intuition, but merely *empirical-Existence (Dasein)* and the mutual *Relation* of Phenomena with reference (*in Anehung*) to their empirical-Existence. (III, 159, 34–7)

FIRST ANALOGY

[FIRST EDITION] – *Principle of Permanence (Beharrlichkeit)*
All Phenomena contain the *Permanent* (Substance) as the *thinglike-Object* itself, and the *Variable (Wandelbare)* as its mere *Determination*, that is, qua *Mode* (Art) in which the thinglike-Object exists (*existiert*). (IV, 124, 19–22)

[SECOND EDITION] – *Principle of the Permanence of Substance*
In all change (*Wechsel*) of Phenomena, Substance remains permanent (*beharrt*) and its Quantum in Nature is neither increased nor diminished. (III, 162, 3–6)

Only through that which is Permanent does empirical-Existence receive, in different parts of consecutive Time series, a Magnitude, which one calls *Duration (Dauer)* . . . Therefore, it is the *Permanent* which is, in all Phenomena, the *thinglike-Object* itself, that is, the Substance (*phaenomenon*), while everything that *changes* or that can *change* belongs only to the *Mode* in which this Substance or Substances *exist (existieren)*, that is, to their *Determinations*. (III, 163, 18–20 and 29–32)

The *Determinations* of a Substance, which are nothing other than its particular *Modes* of existing, are called *Accidents*. These are always real, since they concern the empirical-existence (*Dasein*) of the Substance (Negations are merely Determinations that express the Non-being of something in the Substance). If one ascribes to this Real in Substance [that is, to the Accident] a particular empirical-existence (e.g., to Motion [taken] as an Accident of Matter), then *this* empirical-existence is called *Inherence*, in contrast to the empirical-existence *of the Substance*, which is called *Subsistence*. Yet many erroneous-interpretations (*Missdeutungen*) arise from this, and it is more precise and correct if one designates the Accident only through the *Mode* in which the empirical-existence of a Substance is positively determined. Nevertheless, it is still unavoidable, due to the conditions of the logical [or discursive] use of our Understanding, to isolate, as it were, that which can *change* in the empirical-existence of a Substance, while the Substance [itself] remains (*bleibt*), and to consider it in *relation* to what is, properly speaking, Permanent and Radical; thus it is also for this reason that this [sub-] Category [of Substance] stands under the title of *Relations* (*Verhältnisse*), [being] more as the *condition* of these Relations than as itself containing a Relation. (III, 165, 10–26)

The mere *Form* of Intuition without *Substance* is, in itself, not a *thing-like-Object*, but the purely formal *condition* of this thinglike-Object ([which] as Phenomenon) . . . (*ens imaginarium*). (III, 232, 28–32)

Several points raised by the texts that have just been cited must be retained.

If the formulae of the general Principle of the three Analogies, as presented in both editions of the *Critique*, are combined, while paying attention to their respective commentaries, it can be seen that empirical-Existence is nothing else but the Totality of the spatio-temporal *Relations* or *Connections* between its own constituent-elements, to the extent that they are 'Phenomena' or, more exactly, 'Things' 'revealed' in and through Perceptual 'contents'. Surely, as always in this context, Kant (explicitly) mentions only 'Time'. But it is undeniable that he is, in fact, speaking, to the same effect, (implicitly) of 'Space'. Therefore, the Relations that constitute empirical-Existence take place in 'Space-time'. But it is clear (and the analysis that follows will confirm) that *Relation* in that context is something altogether different from the *irreducible-Opposition* that constitutes objective-Reality (and which is, strictly speaking, situated in Space-time). The reason being that Opposition, to the extent that it is *irreducible*, excludes Change, in the sense that it conditions the Conservation or the Permanence of objective-Reality in general. Conversely, Relation is a 'mutual Relation *in Time*' or a 'necessary Connection *of Perceptions*', in such a way that it is nothing else but Change as such (albeit one which can be made only on the basis of Permanence). Thus, we must distinguish between Space-time where the irreducible-Opposition of objective-Reality is conserved, and the one where the changeable Relation or the Change in the Relation which constitute empirical-Existence are made. And *that* empirically-existing Space-time (revealing itself, qua Phenomenon, in and through Perceptual 'Content' and no longer merely through Sensation resulting from its Tonal variations or through the Sentiment of Well- or Ill-being which may be implied therein) is no longer called 'Space-time', but 'extended-Duration', notably since, in the cited passages, Kant himself explicitly speaks of 'Duration' (cf. III, 163, 18–20).

Kant says that Change is possible [= in the sense of giving rise to 'Experience', that is, to the coherent Discourse, or *one* in its own self and susceptible of being, by becoming total, the (discursive) Truth] only when grounded upon Permanence (= Substance). In our terminology, this signifies that empirical-Existence is the empirical-existence of objective-Reality [which, in turn, is nothing else but the objective-reality of given-Being] or, which is the same thing, that extended-Duration is the extended-duration of Space-time [which, in turn, is nothing else but the objective-Reality of Spatio-temporality which *is*]. However, in the last-quoted passage [excerpted from the appendix of the 'Analytic', where Kant applies his four Categories to the notion of 'Nothingness', accordingly defined qua Non-Being (Nothingness), Non-Reality (the Unreal) and Non-Existence (the Inexistent), and finally qua Non-Discourse (the Ineffable)], Kant admits in fact an empirical-existence [and everywhere a given-being] 'without Substance', that is, deprived of objective-reality (that is, comprised in the Space-time, which he calls *ens imaginarium* and defines as 'purely formal condition of the Phenomenon'). If, therefore, all that is objectively-real necessarily *is* and *exists-empirically*, an empirical-existence [which necessarily *is*] may *be* albeit without an *objective-reality*. It is obvious that this *Unreal* that exists-empirically and thus has an extended-duration (that is, a *hic et nunc*) is nothing else but Discourse taken solely as *Meaning* {*Sens*} (to the extent that the Phenomenon has, needless to say, an objective-reality lying at the basis of its empirical-existence), the empirically-existing Sense, insofar as such Sense, in *a hic et nunc*, is nothing else but that which is specifically human in the flesh-and-blood Human being. Hence, Kant's empirical-Existence is, in fact and for Hegel as for us, not only inanimate-Thing and living-Organism (both grounded upon a 'permanent' or an objectively-real basis), but also human-Individual or 'Person' ('essentially' *unreal*, indeed 'free' vis-à-vis all that is 'real' and 'objective', that is, 'necessary'). But we will see later on that Discourse and its Meaning {*Sens*} do not intervene, at least explicitly, in the Kantian 'System' of the Categories and that, for Kant himself, empirical-Existence (= 'Relation') is reduced to the empirical-existence of the extended-duration of the inanimate-Thing (to the extent that the living-Organism itself is merely a 'regulative' notion, developable discursively only in the mode of As-if, and not strictly speaking a Category, developable discursively in the mode of Truth).

That said, Kant posits empirical-Existence (= 'Relation'), which is necessarily endowed with an extended-duration, *firstly* as 'Relation' between the (permanent) 'Substance' and its (changing or variable) Attributes. The development of this first Sub-Category of 'Relation' into Principle clearly shows that what Kant calls 'Substance' is nothing else but the objective-Reality lying at the basis [of one part] of empirical-Existence and which exists-empirically qua objectively-real, in and through, or as, this very empirical-Existence. As for empirical-existence per se, it is, as Kant says in one of the cited passages (III, 165, 20–6), not the Relation between the (objectively-real) Substance and its Accidents, but the Relation between Accidents taken as such, that is, as 'the Substance's modes of empirical-existence' (to the extent that this Substance is only the 'condition of these Relations'). In other words, the empirical-Existence [of the inanimate-Thing, Kant would say; whatever it may be, we would say after Hegel] is nothing else but the multiple (= extended) and varied or even variable (= durable) *Relation* between the constituent-elements that are re-united or integrated into one single Totality (differentiated in its extended-duration or with reference to it) in and through, or even qua, this very Relation. Which means, in our terminology, that empirical-Existence is a 'Monad', that is, the *structured*-Unity or 'non-homogeneous' or 'discontinuous' *Totality* in which every [thinglike, organic, or individual, indeed, 'personal'] constituent-element is in turn a Monad 'qualitatively *differentiated*' within itself and 'qualitatively *distinct*' from all that is not it. Besides, Kant himself refers on several occasions to the notion of the Hegelian *Monad* (cf. e.g., III, 217, 29–218, 11). He rejects it only insofar as it is interpreted by Leibniz as 'thinking Subject', that is, in fact and for us, as human-Individual or 'Person'. In so doing, Kant would have surely been right if he reduced the notion of empirical-Existence to that of the inanimate-Thing, but he is wrong to limit his Sub-category in this manner, because in so doing, he introduces a *gap* in his purportedly categorial 'System' and thus renounces the possibility to de-monstrate its 'circularity', that is, its uni-total or its truly 'systematic' character. Not only that, but this arbitrary limitation goes further still, since Kant's Category of empirical-Existence (= Relation) is supposed to exclude even the notion of the living-Organism.

But we will have the opportunity to go back to this question. Let us firstly see what the second Sub-Category of the Category of Relation is (= empirical-Existence having a *structured* extended-duration).

In his *Table*, Kant defines the second Sub-Category in question as the category 'of the Relation of Causality or of Dependence (Cause and Effect)'. And in developing that definition into Principle (by means of the application of that Sub-Category to 'Time', that is, in fact, to extended-Duration), he says, among other things, this:

> The Schema [purportedly temporal, but in fact spatio-temporal, of the notions] of the Cause and of the Causality of a Thing in general is the [empirically-existent] Real which is always [and everywhere] followed by something *other* [existing-empirically] if it is posited (*gesetzt*) arbitrarily [that is, as soon as it exists-empirically in a *hic et nunc*]. This Schema therefore consists in the *Succession* of the Manifold, insofar as it is subject to a Rule. (III, 138, 1–14)

SECOND ANALOGY

[FIRST EDITION] – *Principle of Production* (*Erzeugung*)
Everything that *happens* {*se produit*} (*geschicht*) (begins to be) *pre*-supposes something which it *follows* in accordance/in conformity with a Rule. (IV, 128, 24–7)

[SECOND EDITION] – *Principle of temporal Succession according to the Law of Causality*
All Changes (*Veränderungen*) happen {*se produisent*} (*geschehen*) in accordance/in conformity with the Law of the connection {*Liaison*} (*Verknüpfung*) of Cause and Effect. (III, 166, 31–3)

We can see that the text of the second edition is more precise than its counterpart in the first edition. If one is to stick to the latter, one can say that therein Kant is articulating what we call the Principle of Legality, which is nothing else but the Relation (between the 'Substance' and its 'Accidents' or, more exactly, between the 'Accidents' of a given 'Substance') that constitutes the empirical-existence or the extended-duration of the inanimate-Thing, or even *the unity* of the constituent-elements qualitatively *differentiated* from the thinglike Monad. But the second edition speaks expressly of the Relation between the Cause that *precedes* its effect and the Effect that *follows from* its cause. It is therefore a question of what we, too, call the Principle of Causality. But for us, this Principle constitutes the empirical-existence or the extended-duration of the living-Organism, which is, for Kant, constituted by the Principle of Teleology, to the extent that this Principle has only a 'regulative' value (valid in the mode of As-if) and does not constitute a Category or a notion discursively developable in the mode of Truth.

Whatever one makes of this [erroneous] interpretation that was made by Kant himself, the second Sub-Category is correctly derived from the first one and, accordingly, from the Category of Relation itself (= empirical-Existence). For this is most obviously about the Negation (Antithesis) of the first Positing (Thesis) of the latter, which is the Sub-Category of the (thinglike) Monad or the structured-Unity. The notion of Causality is indeed a *negation* of the notion of 'Substantiality' or of the (thinglike) Monad because it negates, on the one hand, its *unity* by *distinguishing* inside its extended-duration, the Cause from the Effect, and, on the other hand, its 'structural' *multiplicity*, since the Cause is supposed to produce its Effect qua *indivisible* unity and independently [?] from its own 'structure'. But since the Non-one is Manifold and the Non-multiple is One, Causality reinstates the 'monadic' structured Unity which it has negated qua *thinglike* Monad. This *second* Monad is the living-Organism, which is no longer *one* in its duration and ('structured') *multiple* in its extension, but (insofar as it *lives* and is not merely inanimate Thing), {rather} (structured) multiple in its duration and *one* in its extension (thanks to the 'differentiation' of its *living* duration and despite the 'differentiation' of its purely *thinglike* extension: an Animal remains *the same* with regard to the duration of its *life* despite the fact that, in its inorganic extension, it is vacated of its 'molecules' to be replaced by *other ones*).

To be sure, for reasons that we will have to come back to, Kant would not admit this interpretation of his second Sub-Category of Relation. But we will see that he would have been *wrong* not to admit it, and we have just seen that this interpretation is in any case legitimate in the sense that it fits in perfectly well with all that Kant himself says (explicitly) about the Sub-category in question.

It remains to see what the third and last Sub-category of the Category of empirical-Existence (= Relation) is.

In his Table, Kant defines it as the Category of 'the Relation of Community (*Gemeinschaft*) (Inter-action between the Agent and the Patient)'. And he comments on this definition in the following manner (in the new §11 of the second edition of the *Critique*):

Community [= Synthesis] is the Causality [= Antithesis] of a Substance [= Thesis] in the determination of others [and] reciprocally [the Causality of all the other ones in their determination]. (III, 96, 10–11)

Now, a similar Connection {*Liaison*} (*Verknüpfung*) [to the one found in the discursive Judgement providing the logical basis for the Sub-category in question] is thought of in an *Entirety* of Things, where a Thing is not *subordinated* as effect to another one [taken] as the Cause of its empirical-existence (*Dasein*), but rather *coordinated* with it simultaneously and reciprocally as Cause, with reference to (*in Ansehung*) the determination of the other [Things] (e.g., in a body, the parts of which reciprocally attract yet also oppose/resist each other), which is an entirely different Mode of Connection from that which is to be found in the mere Relation of Cause to Effect (of Origin (*Grundes*) to Consequence (*Folgel*)), where the Consequence does not (in turn) reciprocally determine the Origin once again and therefore does not constitute a *Whole* with the latter (as the World-Creator [constitutes one] with the World [that he creates]). (III, 97, 3–12)

Lastly, Kant develops this Sub-category into Principle in the following manner:

> The [supposedly 'temporal' but in fact 'spatio-temporal'] Schema of Community (Inter-action), or of the reciprocal Causality of Substances with reference to their Accidents, is the *Simultaneity* of the determinations of one [of these Substances, taken as one set of these Accidents] with those of the other [Substances as sets of Accidents], in accordance/conformity with a universal Rule. (III, 138, 5–8)

THIRD ANALOGY

> [FIRST EDITION] – *Principle of Community*
> All Substances, insofar as they are *simultaneous*, stand (*stehen*) in a thoroughgoing (*durchgängiger*) *Community* (that is, in Inter-action with one another). (IV, 141, 8–11)

> [SECOND EDITION] – *Principle of Simultaneity, according to/in conformity with the Law of Inter-action or [of] Community*
> All Substances, insofar as they can be *simultaneously* perceived in Space, are in thoroughgoing (*durchgängiger*) *Inter-action*. (III, 180, 23–7)

Here, again, there are two equally possible interpretations. According to one of them, the Principle of Community would be nothing else but a paraphrase of the Principle of Substantiality, which constitutes the empirical-existence or the extended-duration of the inanimate-Thing, except that now the question at issue is no longer (or not only) posed in reference to the Relation between 'Accidents' within an *isolated* inanimate-Thing (or thinglike Monad), it rather concerns the (equally 'simultaneous' and non 'consecutive') Relation between 'Accidents' (or *sets* of 'Accidents') of inanimate-Things *distinct* from one another. In other words, this Principle would make (thinglike) empirical-Existence appear as a 'Monad whose (simultaneous) constituent elements are also Monads [in full agreement with Leibnizian 'Monadology' (cf. what Kant says about the 'World taken as a whole'; III, 185, note)]. According to the second interpretation, the Principle of Community would consist in the application of the Principle of Causality to *extension* (even though, in

Kant, it is valid only in and for *duration*). It would then be a question of what we would call the vital-Activity that every living Organism entertains at every instant in its biological-Milieu, that is, in the World wherein it *lives*. And this second interpretation, although rejected by Kant, is in fact as valid as the first one within the frame of his own categorial System.[27]

But, even if we accept both interpretations at once, we obtain only one ancillary discursive development of the first two Sub-Categories, rather than a third Sub-category, derived from the other two qua their 'Synthesis', in the way Kant intended.

This crucial gap in Kant's categorial 'System' was filled by Hegel, who introduced the third Sub-Category in an explicit manner, thus rendering the Kantian 'System' truly *systematic*, that is, uni-total or 'circular' and therefore *true* as the 'irreducible summary of the discursive Truth'.

What is remarkable is that Kant himself (implicitly) defines the Hegelian third Sub-category in question while commenting on his own pseudo-third Sub-category of Community. Indeed, in one of the above-cited passages (III, 97, 10–12), Kant *defines* Community in *opposition* to Causality, whereby 'the Consequence (*Folge*) does not reciprocally determine the Origin (*Grund*)'. Accordingly, he should have said that Community is *defined* by the fact that, in that case, the 'Consequence' determines the 'Origin' (while being determined by it insofar as it is subjected to the Principle of Causality). Now, to say so, would come down to defining Community as the Principle of Teleology while admitting the empirical-existence, in the extended-Duration, of the efficacious Action carried out (in a *hic et nunc*) in function of a Project. And it is precisely for this reason that Kant neither *says* so nor was he *willing*

---

27 It is obvious that the 'Inter-action' of which Kant speaks when he develops his Category of empirical-Existence has nothing to do with the Inter-action (in absolute 'equilibrium' owing to the absolute *equality* of Action and Re-action) which constitutes, according to us, objective-Reality. Indeed, if, by speaking of the latter, Kant was wrong to admit that Re-actions 'neutralise' Actions only *partially*, he is perfectly right to draw a distinction between the Agent and the Patient within empirical-Existence (to the extent that the Agent is the origin of Actions which are *not* 'neutralised' by Re-actions while the Patient is the point of application of those Actions which are not 'neutralised' by their Re-actions). In this case, 'Inter-action' is, indeed, no longer *Equilibrium*, but rather *cosmic-Movement* [or biological-Activity and human Action]. (Of course, the mouse 're-acts' when it is being devoured by the cat, but its re-action is comparatively 'almost insignificant' rather than *equal* to the action of the cat chewing on the mouse.)

to say so. Just as well, Hegel was the first to *define* the Sub-category of Community (which, like Kant, he calls 'Inter-action') in terms of the action of the Effect upon the Cause. And right away, 'Inter-action' becomes free, that is, conscious and voluntary or human *Action*, and it presents itself as the grounding Category of *Freedom*, which exists-empirically not only as Action of Struggle→ Work or technical-Oeuvre, but also as discursive Concept, to the extent that the said notion or Category is developed discursively into the Sub-categories of the Concept (in the narrow sense), of Judgement and Reasoning, paving the way for the Kantian notion of Community to thus become the Hegelian notion of History (cf. §§154–159 in the third edition of the *Encyclopaedia*).

Kant fully anticipated all (or at least some) of these consequences, since in the quoted passage he cites (between parentheses) the example of the Relation between the World-Creator and the World created by him; nothing then should prevent Kant from introducing in his categorial System the Category of *human* Community, understood as the (free) collective Action of human beings within the natural World (governed by Legality and Causality), wherein it creates the social and historical human World, which in turn re-acts upon Human beings who create that World by acting upon it to the extent that they live humanly (while remaining subjected to the Causality of the living-Organism that they themselves are, and to the Legality of the inanimate-Thing that, in a certain measure, this Organism is to boot).

Kant was unwilling to embark on that path mainly for the essentially *religious* motives of which I have spoken at length in the third Introduction to my Exposition of the Hegelian *System of Knowledge*. Unwilling to admit the efficacy of human Action (and therefore Satisfaction) in the extended-duration of empirical-Existence, he completely crossed out the notion of the said Action from the list of his Categories (which would come down to not including it in the list of the Sub-categories of Relation, for he fully understood that it is strictly impossible to introduce the notion in question in the first two fundamental Categories). And since he [wrongly] thought that the notion of the living-Organism itself involved the notion of Teleology, he believed he had to negate the 'categorial' character of that basic bio-logical notion, seeing in it only a notion developable merely in the mode of As-if. For he could clearly see that in admitting the Category of vital [pseudo]-Teleology, it would be impossible for him not to admit the notion of [the strictly so called] *human* Teleology, and that admission would have been inconsistent with the fundamental 'Dogma' of any Religion (which does not admit full Satisfaction on earth merely in function of the 'teleological' or 'worldly' Action of Struggle → Work, which *engenders*, in addition to an Oeuvre, the Discourse that ultimately becomes discursive *Truth*).

Now, if the teleological interpretation of the phenomenon of Life is a mere Kantian *error* (which, nevertheless, goes back to Aristotle) that is easily rectifiable and requires neither the modification of the categorial 'System' of Kant nor a correction of his discursive developments of its constituent Categories and Sub-Categories, his conscious and deliberate (not to say 'free') refusal to introduce into that System the Sub-Category of Freedom (or of the human-Individual, by definition free and historical, that is, 'political', 'social', or 'communitarian') has had disastrous and irreparable consequences. Indeed, by refusing to interpret the notion of Community qua human-Action, Kant was unable to turn it into a properly so called third Sub-category of his Category of Relation (= empirical-Existence). The notion of Community is, and can only be in Kant, a further development of his developments of the Sub-Categories of Substantiality and Causality. As such, the place allocated to the third Sub-category remains vacant in the Kantian categorial 'System'. Therefore, this purported 'System' is not, in fact, uni-total, and it is on account of its gap that it cannot be 'circular'. Unable to find (as Hegel does), in and through the discursive development of the third Sub-Category, which is absent {*inexistente*} for him, the notion of 'Judgement', Kant cannot *deduce* the development of the latter from his third Category, nor therefore from any of his Categories in general. The Table of the Categories, deduced from the Table of Judgements, is, therefore, in Kant, deduced from an irreducible or a non-deducible 'Fact' (which Kant himself regards as a mere 'historical Fact'), that is, from a 'Proof' that cannot be discursively de-monstrated or justified. Therefore, the number of the Categories, as well as their order, are not de-monstrated or deduced: just as well, Kant cannot de-monstrate that his Table of the Categories is *complete*, to the extent that it is rather a 'Rhapsody' of notions (to use Kant's own turn of phrase) and not a genuine categorial *System*, by definition complete and well ordered in a unique or even necessary way. And just as well did we have to await the arrival of Hegel to see that we were effectively dealing with a *System* properly so called, and that it suffices to fill up its only gap, or the only one entailed therein, to render it complete and circular, thus de-monstrating that it was such, by showing that it was legitimate to deduce (as Kant did) the complete and well-ordered Table of the Categories from the Table of Judgements because the latter was nothing else but the result of the complete and well-ordered discursive development of the last deducible Category from the first one, to the extent that the latter is the beginning of the discursive development of the basic notion that defines that which is common to every discourse whatever it may be, including Judgements in the proper/narrow sense of the term. In summary, to transform Kant's Table of the Categories into a genuine *System*, by definition, uni-total or circular, that is, *one* in itself (because of its *unique* order) and *total* in regard to its content, nothing should be *modified* therein. It suffices *to add* to the Kantian developments of the first three Categories (or the first nine Sub-categories) a *new* development of the Sub-category of Community, wherein it would be shown as the Totality of efficacious human-Action or as achieved universal History, which involves the uni-total Discourse, including, inter alia, the Kantian categorial System itself (without which this Discourse would not be uni-total in the sense that it would be unable to account for itself as Discourse or de-monstrate itself as discursive Truth). Thus completed, Kant's categorial System entirely covers not only the first Part of our exposition of the Hegelian *System of Knowledge* (where we develop Onto-logy, Energo-logy, and 'general' or 'abstract' Phenomenology), but also its two other Parts (where we develop 'applied' or 'concrete' Phenomeno-logy and analyse Discourse qua *Sense*). This is evident for the third Part, since the Category of Community now involves the notions of Discourse and discursive Truth, which will be set forth therein. But it is easy to see that the same applies to the second Part, where Discourse is presented not only (as in the third Part) qua objectively-(unreal) *Sense*, but also as Phenomenon (which is simultaneously living-Organism and inanimate-Thing, both of which are objectively-real in respect to their ground).

The Discourse of the human-Individual (who exists-empirically on an objectively-real ground) will be presented therein in opposition to the Non-discourse of the inanimate-Thing and the living-Organism (both of which the human-Individual implies and presupposes). And we will develop there these three fundamental notions (in the context of the 'applied' or 'concrete' Phenomeno-logy) through the introduction of the Principle of the 'Primacy' of the Present, the Past, and the Future {*Avenir*} (without being able, by so doing, to avail ourselves of Hegel himself). Now, one can show that the idea of this threefold 'Primacy' is, in fact and for us, already implied in Kant's categorial System as completed by Hegel regarding its discursive development.

Indeed, the Sub-category of Substantiality, or of thinglike empirical-Existence (Monad qua inanimate-Thing), is in fact defined by Kant as the Principle of Legality, which determines the ('necessary') mutual Relation of the Accidents of a Substance. Now, by applying to Substantiality what Kant says when he comments on Community (which is perfectly legitimate), one can see that what is at issue here is the Relation of *Simultaneity* (which is, moreover, obvious without any commentary). In our terminology, Kant is talking there about the *Primacy of the Present* (which allows the cognition of the Present to be derived both from that of the Past and the Future {*Avenir*}). As for the Sub-category of Causality, what is at stake here is most obviously the *Primacy of the Past* (which allows the cognition of the Future {*Avenir*} to be derived from the cognition of the Past, which in turn determines the Present). There remains the *Primacy of the Future* {*Avenir*} and, definitely, Kant does not speak of it since there is no such thing as a third Sub-category of empirical-Existence (= Relation) in his philosophy. But it is obvious that the third Sub-category in question cannot be 'essentially' distinguished from the first two unless it refers to the Primacy of the Future {*Avenir*} (which allows the cognition of the Present determined by the Past to be derived from that of the Future {*Avenir*}). And, indeed, the third Sub-category introduced by Hegel (no less than a *novel* interpretation of the Kantian notion of Community) refers to said Primacy (which Hegel moreover updated in another context and without seeing that it pertained to an essentially and exclusively *human* Principle), since it pertains to *free* human-Action, that is, the one carried out in function of a Project, which is nothing else but the realised consciousness of the *Future* {*Avenir*} in view of its active or acting insertion in the Present; the latter being, for that matter, the Present of the living-Organism which is the Human being, and which is necessarily determined by its biological Past.

In short, it suffices to introduce the notion of the Human being (or the notion of the human in the human being) into Kant's categorial System so that it can be better used as a basis for the entire Hegelian *System of Knowledge*, which we are setting forth right away, albeit summarily (provided that the Sub-category of Causality is interpreted as referring only to the notion of the living-Organism and not to that of the inanimate-Thing, subjected to the Principle of Legality alone, which corresponds to the Sub-category of Substantiality, or to that of the human-Individual, which corresponds to the Hegelian Sub-category of Community or Freedom). Now, obviously it suffices to eliminate from the Kantian System any implication of the (contra-dictory) notion of the Thing-in-itself for that introduction of the notion of the Human being to be necessary and unavoidable. Indeed, it is impossible to deny the fact of the latter's empirical-existence, not least because this would lead to the negation of the very fact of Discourse (which would be contra-dictory insofar as it is being denied *discursively*). And if it is no longer possible to refer this 'empirical' fact to a Thing-in-itself (as in the case of the immortal-Soul of Plato–Kant), one is, indeed, obliged to include it in the categorial System which encompasses virtually the *ensemble* of Discourse, even if the latter is *completely* developed in such a way that it is uni-total or circular or *true* in the proper and strong sense of the word.

Moreover, the complete overcoming of the notion of the Thing-in-itself would leave the discourse to which it refers, and which Kant develops in the mode of As-if, without an object. And then it would be possible to eliminate that mode completely and to treat the System in its entirety in the mode of Truth. It would then be required to introduce therein not only the notion of the human-Individual, but also that of the living-Organism. Now, in doing so, one would easily realise that the Principle of Teleology (or Freedom) is valid only for the Human being, while the living-Organism is completely determined by the Principle of Causality alone (to the extent that the Principle of Legality determines the inanimate-Thing, as well as the Organism considered qua Thing and therefore also the Human being qua living-Organism).

Eventually, it suffices to eliminate the notion of the Thing-in-itself for Kant's categorial System to be somewhat transformed by itself into a Hegelian categorial System, which is also ours.

Indeed, Kant's first three Categories exhaust Hegel's categorial System. Since the latter is circular, or even uni-total or closed in upon itself, the question arises as to what is the fourth and last Kantian Category which, in Kant, seems *to be added* to the first three and *goes beyond* them, while, in the Hegelian transposition, the (new) third Sub-category of the third Category leads back to the origin of the entire System, in such a way that there is no longer any room left for any fourth Category whatsoever.

Now, if one refers to the development of the fourth Kantian Category into three Sub-Categories and into Principle, one notices that, irrespective of Kant's own commentary thereon, the Category in question does not add anything to the three preceding ones and in no way does it go beyond them taken as a whole. In fact, the three so-called Sub-Categories of this purported fourth Category are only new presentations of the first three Categories of Quantity, Quality, and Relation, to the extent that these presentations can, moreover, be found, as they stand, in Hegel.

Kant's 'fourth' Category is that of 'Modality'. Just like the third, it is 'dynamic' in the sense that, unlike the first two 'mathematical' Categories, it supposedly refers to the 'Existence' of the thinglike-Objects of the Intuition and not to those Objects themselves. But, in this context, the term 'Existence' (*Existenz*) must be taken in the broadest sense of the word, for the development of this Category into three Sub-Categories shows that Kant distinguishes three modes of 'Existence' which are: 'Possibility', 'real-Presence' (*Dasein*), and 'Necessity'. These modes of 'Existence' are respectively 'Correlated' to: 'Impossibility', 'Non-being' (*Nichtsein*), and 'Contingency'. Kant notes (without further emphasis) that these 'Correlates' appear only in 'dynamic' Categories, since they do not appear in their 'mathematical' counterparts, and he contents himself with adding that this difference between the two groups of Categories must be 'grounded in the nature of the Understanding' (cf. III, 95, 31–96, 2).

All these remarks call for an interpretation, for they show that Kant himself was aware of the real situation only in a rather vague way.

To begin with, Kant's text (III, 95, 31–2) is not clear as to whether the 'Correlates' would appear only in the fourth Category which is part of the 'dynamic' Group, or in the Group as a whole, that is, also in the third Category. Now, in Kant, the third Sub-Category of the latter (Community or Inter-action) certainly does not have a 'Correlate'. As for the first two Sub-Categories, one may say, if one will, that Subsistence is the 'Correlate' of Inherence, and that Dependence is the 'Correlate' of Causality. But, clearly, these two 'Correlates' have nothing to do with those of the fourth Category, wherein the 'Correlate' is a *negation* of the corresponding

Sub-Category. Now, in the first Category, Plurality is unquestionably a *negation* of Unity (or vice versa) and, in the second, Negation is (as its very name indicates) the *negation* of Reality. It is therefore difficult to see why Kant does not want to admit the presence of a 'Correlate' in *all* his Categories. In fact, the first two Sub-Categories of the first two ('mathematical') Categories are two couplets of 'Correlates', while the third Sub-Category of the third ('dynamic') Category is no less deprived of 'Correlates' than the third Sub-Categories of the first two ('mathematical') Categories (which is rather natural, since, to the extent that it is the Synthesis of the first two, the third Sub-Category is a Totality).

In reality, by discovering the 'Correlates' (grounded in 'the nature of the Understanding'), Kant does nothing more than rediscover the discursive fact already discovered by Plato (and which he opposes to Parmenides), namely, the fact that one cannot say what a thing *is* without saying, through this very fact, what it *is not*. Hence, in particular (or in general), one cannot, as Kant remarks, speak of Possibility without speaking of Impossibility, nor of real-Presence (*Dasein*) without speaking of 'real-Absence' (*Nichtsein*), nor of Necessity without speaking of its 'negation', which Kant calls Contingency (*Zufälligkeit*). Consequently, the presence of 'Correlates' in the 'fourth' Category is certainly not a sufficient reason, nor even a reason to begin with, to see therein a *sui generis* Category, distinct from the first three.

Conversely, there are reasons, which Kant himself (implicitly) admits, that make it imperative to see in the three Sub-Categories of this purported 'fourth' Category a mere resumption of the three preceding Categories. Indeed, the Principle of the Analogies of Experience, which corresponds to the third Category, speaks of the *necessary* Connection {*Liaison*} of Perceptions. It is therefore obvious that, for Kant himself, the couplet of 'Correlates', Necessity–Contingency, which constitutes the third Sub-Category of the fourth Category, characterises, in fact, the third Category as such, since, by all accounts, the link between the 'Substance' and its 'Attributes' is, for Kant, a *necessary* one, to the extent that 'Causality' is always assimilated by Kant to 'Necessity', while 'Community' is expressly defined qua *necessary*-co-existence (cf. III, 185, note). As regards the 'Correlate' of the second Sub-Category of the fourth Category, which Kant calls 'Non-being' (*Nichtsein*), it is, by all accounts, identical to the second Sub-Category of the second Category, called 'Negation'.

For, while commenting on this second Sub-Category, Kant clearly says that 'Negation' (which is '= 0') is the *absence* of the Reality that corresponds to the presence of a (positive) Sensation (that is, different from zero). Surely, the term 'real-Presence' (*Dasein*) intervenes in the commentary on the 'Analogies', which correspond to the third and not second Category (cf. III, 159, 34–7). But, in Kant, the meaning of this term is wavering and it is clear that, in the context of the 'fourth' Category, the couplet real-Presence–Non-Being is equivalent to the couplet Reality–Negation (= 0) of the second Category and consequently characterises this second Category as such. Indeed, Kant expressly says that the real-Presence of Phenomena may not be recognised a priori (III, 160, 4), which means, in Kant, that it is 'given' in 'Sensation'. Now, that which 'corresponds' to 'Sensation' is precisely '[Objective-] Reality'.

It remains to see what the couplet of the 'Correlates' Necessity–Contingency is, to the extent that it constitutes the first Sub-Category of the fourth Category. Now, Kant says that the first two Principles, which correspond to the first two Categories, pertained to Phenomena concerning their only *Possibility* (III, 160, 11). At first sight, the couplet in question characterises then the *two* 'mathematical' Categories. But it is obvious that the second Category pertains, in fact, in Kant, to [objective-] Reality and not to 'Possibility alone'. Consequently, in fact, the couplet Possibility–Impossibility does not characterise the first Category as such.

In summary, and to put it in our terminology, while Kant's 'Category of Modality' is only a fourth Category distinct from the first three ones, it is *the* Category (= Concept) *as* such, which governs the *totality* of Discourse whatever it may be. It is developed discursively in three 'dialectical stages', which are the three 'modalities' of Discourse or the three fundamental 'Categories' (or 'constituent elements' of the Concept) of given-Being (= Quantity), of objective-Reality (= Quality) and of empirical-Existence (= Relation), to the extent that the Human being is able to *speak* effectively only of that which *is*, of that which is *objectively-real*, and of that which *exists-empirically*. Now, in Kant (if not for Kant) as in and for us, given-Being is discursively defined by the pure Difference between Possibility (= Being = Positing) and Impossibility (= Nothingness = Negation), while objective-Reality is discursively defined as the irreducible-Opposition of the Real (= Positive) and the Unreal (= Negative). As for empirical-Existence (= Relation), Kant characterises it by the couplet Necessity–Contingency, that is, in and for him, Necessity–Non-necessity. Now, in Kant's philosophical System, Non-necessity is always identified with 'Freedom'. If, therefore, following Hegel, one puts in place of the purported third Sub-Category of the third Category (= empirical-Existence) of Kant ('Inter-action') the category of 'Community' implying *human* or *teleological* 'community', that is, the Sub-Category of free Action or 'Freedom', one may correct Kant's 'categorial' terminology in such a way that it is brought into line with his System in its entirety, by characterising the third Category as such by the couplet of 'Correlates': Necessity–Freedom. And we will see afterward that in our work as well, as in Hegel's, empirical-Existence is discursively defined by the qualitative-Distinction (or Relation) between the Existent (= Positivity) and the Inexistent (= Negativity), the Inexistant being the *Project* as such (= Primacy of the *Future* {*Avenir*}), that is, precisely the Act of Freedom.

Interpreted in this manner, Kant's categorial System becomes circular, that is, uni-total or truly 'systematic', to the extent that the fourth Category is a mere return of the first three, taken as 'Modalities of Discourse'. But this 'return' from the third Category to the first one through the mediation {*truchement*} of the 'fourth' is possible only if one interprets the latter as the ('dialectical') discursive development of the third Sub-Category of the third Category, understood as the specifically anthropological Sub-Category of the free Action. Now, this is precisely what Kant himself neither does nor is willing to do (for reasons that I have substantiated in the third general Introduction of the System of Knowledge). Thus, his 'Table of the Categories' is a *System* of Categories, by definition circular or uni-total, only in fact or for us (following Hegel), but {not} for Kant himself, who can only present it as a deduction from the 'Table of Judgements', which must accept as an 'irreducible given' or a Platonic–Cartesian 'Proof', barely 'justified' by Kant through the fact of its persistence throughout the history of Philosophy.

However, the fact remains that Kant was the first to present a 'Table of Categories', which is, *in fact*, a genuine *System* and which becomes such for us, that is, for him, as soon as one introduces therein the Sub-Category of Freedom or of the Project, for which a place was reserved by Kant himself, even though he camouflaged the vacancy of the 'reserved place' by the pseudo Sub-Category of 'Inter-action', which is, in fact, only a resumption of his Sub-Category of 'Subsistence' (to the extent that 'Substance' is interpreted as the 'Monad of Monads').

Furthermore, Kant's commentaries on the fourth Category and its discursive development into Sub-Categories and in Principle, verify our interpretation.

Let us first take the first Sub-Category, that is, Possibility:

Here is how Kant defines it in the 'Schematism':

> The [temporal] Schema of Possibility is the harmony/adequation (*Zusammenstimmung*) of the Synthesis of different Representations with the conditions of *Time in general* (e.g. [the fact that] opposites in one thing cannot be simultaneously, but only successively); [this Schema is] thus the determination (*Bestimmung*) of the Representation of a Thing at *whatever Time*. (III, 138, 9–13)

Surely, for Kant, the 'Schemata' are nothing else but *a priori* determinations of *Time* according to *Rules* (III, 138, 26–7), which are precisely the Categories. Therefore, they are applicable only to the Phenomenon (in the Kantian sense of this word) and not to Being as such, which is, for Kant, *non-temporal* Thing-in-itself. But, for us, insofar as we eliminate the Thing-in-itself, given-Being itself is nothing else but the [Spatio-]*temporality* which *is*. For us, being 'at any Time whatsoever' is therefore precisely given-Being as such and the 'determinations of time as such' are rightly the 'determinations' of that given-Being. Thus, for us, Kantian 'Possibility' does nothing other than characterise given-Being in its difference from objective-Reality and empirical-Existence. It has, besides, always been agreed to admit that all that *is* in any manner whatsoever is, on account of that very fact alone, '*possible*'. However, in our time, one would still have qualms about saying that *all* that is possible *is*, on account of this very fact, *possible* being (that is, non-impossible). But Aristotle had already rightly pointed out that what is *never* and *nowhere* is, by definition, *impossible* rather than 'possible'. Now, if Being is the Spatio-temporality which *is* in the *Totality* of its being, it is obvious that, as we have said in our Onto-logy, given-Being *is* the Possible, to the extent that the Impossible is Nothingness or the Nothing.[28]

---

28   Here, again, Kant is also 'Aristotelian', and he admits that the *spatio-temporal* Possible does not go further than the Objectively-real (as he says in the relevant context,

Moreover, Kant himself says that the Impossible is the Nothing:

> The thinglike-Object of a Concept that contradicts itself is [the] *Nothing* [= Nothingness] (*Nichts*), because the Concept is *nothing* [in this case], [it is] *the Impossible*, like for instance a rectilinear figure with *two sides* (*nihil negativum*). (III, 232, 33–5)

But this does not imply, *a contrario*, that Kantian 'Possibility' is an outright 'Non-contradiction', in the sense of pre-Kantian so-called 'formal' logic, which believes it can do without Spatio-temporality. Indeed, in the three 'Postulates of empirical Thought in general', which qua 'Principles' correspond to the three Sub-Categories of the fourth Category, the definition of Possibility in the first Postulate is presented as follows:

I. FIRST POSTULATE

> Whatever coincides (*über-einkommt*) with the *formal* conditions of *Experience* (in accordance with [spatio-temporal] *Intuition* and Concepts [= Categories]) is *possible*. (III, 185, 22–3)

Possibility must, therefore, conform to the 'conditions' of Spatio-temporality in general. Therefore, in Kant's as in our own work, there is identity between *all* that is possible and all that *is* qua *spatio-temporal*, given that the Impossible, for Kant, is 'outside' of *Spatio-temporality*, that is, for us, 'outside' of given-Being and thus, as in Kant, Nothingness (= Nothing).

Things become clearer if one refers to the commentary on this first Postulate, where Kant says, among other things, this:

> That no *Contradiction* must be contained/implied in such a Concept [to wit, in the Concept of a *possible* thinglike-Object] is, to be sure, a necessary *logical* condition [in the sense of traditional 'formal Logic']; but it is far from *sufficient* for the *objective-Reality* of the Concept, that

---

while *in fact* having in mind what we call empirical-Existence [and what is, in him, *in fact* the 'Necessary']). [For us: Possible (= given-Being) = Necessary (= empirical-Existence) > Objectively real]. But Kant also understands the 'Possible' as the (non-spatio-temporal) 'Thing-in-itself': thus, according to him, the Possible (in a broad sense) extends beyond the (spatio-temporal) Real (cf. III, 195, 24–197, 4).

is, for the *Possibility* of such a *thinglike-Object* as is thought through the Concept [in question]. Thus [for example] there is no ['logical'] contradiction in the concept of a figure that is *enclosed* between two straight lines, for the concepts of two straight lines and their intersection involves/contains no negation of a figure; rather *the Impossibility* rests not on the Concept in itself, but [on] the *Construction* of the Concept in Space, that is, [on] the conditions of Space and its determinations; now, these determinations, in turn, have their *objective Reality*, that is, they pertain to *possible* Things, because they contain in themselves *a priori* the Form of Experience in general [which is necessarily *spatio* (-temporal)]. (III, 187, 4–15)

Obviously, the 'objective-Reality' that Kant is talking about here has nothing to do with our objective-Reality. It is simply the Sense of 'something' 'referred' to as Notion (this 'something' being something other than the Phenomenon that incarnates Sense). Here, this 'something' (that Kant wrongly calls 'Reality' or 'Thing' or 'thinglike-Object') is, by definition, 'objective', but this is just an 'objective' *Possibility*. Now, according to Kant, this 'Possibility' is nothing else but the inclusion in Spatio-temporality in *general* (within which 'Experience' also lies, that is, Perception 'revealing' empirical-Existence through its trans-formation into a Phenomenon). It is therefore indeed a question of the Spatio-temporality that *is* (but taken as *being* {*étant*} only, and not as objectively-real or existing empirically), that is, in our terminology, it is a question of given-Being. Accordingly, Kant's 'Possibility' coincides with our given-Being, to the extent that his 'Impossibility' is (at least in *this* context) the 'transcendent' with reference to Spatio-temporality [and hence, for us, to given-Being], of which he says (in agreement with us in *this* context) that it is *nothing* or that it is *Nothingness* (*Nichts*) [even though, in Kant, this 'impossible Nothing' is *moreover* defined discursively as 'Thing-in-itself'].[29]

---

29 Obviously, the contradiction between the two cited passages, concerning a figure enclosed by two straight lines, is only apparent. In the second passage, Kant explicitly speaks of 'logical' contradiction (in the sense of Traditional 'formal Logic') and denies it, while in the first passage he (implicitly) speaks of 'objective' or 'thinglike', that is, spatio-temporal contradiction, which he also admits in the second passage. The Kantian Impossible (= Nothingness) is therefore indeed the Non-spatio-temporal and not the Contra-dictory in the so-called 'formal sense of this word'.

Let us now cite a few passages excerpted from various commentaries on the second Sub-Category of the 'fourth' Category:

The [temporal] Schema of objective-Reality (*Wirklichkeit*) is existence [= being] (*Dasein*) at a *determinate Time*. (III, 138, 14)

2. SECOND POSTULATE

That which is *bound* up {*en* liaison} (*zusammenhängt*) with the *material* conditions of Experience (of Sensation) is objectively real. (III, 185, 24–5)

The Postulate [which demands] to cognise the *objective-Reality* of Things requires *Perception*, and thus Sensation, of which one is conscious; not, it is true, precisely, [an] *immediate* [Perception] of the thinglike-Object *itself* the existence of which [= objective reality] must be cognised, but still [of] the *connection* {*liaison*} (*zusammenhang*) of the said object with some *objectively real* Perception, in accordance with the Analogies of Experience [which correspond to the third Category, that is, to empirical-Existence], which present (*darlegen*) all *real* (*reale*) links (*Verknüpfung*) in one [single] experience in general.

In the mere *Concept* of a Thing, no characteristic of its [possible, objectively-real or empirical] existence can be encountered/found (*angetroffen*) at all. (III, 189, 23–30)

The mere, but *empirically* determined, Consciousness of my own [empirical-] existence proves the [empirical-] existence [as well as the objective-Reality] of thinglike-Objects in Space *outside* me.

PROOF

I am conscious of my [empirical-] existence as [being] *determined* (*bestimmt*) in *Time*. All *determination* of *Time* presupposes something *permanent* (*beharrliches*) in Perception. Now, this permanent cannot be something *in me*, since, precisely, my own [empirical-] existence in Time must first *be* determined by *this* Permanent. Thus, the Perception of this Permanent is possible only through a *Thing outside* me and not through the mere *Representation* of a Thing outside me. (III, 191, 18–28)

If, on the contrary, we want to think [empirical-] Existence (*Existenz*) [or objective-Reality (or even given-Being, for it is, in this context, a question of God's existence)] for the *pure* Category alone [that is, without 'schematising' or 'spatio-temporalising' this Category], then it is no wonder that we cannot indicate any character [to help] distinguish this *Existence* from mere *Possibility*. (III, 402, 22–5)

These texts, without even being interpreted, clearly show that, for Kant, the second Sub-Category, characterised by the couplet of 'Correlates' Existence (*Dasein*)–Non-being (*Nichtsein*), is nothing else but our notion of objective-Reality, which we were able to identify with what Kant calls the Category of 'Quality', to the extent that it is his second Category. And one can see that, for Kant as for us, objective-Reality is 'given' or 'revealed' not through Perception that 'gives' or 'reveals' a thinglike-Object in an 'immediate' or 'direct' manner, that is, in its empirical-existence or qua Phenomenon (in the sense *we* ascribe to this term), but through the mere 'connection with the *material conditions* of Experience or Sensation'. It is therefore a question of something *common* to *all* Perceptions or 'Sensations' upon whose 'content' the said something does not depend. And if we also consider the fact that this something in question is a 'Permanent' that determines self-Consciousness independently from its 'content', we find it difficult to deny that Kant has *in fact* in view what we call Tonal Variation. Without the Sensation of such Variation, the meanings of the terms 'objective-Reality' and 'Possibility' would be indistinguishable from one another to the extent that the latter is only a derivative from the meaning of the word 'given-Being' 'revealed' through the Feeling of Well or Ill-being.

Except that, in certain cited texts, Kant speaks of the *totality* of Experience, determined by the 'Analogies', that is, by the third Category, which is for us, empirical Existence. In *those* texts, the term 'Existence' signifies then, in our terminology, empirical-Existence and not objective-Reality. Now, it is, *in fact*, the third and not the second Sub-Category of the 'fourth' Category that corresponds to the third Kantian Category.

This should not concern us unduly, for, in this instance, we are dealing with the frequent conflation of objective-Reality and empirical-Existence, which is quite common not only in Kant, but also in all philosophers [who could not benefit from the lessons of twentieth-century Physics]. For the direct interpretation of the commentaries on the third Sub-Category (= Necessity-Contingency) clearly shows *that in fact* it is indeed the latter, and not the second one, that corresponds to the notion of empirical-Existence, which Kant calls the Category of Relation.

To make this clear, let us first cite a few texts:

Necessity is nothing other than the *Existence* [= objective-Reality, since the context of the cited passage presents every third Sub-Category as a synthesis of the first two categories, and besides, what Kant says shows, however, that 'Existence' signifies here 'empirical-Existence'] (*Existenz* [= *Dasein*]) that is given by *Possibility itself*. (III, 96, 11, 13)

The [temporal] Schema of Necessity is the Existence [= being, if one considers the terminology of the Schema of objective-Reality, but *in fact* = empirical-existence] (*Dasein*) of a thinglike-Object at *all Times* [since the Schema of objective-Reality is *being* in a *determined Time*]. (III, 138, 15–16)

3. THIRD POSTULATE

That whose *connection* {*liaison*} (*Zusammenhang*) with the Objectively-real [= the empirically-Existent] is determined in accordance with the *general* conditions of Experience is (exists (*existiert*) [-empirically]) *necessary*(ily). (III, 186, 1–2)

Finally, as far as the third Postulate is concerned, it pertains to *material* Necessity in [empirical-] *Existence* (*Dasein*), and not [to] the merely *formal* and *logical* connexion (*Verknüpfung*) of Concepts . . . the Necessity of [empirical-] Existence (*Existenz*) can thus never be cognised from *Concepts*, but rather always [cognised] only from the connexion, in accordance with *general* Laws of Experience, with that which is *perceived*. Now, there is no [empirical-] Existence (*Dasein*) that could be cognised as *necessary* under the condition of other given Phenomena except the existence of Effects from given

Causes, in accordance with Laws of Causality. Thus, it is not the existence (*Dasein*) of *Things* (Substances), but of their *state* (*Zustandes*) of which alone we can cognise the *Necessity*, namely from *other* states, which are given in Perception, in accordance with *empirical* Laws of Causality ... *All* that *happens* {*se produit*} (*geschieht*) is hypothetically *necessary*; that is the basic proposition (*Grundsatz*) that subjects *Change* in the World to a *Law*, that is, to a *Rule* of *necessary* [empirical-] existence (*Dasein*), without which not even *Nature* itself would take place (*Stattfinden*). (III, 193, 25–7; 193, 32; 194, 8; 194, 20–4)

These passages should be *interpreted*, for they attest to the 'classical' confusion between the notions of objective-Reality and empirical-Existence, not to say between these two notions and the notion of given-Being. An interpretation is, besides, all the more indispensable because without it, the cited passages would appear to contradict one another.

Indeed, if we limit ourselves only to the 'Schema', we might be led to believe that Kant calls 'necessary' the being (*Dasein*) of an *isolated* thing-like-Object *co-eternal* with Time (that lasts as long as does Time itself).

Let us first see what the term *Dasein*, to which Kant resorts in this context, in fact signifies. In the 'Schema of objective-Reality' (*Wirklichkeit*), Kant says that 'objective-Reality is the *Dasein* in a *determined* Time (*in einer bestimmten Zeit*)'. Here, *Dasein* can only signify 'given-Being': the being-given at a *determined* moment of Time is objectively-real. Now, in the context of the 'fourth' Category, the given Being is defined as Possibility (*Möglichkeit*), which is defined by its 'Schema' as 'the determination (*Bestimmung*) of the Representation (*Verstellung*) of a Thing (*Dinges*) at *any* Time' (*zu irgend einer Zeit*). Given-Being (= Possibility) is therefore the being-given (the 'given-ness' of being is defined by Kant as '[any] Determination of [any] Representation)' of *any* 'Thing' *whatsoever* (in the general sense of 'entity') *at any* moment of Time.

Given-Being is therefore common to *all* that *is* in any manner *whatsoever*, *wherever*, and *whenever*. And the Being-given (= Possibility) is that given-Being taken in the spatio-temporal *totality*. But the given-Being at a *determined* moment is *objectively-real*. It therefore seems that the *spatial totality* of given-Being is *objectively-real* insofar as it is given at a *determined* moment in Time, to the extent that this moment is, moreover, *arbitrary* (in regard to its 'content' or its 'determination', as Kant says, as in regard to its 'situation' in the total temporal duration). Objective-reality is therefore that which allows (any) given moment of Time to *be opposed* to all the other moments: one can say that it 'determines' the (instantaneous) Present in opposition to the ensemble of the Past and the Future {*Avenir*}. But this present is *arbitrary*, in such a way that *any* (instant) moment of Time and hence *every* moment in Time *may* be and therefore *is* the *present* moment. Just like given-Being, objective-Reality is therefore common to *all* that *is* wherever it may be and whenever it may be, except that being in the Present is here *opposed* in an *irreducible* manner to being in the Past and in the Future {*Avenir*} (while the merely possible and not the objectively-real given-Being is everywhere and *always* the *same*, that is, *homogeneous* in itself or *continuous*). One can therefore say that objective-reality *maintains* itself in identity with itself, *despite* the *difference* (= irreducible opposition) between the moments of Time during which it thus *maintains* itself. Objective-Reality is then the *totality* of Space-time where the Past and the Future {*Avenir*} are (irreducibly) *opposed* to the Present *whatever it may be*. And this Present is given or 'revealed' as objectively-real presence in and through Sensation, as Kant says (or as Sensation of Tonal Variation, in our terminology).

In the 'Schema' of Necessity, the term *Dasein* cannot signify 'objective-reality', seeing that the latter refers to *one determined* moment, while Necessity refers to *all* the moments at once. It is therefore a question of the term 'being' taken either in the very general sense of 'subsisting' (an entity being capable of 'subsisting' as given being, as objective-reality, or, lastly, as empirical-existence), or in the precise sense of 'given-being'. In the latter case, given-being would be *necessary* if it is the given-being of a *particular* and *isolated* thinglike-Object (*das Dasein eines Gegenstandes*) that lasts as long as Time itself does (*zu aller Zeit*). Objective-Reality would therefore be the *spatial-totality* of given-Being (= Possibility) as it subsists at the *present* moment, while Necessity would be the *temporal totality* of *isolated* thinglike-Objects, which are coeternal with Time.

But this interpretation is rendered untenable by the statement of the third 'Postulate' which expressly says that the 'necessary' is *Bound up* {*en Liaison*} (*Zusammenhang*) with the Objectively-real *taken as a whole* (*mit dem Wirklichen*), to the extent that this Bond {*Liaison*} is in conformity with the '*general* conditions of Experience' *taken as a whole* (*nach allgemeinen Bedingung der Erfahrung*). And Kant emphatically states that the 'Bond' in question is 'material' and not 'logical' in the sense of 'formal'. Far from being *isolated* from everything else, the thing-like-Object is therefore 'necessary' only in and through these *bonds* with *all* that is not it; Kant says: in and by these connections {*liaisons*} with the *Objectively-real* taken in bloc. If one takes him literally, this means that *only objective-Reality* can be 'necessary' and that *any* objective-reality is *necessary*: the *Present* (or, if one will, the 'content' of a 'present' moment) is, by definition or necessarily, that is, everywhere and always (since *every* moment of Time was, is or will be 'present'), *objectively-real*, and the maintaining (during *all* of the duration of Time) of that Present (or of the spatial totality of its 'content') in *total* identity with itself is *necessary*. But one can take the words *mit dem Wirklichen* in a broader sense, one which is, moreover, consistent with what Kant himself says thereon in his commentary, wherein he speaks not of objective-Reality in the precise sense of the word (that is, of 'intensive Magnitude' in his own terminology), but of that which is 'given in and through Perception (*Wahrnehmung*), that is, in our terminology, of empirical-Existence (which he himself calls 'Relation'). Necessity would then be the *permanent* 'Bond', as far as its *duration* goes, with (or, which is the same thing: of the) *spatial* or *extended* totality of that which *exists-empirically*. Thus, Kant's 'Necessity' would be nothing else but the *totality* of the *extended-Duration* of *all* that *exists-empirically*. Now, for us (as in Kant himself for that matter), *the* extended-Duration-that-exists-empirically is nothing else but empirical-Existence per se. Consequently, '*empirical*-existence' and '*necessary*-existence' would be two equivalent terms as far as their meaning {*sens*} goes, along with the terms 'Necessity' and 'empirical-Existence' (= 'Relation'). Now, this is precisely what Kant admits when he says (in the cited passages) that *all* that *happens* {*se produit*} (*geschieht*) is hypothetically [that is, by definition or 'necessarily', that is, everywhere and always] *necessary* (III, 194, 20–1). For, in this context, the term *geschehen* has the very broad sense of *enduring* in Time qua spatially *extended*. But if, according to Kant, empirical-Existence is 'given' in Perception, this is precisely what he defines in the (cited) 'schema' of Possibility as the Determination of the Representation of any Thing [whatsoever, that is, of the 'Representation of *all* 'Things' whatever they may be] (III, 138, 12–13). Now, Possibility is this 'Determination' in *any* Time (*zu irgend einer Zeit*), that is, at *whichever* moment of Time and therefore throughout *all* the *duration* of Time. One can thus see that, for Kant, as for us, *all* that is *possible* exists-empirically by definition or *necessarily* (in any place of the Extent that endures and at any moment of extended-Duration), in the same way that *all* that exists-empirically is by definition or necessarily *possible* in such a way that the *totality* of given-Being *exists-empirically* and that the *totality* of empirical-Existence subsists in the mode of *given-Being*. But in *our* interpretation of the Kantian text, all that is *possible* is not, by definition or necessarily (that is, everywhere and always), *really present* or, if one will, does not necessarily have a *real Presence* (as the 'content' of a Present opposed to the Past and the Future {*Avenir*}, that is, as the 'content' of a present instant of Space-time), even though *all* that is really present is necessarily *possible* or *necessary* (in this sense that it *extends* spatially in its temporal presence and *endures* throughout its extent, its future becoming past after it was present). In other words, in *our* interpretation (even though Kant himself does not say so, without nevertheless denying it either), given-Being (= Spatio-temporality) and empirical-Existence (= extended-Duration) entirely 'overlap', while objective-Reality (= Space-time) is 'surpassed' by them (without itself being able to 'extend beyond' them) in such a way that what *is* and *exists-empirically* can be either objectively-*real* or objectively-*unreal*, to the extent that the objectively-*real* necessarily has to *be* (qua *given*) and *exist-empirically* [to the extent that empirical-Existence is the extended Duration of the (structured) 'content' of the (homogeneous or continuous) Spatio-temporality that *is* (by being given or revealed as Perceptual Feeling of Well or Ill-being), this 'content' being given or revealed (qua Phenomenon) in and through Perception (to the extent that objective-Reality reveals itself or is given as Sensation of the Tonal Variation of this same Perception, if any Variation there is)].

However, it might appear as if the interpretation that makes Possibility (= Quantity = given-Being) coincide with Necessity (= Relation = empirical-Existence) is not consistent with Kant's texts in the sense that therein he identifies Necessity with Causality alone (= second Sub-Category of the third Category) and not with the Category of Relation as such, that is, with the ensemble of these three Sub-Categories. And this in addition to the fact that Kant in one of the cited passages expressly denies the 'necessity' of *Things* taken as *Substances* while affirming it only regarding the 'State' (*Zustand*) of these 'Things' (cf. III, 194, 5–7).

One could therefore interpret the said passage in the sense that only the *Duration* of empirical-existence (or the 'content' of that duration) is *necessary*, while its *extension* (or the 'content' of that extension) would be *contingent*, in the sense that there would be no '*necessary* bond {*liaison*}' between the *simultaneous* constituent-elements of the empirically-existing extent as far as all 'bonds' between the 'Substance' and its 'Attributes' go [that is, in our terminology, between the constituent-elements of the structured-unity of a Monad], as those between the 'Substances' of the 'inter-acting Community' [that is, in our terminology, between the constituent-elements of the World (Cosmos) conceived as 'Monad of Monads' or structured-Totality)]. This interpretation would surely be consistent with the ideas of 'classical' or 'Newtonian' Physics to which Kant was very attentive [and rightly so, for that matter, because every Philosopher must take account and give an account of the *Physics* of their time, even if they reject the purportedly 'philosophical' ideas of *Physicists* in general and the contemporary ones in particular]. But, *in fact*, this interpretation leads to an untenable result (philosophically speaking) and it accords neither with the context in which the passage in question appears nor with what Kant otherwise says about the Sub-Categories of Subsistence and Community.

In fact, it is contra-dictory to say that a given 'configuration' at a (present) moment t_0 is *contingent*, while that which will be given at moment t_1 ('immediately consecutive' to moment t_0) is *necessary* in the sense that it is 'necessarily determined' by the 'configuration' given at moment t_0. For the moment t_1 is *arbitrary* (= whatsoever) and one can take the moment t_1 as 'initial' moment t_0. Otherwise, the configuration at moment t_1 ($= t_1$) is *contingent*, that is, random, and it follows that the 'anterior' configuration given at moment t_0 ($= t_1$) and considered as 'cause' may have *any* 'effect' *whatsoever*, in which case the very notion of 'Causality' will no longer make any sense. Or else this notion has a (true) meaning, in which case the configuration at moment t_1 is *necessary* in this sense that it is univocally 'determined' by the configuration given at moment t_0, in such a way that it *cannot* be otherwise than what it is in fact. Now, if the configuration is *necessary* and not *contingent* at moment t_1, it is so at moment t_0 as well, and at any moment whatsoever, that is, at *all* moments, since moment t_1 is *arbitrary*. The *momentary* (or *instantaneous*) *spatial* (or *extended*) configuration is therefore *necessary* at *any* moment of its *duration*, which precisely means that it is *necessary* in *all* the moments or in *all* its duration, in the same way that the necessity of the *duration* of a configuration, which is equal to the duration of its *necessity*, means precisely that it is *necessary* at *every* moment of this duration, that is, particularly, at the 'present' moment qua simultaneous or *spatial* configuration.

And this is exactly how Kant himself conceives things. Concerning firstly the 'connection' between the 'Substance' and its 'attributes' (*Accidenzen*), he could not obviously deny its *necessary* character; for otherwise, he would have returned from the (Greek) 'scientific' and 'philosophical' notion of the *Essence* to the magico-mythological [pre-] notion of the *Mana* [which becomes contra-dictory as soon as one develops it discursively].[30]

Indeed, to say that it is not *necessary*, that it is *contingent* that a cat has legs, for example, is to admit that one and the same 'Mana' can be incarnated in a cat and a snake, that is, in any Animal or in anything in general, which would result in the denial of the very possibility of discursive *Truth* and therefore of Philosophy and every 'Natural Science' whatsoever [unless one admits that this Mana itself is revealed by a Discourse susceptible of becoming circular or uni-total, which is, for us, as in Kant, the case for Human beings and them *alone*]. Obviously, Kant does not think anything of the sort. He even finds it dangerous (although discursively unavoidable) to *distinguish* the 'Substance' from its 'Accidents' and to attribute to the latter a particular or separate empirical-existence (*besonderes Dasein*). For him, one speaks in a more precise and correct manner if one designates an Accident only by the mode (*Art*) in which (*wie*) the Substance's empirical-existence (*Dasein*) is positively determined (*bestimmt*) (cf. III, 165, 10–26).

---

30   Undoubtedly, this notion is applicable to the Human being (but not to the Thing or the Organism). It remains nonetheless contra-dictory: 'Human beings are what they are not and are not what they are', says Hegel. But *this* Contra-diction is precisely Negativity that exists-empirically, that is, the Freedom that (actively) contra-dicts the (Essence-endowed) Given whatever it may be. Negativity is therefore Contra-diction, that is, the Impossible or Nothingness (which *is* insofar as it is *identical* with Being and *exists-empirically* insofar as it *annihilates* the Given, but which is necessarily, that is, everywhere and always, objectively-unreal).

The 'link' between the Substance and its Attributes is therefore, in Kant, as little *contingent* as it is possible, since the latter are integrally formed with the former, to the extent that their ensemble is nothing else but the Substance per se, which is nothing outside of its Attributes.

As for 'Community', Kant defines it as 'Inter-action', that is, as reciprocal *Causality* of Substances (cf. III, 96, 10–11), and he expressly says that the World taken as a whole (*Weltganze*), which is the Community of all *simultaneous* Substances, is a Whole made of Parts whose connexion (*Verknüpfung*) (Inter-action of the Manifold) [is] *necessary* by the mere fact of *Simultaneity* (*schon um des Zugleichseins willen*) (cf. III, 185, note).

It is, moreover, obvious that the refusal to extend the notion of Necessity to that of Community (in the Kantian sense of the word, that is, to the notion of the 'simultaneous' structure of the 'World taken as a whole' or of the Cosmos) would have the same consequences as the refusal to apply it to the Kantian notion of 'Subsistence'. Indeed, saying that it is not necessary that a cat lives on dry land rather than in water or in the air, or that it feeds on animal flesh and not vegetation, or that it is hot in the equator and cold in the poles, or that there are no rivers on the sun (and this not because it *was* too hot but because it is so *at this moment*), etc., is to abandon the very notion of the Essence and therefore of the discursive *Truth* and to return to the magico-mythological Mana which supposedly allows everything not only to *become*, but also to *be* anything whatsoever. It is therefore quite natural that Kant applies the notion of Necessity also to that of 'Community', even though sometimes it sounds as if he wanted to restrict it to the notion of 'Causality' alone.

Be that as it may, it is obvious that, in Kant, the Sub-Category of 'Necessity' overlaps entirely not only with the Sub-Categories of 'Causality' and 'Subsistence' but also with that of 'Community'. It thus overlaps with the ensemble of the (third) Category of 'Relation', which coincides with our notion of empirical-Existence, the latter being the Totality of *extended-Duration* [or, if one will, of the '*structured* content' that endures (while *changing*) and extends (while differentiating or diversifying itself) in Spatio-temporality].

If Kant's terminology is often somewhat wavering and if his texts warrant an *interpretation*, it is because he still confuses the notions of

'Legality' and 'Causality' as did all the Philosophers who were unable to benefit from the lessons drawn from the Physics of the twentieth century. But our interpretation has shown that it is *Legality* that Kant has *in fact* in mind. And he basically says so himself, in the last cited passage, where the purported 'Causality' (identified with 'Necessity') is finally defined as a *Rule* [= Law] of the *necessary* empirical-existence (*Dasein*), without which even *Nature* (= discursive Natural Science) would not be able to take place (*Stattfinden*) (cf. III, 194, 20–4). For this definition of the Kantian Category of 'Causality' could be used as an absolutely correct definition of the 'modern' notion of *Legality* (which is also ours). Kant's 'Necessity' is therefore nothing else but the 'Legality' that enables the discursive development (in a univocal way and without contra-diction) of any notion which 'refers' to the empirical-existence (= extended-given) of any inanimate-Thing whatever, as far as its *extended* 'structure' at a given moment of its duration goes, and equally in regard to the 'structure' of the total *duration* of its spatially structured unity or Monad, to the extent that the 'inanimate-Thing' is able to be the *Totality* of these Things, that is, the 'inorganic World' or the 'material Cosmos', that *we* distinguish from the '*living* Cosmos', alone subjected, according to us, to *Causality* strictly so called (which is the 'Primacy' of the *Past*, that is, of the action of the *Past* over the Future {*Avenir*} by way of the Present). Now, it is precisely the Phenomenon of Life (living-Organism) that is altogether excluded from consideration in the first *Critique* (and of which Kant speaks, in the third *Critique*, only in the mode of *As-if*).

For us, while speaking of Necessity Kant is only speaking *in fact* of *Legality* [which, according to us, is not valid for objective-Reality, nor, even less so, for given-Being], which *we* restrict to the domain of empirical-Existence (= extended-Duration) constituted by the inanimate-Thing. In any case, Kant himself wants to speak only of the inanimate-Thing (*material* Cosmos), for he expressly excludes from his considerations all that pertains to the living-Organism (*living* Cosmos) as to the human-Individual (*human* Cosmos). It is therefore not surprising that he does not find any room for that 'Contingency' which is, nonetheless, according to him, the discursively unavoidable 'Correlate' of 'Necessity' (and thus of 'Relation' [= empirical-Existence] with which this 'Necessity' is identified). He is reluctantly constrained to say that *all* that happens [= all that exists-empirically in the extended-Duration] is hypothetically [= by definition] *necessary* (III, 194, 20–1).

* * *

Broadly speaking, when Kant talks in the mode of Truth (as he does in all the texts presently under consideration), he admits that the domain constituted by given-Being (= Quantity) does not extend beyond the one constituted by objective-Reality (= Quality) and nor is it surpassed by it, in the same way that the domain constituted by the latter is not surpassed by nor does it itself extend beyond the domain that empirical-Existence (= Relation) constitutes, which Kant moreover limits merely to the inanimate-Thing, submitted to Necessity or Legality (= Causality) alone. Contingency is therefore, for Kant, identical to Impossibility, which itself is identical to Nothingness (= Nothing = Non-being; *Nichts*, *Nichtsein*). Under the circumstances, one might therefore ask what the *distinction* between the Possible, the Real, and the Necessary signifies, in and for Kant. We have seen, indeed, that concerning the Phenomenon (in the Kantian sense of this notion, which is used in a broad sense to refer to all that is spatio-temporal), the possible *coincides* entirely with the real, which, in turn, *coincides* entirely with the necessary. If Kant sets them apart from one another, it is only insofar as he applies these notions (in the As-if mode, it is true) to the Thing-in-itself, by definition non-spatio-temporal (in any sense whatsoever). It is therefore only in the context of the discursive development (in the As-if mode) of the notion [in fact contra-dictory] of the Thing-in-itself that the notions of the Possibility and Impossibility [= Contra-diction] of objective-Reality (or real-Presence) (= Existence; *Dasein*) and of the objective-Unreality (or real-Absence) (= Non-being; *Nichtsein*) of Necessity and Contingency (*Zufälligkeit*) [which then becomes 'Freedom' (*Freiheit*)] make *Sense*, in Kant, in the proper and strong sense of this word (that is, a 'content' *identical* to itself and *different* from all that is not it, discursively *developable without* contra-diction) (cf. III, 195, 24–197, 4).

Now, following Hegel, we eliminate the Kantian notion of the Thing-in-itself (that is, of Transcendence with reference to Spatio-temporality). Do we not then run the risk of finding ourselves in the same situation in which Kant found himself when he talked about what he calls 'Phenomenon'?

We have already seen (in the Onto-logy) and we will once again see (in the Energo-logy and the Phenomeno-logy) that this is not the case. To be sure, for us as for Kant, the domain constituted by given-Being does not extend beyond the one constituted by empirical-Existence, nor is it surpassed by it. But the domain constituted by objective-Reality is, in our work and [seemingly] contrary to Kant, more 'limited' than that of the given-Being-that-exists-empirically. In other words, we admit the empirical existence (and the given-being) of that which is objectively-*unreal*. Unreality has, therefore, in our work, a Meaning that it cannot have for Kant (when he brings this notion to bear on his 'Phenomenon' and not on his Thing-in-itself, to the extent that the latter is, for him, a *Nichtsein* in the sense of the second Sub-Category of his purported 'fourth' Category). We can then (discursively) *define* Reality (*the Dasein*) of this second Sub-Category by its *irreducible-opposition* to Unreality (to the extent that the 'opposition' in question constitutes precisely the 'objectivity' of that 'Reality'), which Kant cannot do, since, for him, Unreality coincides with Impossibility, that is, with Nothingness [and this is why he is right to speak of a Non-being, a *Nichtsein*], which is surely *different* from given-Being (taken as *Spatio*-temporality) but which is not *opposed* in an *irreducible* manner to objective-Reality (since it is also *identical* to given-Being, insofar as the latter is Spatio-*temporality*). We can thus (discursively) distinguish the Impossible (different from the Possible and defined as Contra-dictory or as Nothingness, which is *different* from Being) from the Unreal and, accordingly, define the latter (discursively) as the real-Absence of the Possible. Similarly, we can (discursively) define the Necessary as the empirical-existence of *objective-Reality* and distinguish it (discursively) from the Non-necessary, (discursively) defined as the empirical existence of the Unreal (which is, by definition, *possible*, to the extent that objective-Reality is the real Presence of the Possible) [the Non-necessary being thus something other than the Inexistent, which coincides with the Impossible (the latter is by definition the Unreal) and therefore with Nothingness, in such a way that if we wanted to identify the Inexistent with the Non-necessary (= Kant's Contingent), we would obtain the same 'identity' as Kant: Inexistent (= Contingent) = Unreal (= Non-being) = Nothingness (= Impossible), following which we would also obtain the 'Identity': empirical-Existence (= Necessity) = objective-Reality (= *Dasein*) = given-Being (= Possibility)].

In summary, the Kantian couplet of 'Correlates': Possibility–Impossibility is, for Kant and for us, the pure-Difference between Being and Nothingness, which is developed discursively in our Onto-logy; the couplet objective-Reality (*Dasein*)–Non-being (*Nichtsein*) is in Kant, *in fact* and *for us* [but probably *for him*], the irreducible-Opposition between objective-Reality and objective-Unreality, which is developed in our Energo-logy; finally, the couplet Necessity–Contingency is, *in our* work, but not *in Kant's* (insofar as at the very least he does not develop discursively, in the mode of As-if, his notion [in fact contra-dictory[31]] of the Thing-in-itself), the qualitative-Distinction, *inside* empirical-Existence (which *differs* from empirical-Inexistence, in the same way given-Being [=Possibility] purely and simply *differs* from Nothingness [=Impossibility], between Necessity and, not Contingency, but *Freedom*).

For, in the Hegelian *System of Knowledge,* there is an equally limited scope for Kantian 'Contingency' as in Kant's own philosophical System, insofar as the latter is developed in the mode of *Truth*. The notion of '*Contingency*' 'differs', in and for Kant, from that of Nothingness only insofar as Kant brings it to bear on the Thing-in-itself. But then, in his work as in ours, it is no longer a question of 'Contingency' but of 'Freedom' in the Judeo-Christian (and Hegelian) sense of this term.

Indeed, we have seen that it is impossible to separate 'necessity' with respect to duration and 'necessity' with respect to extension. Introducing Contingency in one would amount to introducing it in the other and doing this would, in turn, amount to coming back to the notion of the magico-mythological Mana which, to the extent that it is, by definition, Contra-dictory, may be developed discursively in whichever manner one wants, except into a circular or uni-total Discourse, to the extent that the latter alone is the discursive *Truth*.

As for the Judeo-Christian (and Kanto-Hegelian) notion of 'Freedom', it is surely analogous to that of the magico-mythological 'Mana', and, if one will, as contra-dictory as the latter, when considered and developed discursively in itself, since the notion of 'Freedom' can be defined as the possibility to be anything while remaining oneself, or, as Hegel

---

31 Our notion of 'Freedom' is, if one will, as *contra-dictory* as 'the Kantian Thing-in-itself' or the magico-mythological 'Mana'. It is this same Contra-diction that exists-empirically (by 'overcoming itself dialectically') qua Negativity or Freedom or free-Action (= Struggle → Work). What is specifically 'Hegelian' in our work is the affirmation that Contra-diction (= the Impossible = Nothingness) *is* and *exists-empirically* (while being *objectively unreal*) uniquely and exclusively as the Human-in-the-Human-being, that is, as actualised Freedom in and through the free-Action of Struggle → Work, which gives rise to Discourse (ultimately circular or uni-total), wherein Contra-dictions are 'overcome' qua 'dialectical movement', discursively revealing the human-Cosmos, where, eventually, Struggle → Work 'dialectically overcomes' the Contra-diction of Freedom.

says, not to be what one is and to be what one is not. Now, this is precisely what Kant does when he talks about Freedom as a Thing-*in-itself*, which is, by definition, *transcendent* in regard not only to extended-Duration and to Space-time, but even to Spatio-temporality in general, that is, detached and isolated from *all* that exists-empirically or is objectively-real and even from all that *is* simply qua being-*given* (to the flesh-and-blood Human being). Kant is therefore perfectly right not to speak of the Freedom-*Thing-in-itself* except in the mode of As-if, and his only (philosophical) mistake is to have camouflaged the *contra-dictory* character of this discourse (while insisting exclusively on the fact that *this As-if* discourse cannot contra-dict what is said in the mode of *Truth*). But Kant is wrong (even 'on a human level') for not introducing the notion of Freedom as a third Sub-Category in his third Category, that is, for not admitting the *empirical-existence* (or the extended-duration) of that Non-necessity which is for him, as it is for us and for every 'Judeo-Christian', human Freedom [this mistake being infinitely more serious, philosophically as well as 'humanly' speaking, than his exclusion of the notion of the living-Organism, which is, in fact, alone susceptible of being developed discursively into a notion of Causality (the latter remaining, for this reason, in Kant, vague in itself and irremediably confused with the notion of Legality, which he moreover calls 'Subsistence')].

We have seen in II, 2 the (religious) motive underpinning Kant's refusal to introduce in his Table of the Categories the Sub-Category of Teleology, interpreted as the free-Action or empirical-existence (= extended-duration) of Freedom in the World. We have also seen there that it is because he basically confused Teleology with Life that Kant also excluded the notion of the latter from his categorial System, by definition susceptible of being discursively developed without contradiction. We will not therefore dwell on this any further, and neither do we need to say right away what we will say about Freedom in our (general and applied) Phenomenology. Let us just say that in our work, as in Hegel's, the Freedom-Mana is considered not *in itself* (that is, Thing-*in-itself*), but as indissolubly linked to the Essence (in the 'Greek' sense of this word) of the living-Organism which is the Human being conceived as zoological Species, to the extent that the Freedom-Mana is precisely that which is 'specifically' human (or contra-dictory) in that Human being who can effectively be 'anything' while remaining 'human' or, as Hegel says, not to be (qua 'free') that which one is (qua 'necessary' or 'given') and be ('freely') that which one is not ('necessarily'). The 'Freedom' of the (dialectical) movement of the human Mana is therefore limited to the movements of the Human being's animal body (this body being the [empirical] Existence of the Essence which is that of these Human beings insofar as they *live*). The Contra-diction that the notion of the Mana-freedom entails can thus be said *to exist-empirically* (albeit without an objective-reality) as 'contradiction' between the 'free' human in 'Human beings' and the 'necessary' animal, which is equally theirs, one incarnating their Mana and the other their Essence. This 'contra-diction' exists-empirically (= endures and extends) and is 'revealed' (as [human] Phenomenon in and through Perception) qua Negativity (= Freedom), which actively negates the given Present, in function of the Future {*Avenir*} (by way of the Past), to the extent that the free active Negation is the Action of Struggle → Work that trans-forms the material and living Cosmos into a human Cosmos which is universal History, by populating the *given* World with their Arte-*facts*. It is this Action that engenders the Discourse it speaks thereof, and that Discourse becomes circular or uni-total, that is, *true*, by 'overcoming' its entailed Contra-diction in and through its 'dialectical movement', to the extent that this movement accounts discursively for the *historical* movement during which, eventually, Human beings would 'dialectically overcome' the 'contra-diction' that was there at the start between what they *were* qua *given* (= 'necessary') and what they ('freely') *wanted* to be, so that they could be fully *satisfied* by the sole total development of the consciousness of what they *are* in their empirical-existence.

All this will be developed later. For the time being, it is interesting to note that if Kant deliberately excludes the notion of Teleology (= free-Action) from his discursive development as carried out in the mode of Truth, he sometimes talks 'as if' it is this notion that he had in mind.

While commenting on his Table of the Categories, Kant says (in a passage that has already been cited) that Necessity is nothing other than [empirical-] *Existence* (*Existenz*) given through *Possibility itself* (III, 96, 11–13). Kant himself would have interpreted this passage as we had done above. He would have said that empirical-Existence (= Relation) is *entirely* 'given through Possibility' (the Impossible alone not existing empirically, since it alone is pure Nothingness) and that, consequently, it is *entirely* 'necessary' (since entirely 'causal'). In other words, he would have simply identified the Necessary, the Possible (= given-Being), and empirical-Existence (or even objective-Reality). But we could provide an alternative interpretation of this text (even though *that* interpretation would be 'violent' considering that it is contrary to Kant's own *intention*). We could say that there, Kant defines, for sure, empirical-Existence (since he effectively admits, and rightly so, that all that is necessary exists-empirically), but that he calls 'Necessity' what is generally called 'Freedom' (and in accordance with how Kant himself refers thereto in other contexts), or more exactly, *free* (= human in the strong sense of the word) empirical-Existence. This free or human empirical-Existence would then be defined as an empirical-existence (moreover objectively-real) which would be 'given' in *possibility alone* or in non-contradiction as such, to the extent that this (non-contradictory) 'possibility' is the freely conceived 'Project' (in function of the Desire of Desire, which is the Desire for Recognition) and voluntarily realised by Human beings (in and through their Struggles and Works). For the 'merely possible' is in fact 'given' to Human beings only as their own 'Project' of something that *must* be and perhaps *will be*, but which has never yet *been* and *is* not yet. And it is only the empirical-existence of the Arte-fact 'realising' such a 'Project' that is effectively 'given through Possibility itself', as Kant says, to the extent that the 'Project' is unable to be 'realised' unless it is 'possible', that is, 'non-impossible', which means, for the Human being, not contradictory when developed discursively (to the extent that Human beings alone are able to do so and to notice it, to wit, to de-monstrate it, because they alone are capable of *executing* the 'Project' in question).

Even though unquestionably 'violent', this interpretation is somewhat 'confirmed' by certain passages from the commentary that Kant provides in his [third] 'Postulate' of Necessity, where he says, for example, this:

> Consequently, the proposition: nothing happens/takes place (*geschieht*) by an almost (*Ungefähr*) blind chance (*in mundo non datur casus*), is an *a priori* Law-of-Nature; likewise: no Necessity in Nature is blind, but [they all are] rather a *conditioned* Necessity (*bedingte*), [and] *consequently comprehensible (verständliche)* (*non datur fatum*).
> (III, 194, 24–7)

To be sure, for Kant himself, this passage merely develops his Sub-Category of Causality, which he has just identified, *in fact* and *for us*, with what the 'moderns' call 'Legality' [to the extent that the notion of Causality thus identified with that of Necessity, understood as 'Legality', is in fact broader than that of Kantian Causality strictly so called, besides being very vague; which Kant himself moreover acknowledges since he says, a few lines further down (III, 194, 34–6), that his Law of the *non datur fatum adds* to the concept of Causality the concept of Necessity]. But *we* might say that, in these two purported 'Laws *of Nature*', what Kant has in mind is *in fact* the empirical-existence of Freedom in the form of efficacious free-Action. However, to render it *true*, Kant's text itself would have to be corrected in such a way that it says that nothing happens in the World 'by chance' (or 'necessarily' which is the same thing), but rather there are Arte-facts in that World that are *willed* by the Human being, which are surely 'necessary' insofar as they are objectively-real, but which originate in a 'necessity' (= 'irresistible voluntary desire or incoercible free will') which, far from being 'blind', is on the contrary perfectly 'comprehensible' on account of being 'conditioned' by a non-contra-dictory discursive Project.

But, once again, to interpret the cited passage *in this way* would amount to doing violence not only to the text but to Kant himself. For Kant does not *want* to admit the efficacy of free-Action in the extended-duration of empirical-Existence, and this is why he consciously and deliberately excludes the Sub-Category of Teleology (= Freedom) from his categorial System which is discursively developable without contradiction in the mode of Truth, by camouflaging this gap with the third Sub-Category of his third Category, which he calls Community or Interaction, but which is *in fact* only another presentation of his (second) Sub-Category of Causality [in fact identical to his (first) Sub-Category of Subsistence, which roughly coincides with the 'modern' notion of Legality.]

Be that as it may, the (non 'violent') preceding interpretations have shown that the purported 'fourth' Category of Kant merely repeats, under the title of his three Sub-Categories, the first three Kantian Categories.

Generally speaking, the first three Categories of Kant constitute then single-handedly the *complete*, that is, *uni-total* categorial System. This fact is very remarkable because Kant has, as is known, deduced his Table of the Categories from the Table of Judgements, which was so much scoffed at without it being generally taken seriously (as Hegel did). This fact would be something of a miracle if we did not know, thanks to Hegel, that the last Sub-Category of the System is developed discursively in such a way that it makes explicit the very notion of Judgement, which is itself developed and articulated in such a way that the 'Judgements' which have been distinguished and defined for a long time by the so-called 'formal' Logic (thanks to his analysis of the Discourse that exists-empirically) appear as these constituent elements, which are just as much determined by the whole structure of the categorial System in such a way that they determine this very structure and thus the $3 \times 3 = 9$ Categories and Sub-Categories that constitute the (supposedly *true*) Kantian System [in such a way that it makes no difference whether one *starts* (as we do following Hegel) with Kant's first Category to *deduce* in the end his Table of Judgements, or *start* (as Kant did) with this first category and *deduce* the categorial System therefrom].

However, to de-monstrate this, and to de-monstrate by so doing the circular or uni-*total*, that is, truly 'systematic' character of Kant's Table of the Categories (besides, reduced to his first three Categories), Hegel had to introduce, in the guise of a third Sub-Category of the third (and last) Kantian Category, the notion of Teleology or free-Action. Now, he managed to do so only by eliminating the notion of the Thing-in-itself from Kant's Philosophy. But the elimination of the Thing-in-itself has among other things rendered possible the introduction in the categorial System of the Sub-Category of the living-Organism, which coincides, *in fact* and *for us*, with the Kantian Sub-Category of Causality (adequately specified and distinguished from that of Legality, which coincides, in fact and for us, with the Kantian Sub-Category of Subsistence, it too, adequately specified and distinguished from that of Causality). Lastly, a more pronounced and precise distinction between the Kantian Categories of Quantity (= given-Being), Quality (= objective-Reality), and Relation (= empirical-Existence) allows *us* to eliminate the notion of 'Continuity' from the discursive development of the Category of objective-Reality (as from the Category of empirical-Existence, where Kant also introduces it [cf. III, 194, 36; 195, 23]), while assigning to it its rightful place in the development of the Category of given-Being.

Without insisting further here on these points, which are strictly speaking part of the context of the 'Expositions' of the *System of Knowledge*, we must, nonetheless, underscore the remarkable fact (which clearly shows Kant's unrivalled philosophical greatness) that it suffices to eliminate the notion of the Thing-in-itself, introduce that of Teleology or efficacious free-Action, identify Causality with Life, elaborate on the notion of Subsistence in such a way that it coincides with the notion of the Legality valid for the inanimate-Thing, and finally to overcome the notion of Continuity in the development of the Categories of objective-Reality and empirical-Existence, for the Kantian categorial System to coincide perfectly with the Hegelian System which is ours.

A few points of our interpretation of Kant's categorial System remain to be specified and supplemented with remarks on the *Metaphysical Foundations of Natural Science*.

The aim of our interpretation was to show what becomes of Kant's categorial System when (following Reinhold–Fichte–Schelling–Hegel) all implications concerning the Thing-in-itself are overcome therein. There is, thus, a radical difference between our Hegelian point of view and that of Kant himself. For Kant, there is at the same time the Thing-in-itself, transcendent with reference to all spatio-temporality, and the essentially spatio-temporal Phenomenon. Hence, he admits an essential difference between the Understanding, that *thinks* the Object within the frame of the Categories, and the Intuition, that *gives* this same object within the frame of Spatio-temporality. The Categories are *valid* both for the Thing-in-itself and for the Phenomenon, but they can be *utilised* only in the discursive cognition of the latter, because, since the Object is *given* to the Understanding in Intuition alone, only a spatio-temporal cognition is possible. For, in order for the Categories to be discursively developable within the frame of a Cognition susceptible of being true, they must thus be spatio-temporalised or, as Kant says, *schematised*. It is the discursive development of the *schematised* Categories that constitutes the System of Principles.

Here are, by the way, Kant's fundamental texts referring to the Schematism and to the Principles:

> the Schema of each Category ... contains and makes representable (*vorstellig mache*) Time [in fact: space and time] itself [taken] as the

correlate (*Correlatum*) of the determination of a thinglike-Object [that indicates] whether and how this Object belongs to Time. The Schemata are therefore nothing but a priori determinations of Time in accordance with Rules [these Rules being the Categories]. (III, 138, 17–27)

... although it is the Schemata of Sensibility [= Spatio-temporality] that *realise* the Categories, yet they *restrict* them, that is, *limit* them to conditions that lie *outside* the Understanding (namely, in Sensibility). Consequently, the Schema is strictly speaking only the *Phenomenon* or the *sensible* [= spatio-temporal] Concept of a thinglike-Object in agreement with the Category ... Without Schemata, therefore, the Categories are only functions of the Understanding [which refer to] *Concepts* (*zu Begriffen*), but do not represent any *thinglike-Object*. This [objective] significance comes to the Categories from Sensibility, which *realises* the Understanding at the same time as it restricts it. (III, 139, 11–37)

Now our task is to expound in a *systematic* connexion (*Verbindung*) the *Judgements* [= discursive development of notions] that the Understanding effectively produces *a priori* with this critical caution [which limits the discursive development to the spatio-temporal frame], for which our Table of the Categories must doubtless give us natural and secure guidance. For it is precisely the reference (*Beziehung*) of the *Categories* to possible *Experience* [spatio-temporal by definition] that must constitute *all* pure a priori rational cognition (*Verstandeserkenntnis*) [by definition, discursive and true], in such a way that their relation (*Verhältnis*) to Sensibility in general [that is, to Spatio-temporality] will display *all* transcendental *Principles* (*Grundsätze*) of the [objective or true] use of the Understanding *completely* and in a [well-ordered] *System*.

A priori *Principles* bear this name not merely because they contain in themselves the grounds (*Gründe*) of other Judgements, but also [contrary to what the Rationalists like Descartes, Spinoza, Leibniz, and Wolff think] because they are not themselves grounded (*gegründet*) in higher and more general cognitions. (III, 140, 9–19)

What is traditional ('Platonic' or 'rationalist') in this way of seeing is that the ('categorial') notions that constitute the irreducible elements of Discourse are supposed to 'refer' to the Thing-in-itself, that is, to eternal-Being or to the Eternity-that-is, and to draw from *this* reference their (discursive) Truth. What is conversely novel (at least according to Kant himself, even though this 'novelty', in reality, goes back to the anti-Platonic Aristotle) is the statement of fact that the discursive development of these irreducible notions into Judgements or Principles cannot give rise to a true Cognition, that is, to a (de-monstrable) Knowledge or to discursive-Truth unless it is carried out within the frame of Spatio-temporality. And what is truly 'revolutionary' is the affirmation that 'intuitive' or 'sensible' Spatio-temporality as such is as much 'a priori' or 'apodictic' (truly true) as the 'rational' concept per se [independently from the 'cyclical' character of Time that Aristotle affirmed, and which allowed him to assimilate Time to Eternity, and hence assimilate the 'empirical' cognition to which it refers to 'rational' or true cognition].

It is thanks to the completion of that Kantian 'revolution' that Hegel was able to definitively eliminate from Philosophy all references to Transcendence [by thus transforming Philosophy into Knowledge or Wisdom]. By overcoming the Thing-in-itself, 'eternal' or transcendent with reference to Spatio-temporality, he associated Kantian Intuition with the Understanding [called 'Reason' because of that association], in such a way that the Categories were henceforth 'schematised' in a somewhat automatic way, and thus immediately transformed into 'Principles'. The ['rational'] 'pure' Category in the sense of non 'sensible', that is, non-spatio-temporal, and the ['irrational'] Intuition, have become 'abstractions' of the 'Understanding' (*Verstand*). For 'Reason' (*Vernunft*), which is the organ of discursive Knowledge, there no longer is anything but *schematised* Categories, that is, *Principles*, that this same 'Reason' discursively develops into a uni-total or circular System of Knowledge.

By interpreting Kant's categorial System on the assumption of its removal from the notion of the Thing-in-itself, we therefore were and should have been able to utilise indifferently all that Kant had said as much about the Categories strictly so called as about their Schemata and the Principles resulting from their schematisation. And, by following this approach, we were able to identify (after a few readjustments) Kant's categorial System as a Hegelian System which is ours.

There is nonetheless an important difference between the Kantian

'Schematisation' and ours. On the one hand, Kant speaks uniquely of 'Time', while we speak of *Spatio*-temporality. But we have seen that, in fact, Kant too uses the notion of 'Space', even though he introduces explicitly (as a general rule) only that of 'Time'. On the other hand, Kant knows only *one* temporal, or, in fact, 'spatio-temporal', 'Schema', while we distinguish between *three* types of schemata, namely one for each of the three Categories (to which we have reduced the purported *four* Kantian Categories). We indeed 'schematise' the Category of given-Being (= Quantity = Possibility) by Spatial-temporality, that of objective-Reality (= Quality = objective-Reality) by Space-time, and that of empirical-Existence (= Relation = Necessity) by extended-Duration. In other words, we have specified or 'defined', through differentiation, the Kantian notion of 'Time' or, more exactly, that of 'Space' and 'Time', which Kant himself joins together in the notion of 'Sensibility' (= Intuition), which is in his work, in fact, vague and fluctuant.

Seeing the vague character of the Kantian notion of 'Sensibility', its Hegelian interpretation is perfectly legitimate and in no way 'violent'. The analysis of Kant's purported 'fourth' Category has shown that, in him as in Hegel, there is only one 'Category' (which he calls 'Modality', and which is our uni-total Concept that Hegel calls 'Idea') 'schematised' by one single 'Sensibility' through its discursive development into one single 'Principle' (in turn, discursively developable into a uni-total System of Knowledge). We are therefore merely elaborating on Kant's thought when we say [after overcoming the notion of the Thing-in-itself and thus merging the 'Category' with 'Sensibility', the latter and the former becoming thus the constituent-elements ('thesis' and 'antithesis') of the (uni-total) 'Principle' or 'Judgement' (which is their 'synthesis')] that this one and unique [= uni-total] 'Category' is the (discursively developable) notion given-Being, if its 'schematising' 'Sensibility' is Spatio-temporality (its corresponding 'Principle' developing discursively into Onto-logy); that it is the notion Reality, if it is 'schematised' by Space-Time (its 'Principle' developing into Energo-logy); and that it is, qua 'schematised' by extended-Duration, the notion empirical-Existence (whose 'Principle' is developed into Phenomeno-logy).

More exactly (as we have pointed out regarding our Onto-logy), it is by 'reducing' (through 'abstraction' extended-Duration to Space-time that we 'reduce' empirical-Existence, which alone is given or revealed in an *immediate* manner in and through Perception taken as a whole) to objective-Reality (given in and through the Sensation of the Tonal variation of that Perception), and it is by 'reducing' Space-time (or, more exactly, extended-Duration) to Spatio-temporality that we 'reduce' objective-Reality (or, more exactly, empirical-Existence) to given-Being (revealed in and through the Perceptual Feeling of Well or Ill-being). In fact, the notions (= Categories) given-Being and objective-Reality (and accordingly, those of Spatio-temporality and Space-time) are only 'abstract' forms of the uni-total Concept, which is 'concrete' (that is, total or 'necessary') only as the notion (= Category) of empirical-Existence. Therefore, this notion involves *all* the Categories of Kant (reduced to the first three ones), on condition that they are all 'schematised' by extended-Duration.

Now, Kant effectively utilises *all* these Categories to develop them (after schematisation) into Principles: there are in him as many Principles as there are Categories (four for him, three in fact and for us). In addition, the notion 'Time', which serves in Kant to schematise all these Categories, is in fact closer to our notion of extended-Duration than to those of Space-time and Spatio-temporality. For us, Kant's 'System of Principles' corresponds therefore to our Phenomeno-logy [where the 'generic' part is, for that matter, not clearly separated from its 'specific' counterpart, to the extent that the notion of 'Primacies' {*Primats*} is unknown to Kant in general, while the Primacy of the Future {*Avenir*} is deliberately excluded from the discursively developable categorial System in the mode of Truth, in such a way that the Kantian 'Principles' overlap only with our Cosmo-logy and our Bio-logy, involving nothing that corresponds to our Anthropo-logy]. Consequently, we could interpret the ensemble of Kant's 'Principles' in such a way that we make them coincide with the content of our Hegelian Phenomeno-logy without doing much violence to the text [Anthropo-logy notwithstanding], while nonetheless moving on to more substantial readjustments (as well as to a few corrections). But we could also interpret this text in such a way that we make it coincide with our Energo-logy (by attributing to the Kantian notion of 'Time' the meaning of our notion Space-time) or even with our Onto-logy (by identifying Kant's 'Time' with our Spatio-temporality), even though in these two cases the readjustments and corrections should also be more substantial than they were in the phenomeno-logical interpretation.

These three interpretations are legitimate and pedagogically useful. But we would digress too much from the energo-logical context if we undertake all three here. Moreover, we assumed we could exempt ourselves from the onto-logical interpretation, for it is less interesting than the other ones. As for the phenomeno-logical interpretation, we will have the opportunity to say a few words on the subject here. Concerning, lastly, the energo-logical interpretation, we have already covered the gist of it in the preceding pages and further details will lead us too far. It is then sufficient to recall that by eliminating all involvement of the notion of the Thing-in-itself, and by overcoming the erroneous development related to Continuity, we once again find in Kant's categorial System, as 'schematised' by the 'Sensibility' understood as Space-time and developed into a 'System of Principles', all the essential content of the Energo-logy which we will set forth while taking our bearings from Hegelian texts.

It now remains for us to complete our interpretation of the 'Principles' with a few remarks on the *Metaphysical Foundations of Natural Science*.

Here is what Kant himself says:

> It [the Metaphysics of Nature] can still either treat the Laws that make possible the concept/the notion of a Nature *in general* (*überhaupt*), in which case it is the *transcendental* part of the Metaphysics of Nature; or concern itself with a *particular/specific* (*besonderen*) Nature of this or that kind (*Art*) of Things (*Dinge*), for which an *empirical* concept/notion is given, but still in such a manner that for the cognition of this specific/particular Nature no other *empirical* principle is used outside of what lies (*liegt*) in *this* concept/*this* [empirical] notion [that corresponds to it] (for example, the Metaphysics of Nature takes as its basis (*legt zum Grunde*) the *empirical* concept/notion of *Matter* or of a *thinking Being* and it seeks the ensemble (*Umfang*) of cognition of which Reason is capable [to have] *a priori* about these [two] thinglike-Objects), and then such a Science must still be called a *Metaphysics* of Nature, namely, of *corporeal* or *thinking* Nature. However, it is then not a *general*, but a *particular* Natural Science (*Physics* and *Psychology*), in which the above *transcendental* Principles are applied to the two types (Gattungen) of thinglike-Objects of our Sense. (IV, 469, 33–470, 12)

The 'transcendental *Principles* (*Principien*)' which Kant has in mind here are nothing but the 'Principles' (*Grundsätze*) that he dealt with in the *Critique of Pure Reason*. The 'System of Principles' thus constitutes the 'transcendental Part' of the 'Metaphysics of Nature', which deals with (spatio-temporal) 'thinglike-Objects' *whatever they may be*. The 'Metaphysics of Nature' in the narrow sense of the word (which Kant calls in the *Critique*: 'Physiology') is, conversely, concerned with *specific* (spatio-temporal) 'thinglike-Objects'. The thinglike-Object *as such*, to which the 'Principles' refer, namely those which discursively develop the Categories 'schematised' by 'Sensibility' in general, that is, by spatio-temporal 'Intuition' *per se*, is *specified* by 'Experience', that is, by what we call Perception (taken as a whole). This thinglike-object is therefore *given* (revealed), as 'Phenomenon' in the narrow sense of the word, either as *Body* (*Körper*) or as *Matter* (*Materie*), either as Soul (*Seele*) or as *thinking Being* (*denkender Wesen*). The 'Body' and the 'Soul' are '*empirical* notions' equally susceptible of being discursively developed in the mode of Truth. According to Kant, this (true) development is carried out ('a priori') through the application of schematised Categories, that is, ('transcendental') Principles, to the *specific* (empirical or 'a posteriori') 'content' of these two notions. It thus constitutes a (discursive) *systematic* or *uni-total* cognition of the 'Body' and the 'Soul' *per se*, that is, taken as irreducible 'types' or 'Species' of 'empirical' thinglike-Objects. As for *particular* thinglike-Objects (particular 'Bodies' and particular 'Souls') and their differences, they are given or revealed in and through *particular* 'Experiences' (Perceptions) which give rise to *particular* ('empirical') notions, likewise discursively developable in the mode of Truth, but undefined regarding their number and 'infinite' as far as their 'contents' go, in such a way that their discursive development, without ever being able to contra-dict the discursive development of notions, be they *generic* (schematised Categories or Principles) or *specific* ('Matter' and 'Soul'), extends indefinitely and can never be truly complete, that is, *systematic* ('a priori').

The Metaphysical Foundations develops only the *specific* notion of 'Matter': it is the *physical* Part of 'Physiology'. As for the *psychological* Part, Kant dealt with it only in his Anthropology (of 1798), which is something altogether different from the 'Psychology' he had in mind in *The Metaphysical Foundations* (cf. VII, 119–22). The truth is that the

'Soul' as '*thinking* Being' is the object-matter of the *Critique of Pure Reason*, where the notion of the 'Soul' is obviously not *specific* and even less so *particular*; rather it is merely *generic*, to the extent that it is the 'subjective' counterpart of the thinglike-Object *in general* in 'reference' to the schematised Categories.

Kant even seems to say that the *specific* notion of the 'Soul', coordinated to the *specific* notion of 'Matter', is not discursively developable *per se*, at least in the mode of Truth, so that there can be no such thing as 'Psychology' (*metaphysical* Science-of-the-Nature of the Soul) in the same way as 'Physics' (*metaphysical* Science-of-Corporeal-Nature or of Matter): 'Psychology' is concerned with *particular* notions, which it can develop and set in order, without being able to *exhaust* them in a *System* proper, that is, in a genuine uni-total discursive *Knowledge* (cf. IV, 471, 11–37). Lastly, concerning the 'Soul' taken as free Agent, it is the object of the *Critique of Practical Reason* and the *Metaphysics of Morals* (as well as 'practical' or 'pragmatic Anthropology') (cf. IV, 388, 9–14).

Having said that, the 'Psychology' that Kant has in mind in *The Metaphysical Foundations* is *for us* nothing else but our Bio-logy, which is concerned with Life in general (and the animal 'nature' of the Human beings, including their so-called 'psychic' nature insofar as it is not trans-formed by the free-Action that constitutes the human in the Human being). Now, it is known that Kant dealt with Bio-logy in his third *Critique*, besides, in the mode of As-if (for reasons that I have talked about at length in the third Introduction of the Exposition of the System of Knowledge), where he (wrongly) makes use of the (in fact anthropo-logical) notion of Teleology, instead of utilising the (specifically bio-logical) notion of Causality.

Be that as it may, Kant's *Metaphysical Foundations* can only correspond, in the Hegelian *System of Knowledge* which is ours, to Cosmology. We have seen that the text of the 'System of Principles' lends itself more easily to an interpretation that makes it identical with our *generic* Phenomeno-logy. In addition, Kant says that his 'Physics' (= 'Metaphysics of corporeal Nature' qua part of 'immanent Physiology'), which he sets forth in *The Metaphysical Foundations*, is more *concrete* than his '*System of Principles*' in the sense that it does not refer to *all* 'Phenomena' whatever they may be, but only to 'corporeal' or 'material Phenomena'. Now, in us as well, Cosmo-logy is a *specific* Phenomeno-logy, which solely comprises the discursive development of the notion of the *inanimate-Thing* (or, to speak a language closer to the one Kant uses: of the Concept, that is, of the uni-total Category, schematised by the notion of extended-Duration, to the extent that this notion is *specified* by that of the Primacy of the Present). It is therefore obvious that, at least in terms of what he intended to do, Kant set forth in his *Metaphysical Foundations* what became in our work the *Cosmo-logical* Part of the Hegelian System of Knowledge.

It is therefore in the context of our Cosmo-logy that we will have the occasion to say a few words about Kantian 'Physics'. It will suffice to mention here that only a substantial interpretative adjustment can make Kant's text coincide with ours.

On the one hand, like all pre-Hegelian Philosophers, Kant does not distinguish, in a sufficiently clear and precise way, the irreducible notions ('Categories') from one another [being unbale to distinguish, even implicitly, Spatio-temporality from Space-time and extended-Duration]. Thus, by sometimes conflating the notion of given-Being with that of objective-Reality, he, wrongly, introduces in the development of the latter the notion of Continuity. And by conflating the notion of objective-Reality with that of empirical-Existence, he likewise transfers therein this same onto-logical notion of Continuity that can also be found in his 'Physics' (cf. IV, 504, Note I). That is how, in a general manner, one finds in Kant's 'Physics' developments which in fact belong to Energo-logy or even to Onto-logy.

On the other hand, Kant often confuses specific Phenomeno-logy with generic Phenomeno-logy [not having access to the notion of 'Primacy'], and, within the first one, he sometimes unsuspectingly mixes up the development of Cosmo-logy with that of Bio-logy, by, for example, introducing into the former the notion of Causality, in fact specifically bio-logical [owing to the fact that he is unable to distinguish the Primacy of the Present from that of the Past].

Lastly, even though Kant sees better than all his predecessors the essential difference that separates Philosophy (and discursive Knowledge) from the 'Sciences' in general, which are 'abstract' (since they overlook the fact of Discourse), and 'theoretical Physics' in particular (grounded on Mathematics which is not *discursive*) (cf. for example IV, 472, 13–35; 469, 21–5; and 470, 13–35), we find in his 'Physics', which is purely informed by *philosophical* intentions, arguments which, in fact, form part of the 'Sciences' and especially the Science of *physics*.

Here again a substantial interpretive readjustment should therefore be undertaken with the aim of eliminating from Kant's text all these, in fact non-philosophical, elements, which are both 'scientific' or *abstract* and 'physico-mathematical' or *non-discursive*. But we could discuss this last question in a useful way only in the context of the *Appendix* of our Exposition of the Hegelian *System of Knowledge*.

Before we bring our, already far too long, study to a close, it now remains for us to clarify one final point regarding what, in fact, Kantian Energology is.

Kant maintains the 'Platonic' or 'rationalist' distinction between *a priori* and *a posteriori* (discursive) Cognitions, the former alone having the value of *Knowledge* strictly speaking or of (discursive, or even de-monstrable or *irrefutable*) *Truth* in the strong sense of this term. The ensemble of all *a priori* Cognition is constituted, on the one hand, by the 'System of Principles' and, on the other hand, by 'Physics' (even though the latter borrows from 'Experience' the meaning of its *specific* grounding notion, which is that of the 'Body' or 'Matter', or the 'Solid'). It is only *this* ensemble that constitutes a *System* in the proper sense of the word, that is, a uni-*total* well-ordered Discourse, which develops in a *complete way* its own Meaning {*Sens*} proper and can, consequently, be neither completed nor modified, and even less so replaced, that is, 'refuted' by another (coherent) Discourse. The Kantian philosophical 'System' also admits, it is true, an 'empirical' or *a posteriori* Part. But this one is never *achieved* and is in a perpetual state of *readjustment*, in such a way that it cannot be considered as a constituent-element of the discursive Truth strictly so called, which is, by definition, necessarily, that is, everywhere and always, *identical* to itself.

In fact, this Kantian conception of the philosophical 'System' and the Hegelian conception of the *System of Knowledge* differ less than one might believe at first sight. Indeed, Hegel does not say that *all* that can be said without contra-dicting oneself (in the mode of Truth) is *explicitly* contained in the 'circular' or uni-total Discourse that constitutes the *System* of *Knowledge* which is the [discursive] *Truth*. He only affirms that this Discourse *implicitly* contains all that can be said without contra-dicting oneself by saying that what one says is *true*. In other words, every discourse that is not contra-dictory in itself and uttered with the intention to tell *true* can be truly *true*, that is, de-monstrated as being such (and therefore as 'irrefutable') only on condition of presenting (or having the ability to present) itself as a (coherent) discursive development of the Meaning {*Sens*} of an appropriate constituent-element, explicit or implicit, of the uni-total Discourse, even if this (explicit) Discourse is reduced (as is the case in the *Encyclopaedia* for example) to the bare *minimum* needed for the de-monstration of its 'circularity' (that is, its uni-totality). Now, likewise, Kant admits that the (indefinite) discursive development of 'empirical' Cognition can never contra-dict (if it is itself coherent and congruent with the Sense of the developed 'empirical' notion) the System of *a priori* Cognition, by definition 'complete' and thus 'irrefutable'. For Kant, an 'empirical' or *a posteriori* discursive Cognition cannot therefore be said to be *true* unless it can be ultimately 'deduced' from the categorial 'System', which is precisely to say that this Cognition stems from the (coherent) discursive development of the Category or the uni-total Concept ('schematised' and developed into a 'System of Principles'). That the 'developed' (*a priori* or *a posteriori*) or 'irreducible' (= Category) *Meaning* of any notion whatever it may be can ultimately be given or revealed only through Experience, that is, in Perception (taken either as a whole or by an act of 'abstraction', in one or the other of its constituent-elements), is what Hegel admits just as much as Kant (following Aristotle). But Hegel admits that the Meaning of the uni-total Concept (which he calls 'Idea' and which Kant calls 'Category' [of 'Modality']) involves the *ensemble* of discursive Meanings whatever they may be, in such a way that *any* one of these Meanings (be it 'particular' or 'specific') can be 'deduced' from it or presented qua constituent-element of the ('generic') Meaning of the Concept understood as such. Now, Kant admits this just as much (by only following, here too, Aristotle). In addition, Kant is in agreement with Hegel when he says that the discursive development of the Meaning of 'generic' Notions ('schematised Categories' or 'Principles', developable in fact into Onto-logy or Energo-logy and into *generic* Phenomeno-logy) and 'specific' ones (the notions of 'Matter' and the 'Soul' developable in fact into a *specific* Phenomeno-logy, that is, into Cosmo-logy, Bio-logy, and Anthropo-logy) can be *achieved* explicitly or *in fact* and not merely 'in principle', in the same way that he too also acknowledges that Discourse as such can be *completely* analysed (both qua Discourse of Truth and Discussion of True-semblance, or qua Expression of Recognition or the Language of Accomplishment) in a 'formal' (or 'logical') *effective* Discourse and not merely in a 'possible' one. Inversely, Hegel is in agreement with Kant when he acknowledges that the discursive development of 'particular' Meanings can last as long as Discourse itself does, thus representing an 'infinite Task', that is, a discursive development that can progress throughout the entire length of time a Human being may devote to a Discourse uttered with the intention to tell *true*, to the extent that the Truth of this 'particular' Discourse is de-monstrated through the de-monstration of the fact that it develops the implicit Meaning of the uni-total Concept.

An *essential* difference between Kant's philosophical 'System' and the Hegelian System of Knowledge therefore exists only insofar as the Kantian so-called 'System' comprises in fact irreducible *gaps*, which are *camouflaged* rather than *filled* by the discursive development of the 'infinite Task' of the 'particular' or 'empirical', or even *a posteriori* Cognition. In other words, the Kantian 'System', like every *philosophical* 'System', differs from the System of *Knowledge* only insofar as, rather than being 'circular' or uni-total, it is 'open', that is, either 'sceptical' or comprising heterogeneous discursive elements with a 'theological' character (in fact contra-dictory either in themselves and in reference to the rest of the properly philosophical Discourse [that is, uttered with the intention to discursively account for itself as Discourse], or merely in-themselves, when one develops them, as Kant does, in the hybrid mode of the 'theoretical' As-if which, by definition, cannot contra-dict what is said in the mode of Truth).

But I have sufficiently talked about *this* aspect of the question in the third Introduction of the Exposition of the Hegelian System of Knowledge. What we should see *here* is uniquely the question of knowing what is, from Hegel's point of view, the Kantian distinction (inherited from Plato) between *a priori* and *a posteriori* discursive Cognitions.

Admittedly, the classical definition of *a priori* Cognition makes no sense in the work of Aristotelians like Hegel and Kant himself. 'Platonic' Rationalism (which is also that of Descartes, Spinoza, and Leibniz) admits that there are notions, so-called *a priori* or 'innate', whose *Sense* can be given or revealed (and hence discursively developed) by a 'Proof' that Kant calls 'intellectual Intuition', without the need to call upon *Perception* or any of its constituent-elements whatever they may be.

Now, this is precisely what Kant expressly and forcefully denies (following Aristotle), and Hegel is careful enough not to dispute his claims. Undoubtedly, Kant seems at times to be saying that the Categories have a 'definable' or a discursively developable Sense that can be given or revealed *independently* from 'Sensibility' that is, from spatio-temporal 'Intuition' (cf. for e.g., III, 94, 32–7). But he immediately gets hold of himself to expressly negate the possibility for any Sense (or at least one developable in the mode of Truth) to be assigned to the Categories without it being derived from spatio-temporal 'Sensibility' (cf. for e.g., IV, 158, 9–159, 8; this passage from the first edition of the *Critique* has, for that matter, been removed from the second edition). Surely, he opposes the *a priori* spatio-temporal 'Intuition' (*Anschauung*) to 'empirical' or *a posteriori* (discursive) Cognitions, which rest on the 'Perception' (*Wahrnehmung*) based in 'Sensation' (*Empfindung*). But the distinction is here vague and wavering, and Kant himself generally conflates the 'Intuition' so-called *a priori* with *a posteriori* 'Perception' into one and the same ('generic') notion of 'Sensibility' (*Sinnlichkeit*).

This vagueness and wavering in Kant's thinking, which is conspicuously evolving in this area, clearly show that the opposition of the *a priori* and the *a posteriori* is, in his work, a residue of a philosophical past, which is inconsistent with the outcome of his 'revolutionary' intervention in the history of Philosophy. His purported discovery of the *a priori* character of the spatio-temporal 'Intuition' in fact only paved the way for the fusion of the traditional ('Platonic' or 'rationalist') notions of the 'rational' transcendent in reference to Spatio-temporality with the 'empirical' immanent to Spatio-temporality, undertaken by his immediate successors and completed by Hegel, who will draw all the consequences that follow therefrom, including the overcoming of the irreducible distinction, introduced by Kant, between *a priori* 'Sensibility' (*Anschauung*) and *a posteriori* 'Sensibility' (*Wahrnehmung*). Henceforth, as in Aristotle, all Sense whatever it may be has its origin in Perception or in its constituent-elements, which can be isolated from it by an act of 'abstraction' but which *in fact* have no *anteriority* at all in reference to their integrated Whole, which is Perception itself, and which cannot *exist* outside of this Whole, nor are they therefore able to give rise to a discursive Cognition *independent* from Perception as such.

However, this does not mean that Hegel opts for (Locke's) traditional 'Empiricism' *against* (Leibniz's) traditional 'Rationalism', nor that he abandons the specifically Kantian notion of the 'A priori'. Quite the opposite, it is by adopting and developing this notion all the way through to its last philosophical tenets that Hegel was able to 'overcome dialectically' the opposition between Rationalism and Empiricism. In other words, one can just as well say that in Hegel *everything* is either *a priori* or *a posteriori*, in the traditional or pre-Kantian sense of these two notions. But, precisely, these 'antithetical' notions thus lose all their Meaning or, more exactly, merge in the 'Synthetic' notion of the Hegelian 'A priori', which stems from the coherent and complete development of Kant's corresponding notion. Thus, in and for Hegel, the *ensemble* of the philosophical Discourse becomes *a priori* in the Kantian sense of the word, and this is precisely why it ceases to be what it was still in Kant himself (who opposed, within his purported 'System', an *a priori* Part to an *a posteriori* one), namely a *Philosophy*, to become *Knowledge* or the uni-total Discourse which *is* the discursive Truth.

In traditional or Platonic Rationalism, *a priori* notions 'refer' to that which is *transcendent* in reference to Spatio-temporality (= Kant's Thing-in-itself), while *a posteriori* notions exclusively 'refer' to that which is given or revealed (through Perception or Experience) *inside* this Spatio-temporality. Since the Transcendent is, by definition, 'eternal' or immutable, the *a priori* notions to which they are related are also eternal and immutable and can therefore be considered as *true* in the proper and strong sense of the term. Conversely, all that is spatio-temporal is, by definition, 'changing' {*mouvant*} and the (*a posteriori*) notions to which they refer are accordingly 'changing' as well and cannot as a consequence be considered as constituent-elements of the (discursive) Truth. Traditional Empiricism (of Locke for example) accepts this way of seeing things, except that it denies the possibility of cognising the Transcendent (discursively). It is therefore always, in fact and for us, *sceptical*.

Aristotle believed that he might avoid this dilemma by affirming the *circularity* of Time (both in its cosmic wholeness qua eternal Return, and in its particular existence qua eternity of the Species). He is therefore neither a 'rationalist' nor an 'empiricist' in the traditional sense of these words. And this is also the case with Kant. Except that Kant does not resort to the notion of the *circularity* of Time, the latter being, for him, an 'infinite straight line'. One must therefore ask how he may avoid the dilemma in question.

Admittedly, he does not avoid it insofar as he still maintains himself in the 'rationalist' tradition. When he affirms that his 'A priori' is valid for the Thing-in-itself, he must concede, with Aristotle and the Empiricists, that this A priori is not truly *conceptual* in the sense that it does not give rise to a coherent *discursive* development carried out in the mode of Truth. The discursive development of *this* (traditional) A priori is therefore, in Kant and for him, either contra-dictory or *lacunary*; the lacuna can be filled (in fact and for us: camouflaged) only by a discursive development carried out either in the mode of As-if, or in the form of a purported 'indefinite' 'Progress' towards the solution of an 'infinite Task', that is, one which is insoluble. Now, we have seen that in both cases, it is merely a variant (extremely 'cunning' for that matter) of *sceptical* traditional Empiricism.

But we have also seen that *this* Kantian 'rationalism', which is in fact an 'empiricism', represents only residues of the philosophical *Tradition* that Kant himself was neither able nor willing to entirely eliminate from his *revolutionary* System (which remained a *philosophical* 'System' rather than a System of *Knowledge*, only insofar as these 'residues' still feature therein). In fact and for us, by admitting the *a priori* character of *Spatio-temporal* Cognition, Kant introduced in Philosophy a *novel* conception of the A priori, which precisely allows it to avoid both the ('rationalist') pitfall of non-perceptible 'Proof' (which has turned out to be, in fact, 'ineffable') and the ('empiricist' or sceptical) pitfall of 'Opinion' of which one can never tell whether it is true or false in a 'definitive' way, and which can only be more or less true-semblant, depending on how they are Discussed, which varies in accordance with time and space (the elimination of this double pitfall precisely transforms Philosophy or the Search for Truth into a System of Knowledge which *is* this very Truth). All that Hegel did with this domain of the novel Kantian spatio-temporal A priori in question was to overcome the distinction Kant introduces between *a priori* spatio-temporal 'Intuition' and *a posteriori* spatio-temporal 'Sensibility', which comes down to the definitive and complete elimination of every trace, even when implicit, of the 'rationalist' or Platonic notion of Transcendence in reference to Spatio-temporality, which is, in Kant himself, the 'residual' notion of the Thing-in-itself.

But what, then, is this novel Kantian A priori, which allows the *truth* (= 'immutability') of discursive notions to be affirmed while bringing them to bear on (by definition, 'changing') Spatio-temporality?

Here are a few texts by Kant to initiate an interpretation that may cast fresh light on how the novel Kantian conception of the A priori became Hegelian.

Now, it is said that something is cognised *a priori* when it is cognised [from] its mere (*blossen*) *Possibility*. (IV, 490, 18–19)

Whatever coincides (*übereinkommt*) with the *formal* conditions (*Bedingungen*) of *Experience* (in accordance with *Intuition* and *Concepts*) [= Categories] is *possible*. (III, 185, 22–3)

The Postulate of the Possibility of Things (*Dinge*) thus requires that their *Concept* is in harmony (*zusammenstimmen*) with the formal conditions of an *Experience* in general (*überhaupt*). (III, 186, 25–7)

These texts (the last two of which were already quoted and interpreted above) show clearly that the Kantian A priori has nothing to do with the 'Proof' of (Platonic) traditional Rationalism, and that the 'Possible' that Kant has in mind is something quite other than merely the Non-contradictory. In order for a (discursive) Cognition to be *a priori* or *true* in the strong sense of the term, it is not sufficient that it is 'possible' in the sense of 'Non-contradiction'. It is, for sure, a question of 'Concepts', that is, of notions discursively developable without contradiction. But this development must also be in 'harmony' with the '*formal* conditions of Experience', which is nothing else but the notion of Spatio-temporality (in the broad sense of the term, which involves the notions Space-time and extended-Duration). And it is a question of 'Experience *in general*', that is, *any* 'experience' *whatsoever*, and therefore *all* 'experiences' whatever they may be, insofar as they give rise to a supposedly *coherent* or *non-contra-dictory Discourse*. The 'Possibility' that Kant has in mind when he speaks of the A priori or discursive Truth is therefore nothing else but 'the Possibility of *Experience*' taken as a whole, that is, the 'Possibility' of Discourse whatever it may be insofar as it makes *Sense* (to the extent that this Sense it receives is derived, by definition, from 'Experience') which is not contra-dictory per se, or, if one will, the 'Possibility' of developing the uni-total Concept into a 'circular' Discourse (by definition endowed with coherent Sense) [to the extent that this discursive development can, moreover, take as its starting point *any* non-contradictory notion on condition that it has a *spatio-temporal* Sense and can, when developed 'indefinitely', encompass *all* that can be said without contra-dicting itself]. In other words, Kant calls *a priori* or truly *true all* that one *must* say (without contra-dicting oneself) to account discursively for the *Possibility* to say that which one says (without contra-dicting oneself). Now, all that 'pertains' to the *Possibility* of Discourse is called, in Kant, *transcendental* (to the extent that the 'Transcendental' is not *transcendent* in reference to Spatio-temporality). Saying that a discursive Cognition is *a priori* or *transcendental* is therefore to say, according to Kant, one and the same Thing.

Thus, for example, when one says that a dog has legs, it is a question of an 'empirical' or *a posteriori* discursive cognition. But the fact of *saying* it is *possible* only because there is something that Kant calls 'Intuition' and 'Category', and because the 'Category' merges with the 'Intuition' (that 'schematises' it in this manner) to give us what is called in Kant 'Principle', to the extent that this 'Principle' may be developed discursively in a such a way that one may see and de-monstrate that the Sense of the (supposedly coherent) discourse 'this dog has legs' does not contra-dict any of the explicit or implicit constituent-elements of the Sense of the 'Principle' in question. Now, this 'Possibility' of Discourse *as such* is not determined by its *particular* 'content'. It is the 'Possibility' pertaining to *any* (coherent) Discourse (uttered with the intention to tell true), that is, of *all* Discourses strictly speaking, and this is why one can say that (the philosophical) Discourse that 'pertains' to this ('generic' or 'specific') 'Possibility' is a *transcendental* or *a priori* discursive Cognition.

It is *this* Kantian notion of the *A priori* and the *Transcendental* that is at the very basis of the 'Copernican revolution' undertaken by Kant. It is this same notion that also constitutes the basis of the Hegelian System of Knowledge. Except that Hegel has seen and de-monstrated what the rationalist or Platonic 'pre-judice' (ultimately theistic) prevented Kant from seeing for himself. Namely, the fact, in fact 'evident', that is, 'irrefutable', that one can neither see nor de-monstrate that a *particular* discourse does not contra-dict the 'conditions of Possibility' (*Bedingungen der Möglichkeit*) of the (coherent and susceptible of being *true*) Discourse as such (to the extent that this non-contradiction renders precisely the particular discourse itself *possible*), as long as the *generic* or *specific* discourse which (qua transcendent or *a priori*) develops these 'conditions of Possibility' is not *developed* up to the point where it coincides with the *particular* discourse in question, or, which is the same thing, as long as this *particular* discourse is not *reduced* (by coherent successive 'abstractions') in such a way that it coincides with an (explicit or implicit) constituent element of the *generic* Discourse, so-called 'a priori' or 'transcendental'. For if the *particular* discourse 'this dog has legs' is 'possible' just because it *exists*-empirically, one cannot know if it is not contradictory per se (since it is not good enough that it does not entail an *explicit* contra-diction for it to be protected from the presence of an *implicit* one), nor whether it does not contra-dict another (supposedly non-contradictory) discourse, as long as it has not been inserted (without contra-diction) in the uni-total Discourse, which de-monstrates its coherence (its 'unity') and totality ('unicity') proper, that is, its own *Truth*, through its explicitly *circular* character.

Consequently, in fact, and for Hegel, *all* discursive Cognition whose *truth* (and hence *a fortiori* its coherence) can be seen and de-monstrated is necessarily 'transcendental' in the Kantian sense of the word, that is, both 'a priori' and 'a posteriori' in the sense of traditional or pre-Kantian Rationalism. On the one hand, *all* that one says (without contra-dicting oneself) in the mode of *Truth* (which is, by definition, the *unique* mode of discursive *Knowledge*) is 'a priori' in the traditional sense of the word. For *all* that one thus says *can* be unequivocally 'deduced' from the 'conditions of Possibility' of discursive Truth itself (formulated discursively and reduced to the bear minimum necessary for the de-monstration of their 'circularity', whose coherence and totality it guarantees) in such a way that *nothing* one thus says may be replaced by a discourse which would have *another Meaning*, while not contradicting itself by itself and while not contra-dicting the rest of what one *says* in the mode of Truth. *All* that is discursively *true* can therefore be 'deduced' with the help of 'Logic' alone (and) from that 'Logic' itself. But, on the other hand, *all* discursive truth is also 'a posteriori' in the traditional sense of this word. Because for the Hegelian Sage, the very *Possibility* of Discourse whatever it may be can only be shown and de-monstrated by the *Fact* of the *empirical-existence* of *human* discourses. That is how Hegel's 'Logic', from which he 'deduces' *all* that one may say in *truth*, is not the '*formal* Logic' of Rationalism (which is constituted as, and wants itself to ultimately be, 'formal' only because its 'content' is supposed to be transcendent in reference to Spatio-temporality, while in fact that 'divine' content is strictly ineffable for a 'logically' *coherent* discourse), but the '*concrete*' or 'dialectical Logic' of the uni-total Concept or the 'Idea' that de-monstrates the *Possibility* of 'circularity', that is, of the totality and coherence of Discourse, by allowing this discourse to be *effectively* stated. *All* that is true is *true* only because it is inserted (without contra-diction) in the *uni*-total Discourse. But Discourse can be uni-*total* or 'circular' only because it encompasses (explicitly or implicitly), without contra-diction, *all* that was said by the Human being. Discursive Truth is therefore *a priori* only insofar as it integrates the *totality* of that which was said *a posteriori*, but one can de-monstrate the *total* character of that integration only by *reducing* the A posteriori to the transcendental A priori of the 'conditions of Possibility' of Discourse as such, and by de-monstrating the 'circular' character of that A priori or by *deducing* from the 'circular' A priori all that one wishes to demonstrate the *truth* thereof. But the 'circular' development of the A priori is itself nothing other than the (complete) discursive development of the Sense of the notion that 'pertains' to the *Fact* of the empirical-Existence of (human) Discourse.

The affirmation that the whole of Philosophy and of Knowledge per se (that is, discursive Truth) are reduced, when all is said and done, to the (coherent and complete) discursive development of the Sense of the Concept that 'pertains' to 'given' or 'revealed' *Fact* in and through Perception (= Kant's 'sensible Experience') probably goes back to Aristotle, and Kant is the principal philosophical heir to this 'discursive Empiricism'. The affirmation that Philosophy and Knowledge have as their point of departure *Discourse* (Logos) as such and the search for the 'conditions of Possibility' as their goal, probably goes back to Plato (who precisely reproached Parmenidean Onto-logy with rendering Discourse impossible, instead of enunciating the 'conditions' of its 'Possibility'), but it was Kant who drew all the consequences following from this 'transcendental Rationalism'.[32] As for the affirmation that Knowledge is

---

32 Let us recall that, in the *Timaeus*, Plato 'deduces' his (dualist) Onto-logy, and thus his entire Philosophy, from the Postulate of *discursive Truth* (which he moreover presents as a *Fact* rather than as a *Postulate*, even though this Fact is introduced *ad hominem* in *hypothetical* terms). Plato's Onto-logy is thus a deduction of the 'conditions of possibility' of discursive Truth or Knowledge in the strong and proper sense of the word (cf. 51a–52d).

reduced to the (coherent and complete) discursive development of the notional Meaning 'referring' to the *Fact* of the empirical-existence *of* (human) *Discourse*, it goes back, if one will, to the Cartesian *Cogito* (which is perhaps inspired by Saint Augustine). But it is Hegel who was the first to develop a full awareness thereof and who effectively drew all the consequences following therefrom, which constitute the System of Knowledge that we are setting forth.

Hegel saw that the primordial 'empirical Fact', with which 'Aristotelian' Empiricism claims to be affiliated, must be the Fact *of Discourse* (Logos), and that the 'Discourse' ('Logos') that 'Platonic' Rationalism lays at the basis of Philosophy must be an *empirical* Fact. And he likewise saw that the empirical Fact of (human) Discourse must not be *particular* (as in Descartes), but *specific* or *generic*, if not *universal*. In other words, the 'primordial' Fact of Philosophy and Knowledge was in Hegel, as it has been since, the sum-total of discourses pronounced by the Human being in the course of universal History. Thus, the Kantian *Transcendental* has become, in Hegel, *the Historical*, while remaining *Synthesis* of the A priori and the A posteriori. Indeed, the *historical* discursive Fact is itself both 'a priori' and 'a posteriori'. On the one hand, History exists only insofar as it is *created* 'a priori', out of discursive Projects, which are Notions whose Meanings refer to nothing that is given or revealed through Perception as (already) existing-empirically in the natural spatio-temporal World. On the other hand, History exists only insofar as it is 'remembered' or *cognised* 'a posteriori', out of Oeuvres that exist-empirically qua objective-realisations of the 'a prioric-Projects' in question. But if this is the case, the Notion that 'refers' to the historical Fact of Discourse can take the Meaning of the *uni-total* Concept, in the sense that it can be developed into *circular* Discourse which *is* the discursive Truth, only if this Fact itself is *one* and *unique* qua Fact. In other words, to be able to give rise to or to be the *Truth*, to be the 'Transcendental' that brings together the conditions of the possibility of discursive *Truth*, History itself must not be only *discursive*, that is, consciously willed, but also such that, one day, it effectively exhausts, in and through an empirically-existing discursive Oeuvre, the very Possibility of its empirical-existence, by realising completely and perfectly through and in that Oeuvre the primordial discursive Project which was its point of departure and the unique motive {*mobile*} informing its movement. This final historical Oeuvre will then be nothing else but the uni-total Discourse of Truth, which is a 'transcendental' Discourse in this sense that it de-monstrates (through its 'circularity') the *effective* completion of History which made it *possible*. The 'content' of that Discourse will thus be its own 'deduction', which will make it appear as the 'necessary' term of the historical evolution understood or conceived (after the event) as the empirical-existence of the Primacy of the Future {*Avenir*} in the extended-Duration of the progressive objective-realisation of the Project of a free-Action, whose given-being is the Desire (that is, the Possibility) of the discursive self-Recognition of the Human being, to the extent that this Recognition is complete and definitive, to wit, irrefutable or demonstrated as true, only if it is communicable, communicated, and accepted everywhere and always, that is, necessarily, by all those who speak or understand Discourse.

This fusion of the A priori and the A posteriori in the Hegelian historical Transcendental of the uni-total Discourse, which accounts discursively for its own 'possibility' as true Discourse and which, in thus fully and perfectly de-monstrating its own Truth as being the Philosopher who pronounces it (and who becomes a Sage in and through this very philosophical Satisfaction with their self-Consciousness, *universally* recognised as being true *forever*), is indisputably of Kantian origin. And that is what makes Kant the greatest of philosophers. But Kant himself was unable or unwilling to raise himself to the level of Wisdom, because, for religious motives, he never wanted to admit the *efficacy* of the free or conscious activity of the Human being in the World and consequently refused to identify the (discursive) Truth with History. This is why, in and for Kant, the *Fact* which is given or revealed by the spatio-temporal Intuition or by Sensibility (Perception) remains forever separated and distinct from the categorial *Discourse* of the Understanding (Logos). In other words, Kant's projected merging of the A priori and the A posteriori in the Transcendental remained only a draft in his work. The transcendental Discourse, which was supposed to transform Philosophy into a System of Knowledge, was not understood as Discourse accounting for History taken in its achieved ensemble. Kant's 'transcendental' Discourse did not close in upon itself and it thus degenerates into Scepticism (cunningly camouflaged, it is true). Thus, Kantian Philosophy never knew how to be truly rational or reasonable (despite Kant's tremendous common sense, which was nevertheless offset by his religious temperament), for the purported 'Reason' which was supposed to be the organ of the transcendental Discourse of Knowledge, where the categorial A priori should have merged with the spatio-temporal A posteriori, has never ceased to be in fact the 'Understanding' as *opposed* to 'Intuition'.

Philosophically speaking, this final failure of Kant finds its expression in the upholding of the (Platonic or theistic) traditional rationalist notion of the Thing-in-itself, which remains in and for Kant the genuine *objective-Reality*, as opposed to every spatio-temporal *Phenomenon* whatever it may be. It is probable that Kant upheld this notion because he wanted to save, at all costs, the (in fact contra-dictory) 'theological' notions of God and the immortal Soul. In any case, it is the presence of this notion that turns his 'System' into a *philosophical* one, where the Contradiction could be avoided only by the opening of 'sceptical' gaps, barely camouflaged by developments in the troubling philosophical mode of As-if and by disappointing philosophical perspectives of a purported progress towards a goal presented as getting infinitely further away.

Nevertheless, what is surprising and truly noteworthy is not the perseverance, in Kant, of the Platonic or 'theological' Energo-logy of the Thing-in-itself; rather, what is really 'admirable' is the fact that Kant's Energo-logy becomes strictly identical to the Hegelian Energo-logy which is ours (the error of Continuity notwithstanding, which is relatively speaking secondary), concerning as much its 'place' in the categorial System (as *second* 'Category') and its proper dialectical development (into three Sub-categories), as its discursive 'content' (developed into 'Principle'), through the mere fact of overcoming in the Kantian philosophical System all that pertains to the notion (in fact contra-dictory) of the Thing-in-itself.

Hegel's Energo-logy

I do not need to interpret Hegel's Energo-logy in the present philosophical Introduction as I intend to set it forth further below. Considering, however, that it will be a refresher {*mise-à-jour*} exposition, that is, an *interpretation* of the Hegelian text, a few comments on the topic can and must be made right here.

Updating Hegel's Onto-logy did not require, on my part, anything other than purely formal terminological modifications and minor adjustments, but that does not apply to his Energo-logy. Not only is the terminology . . .

Index

A

Accident, of matter, 170, 172, 174, 176, 181, 198
accomplishment, 6, 48, 53, 98, 105, 134, 137–8, 141
Action, 1, 40n, 41, 45, 71, 73, 78, 95, 101n, 103–4, 119, 123–5, 129–33, 134, 137–40, 178–81, 205
   in Buddhism, 43n, 44, 45–6
   collective, 178
   Contra-diction, 103n
   destructuve, 157
   efficacious, 103, 122–5, 132, 177
   free, 23–5, 32n, 35n, 65, 70–1, 74, 97–9, 124–5, 129–32, 134, 138–9, 181, 186, 204, 207–9, 216, 229
   impossibility in the spatio-temporal world, 124
   inefficaciousness of, 34–5, 80n, 98, 100, 135
   as intentional morality, 26–7, 35, 39, 52n, 90–1, 99
   inter-action, 46, 109, 118, 122–4, 138, 140n, 143, 157–9, 167, 175–8, 183, 186, 199
   negating, 1, 40n, 97, 104, 105n, 137–8, 140, 142
   projection towards future, 27
   pseudo-action, 90–1
   Re-action, 177n
   Struggle and Work, 45, 53, 57, 77–8n, 89, 91, 93, 95, 122, 131, 134, 178–9, 203
Act of Freedom, 32, 168, 186
Adam (first man), 33n
Aenesidemus (Schulze), 142
Analytic of Concepts, 112, 136, 144
Analytic of Principles, 113, 136, 144, 150, 152
Anthropology, 31–2, 73
   Buddhist, 47
   Greek, ancient or pagan, 27, 31
   Judeo-Christian, 1, 28, 31–2, 34, 47, 48–9, 52n, 53, 66, 87, 93, 94, 97, 102, 105, 128
   Kantian, 128, 132
Anthropology from a Pragmatic Point of View (Kant), 73, 75, 215
anti-Platonic Aristotelianism, 1, 6, 16, 211
a posteriori, 113, 116, 119, 120, 122, 215
   distinction from a priori, 222, 225–6
   empirical cognition, 219

a posteriori (*continued*)
 infinite task, 115–16, 120
 Kantian transcendental vs
  Hegelian historical, 227–9
 opposed to thing-in-itself, 114–15
Appearance, 168
a priori, 19, 20–1, 27, 58, 61, 63, 76n,
 79n, 83, 113, 116, 120, 123,
 125–6, 129, 136, 148–51, 154,
 156, 162, 169, 185, 187, 189,
 206, 210–11, 214–15, 218–30
apodictic, 211
Architectonic of Pure Reason, 58–60,
 59–60, 61–3, 72
 art of Systems, 57–8
 uni-total discourse, 59–60
 See also *Critique of Pure Reason*
  (Kant)
Aristotle
 anti-Platonic, 1, 6, 8, 16, 211
 atheistic, 7, 10, 21
 C. /. E, 2
 empiricism, 2, 59–60n, 223
 and Hegelian System, 7, 10, 219,
  221
 Perception, 27–8, 219, 221, 227
 Physics and Philosophy, 167
 Platonic, 49n, 59–60n
 rationalism, 1
 Teleology, 179
 Time, 187, 211, 222
 and Will, 2
Art, 50n, 57, 87–8, 90–3, 94–6, 101,
 123, 198, 214
Arte-fact, 91, 131, 205–6, 208
As-if
 aesthetics and nature, 92–4, 100–3,
  116–26, 133, 143–4
 avoids contradiction, 9–11, 15–18,
  22–4, 43, 49, 69, 74, 76, 80–2,
  86, 92–6, 100–9, 116–26, 133,
  143–4
 from Kant to Hegel, 103–7,
  116–26, 133, 143–4, 182, 201,
  203–4, 220, 223, 230
 moral faith and teleology, 22–4, 43,
  49, 74, 76, 80, 86, 92–4, 116–26,
  133, 143–4, 178, 200, 203–4, 216
 skepticism, 11, 15, 22, 49, 76, 80,
  86, 116–26, 133, 143–4, 220,
  223, 230
 Thing-in-itself, 9, 15–17, 22–4, 49,
  69, 74, 76, 80, 86, 92–4, 116–26,
  133, 143–4, 182, 201, 203–4,
  223, 230
atheism, 1, 3n, 6, 7, 26, 47, 77n, 97,
 106
Axiom of Error, 5, 76n, 132
Axioms of Intuition, 154

B
Bach, J. S., 96n
Beauty, 87n, 88, 91–6
 aesthetic judgments, 91–2
 artistic vs natural, distinction in
  Kant, 92–3
 in Schelling and Plato, 92–3
 silence and artistic production,
  95–6
 teleology and aesthetics, 91–6
 Work and Struggle, 91–6
beginning of philosophy, 107
Bible, 50–1n
Bio-logy, 102, 213, 216, 217, 219
the Bodhisattva, 43n, 44
Body, 67, 104, 113, 140n, 205, 218;
 and Soul, 215
Brahma, 44
Buddhism, 43, 44, 45, 46, 47, 49n,
 52n, 80n

C
calculus, 163–4
The Canon of Pure Reason, 22, 30,
 36, 51, 55, 65–6, 73, 79n, 84. See
 also *The Critique of Pure Reason*
 (Kant)
Cartesian Extension, 67–8, 73, 113
Cartesian Thought, 67–8, 73, 113,
 228
Categories, 4–5, 8, 13–14, 19, 67, 69,
 72, 80n, 111, 113, 115–19, 124,

Index

126, 129, 134, 136–9, 143–5, 147, 149–150, 152, 153–5, 167–8, 171–2, 177–80, 182–8, 196–7, 199, 204–5, 207–13, 215–17, 219, 221, 224
  of Freedom, 118–19, 126, 129
  of Nature, 112, 117, 119, 126, 129, 134
  of the Understanding, 134
  See also Quantity; Quality; Relation: and Modality
Causality, 65–6, 87–8, 96, 102, 111, 117, 119, 123–4, 129, 133, 138, 173–9, 181–4, 196–7, 199–201, 204, 207–9, 216–17
  Principle of, 173, 176, 177, 193
Certainty, 20–1, 30, 32, 33–4, 36n, 38, 51n, 74, 76, 78n, 80n, 81, 99, 100n, 123
  absolute, 20–1
  of Hope, 35, 36n, 42, 54, 56–7, 74, 81, 86–7, 99, 116, 123
  non-discursive, 34
  of Satisfaction, 74
  subjective, 32, 37, 39n, 44, 51n, 55, 56–7, 73, 74, 86–7, 100n, 103n, 123, 133
Charity, 43n, 52n
Christianity, religion, 35–6n, 49, 51–2n, 54–7, 100n, 102, 116, 123, 125
  Imitation of Christ, 56
  morality, 51–2n
  mythology, 28–9
  protestant, 98
  theology, 7, 48
  See also Judeo-Christian Anthropology; Saint Paul
Cogito, 228
Cognition, 5, 14, 19, 22, 33, 58, 61–3, 71, 76n, 113–15, 119, 122, 140, 143, 209–11, 214, 215, 218–1, 223–6
Common Sense, 12, 25, 26, 39–40n, 45, 69, 83, 92, 94–5, 102n, 103n, 162

Community, 138, 175–6, 177, 177–9, 180, 181–3, 184, 186, 197, 199, 207
  Principle of, 176
  as a Hegelian category, 177–9
Concept, 108, 126, 136, 139, 142–4, 147–5, 151–3, 162, 168, 178, 185, 188–90, 192, 210, 212–13, 217, 219–20, 224, 227–8
  conflict between 'Athens' and 'Jerusalem', 66
Contingency 138, 183–6, 192, 200, 201, 203
Continuity, error of, 167, 230
  notion of, 163, 164, 165–6, 208, 209, 214, 217
Contradiction, mode of, 6, 48, 70, 79n, 80, 188, 230
conversion (idea of), 28
Copernicus, N., revolution, 225
Correlate, 183–5, 186, 191, 200, 202, 209–10
Cosmo-logy, 39n, 45, 53, 213, 216–17, 219
Cosmology, 72–4, 76, 81, 4, 88, 97, 99, 107, 111n
  rational Cosmology, 62, 72, 74
  rational Theology, 62, 72, 73
Creativity, creative Action, 2–3, 44, 77–8n, 90, 91, 95, 103n, 104, 123, 131, 132, 137
Critique of Practical Reason (Kant), 35n, 41n, 57, 65, 71, 73, 77n, 79n, 81–5, 86, 88, 91, 94, 97, 106, 109, 116, 125, 132–3, 216
Critique of Pure Reason (Kant), 3, 4–5, 12, 17–18, 19, 20, 55, 57, 58, 60n, 61–2, 65, 70, 71–2, 75, 76–7n, 79–80n, 81–5, 86, 88–91, 93, 94, 96, 100n, 106, 109, 136, 138–9, 143, 146, 167–8, 170, 175, 200, 215–16, 221
Critique of the Power of Judgement (Kant), 55, 57, 65, 75, 79n, 81–2, 83–4, 85–6, 88–90, 91–3, 94–7, 100n, 102n, 106, 109, 111, 116, 133, 140, 144, 200, 216

D

Dasein, empirical existence, 138, 169, 170, 175, 183, 184–5, 190, 191, 192, 193–4, 198, 200, 201–2

Degree, in relation to category of Quality, 139, 155–6, 158n, 160–3, 164

Democritus, 157, 165

Descartes, R., 25, 34, 48, 54, 66–7, 73, 113, 210, 220, 228

Desire, 35n, 43–4, 77–8n, 81n, 82, 118, 119, 129, 130–4, 135, 137, 138, 139, 141, 206, 229
 for Recognition, 35–6n, 39, 78–9n, 80n, 81n, 96n, 97, 122, 129–34, 206

Determinations, of a substance, 169–70

Dharma, 43

Discipline, internal Discipline, 41, 43, 44, 99, 101–2n; religious discipline, 41n, 45–6, 51, 52, 54, 56, 98–9, 100n, 101–2n

Discourse, 1, 2–4, 5, 6–7, 8–9, 11, 13–19, 20–4, 46–9, 54, 59–60, 63, 67, 76–8n, 102, 104, 106–8, 112, 114–17, 139–41, 144
 atheistic, 47
 categorical structure, 117
 circular, 20, 47, 49, 77–8n, 141, 204n, 205, 224, 205
 coherent, 7, 11, 13, 16, 22, 68, 96, 111, 172, 218, 224
 Fact of, 4, 5–6, 76n, 81, 182, 217, 228
 generic, 226
 human, 2, 5, 180, 228
 Meaning, 141, 172
 Modalities of, 185–6
 Nature, 134
 philosophical, 19, 89, 115, 220, 222, 226
 Possibility of, 224–6
 Reason, 130
 theoretical, 53, 111, 112–13

transcendental, 225, 227–30

Understanding, 229

uni-total, 2, 6–9, 11, 14–15, 18–20, 24, 31, 52, 58–9, 59–60n, 61, 77–8n, 84, 102, 105n, 106–7, 115, 123, 128, 135–6, 138, 139, 180, 203, 218–19, 222, 226–9

Dogmatism, dogma, 10, 20, 34, 36, 38, 43, 43n

Dostoevsky, F., 26

Duration, 67, 116, 169, 174–5, 177, 195–8, 200
 extended, 2, 5, 19, 44, 54, 63, 78n, 81, 88, 92, 114, 128, 130, 134, 138, 139, 141, 171–8, 195, 199, 200, 203–4, 207, 212–12, 217, 224, 229
 temporal, 150, 154, 194

Duty, 34, 35, 40, 40n, 41n, 50, 68–9, 73–4, 76, 77n, 78, 80n, 88
 Consciousness-of-Duty, 71
 and faith, 76, 80n
 moral Duty (*Pflichbewusstsein*), 57
 and Nature, 73–4

E

empirical-existence, 2, 19, 27, 35, 39n, 44, 46, 50n, 54, 56, 63, 78n, 81, 90, 91, 94, 97, 103, 105, 106, 108, 114, 128, 130, 131, 133, 135, 138–9, 141, 143, 155, 157, 161, 166, 167–79, 181–2, 185, 189–209, 212–13, 217, 226–9

Empiricism, Kantian, 1, 2, 221, 223
 traditional, 222, 223
 Aristotelian, 1, 2, 228

Encyclopaedia of the Philosophical Sciences in Basic Outline (Hegel), 178, 219

end of history, 2, 27, 32

Energo-logy
 Kantian, 108, 143, 160, 165, 166–7, 214, 217, 219, 230
 Hegelian, 143, 144, 155, 157, 180, 203, 213, 219, 230–1

Energy, 166n
Epicurus, 30n, 42n, 60n, 60
Eroticism, 57
Error, 103, 105n, 107, 124. *See also* Axiom of Error
Essence, 8, 27–30, 56, 66, 77n, 87, 103–5, 138, 157, 159, 168, 198, 198n, 199, 204–5
Esteem
  for the moral law, 35–6n, 41, 118
  feeling of, 119, 128, 130, 132
  self-Esteem, 129, 131
Eternity, 3, 5, 6, 7, 144, 211
Experience, 12, 14, 16–17, 19, 21–3, 25, 59–60n, 62, 65–8, 71, 74, 83, 86, 91, 101n, 104, 113–14, 136, 138–9, 168–9, 171, 184, 188–92, 195, 210, 215, 218–19, 222, 224, 227
Ego, 73, 112–14, 117– 19, 121–2, 134, 136–7

F
Faith, 30, 32–4, 35–8, 39n, 42n, 44, 51–2n, 54–7, 68, 73–4, 76, 78, 80n, 81, 81n, 85–7, 98–9, 100n, 103, 103n, 104, 111, 116, 120, 123, 128, 133
Feeling (Gefühl), 35n, 82, 118–19, 121, 124, 129, 132
Fichte, J. H., 10, 11, 18, 127, 142, 209
formal Logic, 188, 189n, 208, 220, 226
Freedom
  Act of, 32n, 69, 168, 186
  categories of, 118–19, 129, 178, 179, 182, 186
  consciousness of, 76–8n
  creative, 1, 44
  human, 49, 56, 65–6, 68
  notion of, 23, 25, 32n, 34, 48, 52n, 61, 65–6, 68, 69, 73–4, 76–81n, 82, 86–8, 109, 116, 119, 124, 126, 128–31, 132, 134, 168, 182, 186, 198n, 201, 203–7
  transcendental, 25, 65
  of Will, 23, 87, 116, 120

free Will, 2, 65, 66, 67, 68, 87–9, 94, 116–17, 128–9, 135, 137
future world, 50n, 54, 57, 68, 72–3, 77n, 78n, 79n, 94, 105, 108–9, 116, 124, 128, 143
  condition of, 24–5, 26–7, 36–7, 38–9, 41–3
  transcendent, 27, 34, 36n

G
Gautama, 46
geometrical point, 136, 159
God
  in Buddhism, 43n
  in Christianity, 51–2n, 56
  as a condition of morality, 23–5, 26–9, 30, 31, 33n, 36–9, 42, 43, 46, 50–1n, 52n, 62, 68, 72–3, 79–81n, 86
  and contradiction, 93–5, 98, 101n
  fall of Adam, 33n
  free action, 70
  Hegelian, 50n
  imitation of, 56
  in Judeo-Christian Mythology, 28–9
  and Kant's Thing-in-itself, 6–7, 36n, 51n, 77n, 79n, 87, 98, 105, 109, 116, 118, 124, 128, 143, 191, 230
  Law of, 36n
  and Nature, 62, 68–70, 73–4, 79–81n, 95, 108, 140n
  objectively-real, 140–1n
  Platonic Myth, 60n
  plurality of, 124
  problem of 'free God', 69–70
  recognition by, 30, 31
  and Satisfaction, 55–6, 98
  Soul-image of, 38
  supreme one, 44
  temptations, 99
Greek Anthropology, 27
Greek Philosophy, 31, 49, 50
Groundwork for a Metaphysics of Morals (Kant), 75, 76n

H

Happiness, 23, 29, 29n, 31, 32, 33–5, 36–9, 40n, 41n, 43–4, 48, 54
  and worthiness, 30, 31, 69
  worldly, 51n
Hegel, G. W. F.
  the a priori, 222, 224, 225
  Aristotelian, 7, 219, 220–1, 228
  Christianity, 100n
  circularity of Discourse, 11–12n, 17, 20, 21, 84, 94, 180, 218, 219–20
  conception of history of philosophy, 59
  Contingency, 203
  contrasted with Kant on moral law, 77–8n
  Cosmo-logy, 39n, 216–17
  desire for recognition, 35–6n
  Energo-logy, 167, 143, 155, 180, 230
  expression of the Judeo-Christian anthropology, 1, 40–1n
  first three categories of Kant, 183
  Freedom, 203–5; God, 50, 93
  fusion of the a priori and the a posteriori, 222, 229
  given-Being (*Sein*), 145–6, 153, 155
  the Hegelian Sage, 15, 226
  History, 177–8
  Idea, 212, 219
  Kantian Anthropology, 132
  Kantian Modality, 212, 219
  and Kant's Thing-in-itself, 10, 49, 104, 106–7, 127, 142, 144, 158, 182, 201, 208, 209, 211
  and Locke's traditional Empiricism, 221–2
  Logic, 143, 144–5, 155, 226
  Monad, 173
  Negation, 1, 25, 198n, 203n, 156
  Onto-logy, 144, 180, 230
  Phenomeno-logy, 144, 180, 168, 213
  Philosophy of Spirit, 140–1
  Primacy, 181
  notion of empirical-Existence, 167, 172, 186, 220, 228
  Sensibility, 212
  spatio-temporality, 146, 155, 221, 223
  Struggle or Work, 90–1, 122
  sub-category of Community, 177–8, 182, 186
  Synthesis is Time, 153
  Table of Judgements, 208
  Teleology, 177–8, 208
  and the third Kantian Question, 54–5
  trinitarian vs. Kant's dualist system, 84, 146
  violent interpretation of Kant, 3, 47, 49, 212.
History, 2, 3, 25, 27, 28, 29, 32, 59n, 77n, 78n, 97, 105n, 142, 180, 205, 228–9
  end of, 2, 25, 27, 29, 32–3, 77n
  Hegelian, 58n, 178, 228–9
'The History of Pure Reason', 59n
history of Western Philosophy, 1, 11, 25, 59, 59n, 91, 142, 186, 221
Hope, 30–4, 37–38, 39n, 42n, 47, 51, 54, 57, 73, 74, 78n, 80n, 98, 116, 133
  certainty of, 34, 35, 36n, 44, 51n, 54, 56–7, 74, 78n, 81, 86, 98–9, 103, 116, 123, 133
  positive, 41n
  renunciation of, 42
  subjective certainty of, 57, 68, 86–7
Hume, D., 19
Hypocrisy, religious, 99, 100–1n
  in theoretical skepticism, 116, 120, 123, 124, 125–6

I

Idea
  Hegelian, 212, 219, 227
  Kantian, 22–3, 58, 59–61, 79n, 85
Identity, 31, 34, 49, 66 146, 87, 131, 136, 137, 145–52, 154, 202
Impossibility, 79n, 138, 183–5, 189, 201–3. See also Contradiction

Index

Intellect, 27
intellectual Intuition, 76, 220
intelligible World, 54, 71–2, 116, 117, 124
Intuition, 3–5, 62, 67, 76n, 90, 111–12, 116–18, 119–21, 125–6, 136–7, 143–4, 146–51, 152, 154, 188, 209, 211–12, 215, 221, 223–4, 225, 229–30
  Axioms of, 154
  empirical, 160, 164, 169
  Form of, 165, 170
  intellectual, 76n, 220
  non-sensible, 4–5
  sensible, 4–5, 12, 13, 72, 111n, 112
  theoretical, 118
  thinglike-Objects of, 168, 183
Islam, 50–1n
Ivan Karamazov (character), 26

J
Jesus-Christ, 52n, 55, 56
Judaic Religion, 50–2n
Judeo-Christian Anthropology, 1, 28–29, 31, 33–4, 35, 40n, 43, 45, 47–8, 52n, 53, 66, 87, 93–4, 97, 100, 102, 105, 128, 132, 203–4
Judeo-Christian Mythology, 28–9, 93, 128, 132
Judgement, 82, 88, 123, 151, 175, 178, 179, 208, 210, 211, 212
  Faculty of, 88–91
  Table of, 179–80, 186, 208

K
Karman, 43, 44, 46

L
Legality, 66, 88, 96, 133, 174, 178, 200–1, 204, 207, 208–9
  Principle of, 174, 181–2
Leibniz, G. W., 48, 60n, 69, 163, 164, 173, 176, 210, 220, 221
Limitation, 137, 155, 157, 158n
Locke, J., 60n, 221, 222
Logos, 67, 227–9

M
Madness, 29, 42, 103n, 104
Magnitude, 13, 152–3, 160–1, 163, 164–4, 169
  extensive, 154
  intensive, 155–6, 161, 167, 195
  continuous, 166
Maimon, S., 142
Malebranche, N., 69
Mana, 28, 41, 50n, 66, 132, 198, 199, 203, 203n, 204–5
Manichaeism, 45
Marx, K., 100n
Mathematics, 19, 63
Matter, 214–16, 218, 219
  Accident of Matter, 170
  corpuscular, 163
  transcendental, 165–6
Maya, 45
Measurement, 161
The Metaphysical Foundations of Natural Science (Kant), 72, 75, 158n, 166, 209, 214, 215–16
Metaphysics of Morals (Kant), 53, 61, 65, 67, 71, 78, 84, 87, 89, 97, 106, 109, 116, 122–3, 126, 133, 141, 216
Metaphysics of Nature, 61–2, 65, 71–3, 78–9, 81, 84, 87, 89, 109, 111, 115–16, 133, 140, 214–215
Modality, 138, 150 183, 185–6, 212, 219
Monad, 155, 172, 173–4, 176, 181, 197, 200
Monad of Monads, 187
Monadology (Leibniz), 163, 176
monotheism, 99
Morality
  as action, 24–7, 52n
  Buddhist, 43–4
  Christian, 51–2n, 100n
  concept of, 23–5
  condition of future world, 26–7, 36–7
  discipline, 35, 40–1

Morality (*continued*)
  existence of God, 26–7, 29, 36–7, 86
  imperative and categorical, 27
  Judaic, 52n
  Kantian, 33–5, 35–7, 38–9, 40–1, 42–3, 52n, 53–4, 68, 97
  Kant's transcendence requirement, 35–7, 42–3
  moral Law, 36, 37
  religious, 33–5, 54, 100
  as the supreme End, 30, 36
  and Theology, 85
Moral relativism, 27
Mysticism, 57
Mythology; 28–9, 31, 38, 39n, 47–8, 49n, 50–1n, 60n, 69, 74, 93

N
Nature, 24–35, 32–3n, 34, 61–3, 65–7, 71–4, 78–80n, 81–2, 84–5, 87–92, 95–7, 106, 112, 117, 129–32, 134–5, 136, 166, 193, 200, 206–7, 214–16
  categories of, 117–19, 126, 129, 134
  Metaphysics of, 61–2, 65, 71–3, 78–9, 81, 84, 87, 89, 109, 111, 115–16, 133, 140, 214–215
  necessity of, 124
Necessity, 65, 74, 87, 124, 138, 183–6, 192–6, 199–200, 201–3, 205–7, 212
Negation, 44, 137, 145–6, 148, 155–7, 160–3, 165, 170, 174, 184–6, 205
Newton, I., physics of, 39, 63, 73, 163–5, 197
Nietzsche, F. W., 100n
Nirvana, 43, 43n, 81n, 105
Non-contradiction, 188, 224–5
Non-necessity, 186, 202, 204
Non-Reality, 171
Nothingness, 44, 78n, 106, 138, 156, 171, 185, 187–9, 198n, 201–3, 205
  and Contingency, 201, 203, 203n, 205
  opposed to negation, 78n
  relation to Non-being, 202
Noumenon, 4–5, 7, 12–13

O
objective-Reality, 39n, 44–5, 56, 70, 81n, 90, 103, 105, 108, 128, 131, 138–40, 143, 155–67, 171–2, 177n, 185, 187–96, 200–3, 206, 208–9, 212–13, 217, 230
Onto-logy, 53, 57, 106, 108, 143, 155, 180, 187, 201–2, 212, 213, 217, 219, 227n, 231
Opposition, 157, 159, 162, 165–6, 171
  irreducible, 45, 46, 107–9, 112, 137, 140, 142–4, 156–9, 165–7, 171, 185, 202
Otto, R., 42

P
pagan, philosophy, 1, 27, 29, 31–2, 33, 49
  Anthropology, 27, 31
  Cosmology, 66
  religious, 33
  Theism, 31, 48, 92
  unreligious, 30
Parmenides, 84, 145, 146, 156, 184, 227
Perception, 2, 8, 12–13, 19, 27, 50n, 55–7, 62, 71, 74, 81, 86, 90, 94, 107, 113–14, 119, 129–30, 133, 136, 139, 143, 147, 150, 155–6, 160–3, 166, 168–9, 171, 184, 189–91, 193, 195–6, 205, 213, 215, 219–22, 227–29
Phenomeno-logy, 53, 55, 108, 143, 144, 168, 180–1, 201, 212, 213, 216–17, 219
Phenomenology of Spirit (Hegel), 84, 97
Phenomenon, 3–5, 13–14, 17, 32n, 35n, 39n, 56, 63, 67–8, 74, 87–8, 94, 105, 107–9, 111–12, 120, 128, 136, 141, 143–4, 147,

154–8, 160–1, 166, 168, 170–2,
180, 187, 189, 191, 196, 200–3,
205, 209–10, 215, 230
Philosophy of History (Hegel), 106
Philosophy of Nature (Hegel), 97, 106,
140–1
Philosophy of Spirit (Hegel), 97, 106,
141
Physics
  Kantian, 63, 100, 161, 163, 197,
  214, 216–18
  modern, 165, 192, 200
  Newtonian, 64, 163–4, 165, 197
  and Philosophy, 166–7, 197,
  217–18
  quantum, 164
  theological, 85–6
Physiology, 62–3, 72–4, 84, 96–7,
106, 215–16
Plato
  a priori and a posteriori, 218, 220,
  221
  Beauty, 87n, 92, 96n
  Idea of the Human being, 87
  Myth, 10, 48n, 60n, 69, 101, 117
  One-Agathon-Theos, 7–8
  Parmenidean Ontology, 184, 227
  Proof, 10, 76–7n, 186, 224
  Psyche, 50n
  Rationalism, 220, 221–4, 228, 230
  and Teleology, 92
  as theistic, 3n, 7, 9, 12n, 31, 48,
  60n, 92–3, 225, 230
  Timaeus, 87n, 92, 227n
  Unity and Plurality, 145–6
Plurality, 8n, 137, 145–7, 149, 154–5,
184
Poetry, 8, 40, 57
police, 26
Politics, 50
polytheism, 92
Positivism, 11
Possibility, 79n, 114, 138, 159, 183–5,
187–9, 191–6, 201–3, 205–6,
212, 224–9
Postulate of Truth, 4, 5, 32, 103, 132

Pride, 33, 39–40n
Primacy of the Future, 32n, 181, 186,
213, 229
Primacy of the Past, 181, 200
Primacy of the Present, 133, 181, 217
Principle of the Analogies of
  Experience, 184
Principle of the Anticipations of
  Perception, 160
Principle of Causality, 174, 177, 182
Principle of Community, 176
Principle of conservation, 165–66,
  166n
Principle of Legality, 174, 181–2
Principle of the Permanence of
  Substance, 169
Principle of Primacy, 181
Principle of Production, 173
Principle of Simultaneity, 176
Principle of Substantiality, 176
Principle of Teleology, 174, 177, 182
Principle of temporal Succession,
  174
Principles, Kantian, 16, 20, 60–1, 72,
  83, 116, 129, 144, 152, 154, 160,
  169–70, 172–4, 176–7, 181–3,
  184–5, 187–8, 209–16, 218–19,
  225, 230
*Prolegomena to Any Future
  Metaphysics* (Kant), 2, 16, 17, 21
Proof, 2, 10, 71, 76–7n, 80n, 85, 86,
  94, 179, 186, 220, 223, 224
Psychology, 63, 82, 88, 162–3, 214–16

Q
Quality (Category), 137, 155–6, 158,
  160, 162–4, 166, 168, 183, 185,
  191, 201, 208, 212
Quantity (Category), 137, 145–7,
  154, 156, 160, 168, 183, 185,
  196, 201, 208, 212

R
Ràga, 44
Rationalism, 220, 221–3, 224, 226,
  227, 228

Rational Physiology, 72
Reality, 13, 34, 130, 137–8, 155–7, 158, 160–2, 165, 189, 202, 212
  as Being (in Time), 156–7
  and Negation, 156–7, 160, 162, 165, 184, 185
  and Sensation, 161–2
  See also *Dasein*; objective-Reality
Reason, 1, 16–18, 19, 21–5, 36, 51–2, 56, 58, 60–2, 68, 76n, 79–80n, 82–3, 90, 112, 118–19, 124, 129–30, 137, 211, 214, 229
  Fact of, 76n
  practical, 41–2n, 61, 65–7, 69, 76n, 88, 118, 122, 124–5, 129–30, 132, 134
  pure, 19, 21, 23, 36n, 61–2, 66–7, 72, 76n, 79n, 83, 85, 112
  pure practical, 76n, 78n
  theoretical, 42n, 66, 69, 80n, 118, 120–2, 132, 134
Recognition, 6, 31, 35–6n, 39n, 48, 78–9n, 81n, 96n, 97, 100n, 105, 122, 129–34, 151, 206, 220, 229
  Desire for, 35–6n, 39, 78–9n, 80n, 81n, 96n, 97, 122, 129–34, 206
Relation (Category), 137–8, 158, 160, 167–83, 185–6, 192, 195–6, 199–201, 205, 208
Religion
  Buddhism, 43–4, 70, 81, 97
  Christianity, 32–3, 40–1, 54–5, 70, 73, 79–81, 93–102, 116
  concept of, 29–30, 45, 48–9, 54, 73, 79–81, 93–102, 116, 179
  faith and hope, 36–8, 42, 54, 73, 79–81, 93–102, 116
  Judeo-Christian tradition, 31–3, 40, 44–5, 47–8, 55, 70, 73, 79–81, 93–102, 116
  in Kant, 32, 35, 40, 42, 48–9, 55, 70, 73, 79–81, 93–102, 105, 116, 178–9, 204, 229
  Kant's critique of religious postulates, 79–81, 93–102, 116
  and Morality, 32, 40, 42, 54, 73, 79–81, 93–102, 116
  Protestantism and Kant, 97–102, 116
  Religion Within the Limits of Reason Alone (Kant), 73
Resurrection, 55–6
Rousseau, J.-J., 46

S
Saint Paul, 25, 28, 32, 48–9, 51–2n, 54, 55–6, 57, 71
Salvation, 36n, 38, 41–2n, 44, 46, 52n, 98–9, 100n, 103
Satisfaction, 19, 29–42, 44, 47, 49, 51–2n, 55–6, 73–4, 79n, 81, 86–7, 98–9, 100n, 135, 178–9, 229
Scepticism, 11, 15, 19–21, 69, 77, 79, 80n, 82, 84, 107, 115, 116, 123, 125, 142, 220, 222–3, 229
  hypocritical, 120, 123, 125–26
Schelling, F. W. J., 10, 11, 18, 55, 88, 89–90, 91–2, 127, 209
  Fichtean-Schellingian movement, 142
Schema, 60, 113, 136, 144, 154, 155, 160, 173, 176, 187, 190, 191–5, 209–11
  schematised categories, 3n, 213–17, 219
Schematism, 150, 152, 153, 160, 187, 209
Schiller, F., 40n
Science of Logic (Hegel), 139, 144–5, 155, 226
self-Consciousness, 31, 35n, 38, 39n, 40n, 41, 47, 54, 98, 113, 132, 137
self-contempt, 36n, 37–8, 39n, 41, 41n, 42, 56, 73, 79n, 98, 129, 130–1
self-satisfaction, 36n, 37–39, 41, 51n, 98
Sensation, 3–4, 7, 12–13, 56, 113, 119, 130, 136, 139, 155–6, 160–6, 171, 185, 190–1, 194, 196, 213, 221
Sensibility, 90, 112–14, 119–21, 139, 152, 210, 212, 214–15, 221, 223, 229

Index

sensualism, 2, 60n
Sensuality, 119–22, 130, 131–2
sensual Object, 120
sensual Subject 122, 125, 120, 131–2, 139
Silence, 5, 6–7, 10, 12n, 14, 15, 20–1, 40n, 46, 47, 48
Soul, 23, 36n, 38, 39n, 41–3, 50n, 60n, 63, 66, 70–3, 87, 98, 105, 108–9, 113–14, 116–18, 124, 126, 128–9, 132, 134, 140, 143, 148–9, 182, 215–16, 219, 230
Space, 45, 113, 149, 152–4, 157–8, 158n, 170, 176, 189, 190, 212
Space-Time, 44, 70, 128, 144, 157, 159, 167, 168, 170–1, 194, 196, 204, 212–14, 217, 224
Spatiality, 137, 146–7, 151–4, 157
Spatio-temporality 5, 7, 14–17, 22–3, 27, 44–7, 54, 70, 78, 80–1n, 106, 108–9, 111–13, 117–18, 124, 126–8, 136, 141n, 142–4, 146, 151–5, 157, 159, 171, 187–9, 196, 199, 201, 204, 209–13, 217, 221–5
Spinoza, B., 25, 48, 69
State, 30, 32–3, 52
Statesmen, 51–2n
Stoicism, 31, 42n
Struggle, 3, 32n, 34–5, 45, 90–1, 91–2
Subsistence, 138, 168, 170, 187, 197, 199, 204, 207–8, 209
suicide, 26, 30n, 42, 98

T

Taoism, 43–4, 47
Teleology, 86, 87n, 88, 91–3, 94–5, 97, 102, 106, 111n, 178–9, 216
  excluded from Kant's Categories 204, 206–9
  Principle of, 174, 177, 182
  relation to Free-Action, 207–8
Temporality, notion of, 70, 137, 147, 149, 151–4, 157. *See also* Time
theism, 1, 3, 7, 9, 12n, 28, 30–1, 36n, 42–3, 45, 47–9, 49n, 50n, 60n, 70, 77n, 80n, 84, 97, 98, 99, 100, 101n, 105, 108, 123, 125–7, 225, 230
Thing-in-itself, 1, 3, 8n, 8–11, 17–18, 21–2, 24, 27, 36n, 39n, 28, 49, 54, 67–8, 71, 87, 89, 105–9, 111–18, 120, 124, 126–9, 132–4, 136, 140–4, 155, 158, 165, 167, 182, 187–9, 208–9, 211–12, 222–3, 230
  categories inapplicable to, 209
  eliminated by Hegel, 108–9, 208–9
  necessity and contingency, 201–4
thinglike-Object, 12–13, 16, 19, 23, 60, 62–3, 72, 76, 113, 124, 136, 138, 147, 156, 160, 165, 168–70, 183, 189–95, 210, 214–16
Timaeus (Plato), 87n, 92, 227n
Time, 43–4, 113, 115, 136, 144, 148–9, 151–4, 156–7, 160–1, 165, 168–71, 173, 187, 190, 192–6, 209–13, 222. *See also* Duration; Space-time
Tonus, Tonal variation, 2, 139, 156, 161–2, 164, 166, 171, 191, 194, 196, 213
Totality, 19, 20, 58, 74, 112, 137 145–6, 148, 153, 154, 157, 170, 172, 180, 184, 197, 199
Transcendental Aesthetic, 3, 143, 148, 155
Transcendental Dialectic, 7, 136, 144
Transcendental Logic, 84, 136, 139, 143–4, 155
transcendental Methodology, 18–19, 22, 55
transcendental Principles, 210, 214n, 215. *See also* Principles
Truth, 2, 5–6, 11, 20, 59, 70–1, 76n, 80, 95, 101, 103, 105n, 107, 167, 218, 220
  discursive, 2, 3, 21, 23, 31, 47, 53–4, 58, 59, 68, 73, 77–8n, 80n, 82, 84, 86, 101, 104, 105n, 115, 121, 132, 135, 141–3, 171, 177, 179–80, 198–9, 211, 218, 222, 224, 226–9, 227n

Truth (*continued*)
  mode of, 36, 53, 89, 91–4, 96–7, 99, 102, 107–8, 111, 113, 116–17, 121, 123–7, 133, 141–4, 146, 172–3, 182, 201, 203, 205, 207, 215–16, 218, 220, 221, 223, 226
  Postulate of, 4–5, 32n, 103n
  practical, 109
  pseudo, 82
  Search for, 223
  secular, 57
theoretical, 102, 109, 123

U
Understanding, 1, 3–5, 7, 13, 62, 72, 82, 88, 90, 112, 118–19, 121–22, 129–34, 136, 143, 144, 147, 158, 168, 170, 183–4, 209–11, 229–30
Unity, 8n, 112, 136, 137, 145–7, 149, 151, 153–5, 172, 174, 184

Unreality, 70, 138, 139, 156, 163, 165–6, 171–2, 180, 186, 201–2
  non-unreal, 161–2
  objectively-unreal, 196, 198n, 203
  unrealisable, 103n

V
Vanity, 39, 40n
Veda, 50n
Vinaya, 43
Volition, 1, 69, 73–4

W
Wei wu-wei, 43–4
Well-being, feeling of, 2, 56, 57, 171, 191, 196, 213
Wisdom, 16, 33, 42n, 43n, 45, 46–7, 49, 54, 99, 107, 211, 229
Work, 3, 34–5, 45, 53, 57, 77–8n, 89, 90–1, 93–5, 97, 122, 131–4, 178–9, 203n, 205